About the Author

Rabbi Dr Noteh Glogauer began his journey as a school principal at the ripe old age of twenty-nine. He has combined his passions for truly reaching each child, striving for excellence in all he does, and inspiring those around him to do the same at three schools on two continents. He is a committed lifelong learner – a journey he continues with his wife Chaya and his beloved children, Esti, Yossi and Rochel.

Rabbi Dr. Noteh Glogauer

NEVER GIVE UP
A JOURNEY FROM CLASS CLOWN
TO SCHOOL PRINCIPAL

AUSTIN MACAULEY
PUBLISHERS LTD.

A CIP catalogue record for this title is available from the British Library.

ISBN 9781786296337 (Paperback)
ISBN 9781786296344 (Hardback)
ISBN 9781786296351 (E-Book)

www.austinmacauley.com

First Published (2016)
Austin Macauley Publishers Ltd.
25 Canada Square
Canary Wharf
London
E14 5LB

Acknowledgment

As with any journey, there are always ups and downs as well as unexpected detours along the way. This story chronologically ended in 2001 and there have been many more challenges that have come my way. I have always met each trial head on, never shying away from the struggle. That is simply how I was raised. In life there will always be those who will create stumbling blocks. I was taught life skills and strategies on how to navigate the negativity. Above all, I give thanks to the One Above who has allowed me to see past the challenges and see the positivity. This acknowledgment is an expression of gratefulness to *Hashem* for the continuous inspiration and strength that allows me to persevere and never give up, despite those who tell me I can't.

I thank my loving parents for their unconditional support and love. I was never the easiest child and always pushed the boundaries. You have always been there for me and I thank you.

To my brother and his dear family. Mike, I was born looking up to you and you have always been a role model I can count on. The competitive bond has always pushed me to better myself and never take my education for granted. Our fraternal connection surpasses physical distance and I am forever thankful for your love and sagely wisdom.

To my sister and her loving family. Menucha, you are the rock of faith that continues to inspire our family. Your reliance in *Hashem* and devotion is awe-inspiring.

To my brother-in-law, Dave and his family. Thank you for being a support whenever we have needed you. I am honoured to call you my brother.

To my surrogate Bubbie – Bubbie Eleanor. If I am on a journey, you most certainly have been one of the most amazing tour guides. Thank you for always being there for me at the craziest times of the day. *Hashem* sure had a plan when he put the two of us together…Your inspiration and confidence in me has always been one of the greatest motivating factors for me to achieve.

To Dr Laz – the greatest educator I have had the privilege of knowing. I was honoured to meet you way back in 1990 at that crazy *farbrengen*, look at us now! I thank you for your friendship, support and perceptive advice. You have been there for me, guiding me through some great challenges and I appreciate so much your positivity and encouragement. Thank you to you and your wife for opening the door to your home throughout my time in Florida. You are both true emissaries of the Rebbe, spreading light and inspiration.

To my dear children. The three of you have had to endure too many challenges, being the children of a Jewish school principal. Our family chose to move all over the world to make communities and schools better places. Throughout these trials and tribulations, you have remained the true inspiration for me. Your love for *Hashem*, *Torah*, family and each other is all a father needs to know that the sacrifices we have made are worthwhile. May our bond and love as a family continue to grow.

As we say in Hebrew, *acharon acharon chaviv* – the very last one is the most beloved. No words can ever describe how fortunate I am that *Hashem* had a plan for you and me to meet that fateful day in Vancouver. I love how my father thinks that the best thing I have ever done, that will never be surpassed, is to marry you. Thank you for saying yes and for making every day since even better than the day before. May we continue to grow together, breaking all the boundaries and shattering the obstacles placed before us!

Contents

Foreword

"Who said you can't teach an old dog new tricks? I've been teaching full time for almost forty years and this book has opened my eyes and mind to important new ideas and strategies! With remarkable warmth, refreshing honesty, and witty humor, Rabbi Dr G. leads us on a great journey of discovery, growth, and wisdom. This book is a must-read for every teacher, parent, and school administrator. You'll love the new you – and so will your students!"

Dr David Lazerson PhD

2008 National Teachers Hall of Fame Inductee
2007 Teacher of the Year Broward County Public Schools – 6th largest school district in America
1980 Teacher of the Year Buffalo, NY Public Schools

Early Impressions Making a Lasting Impact

I can't say that I was the best behaved child growing up. I loved my parents but as a young child, it was impossible for me to recognize the sacrifices they were making to provide us with better life opportunities than the ones we had living in South Africa. Indeed, they gave up so much to build a better life for us. I was quite young, merely seven years old when we left for Canada. Initially, I simply had no idea why our parents made the drastic decision to relocate to a foreign desolate place, so far away from our family who had loved us and who had been such a stable support mechanism.

In the mid-1970s, South Africa was in utter turmoil. There was always a great deal of tension between the blacks and the whites. This was due to the strict segregation laws of South African apartheid. All of the tension and violent altercations happened outside of my awareness. I was safely in the cocoon of my school and family routines.

My father has always maintained that he was never a very lucky guy. For this reason, he never bought a lottery ticket or gambled. But in one of the first years of the conscription lottery system for the South African Defense Force, my father was selected by lottery to join the army. With many stories of the challenges of being in the army, my father maintained that he would never live in a country where his children were forced to serve. This determination seriously limited my parent's' options when the violence in the early 1970s prompted them to make the decision that it was time to take their young family somewhere else to grow up. Our emigration choices in the 1970s we quite narrow. In those years, America was in Vietnam, Israel had ongoing turmoil with its neighbours, and thus the road to Canada was paved. The 1976 Soweto riots highlighted the writing on the wall and were even more of a motivating factor in my parents' final decision to leave South Africa.

In 1976, my parents informed us that they were attempting to secure a visa for our family to move to Canada. We had taken for granted the natural sense of security, normal routines in school, and the wonderful nurturing connection I had with my grandmother and great grandparents.

We had a very close relationship with my great- grandparents, whom we fondly called Granny and Grandpa. Once a week, we would go to Granny and Grandpa's house for a Friday night dinner or Saturday lunch. I always enjoyed it, walking up the front step, my great-grandparents standing at the porch screen door, eagerly anticipating our arrival. Routinely, they would in unison declare, "Oh! What a surprise!"

Often they would have a gift for us, or a candy or two. My great-grandfather was a decorated soldier in the First World War. His stories were numerous and engaging. He and my great-grandmother evoked a sense of awe in me. They possessed a formality, almost a regal aura from a bygone era. For an impressionable young boy, this awe was palpable, and yet, I felt an intense bond with them, especially my great-grandfather. To this day, I miss him deeply. With the benefit of hindsight, I now cherish a mature appreciation of his unlimited patience and tolerance for my mischievous antics. What a role model for any educator.

Full of energy even then, sitting for long moments was definitely not part of my nature. My impatience is still recognizable at every meal. I'm always kicking about, anxious to finish each course, ready to move on to my next task. As a young child, while sitting at the table, I would have half my mind involved in playing with my older brother in the garden or front porch.

My great-grandparents were very proper and aristocratic. Perhaps it was just the German way. Nevertheless, every detail was taken into account, including the formal seating arrangements. I was always seated in the place of honor. I would sit next to my great-grandfather at the head of the table on his left side. My great-grandmother always sat to his right. Silence was the standard protocol at the meal. Everybody had to sit quietly, very quietly, and just eat. There wasn't much conversation; everyone was just meant to sit and enjoy the wonderful food my great-grandmother and Lettie, her maid, had prepared.

Then it would happen. Grandpa would try not to show that he was wincing in pain. In my innocent nonstop motion, it was far easier to keep my mouth silent if some other part of me was occupied, like my legs. I had, yet again, unintentionally kicked the very leg Grandpa had wounded in the War. My father would get very angry with me. Everyone could see the pain in my great-grandfather's eyes. My father tried to move me away: however, my great-grandfather always stood up for me and made sure I was seated beside him, every single week, without fail. When I was older, my mother told me these stories: how much my great-grandfather loved me, how even though it caused him great pain, at every meal we shared together, he always wanted me to be seated close and near him.

One Sunday, as was quite usual for me, I ended up engaged in a more naughty escapade. As was his way, my father took me to task. My great-grandfather came on the scene just as my father was getting ready to give me a hiding – the belt on my backside. My great-grandfather stood up to his very tall and very thin over six feet height. He vehemently declared that my father was never to raise a hand to any of us in front of him. This was a profound moment that to this very day is engraved in my mind. Admiringly, my father would fondly reminisce about this confrontation he had with my great-grandfather, whom he deeply respected.

Once I was six years old, the rest of my week was spent at a public primary school. To this day, the Jewish community in South Africa is for the most part highly traditional Jewish Orthodox. Most Jewish South Africans, even though they are more traditional than fully observant, sent their children to one of two Jewish educational institutions in Johannesburg. In an effort to minimize intermarriage and to preserve the rich traditional upbringings that most families enjoyed, public school was simply not an option for the majority of the population. As is common throughout the world, the cost of private education made this option prohibitive for many Jewish families and my family was no exception. Therefore, my parents sent my brother and me to the public school, right around the corner from our home. It's not like we realised that we were actually missing something. We were a traditional Jewish Orthodox family, not that I really understood what this meant at my young age.

My parents, all the more so, recognized the critical value of Jewish school attendance, instinctively realizing the link to instilling a strong sense of Jewish identity and ongoing Jewish continuity. Two strong images stand out in my mind as having an impact on me educationally. Every morning in school, students were separated into demographic religion classes. This meant that all of the identifiably Jewish students were separated from the rest of their peers and educated according to a predefined syllabus set by the governmental education system.

From my perspective as a young boy, these classes enhanced a feeling of separateness and difference between my peers and myself. I didn't really understand why I was different, only that there was an identifiable quality that separated our small group from the rest of the class.

Because of the incredible leeway teachers were given in terms of programming and curriculum outcomes, to this very day I vividly recall the sketches and images the religion teacher displayed of a stereotypical Jewish man bleeding from his wrists, nailed to a wooden post. I remember how uncomfortable I felt, not only because of the disturbing pictures we were shown. At some level, I knew that what we were being taught and exposed to was not part of my tradition. I remember looking at my friends to see if they were as uncomfortable as I was.

In these types of situations, children usually look around to gauge the impact the situation at hand is having on their classmates. I now understand that this is a classic response in children. When confronted with conflicting morals and messages, students demonstrate their need to seek validation and confirmation. I know that this was what I was doing, but regardless of the response from my peers, deep down I knew that what we were being taught was not appropriate in the context of our Jewish scripture class.

Today, I recognize something even more alarming. I never told my parents, or anyone else, what we were being taught. And yet, those disturbing images are as fresh in my mind today as if I had just seen them this minute. Thinking now about the power teachers have over their students, and the ability they have to affect their impressionable young minds, how often do similar situations occur in our classrooms today? Do we hear about when our students face moral conflicts? Do we have mechanisms whereby our young students can voice their concerns? Will they feel safe and confident in voicing their confusion or questions?

The 'being different' that scripture classes engendered has shaped my educational philosophy enormously. Given the 'suffering' I experienced and my absolute refusal to inflict those feelings on even one more student, I was forced to think outside of the box and innovate. In every school I have led, there has been incredible diversity in religious observance. Therefore, I have always faced tremendous pressure to segregate – to put the supposedly likeminded religiously together. When I have stood my ground and encouraged buy-ins from key stakeholders, the most amazing outcomes have emerged. Everyone begins to witness the power of integration and appreciation of diversity. The messages are greater for the students when they are in integrated situations such as these. They find ways to seek commonality, rather than staying complacently in their box. This integrated approach promotes tolerance, exploration, discovery of similarities, personal growth and therefore, true celebration of diversity.

The feeling that 'there's nobody I can go and tell' is probably the most worrisome thought a parent could imagine his or her child having. Mine was only about being preached to from a foreign religious paradigm.

Feeling there is nobody you can tell, not knowing that it is ok to tell, is critical to a child's fundamental right to feel safe at all times. And we are all aware that there are situations in which a child feels he cannot tell and that there is no one to tell that are much more sinister than the one I experienced.

It was to that end a few years ago that I encouraged one of my staff members to develop her interest in children's safety. We have made conscious additions to our in-school system to integrate these safety principles into our day-to-day conduct. Students, teachers and parents are fully aware of the hierarchy of safe adults in the school, to whom they can go if they have a question or a concern. There is now a movement to educate children as young as five and six about safe communication and what they can do if they are feeling unsafe. In this way, we are teaching them active skills to be advocates for their own wellbeing.

My great-grandfather, with no words ever uttered, made me know that I was one of the most important people in his world. I felt that somebody cared about me. Somebody would protect me and I was worth protecting. Not only was I different in my 'religion' class, I already felt different from the moment I sat at my great-grandfather's table, but in a way that I couldn't ever articulate. Therefore, it is only appropriate that this is one of my first memories as a child. From these experiences, I've taken on a role I uphold with deep responsibility as a principal. I make it my mission that each of my students and teachers feel that I have their wellbeing at the forefront of every decision I make, that they are celebrated because of their uniqueness and that their voice is worth hearing.

Foundations of Financial Resilience

Once we emigrated to Calgary, Canada, everything changed. Suddenly, we were being raised in a pressured environment integrally dependent upon the financial stability of our parent's' business. The tension over finances certainly had an influence on how my brother and I live our lives today, not to mention impacting the career paths we each chose to pursue. The many decisions we made in life have been a product of our upbringing, and the challenges we saw our parents go through as they tried to do their best for their children, raising them in a foreign land away from family and the culture with which they were familiar.

My parents, from the very beginning, instilled a sense of independence and responsibility in my brother and me. To this day, many of the decisions and conversations we have with our children are a product of these life lessons.

My brother and I also felt compelled to develop a strong sense of resiliency and a deep appreciation of the necessity to take control of our own destinies. We shared an unspoken pact to avoid relying on my parents for the amenities so coveted by growing young boys in North American society. In the early years, we could sustain our youthful needs with some earned pocket money by mowing the neighbour's lawns or shovelling their driveways in wintertime. The demand for significant resources came with age, and so we moved from odd jobs to full-fledged entrepreneurship.

I was always ready to follow my big brother on his zany business plans to raise pocket money. With only one year separating us, we must have been only ten or eleven years old when we began delivering flyers/pamphlets to houses in the neighborhood as our first official job. I think back to how crazy we were delivering hundreds of flyers, one to each house, and only pocketing three to five cents per flyer.

I learned a great deal from my brother; most importantly, to keep my eyes open! It became obvious that somehow my brother was delivering his flyers at twice the speed I was. I became curious why he was choosing the apartment buildings and I was 'assigned' the very long, winding streets. As I doubled back to his apartment buildings, I found stacks of flyers piled high in the lobby, waiting for passers-by to collect them of their own accord.

Needless to say, this venture did not last very long. We soon learned a very valuable economic lesson relating to the ratio of dollars earned to time and effort allocated. However, with our tiny profits from these flyer deliveries, we managed to purchase our most significant acquisition – The Red Wagon.

Turning twelve years old was a big milestone for my brother. He had come of the necessary age to officially acquire his own newspaper delivery route. Of course, he managed to rope me into this new venture with the promise of splitting the profits 50-50. The red wagon assisted us with the much heavier load of newspapers. Dividing the paper route in half on a sunny summer morning, we set out to deliver our newspapers. Of course, being the oldest, my brother unilaterally usurped rights to the wagon and left me with the shoulder bag. We set out on our way with the hopes and dreams of making it big!

Our paper route consisted of five major streets, all surrounding our home. We calculated that by dividing the route in half, my brother and I would be able to successfully deliver our respective newspapers in just under an hour. The two months of the summer went by quickly. In 1985, people did not subscribe to the newspaper by phone. Paperboys would canvass house-to-house in search of homeowners who were interested in receiving the newspaper. Money would be collected on a monthly basis. Some homeowners would prepay. However, most would only pay one month in advance.

It was somewhat a hassle, going door to door in the evening asking for payment for the monthly delivery. Sometimes customers would get a little cranky because their newspaper wasn't properly placed in their mailbox. Or they objected to having to bend down and pick it up from the front step. At times, they might even have to walk one or two steps to pick it up from the front stoop. Despite these frustrations, the tiny rewards paid off in the end. We divided the meagre profits from our subscription collections. After a few months of deliveries, we began to develop quite a profitable venture, at least for youngsters in the 1980s.

Invariably in the morning after my deliveries, I would return home to find my brother already relaxing over a cup of hot chocolate, reading… a morning newspaper! Many times, the circulation department would accidentally give us one or two extra newspapers. I always assumed it was one of these extra newspapers my brother was reading.

One month, my brother asked me to collect the subscription money from one of his customers at the end of his last street. I agreed of course and proceeded innocently, completely unaware of what I was getting myself into. When the elderly lady came to the front door, I identified myself as the paperboy. She let fly a tirade! She angrily chastised me. How dare I ask for payment when throughout the entire month, she had not received a single newspaper! Again, my eyes were opened even wider. The mystery of my relaxed older brother enjoying his hot chocolate and 'extra' newspaper was solved!

It was one thing delivering a newspaper in the summer; it was another delivering newspapers in the Calgary winter. We very quickly learned that the "Ice" season was meant for only the brave and bold of heart. Calgary, with its proximity to the Rocky Mountains, experiences weather greatly altered by the elevation. The winters can be quite uncomfortable. The extremes of both the dipping thermometer and relatively limited winter daylight hours made our newspaper deliveries that much more challenging. Even though temperatures range from a January daily average of -9 °C to a midsummer average of 16 °C, it is not uncommon for a cold spell to visit the winter city. Temperatures could with very little warning plummet into the mid -30s with biting wind-chill factors lowering the temperature well into the -40s.

My brother and I both attended the same bilingual French immersion junior high school. In addition, we both played instruments in the band program. We lived approximately forty-five minutes by public transportation from our junior high school. Band practice began at 7:30 am. Therefore, in order to deliver our newspapers, eat breakfast and catch public transport, we needed to deliver our newspapers by 6:15 am. The alarm went off at 4:30 am. We were dressed in long underwear, trousers, shirt, sweater, toque, scarves, boots and gloves. When it was really cold, we dug out our ski pants as well. We were out of the house by 4:45 am and back by 6:15! If we were efficient enough, we could eat breakfast and get out of the house to catch the bus all in 15 minutes. This may seem quite the impossible feat; however, it was more of a survival mechanism. In wintertime in Calgary, before daylight saving time ends, sunrise is usually around 8:30 am. Maybe that was partially behind my natural desire to be extraordinarily fast. The morning darkness and freezing cold were not deterrents for my brother and me. We were fuelled by our entrepreneurial spirit and the desire for fiscal independence.

Summer and winter, these early, early morning escapades developed a solid foundation of essential skills from which we would draw later in life. It was great training in teamwork, time management, dedication, and efficiency. Whereas I learned the work ethic, my brother learned to delegate. These early entrepreneurial ventures set in motion the early stages of my personal philosophy on administration. The primary skills I developed were based on the need for a strong sense of time management and punctuality through organization; how to delegate work assignments based on the skills of the allocated workers. Overall, however, the most important ingredient in our success was a great attitude, seeing the fun of it all and above all setting a goal and working towards its fulfilment. We probably made what many would, from the outside world, call huge sacrifices. Looking back, I actually agree, but it surely didn't feel like that at the time. As we will see, personal sacrifice is in the eye of the beholder…

Life on the Road with Pops – Sacrifice and Making the Sale

The most valuable treasures in life seem to come through or from sacrifice. As a young boy, my parents always told us that nothing comes easy. But if something is important to you, the value of the struggle to be successful is as important as the result itself.

Sometimes, we only recognise the benefit of overcoming difficult personal challenges when we successfully emerge from the other side. But for me growing up, given our family's circumstances, I somehow appreciated the constant sacrifices my parents were making in the moment of the challenge itself. This awareness had an immense impact on my own development, even though at a young tender age, I couldn't really put into words what I saw.

I grew up in a blue-collar home. My father was a travelling salesman, my mother a book-keeper. Once we emigrated, she also had the arduous task of assuming the dual role of homemaker and business manager. This undertaking was a massive adjustment for my mother as we were all dropped into the last throes of a Calgary winter. All of a sudden, our family did not have a maid, a nanny or a gardener. It was my mother who, all of a sudden, had to assume all of those roles and the responsibilities they entailed. Talk about sacrifice.

The sole reason my parents emigrated was to 'make a better life for their children.' Studies have shown that one of the most prevalent reasons families leave their country of origin is to enhance economic opportunity. My parents' decision to leave South Africa to seek a better life in a new country was based on the belief that the most effective way to improve their children's lives was a better education in a safer country.

There is a stereotypical Jewish anecdote which goes something like, "My son the doctor, my son the…" It was an unspoken yet powerfully felt assumption of my parents that one of their sons would become a doctor and the other a businessman. Since my brother, a mere seventeen months older, had already chosen to become the family's archetypal doctor, my destiny seemed inevitable. The unspoken prophecy: I would become the businessman.

The pressure, never stated outright (albeit strongly implied), was for me to follow in my father's footsteps. Summers were spent travelling around Canada with my father as he made his business calls to various shops selling Western Wear to retail stores. I always felt it must have been quite a shock for the rural Canadians when these two South Africans wandered into town from nowhere with their thick foreign accents, mispronouncing words but trying oh so hard to fit in.

Emigrating from South Africa to Canada was a huge challenge for our family. Back in the 1970s, in order to emigrate from South Africa, a sponsor was needed to ensure a family's financial viability. The picture is vividly imprinted in my mind as a young child. My parents sitting late at night at the typewriter, typing what seemed like hundreds of letters and sending them off to potential employers with the hopes that one of them would be willing to take a chance on a hard-working South African immigrant. After two unsuccessful attempts at securing a sponsor, the third truly proved to be our lucky charm. My father left South Africa with two prospective opportunities – one in Toronto and one somewhere in Western Canada. For over two months, my father was overseas in the hope that one of these leads would secure an opportunity for our family to start a new life.

Word finally came through that we were to start a new life in a tiny Western Canadian town called Calgary. My father accepted the position of a 'travelling salesman' for a well-known cowboy boot manufacturer. The position was a challenging one for my father. He would have to reinvent himself from the travelling South African shoe salesman to a Western Wear cowboy gear salesman. The new job required my father to be on the road travelling, sometimes for up to two months at a time.

The financial pressure my parents experienced was significant. The minute we emigrated, the main focus shifted radically to financial survival for our family. The contrast was obvious even for us. In South Africa, the biggest worry in family discussions was what time the tennis game would be if we had to get to my grandparents or cousins on a Sunday afternoon. All of a sudden, in Canada now looming ever present was the challenging realisation that a guaranteed salary was no longer a certainty. Our family was now dependent upon each and every cold call my father would make to the many retail stores on his route across Canada.

My parents soon began to agonize over raising the necessary capital to open their own business, within the first five years of our immigration.

Growing up, most of my memories were of the tension between my parents relating to financial issues, such as how to pay regular bills, rent payments and eventually the mortgage payment. To this very day, my brother and I recall many of the financial 'discussions' and constant tension that existed in our house as our parents struggled to make ends meet. Perhaps my strongest education came from these home influences. Would these experiences build my resilience? Could I someday come to unleash the potential in these circumstances to enhance my transformational power? These experiences growing up in my parent's' household taught my brother and me to be self-reliant, even as young children. We too shared an unspoken vow: financial security was based on educational achievement; our personal sacrifices would be different to those of our parents. I have always been blessed with a memory for vivid detail. I am grateful to be able look back at times like this, and see the guiding hand of the One Above in all the steps in my family's journey as well. This was, however, not always so obvious at the time.

As a young boy, I remember eagerly anticipating my father's weekly phone calls from his two-month journeys on the road, with the hopes that we would be able to share one or two brief moments talking to him about the goings-on in our new life. Knowing that the phone call was expensive, and that my father had little time to chat, we kept our discussions brief.

In those early years, the house filled with even more anticipation and excitement when my father actually returned from an extended stint on the road. We would all rush eagerly to the door, excited to hear the stories of where he had been, what he had seen and whom he had met. The novel stories and excitement of my father travelling across the country filled my mind with exotic scenes and tales such as those of an explorer, seeking out new civilizations. Each business trip evoked the feeling that my father regularly partook in walkabouts.

My father's tales included exotic adventures. Driving up north to the Yukon and needing to put chains on his snow tires so that the van carrying his samples would be able to traverse the snow-covered backroads in bitter -35°C blizzards. Or the time when the temperature was so cold driving through the Northwest Territories that the petrol actually froze! In the eyes of a young child, my father was a true pioneer, a voyager seeking out new lands, meeting unfamiliar people.

The first year, as my father and mother were building the business, summer school holidays provided us the opportunity to bond with my father and make up for lost time during the school year. The first summer it was my brother's turn, being the oldest, to go on the road with our father. Enviously, I watched as my brother packed his suitcase and headed off early one morning for their six-week summer vacation adventure. We didn't really know what my father did on his trips. The mystery left much to the imagination. Dreams of sleeping in a new motel each night, eating in a different restaurant every day, were almost too much for my vivid child's imagination to contain.

I never understood growing up what happened on my brother's first and only trip accompanying my father. It never really mattered to me what his reasons were. All I remember was my jubilation when my brother returned and declared that he would never again go on the road with my father. This meant not only would I be going on the next business trip, but I also had significantly less competition for the coveted prize of accompanying my father on future expeditions.

My first trip with my father was a five-week journey from Calgary to the west coast of British Columbia. There was a lot of excitement as we wound our way from town to town through the National Parks of Canada. The anticipation mounted as my father went from store to store, meeting new customers and successfully opening up new accounts. In the early 1980s, Western clothing, including cowboy boots and cowboy hats, were in great demand. These were the companies my father was representing, all US in origin. And his product was in great demand.

My father would always call his clients ahead of our arrival to ensure that his customers were indeed willing to meet him. This was especially the practice if it was a 'cold call' and a prior relationship had not yet been established. My father was always quite intense and eager to reach his destination once an appointment time was set up with a potential customer. My father was actually capable of driving incredibly long stretches of road. And Canada, I found out, is full of very, very, very long stretches of road...with nowhere to stop! Like near the beginning of my very first trip out: the road from Vancouver to Bella Coola, British Columbia, approximately a 750 km journey – and that was it... a starting point and a destination. Talk about sacrifice. I sure know about how to manage boredom!

Before leaving Vancouver, my father made sure to top up the petrol and buy some 'supplies' to munch on along the way. My father had already become acclimatized to many of the new slang words for food. However, I had only been in Canada a short while so I was still quite wet behind the ears when it came to 'Canadianisms'.

As my father was filling up the car with gas (petrol), he poked his head into the van and asked me if I was hungry. He told me it would be quite a 'little' journey to our next destination and asked me if I liked pop and cookies. Not knowing what either of these were, and a little intimidated by my father, I told him sure. Before I knew it, my father had come back with a bottle of bright pink cream soda and a giant bag of Dad's Peanut Butter cookies. My father had neglected to tell me that "pop" in our South African vernacular was really "cool drink," and cookies were what I knew as "biscuits." In fact, I don't think I had ever tasted cream soda or eaten peanut butter cookies before. When he said pop, my mind went directly to popcorn, as I had no other context for "pop." I did not expect soda pop and peanut butter cookies.

During that fourteen-hour trip, all I had to eat were those peanut butter cookies with cream soda to wash it all down. To this day, I cannot stand the sight or even the smell of peanut butter cookies. And for some reason, each time I take a sip of cream soda, I get carsick.

As my father entered each store to make initial contact, I would wait in the car for him to come out with a thumbs up, indicating that indeed they were interested in viewing his product. Sometimes this would take ten minutes, sometimes over half an hour. But the wait was worth it once my father gave me the sign to start hauling in the samples. There I was, a tiny little boy, pulling suitcases sometimes twice my weight and size from the van with all my might. It must have been quite a sight for an onlooker. I thoroughly enjoyed how much of a fuss the clients made when I spoke in my eight-year-old South African accent.

I quickly learned the intricacies of setting up the samples for display. My father was extremely precise about how he wanted this done. Some were arranged according to style, others to colour. I soon discovered the "secret code" underneath the cowboy boots, indicating the manufacturer's price, allowing the merchants to calculate their mark-up. It made me feel proud inside as I learned each of my father's little tricks. I became part of the process, and not just the middle son my father had to drag along on the road during summer holidays.

The intensity of sales calls, as I knew how vital each was to our family's survival, affected me greatly. I realised very early on that it was important for me to speak only when spoken to. I would take my social cues from my father. I realised as I watched silently that my father was extremely successful as a salesman because of the individual attention he gave each and every customer. He went to great lengths to get to know his clients on a personal level. Every call took a long time that way. He didn't ever see the sacrifice he made – so much time for one customer, without even the guarantee of a sale. He seemed to know the significant events in their lives, such as the birth of a grandchild or God forbid, the loss of a loved one. My father established a warm connection that was both sincere and genuine. He had the gift of the gab, and his customers enjoyed his infectious good humour and jovial personality.

My father has a deep sense of integrity. Once his clients got to know him, they knew they could trust him to sell them what would be best for their business in his deeply honest opinion. He was not just in it for the bottom line sale. As much as there was enormous financial pressure on him as the family provider in those early years of our emigration, he would not make the sale unless it was good for both the client and him.

My father instinctively knew that one of his most valuable tools for building a successful relationship was his ability to communicate. One of the advantages I felt my father had was his diverse background and experience having also been a salesman in South Africa. Over the years, my father had dabbled in many languages and dialects. We enjoyed hearing my father speak Zulu, Swahili, Hindi, and now French, just to name a few languages in his repertoire. Of course, the family joke was my father truly could only speak three or four sentences in most of these languages! We always asked him what would happen if they started to converse back with him and he didn't understand what they were saying. My father would smile knowingly. It wasn't until I went on the road with him that I actually understood this gift. For 99% of his initial encounters, breaking the ice by conversing in his South African accent in numerous languages was just what was needed to demonstrate his genuine sincerity in wanting to make a personal connection with his client. Many times, especially in the smaller towns we would frequent, we would be invited to their homes for dinner or a cup of tea. It wasn't that often that my father acquiesced, but it was heartening knowing that my father was important enough to these people that the gesture was made.

I think the quality my father possesses of exuding a sincere interest in his fellow human beings has made a profound impact on me over the years. Seeing how for my father his gift for languages and his natural South African accent quickly generated conversation, subconsciously I feel I may have worked a little on keeping my South African accent, because everyone still marvels when I put it on. I consider myself very shy and somewhat uncomfortable in new social settings. When I am feeling particularly shy, I find myself reflecting on what my father would have done in that situation. My wife will say that the older I get, the more I act and sound exactly like my father! The ability to open up a conversation and immediately create a connection is very important as a school principal. My father taught me that sincerity, coupled with a light-hearted icebreaker, is the secret to breaking walls of social unease.

I was very proud of my father and his ability to make the sale. I definitely didn't realise it at the time, but I learned some of the most important guiding principles of my life from those summers on the road with my father. No matter the profession, it is one-to-one contact and sincere concern for another human being that is valued most. Above all else, it is essential to make that personal connection. Using that foundation, you can nearly always find a pathway leading to a successful outcome. It doesn't matter if one is in sales, medicine, accounting or education. If the client does not perceive sincerity and a genuine care for his or her well-being and gets even a whiff that he is merely being sold a 'bill of goods,' the desired outcome will never be achieved. However, the most valuable lesson I learned from those summers with my father is the importance of one's integrity. No matter what the financial pressure, my father was never in the business for himself alone.

A school principal faces enormous pressure to 'make the sale': to increase enrolments and keep the end of year results high every year so the school remains a viable alternative to the competition. It is easy to lose sight of the fact that the principal is there for the benefit of and as the ultimate advocate for the students. Sometimes, this role can even be incongruous with the wishes of certain parents and board members. Sometimes there are no clear answers in this juggling act. What I try to do is be able to put my head on my pillow at night, knowing that I have done my utmost to keep the best interests of my students in mind in the decisions I have had to make. This can only be accomplished by developing sincere relationships.

School Camp – Interfaith Dialogue Gone Wrong

So, now that you have a sense of some of the lessons I experienced prior to school with my brother and summers with my father, I think you are ready to hear a bit about what school itself was actually like once we emigrated from South Africa to Canada.

The educational path for my brother and me was paved by the ongoing constraints our parents faced as new immigrants to Canada. Once we had emigrated away from the supporting infrastructure of an established community and family network, my parents felt an even more fervent desire to instill traditional Jewish values and a strong work ethic in their children. My future was sculpted by what my parents realized were essential qualities necessary for building a solid foundation in our new life.

The primary school my parents chose upon our emigration was a small parochial school, which had a preschool through Grade 6 program. The I. L. Peretz School offered a generous subsidy program and the promise of a community focus to help integrate our tiny Jewish family into a foreign country. My parents signed us up at their first meeting with the school principal.

My parents were not predominantly concerned about my academic placement – how my education would serve as a stepping-stone to further my future employment opportunities. Their motivation was more primal. A small school offered a safety bubble in a new environment that held many trappings for a young boy. A community school would provide a nurturing environment based on traditional Jewish morals. Just what we needed to acclimatize to the new world of North America.

Our parochial school was one of two Jewish schools in a city of approximately 500,000 inhabitants in the late 1970s. The population of our school was around 120 students, preschool through Grade 6.

In 1981, the I L Peretz School launched a pilot program aimed at instilling the value of interfaith dialogue among its students. Motivated by a minority of parents, this initiative resulted in the school deciding to "integrate" with a local public school. The initiative was spearheaded by a few parents who felt that their children were missing the opportunity to socialize with a wide range of children due to the insular nature of the school. By joining up with a large public school through an educational initiative, the exposure to other children and their diverse, multicultural backgrounds would satisfy these parents' guilt about the compromise in having chosen the parochial school as their educational institution of choice. The interfaith dialogue committee decided the best way to implement this initiative was for our school and the public school kids to spend five days at a remote campsite engaging in an outdoor education retreat. What could go wrong?

The program was an attempt to provide new educational opportunities for the I L Peretz School students. The committee parents were aiming to strengthen the resiliency of the students, providing them with limited exposure to the world outside their tiny insulated bubble by integrating Jewish children with non-Jewish public school students.

On the surface, this seemed like a great idea. Often when suggestions come forward, they sound great in a vacuum. However, when not properly thought through with every angle examined, unpredictable situations arise that can have long-range consequences. I'm not implying there was any malice or purposeful neglect. It is just that having been a student involved in the initiative, it was clear that many issues had not been attended to. Because of this, the students became pawns in a public relations stunt gone very, very wrong.

One day, with great excitement, this initiative was announced. Our school would participate in an experimental outdoor education program. Our tiny school's grade six class would join another public school's class at an outdoor education retreat in the Rocky Mountains. The first year of this initiative was my brother's grade six class, as he was just one grade above me. That inaugural year, the plans went off without a hitch.

The next year, when the time came for the outdoor camp excursion, we were excited. We had been looking forward to this for over a year. We would be 'integrating' ourselves amongst the students of the other school and experiencing outdoor life, making new friends, and learning a new set of skills. My class consisted of a total of thirteen students: five girls and eight boys. Only in joining the other school could we have ever benefited from this public outdoor education facility. Therefore, we were very grateful for the opportunity.

I even distinctly remember the thrill of choosing a class partner who would be my bunkroom buddy. Since we were only about 13 students compared to the other school's 150, there were going to be six groups: 3 boy groups of 25 and 3 girl groups of 25. Our 13 students would be integrated, two in a group among the bunkhouses of 25. As our school bus pulled away from our parents, nervously waving goodbye, our tiny group feverishly began discussing what the next few days held in store for us. What activities would there be? What would the facilities be like? What time would we have to go to sleep? But more importantly – what were the other kids like? Would they be friendly? Were they interested in the same things as we were? How many of them would be there?

The hour and a quarter bus ride seemed like an eternity. We were all so eager to get to the camp site. The ride was a familiar one. Most of us had travelled to the Rocky Mountains many times before. This time, the destination was not the ski hills of Banff National Park; it was the Rocky Mountains YMCA's Yamnuska centre. As our bus pulled up to the main campsite administration building, we could see that the other school had already arrived. Our bus came to a stop and a guide boarded the bus. With a broad smile, we were welcomed to Camp Yamnuska. We were instructed to grab our things off the bus and bring them into the main dining room, as the other school was waiting for us. We could hear a lot of noise as we came closer to the hall. I remember the doors opening. The adrenaline was pumping as we walked single file into the dining room. All of a sudden, it felt like three hundred sets of eyes were riveted on us. Huddled together, we moved in a tiny pack to the middle of the room. We felt surrounded and almost engulfed by the intense stares intent on each step we made.

To break the tension, the camp site director called every one's attention to him by blowing a whistle. He covered emergency procedures. Then, we were told it was time to be split into our sleeping groups so we could put away our things and change into our outdoor clothing for our first activity. There were three lodging areas: Pods 1, 2 and the coveted Long House. As the group of eager students' names were called, slowly the pack began to thin out. All my classmates were assigned to one of the pods. All except my partner Boris and me. We were among the remaining children who were left and informed that they would be assigned to the famed Long House. Located at the edge of the campground, this extended building had separate rooms as opposed to the pods, which had a central living room with bunk beds connecting. The pods were located strategically around the campsite with girls and boys in separate facilities. The Long House had a dividing wall. The first half of the dormitory would be occupied by boys and the other half by girls. At the time, this seemed an inconsequential detail. Each time a child who would be bunking in the Long House was called, there was a tiny flurry as they quickly organized themselves into who would be sharing a room with whom. Boris and I quickly realised that we were on our own, literally and figuratively.

We made the long trek from the main dining hall to the Long House, with only thirty minutes to unpack and change for the first activity. The mad dash to select the 'best' rooms had begun. There really was no reason for Boris and me to rush. As we had suspected in the dining hall, it was crystal clear where we would be sleeping. We realised we would not be mixing with the other students, as they had already picked their roommates. Nevertheless, caught up in the euphoria of the choice of rooms, Boris and I too found ourselves running to the Long House in a race whose purpose we could not readily articulate. As we arrived, Boris and I walked into the first room, ready to place our sleeping bags and luggage on our beds, only to be told, "Sorry buddy, this bed is already taken!"

As we moved from room to room, we got the hint that no one wanted to share with us. As each room's occupants repeated the now familiar refrain, we became relegated to the back of the Long House, farthest from the entrance. In that last empty room filled with bunk beds, Boris and I had our pick of where we wanted to sleep. No other students from the public school would stay in this room. Opposite each other, we each chose the bottom bunks. We unpacked our clothing and got settled. Suddenly there was a knock at the door. It was Bunny, the head female counsellor. Bunny announced her arrival and asked if she could come in. A little surprised, we said yes. Bunny entered and introduced herself. She explained that the girls were on the other half of the Long House and the separating wall was right outside our room. The adjoining door would be locked at all times, during the day and at night. Since Bunny was the designated supervisor, her room was right next door. She would be keeping an eye on both the boys and the girls, and there was to be "no monkey business," she exclaimed with a half-smile.

Bunny then looked around. She asked, with a puzzled look, where our roommates were. We confirmed that it was just going to be us. It seemed that all the others' rooming buddies were somewhat predesignated. You could tell Bunny felt a little sorry for us. From there forward, we felt like we had an advocate and a friendly face to keep an eye on us. With a quick wink, Bunny walked into the main hallway announcing her presence to the entire Long House. We were to get changed into active, indoor clothing, ready to meet in the main dining room in fifteen minutes.

We got ready quickly and made our way to the main dining room, again not sure what to expect. By the time we got there, the tables and chairs had been stacked along the walls, and the dining hall was converted into a playroom/gymnasium. The excitement and anticipation of the unknown was palpable. Not knowing what was to come, all the students gathered in the centre of the room. Our tiny group quickly gravitated to each other on the side, hastily sharing anecdotes about the lodging structures and any brief interactions with students from the other school. From what the others shared, nothing significant had occurred, other than a few of our classmates managing to chat up students from the other school; all seemed to be progressing as expected.

Our first icebreaker game was a success. Students were organized into groups based on numbers. The purpose of the game was obviously intended to break down the social barriers and develop camaraderie and teamwork. Running around, expending energy and friendly competition were key ingredients in motivating students to get out of their shells and connect. Laughter and smiles were also ingredients in this successful activity.

An hour or so later, it was time to wash up for lunch. After a minute bathroom break and recruiting of some student volunteers to reorganize the gymnasium, the room was transformed back into a dining hall. We had some of our own teachers accompanying us on the trip; however, they were relieved from supervision during meal times. The students were given a chance to sit where they wanted. Despite this freedom of choice, most of us gravitated back into our class group. There were ten of us together sitting at a table when the food came out. The others were scattered with their newfound public school acquaintances. I distinctly remember the wave of commotion as the food appeared.

In the centre of every table, jugs of juice, plates and cutlery were placed. A few students were chosen to bring out trays of sandwiches, which were placed in the middle of the table. Hungrily, students dug into their sandwiches. The ten of us were very slow to react. With a sinking dread, we recognised the content of the sandwiches. Ham and Cheese. It is important to know that none of us were from observant religious backgrounds. I can't even recall if any of us even kept *kosher*. It was more the principle of the matter. Looking back, it is likely I was one of the few in our group who had never eaten pork – not that we had ever shared these minor details amongst ourselves. Never had a situation arisen when there was a need for disclosure or discussion of our religious practices.

It was quite surreal that we were faced with a dilemma like this. We were trying to fit in. Trying to blend, prevent the spotlight from falling on us. At the same time, there we were. We needed to make a decision on how to act at this very moment. The impact of that decision could affect the success of the entire week ahead. For young students such as us, this was the fork in the road — the ultimate turning point that could have massive implications. The pressure, as I remember, was mounting. We looked at each other, no one uttering a sound. Waiting for someone to speak. None of our teachers were there, of course, as they were off duty during lunch. So, we looked out toward our peers, who had integrated with their bunkmates and were sitting in another area in the dining room. Their decision was pretty clear. They had begun eating their sandwiches along with their new peers. There was something about us all being together that put the question, the pregnant pause, in our instincts. I sat there, knowing that a Jewish school should not be providing pork meals to its students — that it absolutely sent the wrong message to both the Jewish students and also, the non-Jewish students and staff. So, I spoke up. I told my fellow students that we should not eat the sandwiches. Everyone at our table agreed. I got up. I would be the spokesman and tell our counsellor.

One of my friends came with me. Together, we went to the counsellors and tried to explain the problem to them. We simply explained that in Judaism we are forbidden from eating pork. Therefore, the ham and cheese sandwiches were not an appropriate lunch. The counsellors innocently told us to just take off the ham and eat the cheese. Trying not to lengthen the already uncomfortable conversation, I explained that since there was a residue of the ham on the sandwich, it was still a problem for us to consume. The counsellor, honestly trying to find a solution, asked why it was satisfactory for some of our peers to eat the sandwich, pointing out in the dining room how some of our peers were indeed partaking in the lunch, I tried to explain that some were more 'observant' than others. It began to feel like an interrogation. I said it was ok, that maybe we weren't that hungry anyway. I was already feeling like it was best not to pursue the case any further.

We turned to go back to our table when one of the other counsellors said that she would go to the kitchen and see what she could do. It was a familiar voice. It was Bunny, the female counsellor from the Long House who had spoken earlier to Boris and me. I recognized her. I smiled, thanked her, went back to the table, and filled our friends in. There was some debate amongst us if we should just eat the ham sandwiches or not. It was already beginning to cause a stir in the dining hall. The other students were watching us debate amongst ourselves "to eat or not to eat?" I told our group that we had made a path already, and to jump off now and just give in would have even worse consequences. The counsellors, who now understood the situation, would be quite frustrated that we had gone against the very reason why we could not eat the food in the first place. Before we could finish our debate, the cook came out with a few loaves of bread, peanut butter and strawberry jam. He apologized that he was not made aware of any special dietary restrictions and that he would do his best to accommodate us. This seemed really strange to us, since we recalled having filled in under dietary restrictions on our camp forms, not to mix milk and meat and not to have any pork products.

At this point, you could feel every pair of eyes of every student riveted upon our group. The spot light was shining brightly on our alternative lunch. Reluctantly we began making our sandwiches, realizing the potential situation we might have just created. If our goal was to blend in, assimilate and develop some relationships with new people, we would be hard-pressed to retract this highlighted difference and the targets on our backs.

Inhaling our sandwiches, trying to inconspicuously blend with the rest of the group who had already finished their lunch, the head counsellor grabbed the microphone to announce the activities of the afternoon. He explained that we would be separated into groups based on our lodging facilities. We would be rotating among five outdoor activities for the five days of camp. We would be eating as a group as well as doing specific jobs or chores around the camp site on a rotation basis. It was the Long House's job to do dinner clean-up. At the conclusion of the announcements and the explanations, the counsellor drew our attention toward a large poster on one wall. All the counsellors stood up and sang the following song –

"Oh the Lord is good to me
and so I thank the Lord
for giving me the things I need
the sun and the rain and the apple seed
the Lord is good to me.
Johnny Apple Seed AMEN."

The tune was catchy and we all laughed along as the counsellors sang it with glee. Then it was our turn. The entire hall stood up and sang the song in unison. Only years later did it dawn upon me what the purpose was of the non-denominational prayer of thanks at the conclusion of the meal. As naïve kids, we just went along for the ride in what was a cute bonding exercise at the conclusion of the meal.

Stating the obvious, a school must have an educational philosophy and an infrastructure to further and maintain the tenets of that philosophy. It must be clear and articulated in a positive way, permeating all aspects of curriculum and school life. As much as possible, special events should have a formal run sheet, or a scaffold to anticipate potential pitfalls. Time and resources need to be allotted to making those forward plans. Specifically, in relation to Jewish schools, or any other cultural minority who follow a set of values and religious practices, there are two ways of approaching any situation. Either you stand up for something or you wind up falling for anything. Putting it another way, if we are not standing up in a positive way for what we are, we will be forced to stand up in a negative way.

Assimilation is not the same thing at all as integration. If integration is the goal, then knowledge, not blind ignorance, must be the route to achieving that outcome. In the scenario above, it was clear that the school had not developed a clear code of values. Both the staff and the students had not been properly educated about the tenets of their religious philosophy. Had this been integral to the school's philosophy, then the pitfalls of this venture could and would have been anticipated. At the very least, one of our staff members would have been present at meal times. The kitchen staff would have been prepared for our special needs. Our school was not clear enough about its priorities to make this obvious to others, much less to ourselves.

As you may recall, this was already the second year of the camp experience for the I L Peretz school students. The previous year, the kids had also 'thanked the lord, Johnny Appleseed Amen'; I have always wondered whether the goal was integration or assimilation.

The remainder of the afternoon went off without a hitch. We spent the time outside on the lake, learning how to ice fish with our 'Long House' group. Some of the social barriers began to lift as we integrated well among the boys and girls in the group. Our head counsellor, Bunny, tried to spend a little more time with Boris and me — getting to know us a bit better. While walking to the lake, carrying our ice fishing equipment, Bunny hung back with us, chatting about our school, favourite sports and the upcoming hockey play-offs. We could tell she was making an extra effort and we appreciated it. As twelve-year-old boys, it was almost a boost to our boyish egos having the pretty head counsellor pay a little more attention to us, causing some annoyance among the contingent of other boys. The sun dipped behind the mountains relatively early in the late afternoon. Our outdoor activity ended around 4:30 p.m. which left thirty minutes of free time to go back to our cabins, change out of our damp clothing and head back to the main dining room for dinner. As we arrived at the main dining room, the tables were already set and a sign indicating each lodging area pointed to specific tables where we were to sit. Each table was segregated between boys and girls, with the exception of the 'Long House', since boys and girls shared the same dorm, albeit with a dividing door. Boris and I sat beside the two girls from our school, chatting away about some insignificant topic, eagerly waiting for dinner.

We had all worked up quite an appetite from the outdoor activity. As one can imagine, being out in the cold and generating body heat while engaged in physical activity can be quite energy depleting. Each table was required to nominate one student as a server to go to the kitchen window and retrieve food for the table. One of the students from the other school jumped up and nominated himself as our designated waiter. No one had an objection. The boy came back with a tray of ham, peas, carrots and mashed potatoes. This time, however, a counsellor followed behind, carrying a smaller tray of fried chicken. As all the onlookers from each table watched with bated breath, the counsellor informed the table that the ham was for every student. The fried chicken was only for students from our school.

You could hear the moans and complaints as the students openly objected to eating the ham. Why were *they* getting a much better, more appealing food substitute? This time, there were a number of students who were really up in arms. The commotion became a large growling rumble. The other students were quite vocal in expressing their displeasure about having to eat the ham when a much better substitute was being offered to the "Jewish" students.

Once again, we just wanted the floor to open up and swallow us and our distress. Luckily, we were so famished we tried to ignore the stares and comments and eat the chicken nonetheless. There were a few leftovers that were distributed to the other students. However, the damage had been done.

At the conclusion of the meal, once again we sang the "Johnny Apple Seed" grace in some sort of false sense of unity. The song's catchy tune seemed to distract the students from the situation and erase the giant divide that had opened up.

The evening activity was charades. All of us weary-eyed students were ushered off to our lodging with the strict announcement that we had thirty minutes to shower and get ready for bed. Lights out was to be strictly enforced at 9:00 p.m.

Boris and I went straight into our room and began getting ready for bed. Suddenly, our door was flung open. One of the more outspoken students from the other school stepped forward with three or four of his friends behind him. The boy approached me quite aggressively and in a threatening manner said, "You think you are better than us, dirty Jew boy!"

Now might be an opportune time to let you know that I had always been the smallest kid in my class. It never bothered me. But I certainly stuck out of the crowd, being so small in comparison with my peers. I guess this made me appear like an easy target for what was about to come.

I was quite shocked and unprepared for his verbal attack. All I could answer was, "No." I looked at Boris for support, but he just backed away.

"You think you're just so special, you and your Jew friends!"

That's when his posse moved in front of the entrance to our room, blocking our only escape from this very uncomfortable hostility.

I tried to reason with him. "I'm not sure what you mean, we are just like you. We don't want any trouble, please just leave us alone!"

That's when he took his first swing at me. He tried to knock me to the floor with one punch.

Oh, and I forgot one other thing: I learned in first grade that being small means you could also be fast, really fast! I managed to move back just in time and he missed. I rotated away, but I realized his friends were surrounding me. There really was no escape from this frontal attack.

The adrenaline was pumping. The next encounter happened so quickly; I reacted swiftly, without any conscious thought at all. Survival was at stake. As the boy lunged toward me again, I ducked, grabbed his legs below his knees and lifted, thus catching him by surprise and removing his feet from under him, causing him to fall on his back. As he fell to the floor I realised that the other boys were still shouting, "Get the Jew," and, "Hit the Jew." The wind was knocked out of him and I found myself kneeling on top of him, with his shocked expression staring back at me.

At this point, the room had become very silent with absolute shock. The boys could not believe that tiny little me had managed to put down their strongest, most vocal representative. I managed to pin him to the floor. I screamed back: "Don't you dare call me a dirty Jew!"

That image is forever engraved in my mind. I'm not sure where the strength came from, nor the conviction to fight so hard to stand up for myself. Somewhere deep down, I felt like I was not actually fighting for myself. It felt as if something was at stake, something much bigger than me.

The boy just lay on the ground, looking up at me, the same shocked expression on his face. Out of the corner of my eye, I saw Bunny standing in the doorway, taking in the scene. As she came over to me, I released the boy on the ground. He got up and stepped back. No one really said anything.

Bunny sternly told all the boys, "Get back to your rooms." Very quickly, the crowd dissipated. I looked over at Boris, who was white as a sheet. Bunny came over to me, put her arm around me and asked me if I was ok. The simple reassuring gesture was all I needed to regain my composure… and then grasp the magnitude of what had just happened.

Word spread quickly around camp about what had transpired. As we walked into breakfast the next day, everyone was whispering and chatting. No one bothered Boris and me for the duration of camp. On the spot, the camp staff and teachers began to initiate tolerance workshops. Some positive discussion may have come through those reactive initiatives. For me, I realised that this event forever changed the course of my life. It made a tremendous impact on who I was then and the type of person I was to become.

While maintaining my conviction for who I was, my philosophy as to how I would interact with the world forever changed. No longer would I sit back and let others determine who I was, how I would think and what it meant to be a Jew in the world. It would take many years and other incidents to fully formulate and articulate this philosophy. But the seeds had been sown. I think my sleeping inner giant had been awakened. If we accept and fully embrace our uniqueness, the world will respect us for our integrity, bravery, courage and honesty. Only then will we have the opportunity for genuine peace, authentic unity, and mutual respect, allowing for true interfaith dialogue.

Growing Pains, Top Secret Gains

Quite simply, my parents were not prepared to simply drop me into a regular public school after elementary school. The thought of me becoming a teenager in an environment devoid of Jewish culture, coupled with the influences of North American society, frightened my newly immigrated parents. We were still getting used to living in this foreign country and assimilating into a totally new culture. These were the all-important teen years, when peer influences are strong and powerful. Being nurtured in a small parochial school environment and tucked far away from the influences of popular culture appealed to my parents' need to protect us while we were not at home. Actually, I benefitted greatly from the fact that my brother was one grade ahead of me. My parents had to tackle the issue of where they would send both of us after graduation, a full year prior to my completing Grade 6.

There was only one real problem with that line of thinking: my brother and I were two completely different types of students. Michael is an academic machine. Teachers loved him and he was justly rewarded with an academic scholarship in his Grade 6 year. As a reward for his accomplishments, my brother received the B'nai Brith academic award. This was a fully paid summer sleepaway camp experience in the famed B'nai Brith Pine Lake facility. This was the camp that every Jewish child talked of and dreamed of attending. Only the wealthy kids in the communities of Calgary and Edmonton attended. The camp was situated between the two major Alberta cities, just north of Red Deer.

This was only the first of many accomplishments that set my brother in a totally different league to me. My older brother was a very motivated and intelligent student who excelled in school. Early on, I realised that our family already had its scholastic achiever. No family needs two. This unstated conclusion strongly guided my thinking in my early years. So much so that for many years my lack of motivation was due to my firm internal conclusion that there was no point in trying. I could never reach the bar Michael had set so high. I set in motion an alternate route, a different path from my brother. I raised the bar high to be sure. I ensured that I would enjoy every moment in school. School served as the theatre and stage for my dramatic and comedic performances.

My peers would be the judges of my achievements, not my teachers! A good day was determined by how many laughs I received. The truly memorable days were not those when I ended up in the principal's office – that was not relevant in my equation for school. How did I judge a good day? By how long the smiles lasted on my classmates' faces.

This path created a big problem for me, one I was completely unaware of. Instead of planning my future, I was plotting my next in-class screenplay. I didn't foresee how the impressions I had made on my teachers and principal, and my behaviour, would affect my future academic endeavours.

When it came time for Michael to graduate from Grade 6, my parents thoroughly researched an experimental program in the public education system. This elite program, the French Late Immersion Program, was a pilot program designed to stimulate the motivated learner in a totally French environment. The program was widely promoted as an alternate program that created opportunities for the self-motivated student.

Descriptive selling points included expanding the students' intellect, teaching responsible citizenship, and developing enhanced feelings of self-esteem and pride through the mastery of a Romance language. Other educational benefits included the strengthening of English literacy skills, encouraging the pleasure of lifelong learning and, most importantly, providing students with supplemental choices for advanced education and career options. These were all things the standard education program in the public system could not provide. For many parents, this program was an important and viable path, different from that of the majority.

Of course, for my brother, this program of study was perfect for him. There was no doubt he would excel in this type of academic environment. My parents could not pass up the opportunity for my brother to surpass most others his age. Neither could my brother, who was 100% keen to take on the challenge. The problem was that there were only two schools offering the program in the southwest quadrant of the city where we lived. Even though the alternative education program was in its infancy, in only its second year, its popularity was quickly on the rise. So much so that in the third year, the year I was eligible, parents overwhelmed the Board of Education.

One day in late April of my Grade 6 year, registration opened to the public. Parents were to place the name of their child on a list in the designated school that ran the French late immersion program. The students would be screened for eligibility through a simple report filled out by their Grade 6 English teacher, endorsed by the supervising principal. The unsuspecting Board of Education failed to anticipate that there would be such an overwhelming demand, especially with such a simple application process. As long as the child met the eligibility criteria and was approved by their last school of enrolment, they would be accepted into the program – on a first-come, first-served basis.

After two years of success coupled with popularity, high demand, and a lack of places for children in the Late Immersion program, word had spread like wildfire. Because of the first-come, first-served policy, parents resorted to sleeping outside the school the night before registration. Luckily, the registration date was in late April, so the weather cooperated. A line began to form in the late evening prior to the registration date. Eager parents queued up, motivated by the desire to ensure their child's name was placed high enough on the list.

The tension was palpable amongst the throng of parents. Everyone enviously eyeballed the early arrivers, including my mother and me, who had beaten them to the punch and had assembled in an orderly line. We were lined up with some of the parents from our tiny parochial school that had arrived around the same time as me and my mother. With hot chocolate and sandwiches, we took our spot on our lawn chairs, somewhere around sixteenth in line. This more than secured my early registration. Nine hours later, the doors opened. We successfully placed my name on the registration list and handed in the completed application. I was in…

Once the application process was completed, the Calgary Board of Education would ratify the registration lists of applicants for the program. They then placed the authority of determining eligibility onto each individual school. It was now up to the education committee at Elboya Junior High School to determine the suitability of the candidates. The process began with a phone call to each student's elementary school requesting the last term's report and a statement of endorsement from the school principal.

That's when the error of my comical, jovial, non-academically minded ways came back to haunt me. My parents were called in by the principal to discuss my 'choices' upon graduation. It was only many years later that I became privy to what went on behind the scenes of that meeting.

One afternoon, toward the end of my Grade 6 school year, my mother received a phone call from my principal. She was asked to come in with my father for a meeting as soon as possible. Unbeknownst to me, my parents set a time and went to this urgent meeting. No reason for the meeting had been given, and they had not asked for one.

The principal sat my parents down. Using his professionalism and a long history of experience with educating children, he then proceeded to explain to my father and mother that they were harbouring completely unrealistic expectations for me in thinking that I was a suitable candidate for the late immersion program. He himself, having come from Montreal, Quebec, knew very well the difficulties of learning a new language in an immersion setting. The challenge for any student would be immense. Coming from a very nurturing environment such as my current school, the integration into a larger public school, moving from a teacher -pupil ratio of 1:13 to 1:28 would be a challenge for any student. These were all very sound points to consider. The lead up all sounded reasonable.

Then came the blow my parents never could have expected. A conversation that would haunt them for many years – until my graduation from university and ultimately receiving my doctorate– a true testimony to my academic potential realised.

The Principal stated in his very clear, unemotional voice, "As Arnie's parents, it would do Arnie so much better in the long term for you to recognize his limitations. You must realise that he will not become much of anything that is dependent on academic achievement. Arnie is already maximizing his potential. He simply is not intellectually equipped to attain any significant standing to merit even going to university. I suggest you encourage him to focus on a trade and embrace the opportunity that would come from a less vigorous academic program. He is better suited for a practical vocational program." He concluded by saying that he strongly suggested that my parents withdraw my application from the Late Immersion Program and find an alternate, less demanding program of study for me.

As my parents tell it today, this was an all-defining conversation. It had a lasting impact on both their standing in the community and my sister's education, who was three grades below me. If you knew my parents, in this case, especially my mother, you would know that they both saw red. My mother and father both stated emphatically, it was not the decision of the school to determine my future path. The principal had only arrived in Calgary a year prior. He had little knowledge of me and had no right to make this decision about my future with his limited background.

I know this episode cost my parents some friendships. Going head to head with the principal of the school in such a tiny community alienated them from some of the families who were good friends with the principal. I remember that around the time I finished elementary school, a social void opened up. Social activities and get-togethers simply stopped. I never understood why at the time; but I never imagined it was because of a stand my parents took on my behalf.

My parents went to work. Shortly thereafter it came to light that the principal's daughter, who was in my class, had also applied to the very same late immersion program. Her name was much further down the list. Perhaps she was in jeopardy of not being accepted due to her distant placing in the registration queue.

It was to my advantage that my mother was the co-president of the school. Thus, when she pushed for the issue to be brought to the school board, she had some influence over the matter. After a nerve-racking board meeting, the decision was made that the principal was to indeed recuse himself.

In addition, a decision was made that the letter would be more appropriate coming from my 4th/5th grade teacher who had taught me two years prior, who had also acted as interim principal until this principal's appointment. Despite the principal's belief that I would not amount to much, my former teacher (and former interim Principal) sent in a recommendation that I be accepted into the late immersion Junior High School program. She cited my love of languages and the untapped potential that I would achieve when motivated and inspired. More importantly, she felt that when I was placed in an environment where I was nurtured, with the opportunity to excel, she believed I would reach my potential. Because of this reference, which I found out about two months later, I would be starting in the late immersion program at Elboya Junior High School.

Don't get me wrong; despite the principal's lack of confidence in me, I was blissfully unaware of these events. My parents strategically kept this episode from me until many years later when I was well into my successful high school years.

This incident highlights keystone principles of a child's success in school, one that is an absolute imperative for parents. *To the child, the school and the teacher are always right.* Despite how obvious it was that the implications of the school's decision would have a profound effect on limiting my future, it was more important in my parents' eyes, that my respect for the 'educational institution' should not be compromised. Had my parents not kept this secret, my respect for educators and my path in life could have been significantly altered.

There were many experiences in this small parochial school and other similar institutions that shaped my educational philosophy. I have witnessed individuals or school boards push far-reaching, haughty, philosophical goals that are forced upon schools to direct educational policy despite the pitfalls and illogical practicality of the initiative. Having personally experienced how educational policies are sometimes set, it is no wonder many teachers and students become disenfranchised with the 'system'. Too often, decisions are made in a vacuum without the direct input from the teachers and those with educational training as to why a program should or should not take place. Often the principal is the sole educator around the boardroom table. As a lone voice, there can be no platform to stand up to a board, presenting significant reasons why a certain initiative should not take place. When a school board is structured around individual egos that have the 'power' to force these programs into policy without any input from the educational core, critical mistakes are made, which ultimately are paid for by the children. In my experience, I have seen far too many of these examples, both from the perspective of a student as well as a principal.

On the other hand, it is also possible with proper governance and a strict structure, to work successfully with a school board that consistently focuses on the best interests of the students. When the ethos of the school drives the decision-making process of the school board, the students' best interests can be kept at the forefront. The chair or president of the board must be committed to this ethos. If and when an idea or concept is poised to derail this focus, there must be mechanisms in place within the board structure to redirect attention to the tenets of the school. There needs to be a thorough vetting of potential board members to ensure that they are there to serve the best interests of the school and all the students, not simply their own egos or their own children's benefits.

Never Underestimate the Power of Nurturing –
Overcoming 'MCS' by Brawn or Brain?!

My 4th/5th grade teacher's prediction was spot on. Indeed, all I needed was a nurturing environment to motivate me. Of course, there were factors outside the academics that also played a huge role. Prophetically, Elboya Junior High's late immersion program suited my personality to a T. It would take a bit of time to adjust and as expected, 7th grade was full of transitions, which resulted in me receiving a C average.

Today, I am blessed to be in a profound position to effect educational change on a larger scale. Having been a principal of over 500 students, reflecting on my experience as a stray child in the vast educational sea, I have come to know that a nurturing environment is the most essential factor to guide a student to meet his or her potential.

This has proven one of the most challenging sections to write. I could provide a chronological account of how I grew from that unmotivated elementary school class clown, knowing I would never follow in the footsteps of my gifted older brother, to the scaffolding of the person I am today with a rabbinical degree and a doctorate of education. However, that would make for a really long story and might miss the point. As the second son and the middle child, I was used to not having my story heard, so I learned early on how to distil the essence of what I needed to communicate.

It seems I wanted to find and define an identity for myself, to increase my sense of self-esteem, to find ways to stand out from my peer group, to stand out in my family! I was searching for outlets that would provide recognition of my values. I had to identify my skills and talents, which would be rewarded by my family and school. Unconsciously at some point, I realised that I was always intent on making my father proud of me.

It was only in the 8th Grade that I started to realise that I had no idea where I was heading. Once again, it was the aura of my brother's accomplishments that accentuated my floundering sense of direction.

Until now, resigned to be in my brother's shadow, watching his hard-fought determination to pave a pathway to medical school, I suddenly realised I was lost. My brother began discussing his future in the field of science. But then there was that unspoken reality. No two children in a family become a doctor. But even more to the point, no one could even imagine that I had the academic potential to become a doctor. The thought that I would be able to enter a profession such as medicine never even entered my mind. If not a doctor, then what? After all, there are only Jewish doctors or Jewish businessmen; the Jewish professions by default: – one prestigious the other predictably stable.

I realise today that I didn't really believe in myself. How could I? Over the first fourteen years of my academic career, I never even tried. I didn't know how to study or how to even have constructive homework periods. I never worked a day in school, but then again, I didn't fail either. I was able to get by at a B level simply by listening when I needed to. A quick review session before the test enabled a satisfactory achievement, enough to fly under the radar of my parent's wrath. After all, the only method my parents used to gauge our academic standing was the final report card, or if they ever received a phone call from the school because of my misbehaviour (which, by junior high school, I made sure rarely took place).

As I evolved through Grade 8, I started to see that positive academic results felt good. However, you must realise that this boost in self-esteem had a lot to do with my experiencing success and achievement in other spheres Elboya offered, spheres that were of little significance or interest to my older brother especially sports. In terms of being the class clown, I gradually decided I had to pick my moments a little better. I could still make people laugh; however, I had recognised that I had a variety of opportunities, including academically, where I could sense a feeling of accomplishment. All of a sudden, my teachers started to look at me a little differently. I was really coming into my own and my marks were suddenly high B's. By the 9th grade, I had an A average. Not only that, but for the first time, my parents were called to come to the final school assembly. I was an acclaimed all-rounded student; I still have the trophy today, signifying my achievement as the top physical education student in the school that year.

For those many years as an average student, I witnessed how it feels at the end of a school year to sit in a final assembly and not be recognized. One becomes jaded seeing the same students rewarded year in and year out for the same brilliance and God-given talent they consistently display throughout the year. The end of the year assembly for Grade 9 taught me an incredible lesson. That one moment had a profound effect that shaped all my year-end assemblies in all my schools.

There is extraordinary power unleashed in students when they see their unique contribution acknowledged. They feel that deep down there is something special about them that others value. This was how I felt when my name was unexpectedly called. The award was more than just a plastic trophy. The recognition meant that someone saw me for who I truly am. That I am unique and I have a gift.

It takes a lot to erase a deeply-ingrained negative self-image. Even with this newfound confidence starting to bloom, I was still trapped by my "middle child syndrome" (MCS). My brother could always be recognized for his academic accomplishments. I needed to have some area that defined me. I was yearning for something that gave me a sense of accomplishment. One of my God-given advantages, which I was fortunate enough to exploit throughout my schooling, was my speed. I was a pretty good runner, being recognized early on for my very fast, tiny physical stature. As the little Grade 1 student in South Africa, I won the school competition in sprints. I came first in the Athletics Carnival and ended up running in the All-City Championships in the 100-meter dash at the University of Witwatersrand, where I finished second overall.

It had always been a thrill to excel physically above others' expectations. I reaped great satisfaction doing well physically, especially because no one ever would expect me to, because I was such a 'small boy.' To combat my MCS, I mentally declared that my brother would receive the academic accolades while I made my mark athletically, thereby gaining recognition in my family and within myself.

What I experienced was all about the fundamental developmental markers of childhood and adolescence. These milestones are only becoming more challenging to recognize and achieve healthily for a growing majority of young people. The fleeting advances in technology, the 'I' generation, the growing evidence of a plague among parents resulting in an inability to lovingly discipline and set limits on their children, much less their adolescents, are conspiring against the healthy development of our young people. All in all, we are seeing a decline in resilience and self-motivation among our young people.

Resilience and self-motivation were two characteristics I was fortunate enough to have nurtured in me – or to have been born with, in very healthy doses, I am never sure. What I did realise in structuring this chapter of my book is the back story. It has become the role of schools to create opportunities for all students to recognize their strengths, celebrate their aptitudes, be able to problem-solve through challenges and, overall, nurture resilience. These were the outcomes for me from my personal experiences in junior high and high school. These are the outcomes I strive to recreate for my students in my schools. Because, as we are all aware, there were many students who were not as fortunate as my brother or me.

The crisis in education today is no different from what it was years ago. The most economical and perhaps the most convenient method for the average teacher is to teach toward the middle level of the class and expect both extremes to conform. It was in my nature, to rebel against that very premise. I refused to be forced to comply with my teacher's standard expectations, primarily because they were set in a vacuum, not seeing me for who I was. In this model, there was no value for them in recognizing my individuality and the contribution I could make if they saw me for me.

The fact is, however, there are always too many students who don't fit into the 'box.' There always have been, and there always will be. It is a miracle that I did not end up jaded, disillusioned and disenfranchised. I was extremely fortunate to have had a few, amazing, nurturing role models scattered within my thirteen years of education. They ignited in me a belief in myself as a valuable student with the potential to achieve well beyond my past performances – a belief I was able to hold on to. I have now realised that the missing component to change this imbalance in the equation is the passionate teacher who has the ability to nurture individuality. As a principal, this is what I now look for, first and foremost, in all of my staff. There is a passion and realisation in that individual teacher, as corny as it may sound, that they can indeed change the life of a child. And by nurturing that child, they are changing the world. It is becoming imperative for schools to recognise and provide opportunities for the differentiated developmental needs of all students.

In junior high school, I ran in the Calgary Spartan track and field club I achieved my potential by running the 200m and 400m. I ended up being selected for the city team and ran in the Alberta Provincial Games. I was a bronze medallist in the 400m. At some level, I think my father was very aware of how I constantly felt like I was living in my brother's shadow. My father tried to praise me whenever possible. I know he even overlooked some of my academic floundering. I was finding my way, my path, and my identity. Whenever my father was in town, which was quite infrequent, he would attend my practices to watch me run. As a sprinter, however, I was never satisfied. I realised that I would never be one of the best runners.

Having to push myself as a sprinter was taking a toll on my tiny frame. By Grade 10, I realised that I could no longer exert myself further and achieve any greater results in track and field. I had pain in my legs, which reached an all-time high, necessitating significant medical intervention. I had developed muscle hernias all the way down both of my calves. The recommendation was to either do nothing or try surgery on the leg that was the most severe, and through therapy see if there was a significant difference. We decided to perform the surgery on the left leg due to its more acute pain and rehabilitate the right through a change in training regime.

The impact of the decision to have the surgery caused many significant changes in my life. I realised that my competitive track and field days were over. It was time to set my sights on a different sport. I had adopted the persona of an athlete and defined my choices accordingly. It was working for me. Whereas my brother was 'the 'academic',' I felt that I had to have an image that was all mine. When my parents and friends looked at me and the question came up as to exactly who I am, I wanted them to think: the athlete, the jock, the tiny, fast guy who made a giant impact on the sporting field – someone who would be remembered for something. I was a mere year behind my brilliant brother. I still had the academic confidence somewhat knocked out of me. So far, the sports arena was the only realm where I felt I could define myself above the crowd. I had managed to accomplish this on a relatively small scale in my junior high school. In the track club, I had gained a small sense of nurturing that was enough for me to feel like I was more than just another face in the crowd.

As I now had to shift away from track and field, it was critical that I quickly find another canvas upon which to illustrate my individuality. To legitimately build my self-esteem, I had to develop myself as a stand-out in the crowd, define my purpose in my own mind, and gain the sense that I was a winner in my father's mind.

As The Transition Turns…Brains

Due to the rehabilitation from the surgery, I was unable to participate in school sports for two months. I was required to apply for an exemption from my high school physical education class. Instead of taking a sport the first term of my Grade 11 year, I decided to challenge myself and take physics, but there was a twist.

My brother, who was in his final year of high school, was also taking his first physics class. Thus, the two Glogauer brothers were enrolling in the same class with the same teacher that fall term.

That year of physics changed my life. I will never forget Mr Barry McGuire, our physics guru. The structure of his class was novel. It was so powerful that to this day I use his "opening ten minute" rule in all my classes whether I am teaching math, Jewish law or personal development.

At the beginning of every class, Mr McGuire would walk in, fold a stack of loose-leaf paper in half and tear the sheets along the crease. He passed a half sheet of paper to every student and would then proceed to write a question on the blackboard. Mr McGuire allowed 5-10 minutes for us to write our answer on the sheet of paper. The question was always based on the previous day's lesson. The question was always a practical application of the theory taught the previous day, with the same sort of calculation we had learned the previous lesson. The question reinforced our intrinsic understanding of the formula and how to apply it within the overall theoretical picture. It sounds pretty mundane, but here is the genius part: how you answered the question was more important than your final bottom line answer. We were all required to recall the applicable formula and write it out in its original form. We were to show all the steps needed to isolate the unknown variable. Substitutions always had to be shown in parentheses and the final answer had to be written on the bottom line. Every step had to be written on its own line with the 'equal signs' all lined up on the left margin.

At the beginning, it seemed the teacher was just a tad over the line in his pedantic, OCD demands. As his class progressed over the year, severe consequences were meted out to those students who did not adopt these strict parameters. It didn't take long for students to recognize the benefits of the system.

An organized mind, mathematically, has the ability to focus in a systematic way. This allows the brain to weed out extraneous, irrelevant information. The system he established forced us to do just that. It sounds quite simplistic, but the adherence to his system was the stroke of genius. It allowed us students to take the guesswork out of how the teacher was going to evaluate our knowledge acquisition. The students would now be precisely aware of the analytical elements that needed to be retained from the previous lesson based on the question posed the next day. After each lesson, the student understood, because of the teacher's consistency, the exact system of how to pinpoint the most essential outcome of the lesson. There was no guesswork, no "what did we learn today?" Each quiz was handed back in a box for pick up the next day. Feedback was immediate and precise.

After the quiz, Mr McGuire would solve the problem on the blackboard and the lesson of the day would proceed from there. Besides lab work, there were never any tests. We were all very prepared for our final exam because it consisted of a series of questions that were designed in the same style of each daily quiz.

To this day, I use this exact style of class structure and have felt that it automatically encourages the students to review the daily lesson and keeps them on their toes. They become accustomed to thinking about the most critical aspects of the lesson and taking notes during the lesson that focus on those key points.

At the conclusion of our shared physics year, my brother, who naturally was the stronger student, achieved a higher grade. It was amazing how little effort he put in to achieve such a high mark. For me, I had to study diligently to ensure I would be ready for every daily quiz. Every now and then, I would beat him. That was always a personal triumph, a little victory for the underdog. It was close in the end though; there was less than 5% difference in our final marks! We both look back at that year fondly. I must say that it seemed the teacher also got a 'kick' out of having two competitive brothers in the class. To his credit, Mr McGuire never compared me to my brother. I always felt he looked at me with a spark to encourage me to be all I could as a student in his class. I received truly lifelong lessons from a master educator that have stuck with me for almost thirty years.

Mr McGuire also shaped my 'first day of school' routine. He implemented an amazing idea I use today to encourage my students to get involved in their lessons. As all thirty students scrambled and clamoured into the classroom on the first day of school, most students coveted the back seats in the classroom. Mr McGuire looked at us all vying for the back rows. He said, in the calmest and uncaring of ways: "The students in the front row of the class generally achieve 10-15% higher than those sitting anywhere else." He paused, smiled, and added, "Would any of you like to move from the back to the front? Anyone not happy with being in the front?" I too use this at the beginning of the year. I always have a smile on my face as I see those students who ended up under duress in the front, all of a sudden become content, even ecstatic with their selection.

I was not fortunate, nor brave enough to sit in the front row that first year of physics. The next semester, in order to finish off my physics requirements, I was determined to have Mr McGuire as my teacher. I remember that first day of class when he walked in with his swagger and attitude. He began his class with the same intimidating speech. This time I was definitely at the front of the class looking him right in the eye. I noticed a little smirk as he recognized me. I will never forget his opening remarks, "So, I see some of you are back for more...buckle your seatbelts!"

As The Transition Turns...Brawn

Before my surgery, I began to experiment with various other sports. The wait list for surgery was a few months and I had stopped running due to the intense pain. I took up water polo. Some people shy away from physical contact sports and how dangerous they are. For me, I could always take a physical hit. However, as we would say when I was playing defence on the football team in grade 10, "It's always better to give than to receive." Translation: it is always easier to be physical and dish out the blow, rather than to take a hit on the receiving end.

But then I played water polo. What an insane sport! In water polo it is not good to either give or receive! I remember the first time I had to go in the 'hole', as they called it. This was the strategic offensive position. In the 'hole', the main focus was to set up one key player, me, in front of the opposition's net. The team sets up around the player and attempts to feed him the ball. If he is open and manages to evade the opposition, he can take a shot on the net. But if the opposition plays tight, close defence, they are legally allowed to dunk the offensive player, me, when they have the ball. Simply put: In water polo, you have three chances to legally drown a player, me. On the third time it is considered an offense, then the guilty player is sent out for the duration of twenty seconds, and a power play one-man advantage is given to the offensive team.

Once in the hole was more than enough for me. I was not interested in nearly drowning, not a second time. I decided water polo was not for me. So I tried wrestling.

I was quite surprised at the level of fitness needed for wrestling. I quickly got in shape. I was small, strong and scrappy but thoroughly enjoyed the camaraderie of the team aspect. I was fortunate to fit right into the middle of my weight class. While many of the other boys were focused on losing weight to drop down into my weight category, I focused on strengthening my upper body and learning some technical moves. Training was intense at school but I decided that if I wanted to succeed above the students in my school, I would need to join a team. One of the students in my grade, Tony, mentioned that I could come and try out his club. He told me that it would not be my choice but that of the instructor, if I were to be selected to join. I was a bit nervous but in sport, I had a lot of confidence. To that point in my life, I had never 'tried' out for a sport team and not been selected.

On Sunday morning, I joined the team practice for a work-out/try-out. I was introduced to the head coach, I briefly said hello and then joined the team for practice. I occasionally peeked over my shoulder to see if the coach was watching me. Despite this minor distraction, I nevertheless had a good work-out. Just when I thought practice was over, Tony said to me "Now the try-out begins." All the boys sat around the perimeter of the mat and the coach called on two boys to spar against each other. Before I knew it, my name was called and it was time to step up. My opponent was Tony. This was an all or nothing match, up against a wrestler who had been training for years.

I decided to let it all out and be the aggressor. As we began, Tony sat back a little and gave me the opportunity to attack, which is what I did. Before he knew it, I had lunged in for his leg and managed to take hold of it. I spun around and took him down to the mat for a critical point. Tony was strong and a good technical wrestler. He managed to fight me off and not allow me to pin him. This was enough for me to have minimally impressed the coach. I was invited to join the team.

I continued to grow and develop as a wrestler, all toward our first wrestling meet. I really enjoyed the rigorous training, the team camaraderie, and it definitely kept me in shape. I had only fought against a few boys from the club and at school. I still didn't really know what to expect. I learned to wrestle instinctively in keeping with my personality. With the good-natured chip planted firmly on my shoulder, the tiny little athlete with something to prove, it was this frame of mind that, in the end, became my wrestling downfall.

In our second invitation wrestling meet, I was paired against a very strong wrestler who was much more experienced than I was. It was a very competitive match and I was keeping up, move against move. At one point, he managed to twist around me and secure me in a hold with him on top of me. He was grabbing my legs, attempting to twist them to force me onto my back. I refused with all my being to turn, knowing that once I did, my fate would be sealed. Everyone could see the agony in my eyes, along with a steadfast, unwillingness to give in. Then, suddenly, without any warning and with a loud pop, my knee gave out. The cartilage in my knee tore right away and my leg buckled. Under the pressure, my back was turned over toward the mat and I was pinned. In one move, I had lost the battle, and the war.

My coach and teammates came over to me offering comfort, support and first aid. Upset at the loss, I shrugged off their sympathy and resigned myself to rehabilitating my knee and to keep moving forward. Of course, there was the more immediate challenge...how to get home. I was dreading that phone call. It is a theme that has haunted me into my adult life. Whilst my father was the one whose accolades I sought, it was my mother's reactions that I actively avoided. Usually it would unleash for injuring myself or at other times for getting myself into some situation which I always maintained was due to no fault of my own. I knew she would be upset and frustrated... and I was right. I had no choice in this situation, however. I called my mother. When she answered, I already knew how it was going to turn out. There was that tone, that edge that this was simply not a good time. I told her that I was injured and could barely walk. She responded pretty typically. "This is once again an example of you following your own path." I knew the drill already. I had made my choices with full knowledge and acceptance of the responsibility that if I were to get hurt, it was on my sixteen-year-old shoulders to find a way to take care of myself. She said she could not come and pick me up. I was to find my own way home. Which was exactly what I did. Hobbling to the bus stop, I managed to make my way home on public transport. I opted for the long rehabilitation road with many hours of physiotherapy over surgery. It was another tough lesson to learn but like every other hard-won lesson, it gave me even more determination to find an outlet that could provide me with the physical activity to match my active personality and emotional needs. I have also since honed my skill to recognise when to concede the battle to win the war.

As high school progressed, I found my individual academic talents were validated more regularly. I experienced success in achieving with some of my mentors and role models, both academically and athletically. I began to believe in myself. I also learned some very important lessons. It would have to come from within me. I wouldn't receive any handouts. Success only came through tenacious commitment and self-reliance. Because my parents were so busy, and I felt no one was really looking over my shoulder, all I had was myself. I had only myself to blame for lack of success or to pat myself on the back for any accomplishments. Either way, I owned both outcomes. Even if there were huge obstacles, I never gave up.

Climbing the Social Ladder

Every child grows up with a deep, ingrained need to feel a part of something greater than him or herself. It is well-documented psychologically that nurtured children develop a more solid sense of self-esteem compared to children who are raised devoid of a consistent emotional bond. We seek this connection early in our development. Our future social wellbeing and the success of our relationships depend on the maturation of this attachment.

As young children, my brother and I were unique amongst our peers in developing our self-reliance. When I explain to my children how we delivered newspapers in -30°C winter weather in the early hours of the morning in the frigid, pitch dark, dashed to public transport before 7 a.m. in order to make junior high school band practice, it sounds almost like a fictional story right out of a Charles Dickens novel. We never grew up resenting our situation. We only felt that we had to be self-reliant.

We never felt unloved and it never occurred to us to wallow in self-pity. We had the best role models in our parents, who taught us by example. In order to get ahead in the world, you need to get off the couch and make something happen, because no one is going to do it for you. In one simple phrase, nothing comes easy, and nothing comes by chance.

My father was not one for great emotional displays, at least in the early years. Often he would come off the road, his equivalent of a hard day's' work. He would come to the dinner table with the expectation of silence and obedience. There wasn't a lot of discussion–what my father said was the law, and he didn't mess around. We grew up in tense financial times and much of the conversation between my parents was about money and spending. I realise today that many of my frugal tendencies stem from those deeply ingrained words we silently digested at those quiet, tense evening meals.

Despite my father being somewhat distant and intimidating, I admired him and longed for his affection. One of the ways my father lets off steam and demonstrates his passionate personality is through sport. My father had been quite an accomplished athlete in high school, before he was forced to drop out in his final year to go to work and earn money to assist his father in supporting their growing family. My father was selected to be a first string member of his high school rugby team. This was quite an honour. The one prize possession he has treasured to this day is his team rugby blazer. We looked forward to the rare moments of closeness when he would take his blazer out of the closet, show it to us and share some of his stories.

Remember when I came in first place in the entire first grade at school and was selected to represent our school in the All-City Athletics Championships at the major Johannesburg University WITS? What I didn't tell you... one of my most cherished memories is the pride in my father's face when my mother told him how well I had done. A slight schoolboy was able to beat many other youths twice his size. And with this, I began to cement a niche and bond with my father that continues to this very day. My father always praised me on my athletic accomplishments. I think they reminded him a bit of himself when he was growing up. I made the cricket team with my brother, despite being smaller than the bat and the cricket pads sliding off, no matter how tightly we buckled them! Even though I was bowled out in one over, my dad displayed a pride that was sincere and nostalgic. I had found a way to connect. I would seek out as many opportunities as I could within his hectic schedule.

Always squirmy and lightning fast, I would forever be chosen as a first string player, no matter the sport due to my ability to be faster than the crowd. I displayed tenacity with that chip on my shoulder. I would have something to prove with every single chance I got. When I entered high school and the world of contact sport, nothing gave me a better opportunity to do just that.

Of course, there were slight drawbacks, such as my tiny frame and the frequency of injuries that resulted from my deep-seated need to constantly prove my worth. My father didn't see the impact of my injuries. Most of the time, he was on the road. My mother was the one that bore the brunt of my drive to succeed. As a parent, I can now understand the emotional turmoil she must have felt seeing her child injured. Or how her heart dropped out when that phone call came from the coach that her son was on the way to the hospital and could she please meet him at the emergency department. Don't get me wrong: it didn't happen every game, but it was somewhat frequent. And as my wife has learned, and states often, when I do something/anything, including injuring myself, I do it really, *really* well. From high school onward, my mother stuck to her steadfast declaration that she would not stand in my way in playing sports, but she would not attend any of my games or practices. She could not stand seeing me get hurt.

I was quite excited to give football, American gridiron style, a go. We all played pickup football on the weekend although these were never tackle games. In fact, I had never played full contact football ever. And I was only in 11th grade when I made the first string on the senior football team! It was quite unusual for a year 11 student to make it, but I did. I was selected to play wide receiver and I proudly shared the news with my father. Whenever he was in town that year, he made sure to attend our games. Disappointingly, our team was not that good and rarely threw a pass. As it was my position to catch the ball that year, I was rarely involved in any action on the field. Most of my duties entailed 'running the plays' from coach to the quarterback.

I did get to see some action, however. In one of our last games of the year I was thrown a pass. I jumped up to catch it. Immediately I was hit in the back by a defender with his helmet square on my spinal cord. I went down and could barely move. Carted off the field, straight to the emergency department, and some painful x-rays later, I had slightly rotated two vertebrae. To this day, I continue to have back problems stemming from this injury. I realized it was not the wisest choice for me to be such a target. I would have to find a different position if I wanted to survive another season of football.

All the jocks played football, so I would stick to the sport with hopes of developing my image within the popular high school clique. After all this was who I was striving to be. Sport was something in which I had a significant amount of talent, recognizable to others, but more importantly to myself. Having learned a lesson the hard way once again, I made a slight but significant switch in positions. I moved from offence to defence. The psyche of a defensive player is radically different to that of an offensive player. Once again, I would have to prove myself to my teammates, and more importantly to the coaching staff that I had the mental agility to fit this new role. I had been a visible member on offence the year before, but given the talents of our team, I had not really made an impact that lived up to the hype of my speed. At the first practice, players were split voluntarily in half. An imaginary line split the field so that players self-divided themselves into offence and defence. I stealthily positioned myself, hiding behind some of the larger defensive line-backers and slithered among the defensive players. From nowhere came the large booming voice of the head defensive coach, Mr. Thomas. "Just where do you think you're going, Glogauer? Are you defecting? Do you think you've got what it takes to play with the tough boys?"

On the spot, without hesitation, I screamed back affirmatively, "Yes sir!"

He replied, "Well, we will just have to see about that!"

So much for my plan to go unnoticed before the practice even began.

One of the practice drills, which tested your conviction as a player, was called the pit. One offensive player would enter a square zone marked off by some tackle bags. It was the job of the defensive player to tackle the other player and not let him out of the marked zone. This gives coaches an opportunity to carefully evaluate both the defensive player's tackling technique as well as his toughness. Every player had his chance and the coaches and players all kept a running score. The offensive players lined up, as did the defensive players. Each time a player escaped the zone, the offensive players screamed in delight. You could hear the roar and feel the ground rumble when a defensive player tackled and laid out his opposing competitor flat on the ground. It was intense and the adrenaline started pumping as you inched closer to the front of the line, ready to engage your opponent in the pit.

That first practice, as my turn came in the pit, I felt that this was my one shot to make a lasting impression. I lined up in a three-point stance, put my mouth guard in, looked the opponent square in his eyes through his face mask, and anticipated the sound of the whistle signalling my call to battle. And then it happened, something snapped inside me, each time someone had made fun of my size, each time a joke that was made at my expense for being so tiny, the jocularity at line-up – "little ole Arnie at the front of the line again." Enough was enough. With the sound of that whistle, as if I was shot out of a cannon at full speed, I launched myself at that player in front of me. Before he even had a chance to move, I laid him flat out on the ground. The entire defensive side roared in jubilation as coach Thomas squealed in delight, giving me a pat on my helmet. From that day forward I was knighted "Arnie the Animal."

From then on it all just clicked into place. Okay, so you want to see if I can make it, I would practice each day, giving it my 100% all. I would play with that chip on my shoulder and prove to everyone that I belonged. I love the psychology and camaraderie of the defensive team – "It is better to give than to receive." You could determine the force of impact and will with all your might, without hesitation; a little dynamite was all I needed to make a giant impact. But I would have to continue to prove myself each and every practice in order to jump up the roster to first string.

There were two cornerbacks, the positions that cover the wide receivers. You had to be fast, be able to catch the ball but also be able to hit, and hit hard. I would be a target because of my size and teams would try to test my vulnerability early on in the game. They would throw the ball my way, and throw it often. It was one thing to prove myself on the practice field; I would have to consistently fight to change the minds of the remaining coaches that I deserved a second chance to be a first string football player on the high school team, this time as a defensive player. I felt that due to a very lacklustre performance the year before, the offensive coaches had already written me off.

As the season began, I was assigned a position as a special teams player. My task was running down the field on kick-offs, attempting to be the first player to make contact, slowing down the opposing team's kick-off returner. This was my role for the first two games as I had not made the first string defensive team as a starter. I didn't really let my father know too many details, as he was quite busy at the beginning of the football season meeting clients on the road. Because I wasn't a defensive starter, I felt I needn't bother him as I didn't want to waste his time talking about how I was relegated to the bench for the majority of the game. We had won our first two games in a low scoring fashion and I didn't have more than two or three opportunities to even run down kick-offs.

This all changed in our third game. We were playing one of the better teams – St Francis Xavier. Their team was legendary for not only their size, but also the many championships they had won over the years. Not known for passing the ball, they were a running team simply because they could steamroll over their significantly smaller opponents. Midway through the third quarter, the corner back that played in my position had been laid flat out by St Frances Xavier's offence!

Before I knew it, my name was called to take over his position. I eagerly ran onto the field. My heart was racing a million beats per minute – I could feel it in my chest. I had to calm myself by taking a knee in the huddle. After one or two plays, not really needing to do much but maintain my position, we were called into the huddle to talk strategy. The opposition had called a timeout as they were on our 35-yard line in a close game, ahead 21 to 10 but it was third down. Would they punt the ball and try to pin us deep in our own end or would they go for the touchdown?

As they lined up to kick the ball, I saw one of their blockers motion ever so slightly in my direction. Whether it was my paranoia or excitement, I felt that they were going to fake the kick and try to sneak the ball my way. I screamed, "watch the fake, watch the fake" and before I knew it the ball was hiked to the blocking back and the fake was on! I was so hyped up, I managed to run past, averting the blocker and I launched myself at the ball carrier. I must have shocked everyone as I laid into him so quickly that before anyone knew what had happened, I had tackled the ball carrier clearly behind the line of scrimmage. My defensive teammates were jumping on top of me for joy. As I ran off the field after engineering this fortuitous change in possession, both the offensive and defensive coaches came up to me, patting me on my helmet signifying a job well done. I had seized the opportunity and made a turning point in the game. Our offence marched down the field and quickly scored a touchdown, closing the gap 21 to 17.

I was put back on the field for the fourth quarter, and it seems I wasn't done yet. Trying now to put the proverbial nail in the coffin, our opposition went aerial. Instead of trying to run the ball, they attempted to make large gains by throwing the ball. For the most part, they were succeeding in passing the ball down the middle on the opposite side of the field from my position. I was fast enough to quickly fall back into my coverage zone, thus taking away the possibility of a successful completion by the opposing team. Before we knew it, the opposition was on our 20-yard line with less than five minutes left in the game. They had not run the ball my way throughout the series of downs, and I felt it was only a matter of time before something came my way. I dropped back a little deeper this time, and my eyes connected with their quarterback. I felt like he was looking right through me and before I knew it a receiver was running my way with the ball spiralling through the air. I aggressively cut in front of their receiver. Before I could process the commotion around me, I had instinctively jumped in the air, intercepted the ball and now was running up the field with twelve players in opposing jersey colours chasing me in hot pursuit. Running up the sideline, from our 5-yard line where I had intercepted the football, I managed to make it all the way to our opposition's 30-yard line before being pushed out of bounds by their team's speedy running back.

Our entire team, including the players on the field and those on the sideline, were euphoric. There was so much noise. But it was quite overwhelming to hear the game announcer over the loudspeaker call out "interception by Western Canada Redmen, #28 Arnie Glogauer with the return of 75 yards, first down on the St Francis Browns 30-yard line at the two-minute warning." As I made it to the bench, every player and coach came over to me and congratulated me on an amazing play, putting us into scoring position with two minutes left to go in the game. And score we did, winning the game 24 to 21. I was presented with the game ball as player of the match by the coaches and a great write-up was posted on the wall outside the PE offices where scores and notices were regularly displayed.

I was not prepared for my reception walking into school the next day. I was an instant celebrity, on the receiving end of high fives from not only my teammates, but from most of the students who had heard that our team was now in play-off contention among the high school teams in our division. I had now solidified a starting role on the football squad and would maintain this status for the remaining part of the season.

We actually ended up in the play-offs in what would be a momentous game for our entire school. It had been more years than anyone remembered since our school, Western Canada High School, had made it to the semi-finals playing our archrivals at the professional football stadium – McMahon Stadium. It was an evening game and many fans came out to cheer us on. My father was out of town that week and sadly could not make this momentous game. We ended up losing anyway. But the thrill of playing in such an atmosphere was something I will always cherish.

The football experience would prove to be so powerful in my overcoming the challenge of my size and persona of being the "little" athlete. It would have a profound effect on my journey of self-development. I had become one of the jocks. All the high school stereotypes of the social cliques and influence each group had on the hierarchy of the high school student body were consistent in our high school. Those who were on the football team were seen as the school heroes and could do no wrong in the eyes of their fellow students. Rightly or wrongly, students revered the jocks because of the glory and positive publicity they brought to the school.

Western Canada High School had come under some serious scrutiny over the years due to its significant battles with drugs and a well-publicized episode of an underground narcotic marketing network within the student population. With the infiltration of some student narcs and a very well-publicized drug bust, it had taken a few years to move past the negativity and re-establish a positive profile. The recent sporting successes aided immensely in rebuilding the school's reputation. The students attending the school longed to have some impact aiding the move past the negative stereotype of being the Western Canada Druggies. The football team's success was one significant mechanism to change this image.

You must understand, I am not the most outgoing of people at the best of times. This fortuitous rite of passage into the world of the social elite was one of the most valuable experiences of my life. I now have the privilege of understanding the complicated intricacies of social hierarchies and how they can make or break a young adolescent. This awareness has stood me in good stead wherever I have been. As a teacher, as a principal, I have used this knowledge to sensitize my staff. It is possible to establish a more cohesive social environment, one in which there are safe outlets for students to be themselves and to seek out a trusted adult when they are struggling. This type of school environment values every student for their unique contribution, not for where their rung is on the ladder of popularity. When we strive to develop this socially acceptable atmoshpere and when we all work together with this purpose in mind, everyone succeeds.

Dual Identity

Being a part of this football success, being labelled as one of the heroes, had a significant personal impact on me. At the very same time, I was embarking on another set of experiences that would shape who I was to become in ways I could never have imagined. During the entire football season, I was a somewhat hesitant, but active member of my local synagogue youth group. The reluctance stemmed from the reasons I attended in the first place. It seems that my 'active' affiliation with the youth group nearly silenced the major, vocal consistent pressure from my parents. I felt it kept them off my back. Specifically, the pressure was about their prohibition against any personal relationships with non-Jewish girls. At some unarticulated level, my parents were petrified with worry about the increasing lack of control they had over our social affiliations and our integration within the Jewish community. It was another unforeseen outcome of immigration that terrified my traditionally Jewish parents. In South Africa, there was a strong, familiar infrastructure to engage Jewish youth. In Calgary, in short, there wasn't.

Despite having been quite active members of the Jewish community in our primary years, once we graduated in Grade 6 from our parochial school, the only connection we had to the Jewish community was dependent on our weekly Synagogue attendance on Saturday, *Shabbos* mornings. As junior high and high school activities increased, *Shabbos* mornings became less about Shabbos and more about track and field and then football.

In Calgary, our family was seen as observant. We were labelled as very traditional with a strong influence from the Orthodox perspective. In our home, Friday nights were sacred. My mother ushered in the *Shabbos* by lighting candles. My brother or I recited the Friday night *Kiddush*. There was a strict obligation on our entire family to attend the Friday night meal, despite the ongoing social pressures from our non-Jewish peer groups to go out on a Friday night. From our primary parochial school, our minimally-sized peer group assimilated quickly into the many 'groups' in the public junior high school. I quickly drifted away from connections to my Jewish classmates. From that point forward, my peer group at school was primarily made up of non-Jewish friends with stronger shared interests such as sports.

Thus from my parents' perspective, the pressure was even greater to maintain a hold on any influence they could that would foster a direct link to our Jewish heritage. For my parents, particularly my mother, the antidote to assimilation was our Friday night dinner. For many years, my mother and father successfully kept that stronghold on us, maintaining this tradition until mid- junior high. It was then that the pressure to keep us home crumbled away.

There were a couple of factors at play. My father was often not home for weeks at a time. His absence was coupled with the strong social pressures of being a teenager in public school. Slowly, our traditional Friday nights became a thing of the past. My brother and I had very strongly assimilated into the social scene at school. My mother's only influence at that stage were the many verbal threats of what she would do, should she find out we were involved with dating non-Jewish girls.

My strongest mechanism to deflect her scrutiny was my strategic participation in the synagogue youth group. Whether or not I was successful in fooling my mother, it was a way for me to overtly demonstrate an obedience and acceptance of my mother's expectations. In my other life, I was fully immersed in the social scene that was just too naturally a part of high school. The junior high and then the high school social pressures were of conformity, acceptance and fitting in. Every social activity pitted the social haves against the have-nots. Survival depended on a student's ability to blend in and conform to the group's established norms. Those who did not fit in were harassed and reduced to being labelled social outcasts.

With my successes on the sporting field and notoriety in the classroom, I had pretty much actualized the image of the athletic jock and all-round entertainer. All that was about to change. And I was about to change it, all by myself...

Enchanted Encounters at 17 – Meeting My Soul mate… and…My Soul

In the fall of 1987, at the beginning of the 12th grade senior football season, I received the phone call. Was I interested in joining the USY (United Synagogue Youth) Annual Fall Convention in Vancouver? The entire conference fee was covered by a donation. What was the catch? All I had to do was commit to run the USY junior high synagogue youth group the next year.

I thought it through and accepted the offer, as well as the youth leader position for the following year. Who could turn down a trip away from home? I packed my bags and flew west over the Rocky Mountains with seven other Calgary high school students. We landed in Vancouver, representing the Calgary chapter at the Annual USY 1987 Fall Convention.

We were very well received. Actually, ours was the first contingent of students from Calgary to ever attend the USY National Convention. As we arrived at the hotel, a greeting party had assembled in the main hall welcoming the different chapters from all over the Pacific Northwest. Right away, I hit it off with a few students from the Vancouver organizing. The theme of the convention was *Tikun Olam* – making a difference in the world, and in your individual community. The specific splinter themes related to making an impact in our communities through sensitivity to those less fortunate than us.

I became inspired at this West Coast Annual Convention. I felt very much part of a brotherhood. As we walked into the hotel Friday morning with the Calgary contingent, we were bombarded with hugs and high fives from the welcoming committee. It was like walking into a family reunion at long last. Family members, most of whom you had never met in your life, were happy to see you. You were overjoyed to connect to people with whom you shared some invisible bond. I couldn't quantify my emotions but I felt some link to a chain, which was beyond my ability to describe. It was an emotional experience and the entire weekend only strengthened this attachment and longing desire to maintain hold of this link.

Throughout the convention, I struggled with the realization that I would be coming back to Calgary. All of a sudden, I wanted to maintain the level of inspiration and connectivity to my new family. How would I accomplish that?

At each discussion group, I personally challenged myself to open up and talk about the conflict of living in two worlds, the public arena – my non-Jewish world – and the Jewish community. Specifically, how could I spiritually navigate through the dichotomy of living in two conflicting realms? It was in the Thursday night open discussion that I would, for the first time, publicly get up and openly talk about my experiences of anti-Semitism in primary school and beyond. I talked about what it felt like to be in an environment of blatant discrimination. I opened up about sometimes not having the guts to step up and address the persecution and perpetrators. Whether it was "dirty Jew" or being hurled a confrontational comment, a discriminatory expression, "Jewing someone down," sometimes it was all around me. It was an emotional session. For once, I had the support of my peers to help me to open up and share my personal journey. I felt close to this new family. The guiding advisors were nurturing and encouraging.

The Vancouver convention experience taught me a lot about how to reach teenagers. Too often, we think that the most confronting experiences will turn off our youth; however, I have found the opposite to be true. Today's adolescents want real experiences stripped of false appearances and fake contrived relationships. From my interactions with teens over the years, it is more than obvious that teenagers depend greatly on input from their peer group. Decisions are rarely made independently without direct consultation with their close, intimate group of friends. Decisions seem to be made based on the shared values of the group. Instead of peer pressure defining their model of actions, a consensus is reached through peer interaction, discussion and group experience. A sort of collective bargaining discussion usually develops. The resulting consensus determines the direction of conduct. This is what usually occurs amongst a fairly healthy cohort of teens.

One of the most inspirational mentors was a female university student named Chaya from Victoria. She seemed very warm and interested in my story. Coincidentally, during the Friday sessions, she and a friend happened to act as moderators. She seemed very skilled at nurturing the discussions of the forums. Not only was she posing follow-up questions to the discussions, she encouraged all the participants to strive to make connections between their shared personal experiences. She directed all of us to think globally where appropriate. It was more than just sharing individual stories. She demonstrated how we were all linked together despite our distant geographical homes and varying backgrounds of observance. Through her guidance and wisdom, we all came out of the sessions more connected and focused toward the potential of uniting our tiny groups into one global community.

That Friday night after dinner, some of the community youth leaders, including myself, gathered round the table in one of the banquet rooms to talk further about our personal stories. Inspired from our morning sessions, we couldn't let go of delving into the differences in our backgrounds – all the varying challenges we had experienced in our Jewish struggles for maintaining our identity in the vast assimilated world. Yet these apparent differences highlighted more how much we were essentially so similar. I felt comfortable to open up about my primary school story and how I had faced discrimination with public school students.

During that powerful evening, another chapter of my story was beginning, unbeknownst to even me. Across the table, I met the eyes of Chaya, our moderator from the morning. As we made eye contact off and on that long and life-changing night, it seemed to me she was hanging onto my every word. We seemed to really click. We continued talking for a while late into that evening. She was really easy to talk to and seemed genuinely interested in what I had to say. Little did I know, that three years later, this individual would become my wife.

The strength I gained from the connectedness that weekend was very strong. As the theme of the convention aimed to do, it stirred up and awakened a spark within me. I left Vancouver inspired to take a stand and make a difference. It was on the plane back to Calgary that I made my decision. In keeping with the theme of the conference, I decided to leave on the *yarmulke* which I had proudly worn on my head all weekend. I had plenty of time to review the social consequences of my actions. Even still, that Sunday night before going back to school, I simply could not sleep. The anxiety and fearful anticipation of the unknown kept me wide awake with the questions and scenarios running through my head. What would be the response from my peers Monday morning when I would walk through the entrance hall to Western Canada High School? I imagined the very extreme. I played over every possible scenario in my mind. Each one ended in humiliation and social suicide. Somehow, I didn't lose my resolve. I hung onto the inspiration from the conference that it was the right thing for me. Somehow, despite risking being dropped by my peer group, and even worse, the entire football team, I was prepared for that Monday morning. I got up, ready to make the 8:30 a.m. walk of room with my *yarmulke* proudly worn in plain view, for all to see.

I drove into the parking lot that Monday morning, found a spot and parked my car. I peaked in the rear-view mirror to make sure my *yarmulke* was properly clipped to the back of my head, realising I had hand-picked myself as a prime target. Here, I had thought I was part of the in crowd. I had worked pretty hard to attain that status. I would surely be testing my social status. I walked in that day with the full knowledge I had painted a social bull's-eye right on the back of my head. Now all I had to do was be ready for when my 'friends' might take aim. With a deep cleansing breath, I gazed into the front mirror and said out loud, "Here you go. No looking back. You are alone, but you can do this!"

I stepped out of the car. Trying to seem casual as usual, I walked toward the main door leading into the central hallway outside the gym. This was the hangout spot for the football team, leading into the cafeteria. Everyone congregated here before the beginning of class, outside the main bulletin board where football practice, regular announcements and game stats were posted for the beginning of the week.

As I walked toward the bulletin board, it looked like I was ready to check out the defensive backs' meeting schedule for the coming week. As you can guess, I only pretended to be interested in that schedule. In truth, all I was really focused on was those who were potentially watching me, fixating on the giant spotlight on the top of my head. I acted as if nothing had changed. The night I spent awake had been productive. I was ready with a torrent of quick retorts. But it was as if a pin dropped. No one noticed the silence as the significance of the giant personal decision I had made in my life sunk in wordlessly to everyone around me in that first fateful moment. It was incredibly anti-climactic, almost disappointing. No one said a word! Then the bell rang and shattered that silence of which only I was aware. It signalled the first period of the day. I continued on my way, touching my head every so often to ensure that I had indeed still come to school wearing my *yarmulke*.

Outside our first period class, there was chitchat among some of the students about our weekends. Then it began: "What's up with the head cover?" I mentioned my conference in Vancouver over the weekend. How I had been inspired and wanted to get closer to my roots. Miraculously, most of the guys just calmly responded with a quick "cool." That was it.

And we got on with the rest of our day. I was amazed that the day just progressed as normal. I still had one major obstacle to pass through – the football team. More specifically, the changing room before practice. The boys prided themselves on giving each other a hard time. I knew I was no different, especially today. It would be important for me not to take any of the gentle ribbing too personally or overreact to their usually friendly hazing.

The 3:30 bell rang. I walked into the locker room. I must have walked more slowly than I thought, given what I anticipated facing, because when I got there, most of the defensive team had already congregated and begun to change for practice. "Hey, Glogie, is that you or your rabbi showing up for practice?" Absolute silence. Time seemed to stop. The bomb was dropped in the middle of the locker room. This was my one chance to put the issue to bed and move on. If I showed any weakness, I would become the target of merciless persecution for the remainder of the season. I looked around to see where the comment came from – it was from one of the toughest defensive players, notorious for pushing his teammate's buttons. Before I got to know him, I thought he was just an obnoxious person. I had come to respect him for his efforts to get the most out of every teammate.

All that played out in a split second because without much hesitation I responded, "The way our offence is playing, I think we need all the help we can get!" That was enough. I deflected. I didn't let it get personal. I highlighted my allegiance to the defensive team. I threw the gauntlet down to the offence, changing the focus in that room. I got a huge chuckle out of the entire defensive core and I challenged the offensive players. There were a few feeble attempts at some comebacks, but it turned out no one was really in the mood to challenge the defence and their loudmouth wisecracks. My comeback seemed to ignite an 'us versus them' feud. Somehow, I was now more strongly aligned with my defensive comrades in arms. After a few high fives, we had to quickly finish suiting up to take the fight onto the field.

I had passed the test. No one commented further about my *yarmulke*! My teammates had my back! I felt a huge wave of relief rush over me. I was proud to have taken such a significant personal stand, that I could be who I wanted even at the risk of standing out like a sore thumb. What are the life lessons? I have developed the personal motto that one "must stand up for something, or risk falling for anything." I knew my decision was right for me. I didn't waver, despite my hesitations. Of course I was scared. But being brave is not about being fearless. Being brave is about doing what is right whether you are afraid or not. I acted from a position of strength – calling out those around me to rise to the occasion. These are all lessons, which can be taught. They are leadership characteristics I expect to be modelled by my staff and, of course, lead by my example.

The football season came to a close. I had solidified my social status as "one of the guys," even with my *yarmulke*. Talk began to resurface around the upcoming rugby season. We harboured hopes for revenge after last year's painful loss. But that is yet to come. Rugby is a whole chapter unto itself.

Rugby – A World of Opportunity

It took me many years to satisfy the burning desire to make my father proud of me. My father was a great athlete in his time at school, excelling in rugby. It was not until high school that I would get my chance to try this fabled athletic pursuit. Despite success in numerous other sports, including football, the first time my father really paid attention to my sporting prowess, was when my rugby career took off. My playing rugby deepened my connection with my father, because it was something to which he could relate. When I made it to the Canadian National Rugby Championships, my father gave me his rugby-lettering jacket from his high school years, the one he used to take out every once in a while when we were little, much to our awe. To this day, I have it with me wherever I go. The jacket still doesn't fit me… my Dad is built like a flanker and I, a winger.

It was a natural progression for the majority of the football team. Football season ended in the autumn, rugby season began in the spring. In my first year of junior rugby, somehow, things just clicked. I became the leading scorer in the city. My coach rather quickly discovered how to exploit my speed. I was soon assigned to the flashier position of winger. Most of our plays revolved around getting the ball to me on the outside. This allowed me to either run through the defensive line of backs, or I could kick the ball downfield, dash through the defence, pick up the ball and run in for the score. It was a simple but effective strategy. That first year, on the junior rugby team, we successfully lead our team to the city championships. It was quite a thrill to win the city finals in my first year of rugby. My Dad was on the road for most of that first season. But there was a difference in how many phone calls there were asking how our team fared after each game.

As the football season ended, everyone was quite excited that to get to the play-offs in football, we had knocked out our biggest rivals – Henry Wise Wood High School. However, our school was not as exuberant as could be expected. This was because Henry Wise Wood High School was still our nemesis in rugby. Our senior rugby team had lost once again in the finals, for the third year in a row to Henry Wise Wood High School. An incredible rivalry had developed between our two schools.

A few of the guys on the senior rugby team encouraged me to try out for the Irish Rugby club as well as the senior school rugby team. I was now a confident rugby player. That fine spring afternoon, after school, I showed up at the Irish club field. I was introduced by my friend to Mr Derek Wright, a Welshman, and the head coach. It turned out he was also the coach of Western Canada High School's senior rugby team. With a wide smile and a firm handshake, he welcomed me with, "I've heard a lot about you; let's see what you've got."

Mr Wright put the players through many drills. It was probably the toughest practice I had ever been through. At its conclusion, Mr Wright called me over. I vividly remember his smile as he put his arm around my shoulder and said, "Son, we're going to get along just fine." We had forged an instantaneous relationship. I would always feel he took a very personal interest in me. Perhaps everyone felt that way; I was oblivious to the connections everyone else had. I only ever knew the depth of his personal care and nurturing nature toward me. And I had the benefit of his coaching both on the Irish and on my school's rugby team!

A true sign of an effective educator is to make personal connections with each student in such a way that the student feels that core connection. Ideally, a student should view every teacher as his mentor and never want to disappoint his personal guide by committing less than 100% effort. This is how each player felt toward our coach. At each practice, it was our goal to give him every bit of energy we had, ensuring that each and every day he would be proud of us. It was under his direction that I learned the deep value of making mistakes if you recognize, accept and learn from them. And Mr Wright taught me the importance of a team and working together. Running a school where individual success is celebrated by all qualitatively changes the nature of the classroom. Instantly, focus is shifted to personal best and how to assist each other in reaching our collective best together.

His advice would prove golden. Over that year, I would learn both how to play the game better and, more importantly, learn valuable life skills through our many personal interactions. He became more than a coach; he became my mentor. He took a sincere interest in my academic achievement, ensuring I kept up my grades. He would address the entire team about our extracurricular pursuits on the weekend, making sure we were never getting into trouble at parties. He was very strict about drinking alcohol under age and would bench any players if he found out they were in breach of his strict lifestyle directives. No one wanted to disappoint Mr Wright.

During the rugby season, his influence even rubbed off on how his players would dress at school. On game days, our entire team wore button-down shirts and ties. This subtle ritual generated a significantly higher level of self-respect, not to mention the reverence we ended up commanding from others around us. Our coach would always say that the best-dressed team walking on to the field before the game automatically received the benefit of the doubt on close calls from the referee. Before we walked out of the locker room, our shirts would be tucked in and our socks pulled up. We ran in formation as a group, as a team, as a community united toward one common goal, to work as a cohesive unit. If we were successful, it was not because of one person, it was because of the team.

That season was a gruelling series of battles. We emerged undefeated, leading up to the mid-season confrontation with our archrivals. It was drummed into us how significant this battle was, since their senior team had beaten our team the year before in the city finals. We did not want to let our coach down and sought revenge on his behalf. Our opposition was known to have some strong forward players and a very speedy winger – my opposite number. My personal mission was to contain him throughout the game. For the majority of the match, it was a scoreless back and forth contest. I had successfully kept the speedy winger playing opposite me in check, matching him stride for stride. As the end of the game approached, they managed to score on a penalty kick. They secured the win by a final score of three to nothing.

We were all very upset, feeling like we had let our coach down. Surprisingly, after the game our mentor had only motivating feedback and was very encouraging. His final message was, "Boys, let this feeling sting. We played well and they capitalized on one of our mistakes. If we continue to work hard and commit ourselves to grow from our mistakes, they will see a different team in the finals. I'm proud of you and I can't wait for our rematch. Before then, though, there is hard work to be done!"

That was it – short, sweet and to the point. In one simple address, we were able to channel the energy of this potentially demoralizing loss and focus our energies toward working that much harder. Just when we thought we had expended 100% of our efforts, from some unknown place, deep down, we mustered even more energy to commit ourselves toward the goal of defeating our rivals.

With this loss, we would have to win all of our remaining games to remain in second place in our division to secure a pathway toward the city championship finals. We managed to accomplish this massive task. Sure enough, we won all our play-off games and made it to the finals that were held 11 June 1988 at the main city rugby fields.

Before that fateful game, you could cut the tension in the locker room with a knife. We all sat around the room, impeccably dressed in our uniforms, silently waiting for the signal to run out of the dressing room onto the field. Mr Wright quietly walked up to some of the team members, whispering final words of encouragement. He came up to me, put his arm around me and simply said, "Today is your day. Play hard. Play big. Leave nothing on that field. Be fast, be swift and play your game." He patted me on the back and walked slowly to the centre of the dressing room. Every single player looked at him, intently waiting for his words of inspiration. He looked around into each and every player's eyes. One could hear a pin drop from that anticipation. And then he spoke: "Boys, I'm so proud of each and every one of you. Today is our day. Scott, they are in your hands." And with that, he left the room.

Our captain, Scott, had played rugby for Western Canada High School for the past two years. He had experienced two of the three crushing defeats at the hands of Henry Wise Wood. This game meant about as much to him as it did to Mr Wright. Scott addressed us with the most inspirational words. "Vince Lombardi said these words, and today for us, they say it all... There is no room for second place, there is only one place in my game, and that is first place. I have finished second twice at Western Canada and I don't want to finish second again. Coach Lombardi said – there is a second place bowl game, but it's a place for the losers. It is and always has been a Canadian zeal to be first in anything we do, and to win, and to win, and to win. Today, we will be great and today we will win. Now let's go and be great!"

What a stirring twist on a most legendary speech from an iconic football coach, Vince Lombardi, with his immortal words of what it takes to be number one. Filled with those inspirational thoughts, in unison we ran out of the dressing room and onto the city rugby pitch. On one side of the stadium sat students from Henry Wise Wood High School. On the other side were our friends and fellow students from our Western Canada High School. The stadium was packed and the cheers were deafening. In the distance, I spotted my father and my brother as we ran into our stretching groups on our respective sides of the field. Both had come to watch me play. Even more amazingly, my father had been asked by the referee to act as line judge for the game.

After stretches and a couple of formational runs with the ball, we were set for kick-off. To begin the game, I was matched up once more against their speedy winger. I was positioned on the 'blindside', closest to our opponents' sideline. Each time I came close to the sideline, I could vaguely hear their crowd boo me, shouting my name. I became a targeted villain of the opposition. The first half proved to be a very tentative match, played carefully and strategically by both teams. Each side was reluctant to take any risks, keeping the ball in the forward pack. For the most part both teams were kicking for touch, trying to press the other team in its defensive side of the field. There was not a lot of action. Their team tried a couple of times to press against us and try to run the ball past me on their wing, but I held my ground. At least twice I had put my opposite man flat on the ground with two punishing open field tackles. At the end of the half, there was no score. Neither team had managed to break the deadlock zero to zero.

As we began the second half, their team, frustrated that they were not able to execute their game plan, made a strategic move. They switched their speedy all-star to the other side – furthest away from my position. Their plan was easy to read. They hoped to pass the ball to the outside and run their winger past our last player at the end of the back line for a score. Moving their winger away from me was their best shot at scoring a try. I looked over at the sideline wondering if I should also move to the other side maintaining my positional coverage, shadowing him. Our coach told me not to make the adjustment and to stay exactly where I was.

At the next scrum, our fly half motioned that he was going to fake a kick. Instead, he would spin the ball out to me with the hopes that I could break their line. Despite being close to our end line, they would most likely not expect us to run the ball. Indeed, this is exactly what happened, and they fell for it hook, line and sinker. Our team successfully spun the ball out to me on my end. Now I had the ball and I was running toward the new opposite winger with their defensive line coming right at me. Instinctively, as they closed in for the kill, I kicked the ball high in the air, as far as I could possibly launch it down field. Running full speed trying to catch up with the ball, two of the defendants in the area just stopped in their tracks waiting for the ball to drop. Indeed, it did; however, without hesitation I ran onto the ball and caught it in full stride. Running at full speed, I sped past every player who stood flat-footed as they could only watch me sprint right by toward the try line. Their speedy winger was way offside. He knew what was going to happen. But all he could do was sprint across the entire field in a vain attempt to catch me. Coming from the far side, for his team it was to no avail. I had successfully scored the only try in the game with less than fifteen minutes to go!

My entire team ran into the end zone and jumped on me in jubilation. At the bottom of the pile, one of my contact lenses popped out as the referee came in to mark the spot from where the conversion kick would be attempted. My father was called in to supervise the kick. To this day, I recall the smile and the emotions on his face were something I had never before seen. I could see his struggle to keep his composure, as he needed to maintain a sense of impartiality – being the line judge. As I kept looking for my contact lens, he managed to whisper, "Unbelievable – well done, son!" Those four words meant the world to me. To this day, we still reminisce about the event as the most incredible sporting happening of which we had ever been a part.

I gave up looking for my lens and decided to play without it. With the successful conversion, we were in the lead, with not a lot of time left on the clock. We restarted the game. Our opposition was playing in desperation. They were taking a lot of risks and at one point with a penalty called against them, we were able to capitalize and score some additional insurance points to their still zero score. At the restart, they kicked the ball to me and I got caught up in a ruck. I remember placing the ball but getting pulled to the ground. All of a sudden from nowhere I was being hit in the head by the opposition. One of the players stood on my head and ground his cleats into my scalp. Too injured to continue, I was sidelined by my coach, mandated to participate as a spectator from the sidelines for the last five minutes.

Henry Wise Wood never scored a point against us that game. Our team managed to hold on and win the city high school championships, 9-0. I had scored the only try. But I had become a victim in my own right. The adrenaline was still pumping and I was euphoric despite an absolutely splitting headache. We all lined up for the medal ceremony and trophy presentation. Each of our names was called out as a medal was placed around our necks. The city newspaper reporter cornered me and asked me for a quick interview. They asked me a couple of questions and before I knew it, my friends were carrying me off the field as the hero of the game. My Dad and brother caught up with me before I went into the dressing room to tell me how proud they both were of me.

I was excited to go to the after-party with my friends so I told my Dad that I would be back home late that night. Full of excitement and looking forward to a well-deserved and just reward, we parted as I went to the dressing room to join my team. We were about to be addressed by Mr Wright. It was incredibly emotional. As our role model, his tears of joy affected us all deeply. It was a short speech but we knew how much our victory, and we, meant to him.

We showered and got dressed, ready to meet our friends outside the locker room. A few of us were going to get a bite to eat together and then head off to the afterparty celebration. Despite the hero's welcome and incredible desire to celebrate with my friends, I suddenly didn't feel too well. I could not understand why I would all of a sudden feel so incredibly ill. Perhaps it was all of the excitement and my needing something to drink and perhaps some food in my stomach? Exiting the locker room, I got into a friend's car, and we headed up to grab a quick snack and drink before the party. I got out of the car and purchased an apple juice to quench my thirst.

And then it suddenly hit me, like ten tons of bricks. It was impossible to even slightly move my head to the left or to the right. It was more than just a headache; it was beyond the most painful migraine. I told my friends that I needed to forego the celebration. I needed to go home. I was in far too much pain to even think about celebrating. The ride home was excruciating. I felt every slight bump in the road reverberating endlessly in my head. Somehow I walked into the house and instantly fell onto the couch succumbing to tears from the pain. My parents came rushing in to see what was wrong. Right away, my Dad came over and said he was taking me straight to the hospital. It was probably the only time I ever agreed without resistance to go to the doctor or hospital after an injury. When we entered the emergency room a few minutes later, my father described my symptoms and how I had been injured in a rugby game. Only then did I recall the full impact of having been caught in that ruck. Lying down on the hospital bed, I was asked a lot of questions, most of which I could easily answer. I knew my name, the date, where I was etc. All of a sudden, a wave of nausea came over me and I threw up in the tray beside my bed. Immediately the doctor told me I had a severe concussion and that I would be spending the night for observation.

My father and brother came to see me in my room to make sure I was alright. I told them I would be okay so they could head off home for the night. Really, my head was spinning and all I wanted to do was go to sleep and wake up in the morning feeling better. The only problem with that idea was the concussion. I was not allowed to sleep for more than few hours at a time. Just when I was comfortably drifting off into a deep slumber I was woken up time after time that night by the nurse to have my vitals checked. This stop, start, jerking sleep carried on until the morning when I awoke to the strangest sight.

I could never have imagined in my wildest dreams that I would wake up in the hospital from a concussion, and the person who would set a vigil beside my bed would be none other than Mr Wright. It was quite a thrill when a few nurses came into my room to check on me, asking how the "Champ" was feeling.

I was asked if I was up for reading the morning newspaper. Somehow, I responded in the affirmative. My coach handed me the sports section. It was an incredible sight. There in front of me was the headline: "Glogauer Sparks Western Canada High School Rugby Championship." I was both excited and embarrassed at the same time. It was quite an honour to have my coach sitting with me in the hospital. It was quite another to fathom that our accomplishments were being flaunted for all to see, having our victory spread over the sports section in the city's newspaper.

Together we sat for a while just chitchatting a bit more about general things besides our recent victory. It was a comforting feeling, one I will cherish for many years, realizing the care and the bond I had developed with that special man. I'm sure he had many things to do, but now I was a priority and it made me feel a lot better. I was able to keep the food down from breakfast. My throbbing headache was letting up. The neurologist arrived with my father to check how I was feeling. I was finally released and sent home with strict orders not to do any physical exercise for at least four weeks.

My coach told me that I should rest up and not worry about my placement on the team. There were two months until the trials for the provincial team and he would ensure my placement on the City Select Team without any further need of evaluation. In front of my father, Mr. Wright said that the try I had scored was one of the most beautiful things he had ever seen, and it had solidified a spot for me on the city team. In two months I would play in this City Select game upon which the provincial team would be decided. The coach sternly explained that if I broke the doctor's orders in the next four weeks and engaged in physical exercise of any sort, he would personally revoke the invitation. I had to comply and make sure I fully recovered from the injury. I spent the next month watching many practices, itching to get back into the game.

It was June of 1988 and my last month of high school. My final year at school was ending up on quite a positive note. I had a strong enough GPA to be accepted early into the University of Calgary's Pre-Business

Management program. I learned that the hard work and effort did pay off in the end. I was eternally grateful to Mr Wright for pushing me in my efforts on and off the field.

Under the watchful eye of my coach, I made a full recovery, and six weeks later began lifting my fitness level in order to be ready to play in the City Select game. All of the eligible high school players in southern Alberta under the age of 21, endorsed by a personal invitation from their high school coaches, formed one team. The high school students from northern Alberta formed the opposing team. The two teams played against each other in a match in front of scouts from the provincial rugby coaching team. I played well in my first match back since my injury, even scoring a try. It was a very close game played in severe rain and storm conditions. So it was a low scoring game with not many opportunities for players to display their individual talents. There were a couple of good tackles, but the game ended with many of us in doubt as to who would be selected to the provincial team.

We showered, dressed and gathered in the main room of the clubhouse after the game for the announcement of the 1988 Alberta Provincial Rugby Team. It was at this time that we were also introduced to the coaching contingent responsible for the development of the team. To our surprise and delight, unbeknownst to any of us players, our own Mr Wright was introduced as the head coach of the provincial team. My heart skipped a beat as I secretly hoped this would put me one step closer to making the team. Not necessarily because of my relationship with him, but because he was deeply aware of my abilities, regardless of my performance in the select game that afternoon. Indeed, it was so, I was elated when my name was called among my fellow team members.

That summer we would take part in development camps in Red Deer, the halfway point between Calgary and Edmonton. In addition, we would travel to Saskatchewan and play against their provincial team and other club teams in an effort to bolster team unity and experience. I felt like royalty, having been selected to the provincial rugby team and experiencing such a public display of exposure as the newspapers covered our build-up to the National Championships in Ottawa. During those weeks, I was training four days a week, playing one game for our Irish club team and one game a week for the provincial team. It was a lot of rugby and it was pretty much all consuming.

The inevitable happened. In one of our games against a touring English team, I severely twisted my ankle. The injury required significant rehabilitation. With only four weeks until nationals, my selection for the team was now in jeopardy. For the next four weeks, I was unable to train with the team. It would require my passing a complete physical before I would get the okay from my coach to remain part of the team that would compete at the national level.

I was extremely disappointed and I could tell my coach was equally distressed. A week before the trip, I managed to mask my discomfort and pain despite having only recovered about 75%. My coach reluctantly gave me the green light. I naïvely thought I had successfully fooled him. I felt at some level he could see that I wasn't wholly rehabilitated to the high level I was accustomed to playing before the injury. Perhaps due to some level of allegiance to me, he nevertheless gave me the go-ahead.

This experience of playing at such a high level of rugby was amazing. The camaraderie of playing on the provincial team was a great learning experience. I gained significant confidence to push myself to the limit. At the same time, I learned how to rely on a team to push through adversity. In our allocated conference, we had lost only two games, to British Columbia and Ontario. Both of those teams made the finals and we were relegated to the bronze medal match against the very tough Nova Scotia team. I played three games and my ankle held up in all three. In our fourth game, our bid to make the final, my attempts to hide the pain and discomfort couldn't last any longer. My ankle gave out. Despite our winning the bronze medal in a very close match, I would always wonder how my future would have ended up if my ankle had been 100%. Our third string winger replaced me. He was nominated as an alternate on the national team, replacing me. My coach pulled me aside to assure me that, had I been healthy, the position would have been mine. I came home somewhat relieved. Now I did not have to make a decision whether to play on the national team and tour Europe that year, forgoing my university entrance in September. This decision was made for me. My path toward my first year of university study was predetermined.

I returned home from Ottawa and those fateful National Rugby Championships. I was resigning myself to the road toward full rehabilitation of my ankle and not making the national team. It was then that I received a call from the Canadian Maccabi Rugby coach. He was inviting me to fly down to Vancouver to try out for the Jewish national team. It was an incredible honour to receive that call. I quickly took stock of my injury and the amount of time I would need to fully recuperate before saying when I would be available to accept this amazing offer. It turned out that I had a couple of months before the Maccabi evaluation camp, more than enough time for my ankle to be fully rehabilitated. The

Calgary Maccabi chapter paid for my flight. I was able to make a strong performance in a scouted game, playing for a local club team who had invited me to play for them that day. I was back to my old fit self so I gave a strong demonstration of my skills that Sunday at the evaluation camp. I was formally selected to the Canadian National Maccabi Rugby team to compete in Israel July 3, 1989.

Little did I know that my life would take such a different turn that it didn't even faze me to push rugby to the side. I would encounter one of the most significant forks in my road of life. It would pave my journey, taking me on a significant path, one that would be much more life-changing than an athletics competition, even a Jewish one, and representing my country in Israel. It became a very easy choice: represent Canada at the 13th International Maccabi games in Israel, or announce my engagement to Chaya.

Heart & Soul…and a Teacher?

I haven't talked that much about my high school academics. But I know you read between the lines. Yes, once that spark was lit in junior high, true to my personality, I became unstoppable in my quest for proving myself academically too. I continued in the French immersion in high school, a prestigious initiative aligned with the International Baccalaureate program. Of course there were those select few who still have no idea of the influence they had on my future: Barry McGuire, and as you know, Mr Wright, with his ironclad insistence on grades being where they should be. High school was all about my studies, sports, and oddly enough, my soul. I was very keen on doing well in my studies. This motivation was not affected at all by the fact that I was not at all sure what my future direction would be! This was also despite the fact that I applied to two business studies programs because that was my destiny, right? In the end, I applied to two universities, Queens University in Kingston, Ontario and the University of Calgary. It was a true testimony to my mending my ways in 8th grade that I received acceptance letters from both!

You can probably guess who was going to be paying for my university tuition, room, board etc.. That's right! So, of course, I opted to accept the early admission into the University of Calgary (U of C). I was accepted for business studies and signed up for the prerequisites for the Bachelor of Commerce program. My mother was over the moon with pride.

This pretty much set the course for my first undergraduate year. I was comforted knowing that I had a place to go. There was very little pressure on me after my early acceptance at U of C, to achieve above my already 80% GPA.

Looking back, the odds had surely seemed stacked against me from the start. It was around this time that my parents actually broke it to me…the solemn pronouncement of my Grade 6 Principal relegating me to a trade school candidate because he thought an academic career was a completely unrealistic possibility! With each academic milestone I surpassed, we shared a good laugh – the irony of his utterly erroneous judgment! My parents told me they never believed him for one second and they surely never gave up hope. I will never know how many nights they lost sleep worrying for my future.

There is no room to predict a child's future or potential. There is nurturing, there is rewarding strong effort, there is fostering curiosity, cultivating openness to see mistakes as the best opportunity to learn, modelling mutual respect and first and foremost, cherishing the privilege of having an impact upon a child's destiny.

With summer coming and all that rugby to look forward to, it was this summer where I was to injure my ankle, make the provincial rugby team, play at nationals but be unable to join the Canadian national team because of my ankle. With my early acceptance from the University of Calgary already awarded, I was coasting through my last few weeks of the 1988 school year without really doing much besides having fun.

What was foremost in my mind was the inspiration I was filled with at the Vancouver USY convention. I was still incredibly motivated to share and pass on that feeling I had experienced. I still felt very committed to develop opportunities for the Jewish youth in Calgary. I truly hoped I could set things up for them to be able to experience even a small part of what I had at that convention. I was so enthused that even with all of my intense summer rugby hopes and aspirations on my mind, I decided I would make two promises to myself. My first goal come September was to try, as their advisor, to build the synagogue youth group to over 30 students. My second goal was to make sure that I investigated and became a part of the university's Jewish students chapter.

The following February, five months into my term as advisor, we were looking forward to actually hosting the winter USY convention in Calgary and I had about 30 students registered. Everyone I had met and connected with from the Pacific Northwest came to Calgary, including Chaya. It was an incredible experience. Mostly because when the winter wonderland weekend was over, I went home and told my mother, "Ma, I think I've met the girl I'm going to marry."

I made good on my commitment to join the university student's group. Although many initiatives were put forward to develop opportunities for social interaction on campus, after February somehow my mind was more focused on developing the long-distance relationship with Chaya.

From the start, there was another plot afoot. I realized early on that I was not driven to the point of excitement about the business world. At first, I just ignored that feeling. It was enough just knowing a pathway to my destiny had been forged. I was able to be positive because I had some direction. Looking back, I realise that the source of my 'happiness' in that stage came from the contentment I was giving to others. I was coasting on the sense of relief and comfort my parents took in knowing that I had come from a very turbulent, shaky academic beginning to a point where I had received my high school Advanced Bilingual Diploma and landed up with acceptance to both universities to which I had applied.

There was just one problem. Wasn't I supposed to be enjoying what I was doing? Was this going to be my lot in life? My future! Was it to be filled with staring at numbers and interacting with spreadsheets, reconciling statements and posting journal entries?

One day, I had an hour before my next class. It happened to be my French phonetics class, one of the classes I signed up for, just to boost my GPA as I had the French skills already. It turned out that I really enjoyed the teacher who purposely presented the theoretical material using active interaction. He would pose questions and involve all the students, no matter what the context. We always used to laugh as he would say, "Imagine someone walking into our lecture, seeing the students and teachers with their mouths wide open, tongues sticking out making grunting and guttural sounds at each other! One would think they had walked into an African tribal dialect class where the natives were learning about hunting for their meal."

On my way to this class, I met up with an old friend from high school. She asked me how things were going because she saw I looked kind of down.

Random side note: whenever poker night came to campus, I was always the most sought-after player! Why? One of my God-given characteristics is that I wear my heart on my sleeve. Not to my advantage in poker, but definitely one for my fellow players! Whilst in some situations this character trait worked to my detriment, today it turned out to be one of my greatest assets. My friend only needed to look at me to know how my day was going. Moreover, it seemed that very moment was the time and place for me to talk about what had been on my mind and heart for so long.

That's when the truth finally sank in... so I told her how I didn't like my business course, and in all truth I actually hated it and could not see myself doing business for the rest of my life.

I went on to say what I really enjoyed was my French and even my math classes, which I was taking as part of the business degree. She asked me, very simply, "So why not just change your major and do what you love?"

How would I make a living?

How would I support a family?

How would I tell my parents?

But…how would I feel as a businessman?

How would I make myself get up every morning for the rest of my life?

How would I find motivation when I felt stuck, uninspired, unfulfilled, but with lots of money in the bank?

How would I tell my parents?

I knew at that second, business was not my path in life, nor was it what the future had in store for me.

"What do you really want to do?" she asked. "Teach!" I responded instinctively.

She went on, "You've got it made. You enjoy French and math. Don't you remember there was always a huge shortage of math teachers in our French immersion program? Why not make a change? Switch to the Faculty of Education, major in French and minor in math. I'm sure there will be positions available, especially for men. Don't you remember? We hardly had any male teachers in school. I'm sure you would have a leg up, especially since you went through the French immersion program yourself. You have first-hand experience."

I remember this being one of the most uplifting conversations I had ever had. It felt as if the sun was shining! Not a cloud in the sky. Even if it had been a totally overcast day, the memory of that lifedefining moment, of me finally discovering my intended direction in life, that feeling of being totally at peace with the decision evoked a sense of tranquillity and excitement. I thanked her so much for her help. I told her I was now determined to set that path in motion.

It just so happened that we were standing outside the Office of the Registrar. I ran up the stairs to the pay phones outside the main office and called Chaya. It was another sign from the universe approving my decision. Despite Victoria, British Columbia being an hour behind Calgary, Chaya was actually home and answered the phone herself. She must have sensed the excitement in my voice because I could not contain my enthusiasm. I burst out the whole story of what happened. I explained my reasons for changing my major and taking the plunge. I was going to be a teacher – I was going to teach math in the French immersion program.

My mother's words still echo in my mind today: "How will you ever be able to support your family? You will forever be scraping by as a teacher. Stop fantasizing and realise that you have a great opportunity to grow in the business world with what you have already accomplished with your internship at Nova Corporation!" For me to have declared my major in education in the midst of a tumultuous educational climate in the province of Alberta was, as my mother put it, "irresponsible."

Temporary or Permanent Insanity?

My mother went on and on: "Arnold, this is just a fad, how can you support your family with a teacher's salary?" Of course, the most relevant question she could and most surely did throw at me was, "There aren't any jobs out there right now in education! You've been following the news, Arnold, just read the headlines in the newspaper for the past few months!"

This was all true. But I had a plan.

The education climate in Calgary in the 1990s was less than stable. The Teacher's Union was engaged in a fierce battle with the Calgary Board of Education. The Government had threatened to step in and legislate teachers back to work if the union threatened to strike. At one point, a blanket hiring freeze was placed over the entire province with the expectation that more lay-offs would be necessary in the coming years. This made all my closet critics charge out of their closets! No one could understand why I had made the unfathomable change to the Faculty of Education from the Faculty of Commerce. No one except Chaya...

Once I had committed to the idea of switching faculties, I had to be strategic in my approach. Surely, my parents would not be very happy. Once I got past their emotional reaction, I would have to have some pretty well-thought-out answers to the very pointed questions they were already raising.

Even my peers from my former faculty were monitoring my change of career path. From a logical standpoint, they were right. According to the front pages of local and national newspapers, all the evidence of my dead end career path was laid out in gory detail. "Education is suffering," screamed a 1992 headline. Funding for education fell to a dismal state in our home province of Alberta. The statistics cited that the provincial government was spending, at the time, less of its gross domestic product on education (6.6%), than any other province in the country. Even more damaging to the confidence in my choice, Alberta was ranked absolute last among provinces in education expenditures as a percentage of provincial and local budgets. All this proved that as 1993 loomed as large as my graduation date, the chance of the largest public school district in the province hiring new graduates was less than remote. I'd probably have better odds of winning the lottery. Nevertheless, I was insanely confident that I could beat the odds. I told myself that I was not like the others. I was different not because I had some secret talent, but that I was more creative than the others, I believed that I was more calculating then my peers and somehow I had known all along that I was going to find a crack in the system.

Throughout all my schooling in quite a variety of settings, I, like many other students, had distilled the ingredients to being a good teacher. To me, this was not rocket science. In fact, this "secret" has guided me as a principal to this very day, whenever I faced the daunting challenge of having to select teachers to be part of my school's educational team.

If you weigh up all the other factors, this one quality is fundamental to being a good teacher. The best teachers truly like kids. They believe in kids.

I did not see myself spending eight hours a day doing something I detested with people I didn't find inspirational. I could not see myself working in an office, doing the mundane. It only made sense to do something I truly loved. Somewhere, my destiny, the cosmic plan was for me to enjoy my life, waking up every day and going to work. The only thing I could see myself doing which I would truly enjoy was to be around children, making an impact in their lives, being that person that made them feel that they had a purpose. Like finding that special quality of which perhaps even they were not aware, uncovering a hidden talent, or helping them overcome a personal challenge. Teachers talk about that "light bulb" moment – the providential time when a student connects the dots. It's that second when the spark of the hitherto unknown is ignited. It awakens a sense of purpose, in themselves and in the teacher. When you, the teacher, are the catalyst of this awakening, in life, there is no better feeling of satisfaction. When someone is privileged to guide children into this realm of possibility where they feel invincible, the awakening of the potential that they can believe in themselves is the greatest gift one could ask for. These enthused students begin to develop self-worth and that their infinite ability is not dependent on anyone else, not their parents not their peers, not the teacher himself. This is education.

I was a student who had to search a long time to discover this feeling. I realize looking back; there were one, maybe two teachers who gave this gift to me. It didn't ever matter that there weren't so many. They had given me an incredible endowment and I too wanted to pay this feeling of gratitude forward. This would be my greatest tribute to those two teachers who took me from nothing and made me feel like I was worth something. A feat no one else could do for me, I wanted to be that teacher for others. I knew there were not a lot of educators out there who were truly dedicated to this purpose, but I wanted to be one who could and would make that difference.

And here was the crux of my plan…mathematics, the most challenging subject. I had always felt like I was a failure in school and in life because I forever had a problem in math class. Somehow, the way others were able to process the material just didn't work for me. I could never do it their way. All my mathematics teachers demanded that the problem be solved their way. "Do it like this," "try this," but it never worked out for me. Not once was I ever asked, "So how do you think it should go?" until I met Mademoiselle Julie Marchand. Mlle Marchand, with her sense of humour, touched with just the tiniest bit of sarcasm, made an incredible impact on me. She found an incredibly individualized way to challenge me and inspire me to show her how I could do the math she assigned my way. It was Grade 10 before I had the privilege of being taught by Mlle Marchand. I had the basics but was never confident because of my struggles throughout elementary and junior high school. Still in the French immersion program at Western Canada High School, Grade 10 pushed the boundaries of algebra for me.

At first, I struggled, falling back into my default position: paralysing self-doubt. Lacking self-confidence and unwilling to take on yet another risk after two zeros on quizzes, Mlle Marchand asked me to see her after class. Thus began our tutorial relationship. She assured me during class, if I didn't understand, I had a backup plan. Someone cared to make sure I had the understanding that would build my self-confidence. What I did mattered. Then, she asked me, "Explain in your own words what you're trying to do." I felt my eyes opening to a new world. Working together, Mlle Marchand helped legitimize my strategies and gave me the opportunity to understand my style of mathematical reasoning. A few times in class, I was even called upon to explain an alternate method to solve difficult problems. Through our relationship, I realised some incredible facts. Not only could I do math, I actually had a gift in mathematical reasoning. This gave me the confidence that it was okay to think outside of the box mathematically and go against the grain of how the collective was processing. From that time forward, with my confidence fostered, I developed more and more faith in my ability. For the next two years, I made sure to have Mlle Marchand as my math teacher. On the 12th grade government exam in 1988, my final math score was a 98%, the top score in our entire year's cohort.

And remember, at U of C I had chosen some additional classes as 'fun' fillers. My criteria for choosing these 'fun' classes consisted of not too many additional assignments, minimal exams and GPA boosting potential. I had decided to go with my strengths, so I chose French language courses, including French phonetics and dramatic literature. These 'fun' fillers turned out to be a foundation stone in my Bachelor of Education plan.

I worked about as hard on my graduation strategy as I did on my class work as I made the move into the education faculty. I found myself plotting on how to break into the job market and get a teaching position right out of university. The crack in the system was staring me right in the face. I felt it was a tapestry that had been woven since I miraculously left the I L Peretz School in Grade 6 and was accepted into Elboya Junior High School.

I would apply to teach mathematics in French. I just had a gut feeling there most likely would be vacancies in the growing French immersion program. Most definitely for mathematics teachers. I knew without a doubt, looking around in all my classes, there were not too many male candidates. I could tick all the boxes. I would capitalize on my strengths in becoming part of the sought-after minority...a male teacher, with a minor in mathematics and a major in French immersion education. Not only that, I realised that my favourite age group to work with is the age group that most teachers despise – Junior High. So I concentrated on a secondary school qualification so that I would also be qualified to teach Grades' 7-12. There was the niche: a male, junior high French immersion mathematics teacher.

My plan was to use my business courses, such as statistics and linear algebra, Bachelor of Commerce prerequisites, and apply them toward a minor in mathematics. It turned out that because of the heavy mathematics requirement in my first years in the Bachelor of Commerce program, I would not be too far off from the requirements for this minor. And since I had continued taking French courses, I found myself also well on the way toward the necessary prerequisites for a major in French language. All that just left the courses for a Bachelor of Education. My road was paved.

The Most Rewarding Profession

Perhaps everyone has a defining moment in his or her life. My very first experience as an education student was one of those defining moments. Because of that, it is most memorable. I am transported back to my first education class at the University of Calgary. It was a first year introductory education class on the first day of the brand-new semester – the very first semester after my life-altering decision to drop business studies and become a teacher. All of us on that very first day of class were starting along a career path that, given the economic atmosphere, seemed doomed to end at the unemployment office, not in a classroom. In order to paint a vivid picture of the competitive education job market at that time, the principal of a well-known and highly successful Calgary Board of Education public school was invited as that year's opening guest speaker. He was present that first day to address all of the first year of education students.

His name was Alf Boldt. He was tall, an imposing figure, somewhat heavyset, with a trimmed beard. He stood, commandingly, at the front of the lecture hall, like the inspector general eyeing the troops. His introduction was the following statement: "Each and every education student has some personal motivation for pursuing a job as a teacher and heading down the career path in education. I am the gatekeeper and protector of the young souls that you may or may not have the privilege of inspiring. Some of you are here today, because you believe that the perks of being a teacher are great enough to outweigh the challenges. Maybe it's the two months of summer holidays, two-week winter vacations and spring break. Perhaps it is the seven-hour workday with a guaranteed lunchtime and occasional coffee break. If any of these thoughts are your motivation for becoming a teacher, I will do whatever is in my power to get you *out* of this faculty. But, if you are here to inspire a child who has yet to realise his or her own potential, if you are the eager, selfless nurturer who is going to stay up each and every night, devising new ways to motivate that struggling child at the back of the classroom who, for some reason, unknown to anyone else, just hasn't turned the key and unlocked the door of his or her potential; if you are prepared to lose sleep because you have not solved the mystery of how to make yourself better in order to improve the educational experience for your students, then I will do everything in my power to get you *in* to the most giving, rewarding profession."

I don't remember much more from his address, because that was all I needed to hear. That touched my soul. This message became my mantra. As I meet new educators as well as veteran teachers, I feel it is my duty to uphold the 'code of conduct' articulated by Alf Boldt. Little did I know that my path would soon cross yet again with this charismatic icon.

During the final Bachelor' of Education year, students are placed in two different schools for trial opportunities, two varied length practica, teaching in one's major area of study.

The teaching practicum is designed to provide the budding teacher with hands-on opportunities to learn and grow by both observing and engaging in the day-to-day realities of the classroom and school environment. Through the guidance of carefully selected mentors, the student-teacher is able to question, reflect and entertain uncertainty in real-life scenarios of the up-to-now mere theoretical understanding of what it means to be an educator.

The first practicum was a mere four-week field experience, simply designed to give an overview of the complexity of the classroom. The main focus of this first practicum is largely observational, with the chance to do actual teaching only in the last week. Specific note-taking tasks are required during the observations to foster engagement on more than a superficial level. I excitedly planned for my first practicum placement with a "real" class, eager to leave the clinical education laboratory, the artificial lecture halls of academia, and enter the 'Blackboard Jungle' at Branton Junior High School.

My first day at Branton arrived. I nervously awaited my introductory meeting with the principal of the school in the main reception area. Through the frosted glass window of his adjoining office, I could vaguely see two individuals engaged in a discussion. I surmised that this must be my mentor, receiving some last-minute directives from his principal. After what seemed like ages, the door opened. The secretary informed me that this was my cue to go in. To my shock and disbelief, I instantly recognized the principal. His face was unforgettable.

With his hand extended, he introduced himself, "Welcome to Branton Junior High School – bienvenue, I'm the Principal, Mr Alf Boldt." I hardly heard him when he said, "This is your supervising teacher, Wayne Pope." It was quite the intimidating introduction, not at all from anything he said. It was all from my instant flashback to three years prior...my very first lecture in the Faculty of Education.

After some further pleasantries, I boldly spoke up. I reminded Mr Boldt of those fateful words at our introductory education course. I told him what an inspiration those words were and how they provided a sense of guidance throughout my learning. How they solidified my resolve and provided a direction for what I was sure was my destined path.

Kindly he responded that I was very highly recommended by the associate professor in charge of practicum placement. He shook my hand, smiled and delivered those echoing words, "I'll be keeping my eye on you!" I smiled nervously. And yet, somehow I had a spark of confidence knowing that we had hit it off. Thus began my journey as a teacher.

You've Got the Job!

Even though I had made my decision to switch faculties a year into my Bachelor of Commerce program, I could still finish in the standard four years by June 1993 by taking some extra spring and summer courses. In the fall of 1992, I applied to the Calgary Board of Education as a bilingual secondary mathematics teacher, able to teach Math in French in Grades' 7–12. My expected graduation date was determined to be the end of the summer semester, as I still had to complete my final French course. Once the application was signed, sealed and delivered, all I had to do was sit back and impatiently wait and pray that my supposedly "well crafted" plan was enough to get me through the front door of the Calgary Board of Education Human Resources Department and shortlisted for an initial interview for what most likely was but a mere fraction of job openings.

No sooner was my first practicum successfully completed in October that I arrived home one day to find an envelope from the Calgary Board of Education. I tore open the envelope, excitedly scanning the letter to see if there was good or bad news. There it was. My interview was scheduled! I had a date with the Human Resources Department. My foot was in the door to my future! That first step – I could tick that box, I had made it to the starting line. To even begin the process, I had to get to this stage. I knew I was ready, and yet I had only a week and a half to prepare for one of the most important meetings in my life.

I assembled my portfolio as my professors had instructed me. I also took their advice and did mock interviews with my classmates. This was a valuable part of my preparation. I knew why I wanted to be a teacher and what I had to offer. Rehearsing why I wanted to be a teacher, but more importantly, where I saw myself, and what I was prepared to teach allowed me to crystallize and summarize what I wanted to say. I needed to be precise and succinct as I had only one opportunity to seize my chance. I needed to be clear, without saying it in so many words, that I would be indispensable to the one or two vacancies in the Calgary Board of Education staffing grid. I was confidently armed with my spiel.

I was a French immersion graduate from the very system to which I was now looking to give back. I was now a confident mathematics teacher, ready to 'pay it forward.' Even as I write this today, I chuckle thinking about how little I really knew. I was just too young and confident to know it. And truly, I was completely unprepared for the challenges that lay ahead. Deep down I think I knew this, but then I was in the same position as every other candidate in the running. How could I really think that I was utterly prepared? I had not even graduated and fulfilled my degree requirements. The graduation wouldn't officially happen until after the summer. I had also only completed one practicum. Yet, I knew that this was what I was born to do. There was nothing anyone could do to dissuade me, not even my own tiny seeds of doubt. I would keep this affirmation in mind when those seeds would, every so often, begin to sprout. This affirmation has often strengthened my resolve over the many years. Knowing you are destined to accomplish something creates great confidence, allowing you to put the full effort in to conquer overwhelming odds and obstacles.

With this naïvely firm spark and resolve, I walked into the Board of Education, ready for my initial interview. I felt the preparation beforehand was time well spent. The opportunity for me to express my philosophy and born desire to become a teacher came through in many of the open-ended questions posed throughout the interview. The most pertinent aspects of the interview seemed to be my experience as a student in the late immersion program leading to my intention to teach in the same program. The interviewer seemed genuinely interested in my background. I summarized the whole story: coming as an immigrant to Canada, becoming fluent in French and having made such a significant change in career path from a promising career in the business sector to education. The other focus of the interview was on my extracurricular background, specifically my athletic sporting success. I hadn't realised how significant my receiving the Calgary Herald Scholarship for Academic Achievement and Outstanding Involvement in Extra Curricular Activities truly was. It appeared that they really did their homework in not only reviewing my resume but also thoroughly checking my references. I left the interview very confident despite the standard "thank you, we will be in touch," as I walked out that door.

The next hurdle was completely beyond my control. The human resources department had to sift through the candidate pool and make recommendations to school principals depending on their requests and specific staffing needs for the 1993 academic year. In all likelihood, any potential positions would only be communicated in the spring. I would have to anxiously wait until May before hearing from the Board of Education that I was sought after for an interview from a school principal.

It was the middle of May, nine long months later. That afternoon when I arrived home, I noticed the indicator light blinking on our telephone message machine. Nonchalantly, I pressed the play button to retrieve the message. "Hello Mr. Glogauer, my name is Gary Jeffrey. I am the Principal of Elboya Junior High School. Can you please give me a call back at your earliest convenience?" I quickly took down the number and prepared myself for making the call. Except I was so excited and nervous that I could have jumped out of my skin! I knew I needed to be calm and calculating. But how? Deep down I knew you get only one chance to make that first impression – even over the phone. Between excited asides of "what ifs" and "I can't believe it's," running over the script with Chaya, I just decided to make the call. It was a brief conversation. Mr Jeffrey sounded nice, quite pleasant actually. He was short and to the point. "We have a vacancy for a late immersion mathematics teacher. Would like you to come in for an interview? How does June 10th at 9 am sound?" Was he kidding? "Sounds perfect. I look forward to meeting you then. Thank you so much for the call!" I was ecstatic – I might have screamed I was so excited. Here was my chance. Now I only had one giant question. Would I graduate on time?

Expecting a Miracle

How were we going to tell Mom and Dad? We had been married in September 1990 and due to the pressures of university and certainly our finances, we hadn't really thought of having children, at least not yet. We had only been married two years. The timing had to be right – it had to fit into our five-year plan. It seems we always had a plan. Get engaged, make sure Chaya got accepted into the doctorate program at the University of Calgary. Secure funding for her PhD, which would include living expenses. Use student loans to fund the gap for covering our living expenses. Work in the summer to make some more money to close the gap. Children would come after Chaya finished her doctorate.

Everything was moving according to plan. Despite challenges with Chaya's advisor and continually shifting deadlines, both Chaya's dissertation and my bachelor's degree were progressing according to plan. My graduation date was June 1993, a year away; I would soon be applying for a job with the Calgary Board of Education. Our life and five-year plan was on track.

One evening, after a long day at University, Chaya said we needed to talk. As usual, I needed a bit of time to chill out and Chaya, in her infinite wisdom, laid the foundation for a potential intensive conversation. I should have realised what was up. Arriving home, the table was set and food was cooking on the stove. Instructed to relax on the couch, she brought me a snack and a cold drink. I could have guessed what was going on – I was being watered and fed. This meant something was up. I didn't argue as I certainly appreciated and enjoyed the pampering. I fit all the silly clichés about how to soften up a husband by feeding and cajoling him…before hitting him with a bomb. I didn't push, as deep down, I knew that I needed to be prepared and in the right frame of mind for whatever I was going to be hit with. It was essential to play my role and go along with the expectation that I submit to the pampering. I felt loved and cared for despite realizing that I was being strategically set up.

When I was well fed, Chaya joined me on the couch. Prepared for almost anything, I don't think Chaya was ready for my response. Apprehensively, perhaps even afraid of my response she began her obviously well-rehearsed monologue. "I know we had a plan and we were going to wait a little longer, but I don't think I can wait any longer. It is hard knowing how long I have to go with my PhD and I'm not getting any younger. I think it's time we try and have a baby." The pause was very long. As I looked into her tearful eyes, she knew it was my Achilles heel. I could not hold back my rush of emotions when she cried.

Looking back, this conversation set the wheels in motion down a road that would change the course of our lives in untold, unbelievable ways. It was not as straightforward a process as one would think for us to successfully conceive. After three to four months and advice from our local doctor, we finally reached the day when enough time had passed to purchase a home pregnancy test. We had tried a couple of times unsuccessfully, waiting in great anticipation for the blank slot on the plastic stick to turn into a plus sign. Many times before, a disappointing negative sign appeared after what seemed to be the longest 120 seconds of our lives. This morning though seemed different. Chaya woke up and followed her regular routine. I was slowly waking up when she came into the bathroom. "I think today is the day." It was 7 am and we didn't have a kit. Eagerly I said, "So what's stopping us, let's go and buy one." And so we did.

That morning, we were the first customers at the Glenmore Landing Pharmacy when the doors opened at 8 am. I can only imagine the thoughts of the sales cashier as she opened the doors to a waiting customer rushing first thing in the morning to the home pregnancy kit aisle. What was she thinking? Was this a positive, excited, anticipatory purchase? Or was it an anxious, hopefully relieving acquisition? She would never know.

We couldn't wait to get home, as I would need to get to a 9 am University lecture. Dipping in the stick, we carefully set it down. We looked at the clock radio: 8:10am. Two minutes and counting. "When the clock gets to 8:12am, let's take a look, but not before that". We were both completely silent for two minutes. You could hear a pin drop as we sat there anxiously. Neither of us wanted to speak for fear that we could jinx the outcome. "8:12am, well, what does it say?" I anxiously cried out.

And there it was, for the first time, it was a plus sign. I looked at Chaya and she at me, with tears in both our eyes, I exclaimed, "We did it, OMG, we are having a baby!"

Carefully we disposed of the evidence. We wanted to just stop time and savour that moment, and all the hopes and dreams it held for what was to lie ahead. Instead, we were off, buckling our seatbelts again on our way to my 9am lecture. With the pull of routine beckoning to continue as if it were a regular day, we knew that it was not and would never be again. We couldn't hold in the excitement the entire way to the University. We got sensible after a while. The first thing was to call our doctor's office and get a confirmation test. That morning as Chaya dropped me off at my class, I looked into her eyes and told how much I loved her and that our lives would never be the same.

Once the good news was indeed confirmed by the doctor, the excitement certainly was building. Next step, we plotted how we would share the news with my parents. Despite being the second couple in my family to marry (my brother Michael married his wife Deborah in May, three months before us) we would be the first to have a child. My sister got married a few months after these events, twenty weeks later to be exact – just when we were able to share with everyone else (outside immediate family) the good news. Funnily enough, while we had the first grandchild (today we have three wonderful children) my brother has nine beautiful children and my sister sixteen gems, all healthy, thank God. Ever the one for revering traditions and special moments, I felt it would be significant how we would ultimately disclose the pending arrival of the first Glogauer grandchild.

That evening, we told my parents we had some news to tell them and could we come over for dinner. We had something quite important to talk to them about face-to-face, over the phone just would not be appropriate. This wasn't necessarily an unusual request, as over the past two years we had sought out the wisdom of my parents over many issues. We have always had a strong, communicative relationship with my parents who have always given us sage advice. Over the course of our marriage, we have often consulted with them before making any final life-defining decisions. Not always have we followed their advice: however, we have always considered their point of view and weighed it considerably before arriving at a final decision. They would not necessarily see what was coming despite my fairly well-known flair for the dramatic.

After dinner, we sat them down, and I began. "Mom, Dad, we both love you very much. We have something to tell you, but before we do, we think you're going to need this..." We handed them a gift-wrapped package. Seated together on the couch, my father took the gift with his characteristic flair for the dramatic (I come by it honestly). He took it, and with his best mock reverence, painstakingly slowly opened the wrapping paper in front of my mother. Inside was the first book in the series titled "What to Expect" by Heidi Markoff. To this very day, that book still sits on my parents' bookshelf. They didn't get it just yet. That initial perplexed look contorted my father's puzzled face. His elation and emotion caused him to immediately well up. He showed the book to my mother and then he immediately began to sob. "Is this what I think it is, does this mean what I think?" "Yes, it sure does!" Chaya and I responded in unison. We all stood up and hugged each other. *Mazel tov*, congratulations! Are you alright? How are you feeling? *Mazal tov!* Oh, we are so happy!

This was certainly one of the most exciting times of our lives. The many doctor appointments, the anticipation leading up to the delivery day. Part of the excitement was watching my parents' enthusiasm and anticipation of the arrival of their first grandchild. A decision Chaya and I made right away was not to be told the gender of a child. It would certainly make the delivery so much more special finding out at that precise moment the gender of our first-born. If you think about it, it doesn't really serve any purpose knowing the gender, other than to spoil a nine-month-long anticipation of a massive surprise – a surprise that comes only that once in a lifetime. You have the rest of the child's life to know that answer. Therefore, we certainly could wait nine months. We weren't yearning for a boy over a girl or vice versa. We really meant what we said. We just wanted a healthy baby.

One of the challenges we had to endure during the pregnancy was the response of Chaya's PhD advisor. Chaya had completed all of her coursework for her doctorate, but was now in the proposal stage of her dissertation. Things were not progressing according to plan due to the demanding expectations of her advisor. It seemed that Chaya could not satisfy the needs of her advisor and this obvious disruption would only cause more friction between the both of them. Chaya was extremely anxious about sharing the news and delayed telling her as long as possible. Since Chaya was so petite, she could only hide the fact that she was pregnant for so long. As expected, the conversation didn't go too well.

There was no real fear of Chaya being let go as a graduate student. It was more the attitude and increased pressure for her to produce the work and complete her doctorate according to her advisor's strict and unwavering timeline. Despite the cold reception from her advisor, our excitement and enthusiasm did not waiver. We would persevere through the pressure and expectations of her advisor.

As those forty weeks progressed, we realized the auspiciousness of Chaya's due date. Not only would the first Glogauer grandchild be born in June, my eagerly anticipated interview at Elboya Junior High was scheduled in June. June 10th.

Don't You Have Somewhere Important to Go?

Having committed to Divine Providence, knowing I had done everything possible to open every potential door into my preferred field of education, my focus, other than my final exam, was on the pending arrival of our first-born child. I had made it a priority to attend every possible prenatal care appointment. The first time the doctor located the baby's heartbeat with the Fetal Doppler Stethoscope, Chaya and I could not contain ourselves and became instantly emotionally overwhelmed. I made a personal commitment to be involved in every way possible. We signed up for a Lamaze class as we excitedly prepared for the big day. Little did we know that there would be no real adequate class that could have possibly prepared us for an experience that would truly change our lives.

Be it Murphy's Law or some other axiom, despite the best plans being made things were not going according to OUR blueprint. We were told that it was normal in your first pregnancy to go past your due date and that we had nothing to worry about as the baby was growing according to plan. As I'm sure most parents can attest, nothing can prepare you for the first time experiences associated with the birth of your first child.

With the initial due date having passed by a few days, Tuesday morning, I woke up to Chaya declaring, "This is it, I'm going into labour". I told myself I would be different, not like all the corny Hollywood depictions of clumsy, nervous, first-time fathers to be. I would remain calm and the epitome of cool collectedness.

Putting the pre-determined plan into action, we called the doctor notifying her of Chaya's condition. The doctor said that since she was already at her clinic, instead of meeting her at the hospital, due to the infrequent timing of the contractions, there was no rush and we were to come straight to her office. Chaya had just been there the day before as she was in the weekly appointment stage. She had been excited when she came home because she was already 1-2 cm dilated. The updated examination result was quite anticlimactic: Chaya was only two or so cm dilated. We were told to go home, walk it off and call back when the contractions reached seven minutes apart. With Chaya's labour progressing, or so we thought, we remained in hopeful, optimistic limbo for the next however many hours. Completely torn, I reluctantly rushed off to try to get back to my regular study schedule. Chaya was in good hands for now with my mother and a close friend attending to her. I still had to finish preparing for my final exam, which was to take place that very next afternoon!

The anticipation and excitement were building on so many levels. Of course, for my parents, waiting to meet their first grandchild, with each day beyond Chaya's due date passing, the anticipation grew more and more. We had all hoped that with Chaya beginning the signs of labour, she would give birth before Wednesday. Because guess what? My parents had already booked their trip to Toronto to attend my brother's graduation ceremony. He would be the first Glogauer doctor and this was truly an event not to be missed. The tickets had been purchased well in advance. We had maintained a strong case that my parents should not hesitate to join my brother just because of the impending delivery. Even though our due date was in close proximity to Michael's accomplishment, the birth would take place at some unknown time in the near future. We had no certainty that the delivery would happen before the weekend. Anyway, with the graduation ceremony scheduled Friday, my parents would be back Sunday. Who knew where we would be holding by then.

After a fitful Tuesday night, all that Wednesday morning my mother sat with Chaya at home, going on long walks, hoping to move the labour along before the midday deadline when my parents would have to leave for the airport in order to make their flight. I was so grateful to my mother as this allowed me to focus on my final exam scheduled for 1 pm that afternoon. It was a tearful goodbye as my parents finally tore themselves away and rushed to the airport, realizing that if something were to take place in the next few hours, they would be on a plane across the country. What made it even more emotional for my mother was that Wednesday, June 9 was the anniversary of the birthday of her grandmother – Oma Erna, whose Hebrew name was Esther. It had been Granny Esther who had lovingly raised my mother from an early age. In a remarkable case in South Africa in the 1950s, my mother's father had been given custody of my mother after his divorce when she was only a few months old. His plan had been to have her maternal grandparents raise my mother. Oma Esther had been my mother's 'mother' from the tiny age of about 18 months!

My heart was racing as I attempted to stay calm and focused toward my major final exam. The implications the three-hour exam had toward the future of our family was overwhelming in itself. But now, Chaya's labour was dragging into the 48-hour mark. It started to take its toll.

12:15 pm came quickly and with it the reality that it was time for me to head up to University for my exam and leave my wife in the middle of labour with our first unborn child. Making sure the cell phone was charged, I rushed up to the university hoping to speak to the professor before the exam.

I arrived fifteen minutes early, enough time to bend the sympathetic ear of our professor. Explaining how my wife was in the midst of labour, I asked permission to leave my cell phone on, under my desk, in case my wife's labour progressed to the point of going to the hospital so I would be contactable. In 1993, this cell phone pack was the size of a large volume of an encyclopaedia, with the phone attached to a large battery and a 30 cm aerial. I was quite a spectacle. At any time, it was an unusual request, but then it was quite the novelty to have a cell phone in the first place. After all, it was 1993 and this innovative technology was in its own infancy.

Those three hours flew by as I floated in and out of my zone, trying to keep focused on the task at hand, at the same time realizing my wife was about to give birth, and how I could never forgive myself if I wasn't present at the delivery.

Having completed the exam with no time to spare, I handed it in and thanked the professor for his understanding as well as his guidance throughout the term. I was trying to run to the car, all the while calling Chaya to get an update but the cell phone was just too big and bulky, so I awkwardly made my way there at last.

Thoughtfully Chaya asked about the exam, but I was only focused on how things were progressing. She said that there was no need to speed home, but once I arrived, we would make our way to the hospital. I told her I thought I did well and now I could focus on just her and the baby. I arrived home. We picked up the last-minute necessities and our pre-packed suitcase. With that, we were off to the hospital.

When we arrived, we parked in the long term parking and made our way to the admissions desk. The first stop was a check-in with our doctor and her intern at examinations. Forty-eight hours of labour had already passed by this time. Chaya had been 2 cm dilated at the beginning of that saga. To find out that Chaya was only 4 to 5 cm dilated after 48 hours of labour; to say we were a little disappointed was a grave understatement.

The doctor informed us we had a few options to consider. "We can keep you here, but it could be at least another day or so. We think it's probably better to send you back home where you can wait more comfortably until things progress even more. Even though it feels like the contractions are closer together, really you have quite a way to go. But before you go, we'll just get a better feel for how things are by putting a fetal heart monitor on for a few minutes. We will see all is well with the baby, then we'll send you home to a more comfortable place rather than sitting here in hospital."

Downheartedly, we just looked at each other. We both knew what we were thinking. Just what we needed, more waiting. Chaya was shattered actually. Forty-eight hours is a long time with very little to show for it. We tried to get our resoluteness back and to wait patiently for the results of the monitors of both our infant's heart rate and Chaya's contractions. We got some comfort from watching the printed results flow from the continuous printout while listening to the pure rise and fall of the baby's heartbeat. What we hadn't taken into consideration was the intentions of our unborn child.

At about ten to fifteen minutes of the recording, the intern came in to read the printout. After studying it for a long moment, she tore off the printout and told us to sit tight, she would return in a minute or two. The monitor kept on recording the contractions. I was quite amused to see the recordings and could even anticipate the contractions before Chaya could feel them. It gave me a chance to help her prepare her breathing and relax for the oncoming onset of pain. We playfully amused ourselves somewhat as each contraction came. Observably I was more amused than she was.

The doctor returned with the intern and delivered the unexpected news. It seemed that the baby was a little distressed, perhaps due to the fact that this had gone on somewhat long with little progression. "What we would like to suggest is to break your water and set up an IV with Pitocin in order to induce labour to get things going. Are you okay with that?"

I looked at Chaya and both of us had expressions of deep relief on our faces. We were ready to take things to the next level. With the induction of labour and the close monitoring of the baby through an internal fetal monitor, we were again hopeful, anticipating results…that simply did not materialize. Yes, the contractions were coming more frequently. The baby's heart rate was fluctuating more and more indicating some levels of distress; however, Chaya was not dilating accordingly. This went on for a few more hours. The doctor pulled me aside and gave me the unexpected news. "Look," she said, "we're going to prepare Chaya for a C-section. Things just aren't progressing as we would like so we're going to move her to the operating room, you're welcome to come in if you would like."

What a question! There was no way I was prepared to miss this, especially leaving Chaya alone. By now, the contractions were coming hard and fast and I had been replaced by the intern helping Chaya breathe through the relentless pain of the back-to-back contractions. Chaya, being brave and a first-time mother had decided against any use of medication including the use of an epidural. The intern and nurses came into our room to wheel Chaya into the operating room and prepare her for the C-section. I was given a gown and head covering. Just as we moved into the hallway, Chaya had a massive contraction – at the same moment that the nurses and attendants all said: 'Try not to scream'. It was quite comical to see the nurses and attending doctors trying to convince a pregnant woman in the height of her labour, mid-contraction after more than forty-eight hours of labour, not to scream, to remain silent. There was an incredible look of indignation on Chaya's face coupled with utter disbelief: as the crescendo of the contraction peaked she let out a giant yell.

Trying not to show my insensitivity and embarrassment, I dutifully followed the parade of doctors and nurses toward the operating room feeling quite helpless. I carefully read some chapters of Psalms, praying that both the pain would be quickly over and the birth of our healthy baby would come soon.

Entering the operating room, I positioned myself behind the curtain as the doctor announced she would try one last manoeuvre, making one last effort to avoid performing the C-section. With good fortune, the baby was repositioned and we embarked down the final stretch. With a few final pushes, the baby emerged. At 2:01 am Thursday morning 10 June 1993, the doctor uttered those fateful words. "Congratulations, it's a baby girl!"

I could not believe my ears. My eyes began to well up, as did Chaya's. I was asked if I would like to cut the umbilical cord, but I quickly declined. Our baby was brought to the infant radiant warmer where all the major checks were done. In true Glogauer fashion, she was allocated a perfect Apgar score.

We were concerned that the distress the baby was under would be evident when she arrived into the world. Thankfully, this was not the case. Her heart rate, breathing, skin colour and muscle tone were perfect. While the doctors and nurses were checking her, I clicked my tongue to my cheek hoping to attract some attention or response from the baby. To my amazement, she immediately responded to the sound. I was so taken with

105

her. While they were still looking after Chaya, they wrapped our precious bundle. I was the first to hold our baby. I truly believe the resulting bond I share with our little girl to this day, is a direct result of this initial connection. I think that mothers automatically have this connection as they intimately share the first nine months of life. It takes a significant effort for fathers to establish this bond. Not too long later, Chaya had the chance to hold our little baby. A lactation nurse came too, and the first efforts in trying to feed the baby were set in motion.

In our private room, we were brought a washing kit and basin and I was given the first opportunity to bathe our baby. Thus, the ritual was set. For the first year of our little one's life, it was now my job to bathe her. Once again, this was special daddy and little girl time. Finally, with our little one fast asleep, it was time to announce to the world that our baby was born. It was now close to 4 am Thursday morning. My parents were staying with my brother in Toronto. My sister, at the time, lived in New Jersey so they were all two hours ahead of us. Six am seemed to be a semi-reasonable hour for really good news.

We first placed a call to my parents and my brother's house. I knew it was early and we would be waking everyone, but it was such an occasion I thought they would forgive us. "Hello Mike, so sorry to wake you...Can we speak to Mom and Dad?"

Sleepily he answered, "Sure, is everything okay?"

"Yeah, *mazel tov*, it's a girl!"

He was genuinely excited and told us to wait while he took the cordless phone to my parents. I could hear a knock on my parents' door. My mother abruptly answered, "Is everything okay? How is Chaya?"

"Hi Mom, everyone is okay. *Mazel Tov* it's a girl." My mother immediately started to cry hysterically and passed the phone to my father. "*Mazel Tov* Dad, it's a girl." My Dad, who is also very emotional, asked to speak to Chaya. After enquiring as to how she was doing and how the baby was, they enquired as to what we were going to call her. Next logical question, right? Wrong! We had been so committed to the process of not planning a thing beforehand that we hadn't even planned...names. This was a true challenge for us as we had decided to not make any decisions regarding a name since we did not want to focus on the gender of the baby. All our thoughts were on our desire to just have a healthy baby. We had no preference and were not fussed either way.

The custom is also to keep the name of a baby girl a secret until the name can be announced at a public reading of the *Torah* scroll. There are three days when the *Torah* is read publicly: Monday, Thursday and on the

Shabbos – Saturday. Since this was Thursday morning, we would name the baby at the first possible opportunity, a *Torah* reading that Thursday morning. One thing we had planned was that this ceremony would take place in the Eastern Time Zone, in Crown Heights, Brooklyn, New York. We had learned that the most auspicious process of naming our unborn child would be to have her named at the Torah reading which would take place at the *Lubavitcher Rebbe's* main *Minyan* (morning prayer service), 9 am New York time. Since New York was two hours ahead and it was now about 6:30 am there, we only had two and a half hours to get our act together! We would need to figure out her name and then have someone 'take' her name to the *Rebbe's* Torah reading in Crown Heights.

Secretly we knew that since our baby was a girl, born the day after my great-grandmother Esther's birthday this would certainly become our baby's first name. We wanted a second name for her and we knew exactly who to call. We said our tearful goodbyes to my parents, telling them we would call them later that morning with the name of the baby. We shared how excited we were that they were returning Sunday, so we would see them soon. They planned on coming directly from the airport to the hospital. We were told that Chaya would be discharged midday Sunday, plenty of time for my parents to arrive after catching the red-eye flight Saturday night back home to Calgary.

Our next call was to my sister in New Jersey. After a quick exchange of *Mazel Tovs*, we jumped to the dilemma of what would be our precious bundle's second name. We were careful not to divulge our chosen name. First, we wanted to explore which combinations might sound right coupled with our selected first name choice. In the coming eighteen years, how were we to know that my sister would become an expert in baby-naming as today she has sixteen healthy children of her own. Menucha was full of suggestions and the sources for each. Once we heard "Dinah," Chaya and I looked at each other and just knew without having to say even one word that this was meant to be.

My sister was well aware of the custom to officially have a Jewish baby girl's name announced by the special prayer and that we would have the supplication recited at the *Rebbe's Minyan* in Crown Heights. We were absolutely thrilled with her incredible offer that my brother-in-law Yehoshua would do the honours. Yehoshua, by Divine Providence was actually able to make the journey to Crown Heights, Brooklyn, New York with enough time to attend morning services at the World Lubavitch headquarters. He would, of course, attend the *Torah* reading at the prayer service and on our behalf, name our baby girl there. That would mean that by 7:30 am our time, we could publicize our baby's name as the naming ceremony would take place at approximately 9:30 am New York time.

We communicated the name to Yehoshua, as he got in the car on his way to Brooklyn. We thanked him profusely for taking this on. It was not a simple favour. He would have to leave right then to fight the traffic from Morristown, New Jersey into Manhattan and then over to Brooklyn – not a fun morning commute. Nevertheless, we hung up the phone very relieved and content with our decision for her name and our gratitude to Uncle Yehoshua for being our emissary. We were so amazed at our good fortune. We felt confident that this was the most appropriate way to begin our new family.

By now, it was well after 4 am I could see Chaya was extremely exhausted. I was trying very hard not to show the overwhelmed feeling I was experiencing. I was only now realizing I had exactly three days to prepare our home for the new arrival! Not only did we refuse to have the gender of the baby revealed until the birth, we also adopted the *Chassidic* custom not to purchase a single item or set up any part of the intended baby's nursery until the baby is born. We had superficially made plans for a baby's room, however we had exercised great self-control not putting any concrete plans in motion. I had nothing else to do! I had finished my last university course that same night…it felt like literally a lifetime ago! Now we had our little baby. I had nothing to do other than race through the blueprint Chaya and I had discussed for what we envisioned if our baby was to be a girl.

One of Chaya's most amazing skills that she has mastered to this very day, one that she has successfully and generously imparted to myself and our children, is her ability to make organized lists. Whether it's the Friday dinner menu with all of the details that need to be taken care of simply to eat a scrumptious meal, or the famous 'to do list,' I certainly had great direction now! I would have a clearly focused mission for the next forty-eight hours, methodically accomplishing the many tasks, checking them off the list one by one on my fun-filled-marathon-new-baby-girl shopping spree. That might have been the only time I ever enjoyed shopping!

With our precious little princess sleeping, bundled up under the heat lamp beside Chaya's hospital bed, it was time for me to head home. I planned to catch a bit of sleep myself before tackling the list of shopping in the day ahead. On my way out, Chaya exhibited another one of her astonishing qualities. We still chuckle over those most incredible five words over which she uttered as I walked reluctantly out the door, "Don't forget your interview today!"

Now, on the one hand it is completely understandable how I could have forgotten about the interview. On the other hand, that day's interview also had the potential for being life changing. I had been waiting for the 10th of June since I received that initial phone call from the principal Mr Gary Jeffrey over six weeks ago. So from that perspective, how could I forget? What was more, with all she had gone through, how could Chaya have remembered?

Promising to get some sleep, I left in a daze now. I felt very delirious leaving the hospital. I still had adrenaline rushing through my body with the excitement that I was actually a father. But all I had in my head now was the realization that I had better get my "A-game" on for the morning! This interview was my only real clear chance for employment for our now expanded family come September.

I really didn't want to leave my wife and new little baby! I was feeling very much alone. The murky night only hardened this sentiment. In the dark of 5:00 am, in the deserted streets, not a soul was out and about to break down the sense of solitude I was experiencing.

These mixed emotions were racing through me as I arrived home that morning. Thankful that Chaya was well and that we now had a new beautiful child, I carefully set two alarms, five minutes apart. I hoped to ensure I would have enough time to wake up, shower, say my morning prayers, have something to eat and, of course, call Chaya to find out how she and our little baby were doing. Of course, this was all to occur before my interview, scheduled for…9 am! A mere 4 hours away!

I didn't need both alarms. With the first ring at 8 am I was up and ready to go, realizing the magnitude of the day ahead. Thank goodness the euphoria and adrenaline were lasting. I excitedly called Chaya to enquire how her night went. It didn't take long for her to answer the phone. It turned out she had a very eventful night. I hadn't realised the magnitude of the learning curve a first-time mother and her newborn infant would undertake. Both in the bonding process and the bare essentials of life as a team, they were learning how to navigate the first steps of nursing, and other natural bodily occurrences.

Chaya had decided to keep the baby in the room the first night. However, she quickly realised that in no way would she be able to recover from the delivery by tending to her every needs, and waking to every movement of our little one. Tomorrow night, Chaya posited, would be different. For the first time though, Chaya asked me if I would like to put the phone beside our little one, if I would like to say good morning to our precious Esther-Dinah. The tears welled up quickly as I emotionally said

109

good morning and clicked my tongue, calling her by her name for the first time. I realised that while I was sleeping she had officially been named and we could now refer to her by her divinely-inspired name. Chaya had already called her mother and father and had settled into her day. Despite feeling a little tired, she took a shower and dressed more comfortably in her own personal clothing. And, she was doing really well.

I needed to get up and shower also. With a cup of coffee in me, I too would be ready to take on the day. It would not be too long from now that I would be pulling up at Elboya Junior High School, arriving promptly for my 9 am interview.

It was quite surreal approaching Elboya that morning. I had done so for three years, as a student. Now I was parking my car as a visitor in the staff parking lot! I arrived with a few minutes to spare, so I decided to take the long walk around the outside of the school. I had many positive memories as a student at Elboya. Now I was seeking a position as mentor to the many students coming into the late immersion program just as I had been, a short ten years ago. I knew what it was like to be a frightened nobody, not knowing a single word in French in a program with ninety other students just like me. Full of desire for a peer group, desperately wanting to fit in, I felt those challenges of adolescence. Now I was hoping I would have the opportunity to experience it as a teacher.

On my way to the office as I was walking around the school, I realised I had no idea what the official offer of employment even was. When I received that phone call, so many weeks ago, I was just so excited to have been granted an interview. I smiled to myself, took a deep breath, and walked in the front door of the school, full of hopes and dreams of what a full-time teaching position offered. In the main office, the head school secretary greeted me warmly: "Well if I didn't see it with my own eyes, I wouldn't believe it. Hello, Arnie Glogauer!"

It was Liz Bolton, the very same head school secretary from when I was a student. Seeing her and her warm welcome was exactly what I needed to ease the tension I was feeling. I smiled as I recalled the overall impression I must have made when I was a student. It was most certainly memorable, and generally positive. My initial year at Elboya started out quite rocky, but I sure made up for it in the last half of my attendance in the school.

As I sat down in the waiting room, the familiar smell of that office, now empty during summer vacation, evoked so many memories of the past. I had a fair few occasions where as a student I was required to sit in that very same chair, waiting to be summoned into the antechamber of the principal's private office.

The time I was caught running after a female friend whom I accidentally knocked over in the hallway, causing her to fall and knock her head on the ground popped into my head as I was sitting there anxiously waiting. Of course, she cut her head and there was concern about a concussion, so I was called into the principal's office and suspended for the day. Luckily for me, my father had been on one of his business trips. My mother, who was quite busy by that time, didn't make much of a fuss out of the situation since she truly knew it had been an accident. Unfortunately for me, however, the girl's father overreacted to his daughter's injury. And then the school responded by an over-exaggerated response to the episode. So, despite my knowing in my heart it was an accident, the entire saga sure left a negative imprint on my mind. So much so, I sat there and could recall and recount every moment of the barrage of questioning from the principal and the girl's father when he arrived to pick up his wounded daughter. From then on, in the eyes of that principal, I was labelled a bully and girl-basher. I forever had a bad taste in my mouth toward that principal, who happened to be female. Luckily, I had a very good reputation with the school's vice principal, who was the basketball coach. Somehow, he communicated to me that a one-day suspension would more than placate the rage of the father and at the same time satisfy the principal's witch-hunt.

This incident popped into my mind as I sat there because it is an iconic example of the difference I wanted to make in education. All I knew then was that I wanted to be the educator in the mold of that special vice principal. There are children everywhere who need educators like him, validating each child's best self, even in tiny ways as he did for me. In so many ways, this is the crux of education.

I switched my attention back to the here and now, warmly engaging in some reminiscences with Liz Bolton, as we waited for me to be called into the principal's office, hopefully under very different circumstances. Before long, that very same door opened. A distinguished-looking man walked toward me with an outstretched arm. With a short introduction, Mr Gary Jeffrey welcomed me into his office. Before me sat the vice principal, Mrs Betty Rose, and then I was greeted by a pleasant surprise. "*Bonjour Arnie, Ca fait longtemps...*" (Good morning Arnie, it's been a long time...)

I immediately recognized Mlle Blackburn's face, even though she had only been a student teacher the last year of my time at Elboya. We had interacted intermittently when she did her practicum and taught some of our French lessons. I remembered we had got along very well in our mutually motivated student/practicum teacher relationship. I remembered I had made a great impression back then as a student. I was thanking my lucky stars, feeling gratefully thrilled I had met her during my good junior high school year, Grade 9, and not earlier.

Now she was introducing herself as the Bilingual Coordinator of the Junior High School, a significant position attesting to her great ambition and substantial aptitude as an educator. She clearly had risen quickly into this position as I had only been out of junior high seven years.

Mr Jeffrey explained that both he and Mrs Rose would be asking me general questions. However, regarding my aptitude and ability to teach in the French immersion program, Mlle Blackburn would conduct the evaluation. I felt very much at home with that arrangement. It immediately became clear that the questions were not designed to stump me but engage me in a dialogue. The entire atmosphere created an opportunity for me to come off as very confident in my ability to present a solid teaching philosophy, even though I had only just begun my formal teaching in my university practica. The panel of interviewers mentioned that they were impressed with my letters of recommendation from my student teaching advisors.

Mlle Blackburn asked me two or three general questions in French. I realised they were open-ended questions to gauge my level of language proficiency so I just spoke to the topics she raised. After I answered the last question, I was quite pleased to catch Mlle Blackburn's approving nod to both Mr Jeffrey and Mrs Rose. The principal and vice principal acknowledged frankly that they did not have strong French skills. Therefore, should I become the successful candidate for the position, I would be working directly under Mlle Blackburn. I smiled and was somewhat relieved since she seemed quite positive toward my responses. Even more so, I felt I might have an advantage over other potential applicants, having had somewhat of a good prior connection. Then Mr Jeffrey threw a pretty massive curve ball.

"Mr Glogauer, the position we are looking to fill is not just a math position. We also have a part-time vacancy in science. How do you feel about teaching introductory Grade 7 science in French? You would be teaching two Grade 8 math classes in French, one Grade 8 math class in English, one Grade 9 math class in French and two Grade 7 science classes in French."

A little taken aback, I replied, "Well, I took science in high school. I did quite well in physics and chemistry, and I studied a little biology as well. I think I could manage. However, I have one request."

Intrigued, Mr Jeffrey replied, "Please continue…"

"I do remember the Grade 7 curriculum and biology component. I would have to request that no reptiles be kept in my classroom." In retrospect, it was more than a little foolish, my making a demand like this considering how desperate I was for that job! If they had said that the reptiles were a prerequisite, I probably would have accepted the position anyway, despite my utter panic and phobia of snakes and other reptiles.

Luckily, they all looked at me, and Gary Jeffrey just chuckled. "No problem; anything else?"

"No, I think that's it."

Mr Jeffrey continued, "There is a requirement that every teacher take up three extracurricular activities. We have four holes and would like you to choose three: basketball, track & field, volleyball, and French immersion winter camp."

I had to think on my toes now. I knew this was a chance to win some points, given my love for extracurricular activities and my athletic ability. I had to be smart and make sure I could become indispensable as a candidate at the same time. "I feel I could do a great job coaching basketball and track & field, not only because I have excelled in track & field in high school and university, but because I know the incredible opportunity I had as a student at Elboya participating in these sports. I was very fortunate as a student to have been mentored by very positive, inspirational coaches."

What would I state as my third choice? Academic pursuits are important; however, in the larger scheme Elboya's philosophy created opportunities to develop the whole child. The excitement I felt at the opportunity to teach at this school was hard to contain, because Elboya fitted very well with my own perspective and outlook on educating children. I always felt it would be critical for my first position in a school to afford me the opportunity to pay it forward. Most appropriately, in the case of teaching at Elboya, I could give back to the institution that had such a profound impact on my own growth and development as an impressionable teenager.

One of the most memorable experiences of coming to Elboya was the French immersion overnight camp. It was this intensive French experience that truly inspired my love for the French language. Camp intensified connections to the teachers who were so intricately involved in my development as a student. Even more so, as Mlle Blackburn attested, the ability to bond with teachers in an informal French environment was one of the essential goals and missions of the late immersion program. "And my third choice would be to co-coordinate the French immersion winter camp."

I felt this choice attested even more so to both my understanding of the inherent goals of the late immersion program but also my commitment as a young professional to be dedicated to its ideals. Once I had identified my three choices, all three members of the interviewing panel smiled and thanked me for coming in. Before they got up, they asked me if I had any questions.

"Not really. I only want to thank you and apologize if any of my answers were shy of the mark. I have been up all night. My wife gave birth to a baby girl this morning, and I have not had too much sleep." Again big smiles, wishes of congratulations and Mr Jeffrey got up to open the door.

Mr Jeffrey told me he had to interview two more candidates and would be in touch sometime early next week. I thanked them once again as I exited his office. I said my farewells to Liz, and left the school office. As I walked down the corridor, I spotted the 1985 graduation photo of my class. It was quite surreal to see my student photo on that wall. Of course, this just fortified my growing desire to be the successful candidate. After all, if Elboya Junior High School were to be my new professional 'family,' perhaps personal photos hanging on the wall would be a hopeful sign from Above. The school felt like home and somewhere deep inside me I knew this was meant to be.

It turned out I would only have to wait three days after my interview for that personal phone call from Mr Jeffrey. "Hello Mr Glogauer, it's Gary Jeffrey calling from Elboya. How are you? How is your wife and new addition?" My heart was beating a thousand beats per minute, almost jumping out of my chest. The anticipation of his next sentence was almost too much to bear, trying not to think of the consequences should I somehow not be the successful applicant. "We are all very well, thank you. How are you?"

"Doing just fine. Hopefully even better, Arnie, depending on your response to my next question. We were all very impressed with your interview and think you would be a fine addition to our team at Elboya. We would be honoured to have you as a member of our faculty this fall. I'm not sure how much time you need to mull things over, perhaps talk to

114

your wife: would you be able to get back to me by the end of the week with an answer? And one more thing, please call me Gary."

"Mr Jeffrey, I mean Gary, no need to think about it any further. We have been hoping and praying for your phone call. It would be a privilege for me to be a part of your team. I accept your offer."

In time, I received the news that I had passed that final course, the exam that I hardly recalled sitting as Chaya was about to deliver our new baby girl. My official convocation ceremony was slated for mid-November 1993. It was a little strange participating in a graduation ceremony, receiving a degree for which I had already been employed for two months. I was certified to teach from the moment I successfully finished that final course, so the ceremony was a mere formality. As I had sensed, Elboya Junior High School was to become the first stepping stone for my future career as a professional educator. It seemed Elboya also set the stage for my leadership skills to come to the fore very early in my career.

A Public School Teacher

I will always remember that very first day as the new teacher at Elboya Junior High School. The school year began with a professional development day, the day before the actual arrival of students. Labour Day 1993 was on Monday, September 6. Tuesday, September 7 was the professional development day. It was quite an unnerving moment walking into the staffroom and being introduced to the faculty. It was a little intimidating, to say the least. Meeting Mlle Blackburn again, now that she was my official supervisor, had its own associations. But then I saw Mr Jorginson, a teacher who knew me all too well from the days when I was a student at Elboya. I'm sure he was thoroughly enjoying the irony, seeing me back at this school, only this time with the shoe very much on the other foot. Mr Jorginson had known me for my entire Elboya career, including when I would definitely have been defined as a rebellious student. Not that I got into too much trouble, but I was certainly known for my reputation as the class clown. Now these two colleagues would follow my journey on the other side of the desk. I was determined not only to succeed but also to make a very strong positive impression.

I very quickly realised that luck was on my side; I was so fortunate to have been assigned a well-seasoned veteran teacher as a mentor. Without her guidance and assistance over that first year, I am not sure I would have made it. That same professional development day I was introduced to Alita Pelle. That first year we shared the "walk-in closet" together, the cupboard-sized space they called an "office." I learned from Alita how to give back and how to patiently guide a first-year teacher. Alita shared all of her resources with me and taught me by example, demonstrating how to connect to students through her variety of differentiated teaching materials. My eyes were opened to many strategies. The confidence I felt to implement them would never have materialized without her support and guidance. I would have never been prepared to take risks in those first few formative, critical years without Alita's calm and encouraging manner.

It is not an easy feat, jumping off a cliff not knowing if there is a lake, or safety net below! Walking into a classroom of my own that very next day, thirty students ready to test me to see if I could withstand the best of their efforts to try my endurance, was forbidding to say the least. Every student knew I was a first-year teacher. There is a theory that students can smell the fear of first-year teachers. The slightest hesitation, the tiniest flinch, and a first-year teacher may be done for the year – never able to get back that which was lost.

As soon as I met Alita, she gave off such a positive vibe, letting me know that she would be with me every step of the way. This sure helped relieve at least some of my anxiety. Nevertheless, the night before my first day was most certainly, as would be expected, a sleepless one; not so much due to the fear I was experiencing, but more the excitement and anticipation that my dream had come true. I made it; I had succeeded in leaping over all the major hurdles. Somehow, my path into the system led me to one of the best schools in the city. Every student wanted to get into the French late immersion program. Students from as far away as the southwest quadrant of the city applied to Elboya Junior High School. The acceptance criteria had not changed very much from my days. I understood very well what it felt like to be the anxious, frightened first-year student coming into this new program. After all, I had gone through the identical process a mere ten years priorly. What made it somewhat serendipitous, even magical, was to walk that main corridor under the watchful eye of my graduation photo among the class of 1985. Despite being a new teacher, I felt like I was at home.

That fateful first Wednesday, I, of course, arrived at school early. I made sure I had plenty of time to assemble my books and supplies for that first week's morning periods. Because I was not allocated my own classroom, I would have a large black plastic tray and supplies I would carry from classroom to classroom. Since the school was full to capacity, it was not an unusual sight to see mobile "homeless" teachers such as myself. Some teachers were "privileged" to have their own classrooms. Others, even veterans, preferred to travel. Many of the seasoned teachers believed not having their own classroom alleviated one more pressure – that of having to focus on the room's daily upkeep. It was simply a matter of preference, not necessarily seniority. Alita preferred not to have her own classroom and I would learn from her how to cope with moving around from classroom to classroom: incredible organization and professionalism. The obvious benefit was less responsibility to maintain the environment, decorating classroom walls and ensuring cleanliness and organization. Not having to continuously update the seasonal bulletin boards, keeping the environment fresh and inviting, left more time for lesson preparation. For a first-year teacher, this would be one significant, time-intensive issue about which I would have no worries.

Arriving to class on time and gaining instant control of the environment was going to be an issue. I realised I would have to utilize strong organizational skills. I wanted to make sure that I lived up to my clearly articulated expectations as well. I also wanted to ensure that my students followed the daily routine I clearly laid out on that first day of class. From the moment we met, I explained the need for a strict adherence to the classroom seating arrangements. I expected the students to be in their places awaiting my arrival with their mathematics exercise book and their textbook placed neatly underneath their desks. Students required only a pencil placed on top of the desk ready for the daily five-minute quiz, which would wake their minds, focus them, orient their brains, sharpening them for my intense mathematics period of "fun."

I was modelling my approach on what I had learned and remembered in the inspirational lessons from Mr Maguire. A regular routine is the easiest way to keep students sharp and focused. The day would begin the exact same way, each and every day. Students could easily self-govern their behaviour and file into automatic routine and frame of mind, ready to function at the highest level, taking comfort in the predictability of the class. I decided I would use this technique in my mathematics lessons as well as adapting it to my science classes.

I gathered my materials. I made a quick stop in the staff room to gain some contagious courage from my fellow faculty members. I was both anxious and nervous to start my first day. The other teachers were all casually sitting down around the common coffee table chatting away about the summer break, eagerly talking about the expectations of the new student body and what the upcoming academic year held. Will there be any surprises? Which troubled students from last year will be back for more hi-jinks? The bell rang and the teachers all rose in unison, and like a flock of sheep responding to the call of the shepherd, we all headed toward the gymnasium. You could almost hear the collective exhalation of the teachers as they all reacted to the bell with a predictable Pavlovian response. All 450 students were gathering in the gymnasium, ready to be welcomed by the principal.

The students all sat in groups in the middle of the gymnasium and the teachers stood around the perimeter. You could hear many of the grade 8 and 9 students reminiscing about the previous year's teachers and speculating who would be teaching them this year. There was much excitement about which teachers would be this year's designated homeroom teachers and which students would be in their class.

I could hear the chatter amongst the students pointing their fingers in my direction, referring to me as the "new one." The way they were looking at me somehow made me feel like I was the sacrificial lamb being designated as the "chosen one", first sent to slaughter. I tried not to smile, trying to hide my rising fear of the unknown, remembering the slogan, "never let them see you sweat!" I stood in front of the school with my untrimmed beard, head covering and traditional *tzitzis,* Jewish fringes neatly peeking out from my hips, eliciting a variety of reactions: intrigue from the non-Jewish students who had never seen such a sight, and pride from the Jewish students who, even though they were not necessarily practicing observant Jews, nevertheless had some familiarity with my traditional garb.

Mr Jeffrey began by calling the students to attention. After a brief inspirational message about student potential, effort and behaviour, the roll call began, introducing teachers to the student body. What followed was the list of students who would fall under the care of a specific homeroom teacher for the year. Some teachers got a rousing round of applause, others a collective chuckle.

At the conclusion of each alphabetical list, students got up from their places and lined up beside their new homeroom teacher. Then it was my turn. Mr. Jeffrey announced "8-16 will line up with Mr. Glogauer, a new teacher to Elboya who will be teaching science and mathematics." He proceeded to call out the names of my homeroom students. Neither applause nor a chuckle; I was relieved to see curiosity in their eyes as they all silently stood up beside me.

At each grade level in Elboya there were two late immersion classes, two continuing immersion classes and one English class. My homeroom was the sole English class in Grade 8. This class was primarily comprised of students who lived in proximity to the school. I was pleasantly surprised to see a few students smile and high-five each other at the roll call when their names were mentioned for my homeroom. After the entire student group was allocated, we were all dismissed to our homeroom classrooms for a brief, first day of class orientation. We made it down the corridors fine. The first task of my first day had begun and I had passed the initial student inspection.

The overly rehearsed, first-day opening monologue, in the mind of the first-time teacher, is the stuff of legends. It's the critical one chance to make *THE* first and lasting impression. The initial introductory speech is practiced over and over, attempted in various styles, all aimed at displaying a calm, authoritative demeanour, demonstrating that it's all business and that the captain is in control of the ship.

Why all this detail? Getting there early, being organized, having a set routine and plan? Rehearsing my opening, seizing that one chance to set the tone for the year with my students? Because, as you can guess, the remainder of that first day demonstrated that I didn't have as much to worry about as I had thought.

Over the first few weeks in our homeroom, I became comfortable to let a bit more of my guard down than in my classrooms. I got to know my students much better on a personal level. I would share a little bit more about myself with the students in the homeroom environment. I would come to know the backgrounds of these students better, and it was my role to advocate for them in the larger school environment.

Given the educational balance of the school, it was the English students who felt like the utter minority. I would find ways to build up their self-esteem and profile in the largely dominant French atmosphere. It helped that I was also their mathematics teacher. Some of the students were extremely strong academically. They were focused individuals on a mission to enter the Grade 10 International Baccalaureate program in high school. I would hold tutorial classes at lunchtime to coach students, being quite familiar with the IB program myself at Western Canada High School. I understood the commitment and desire to both succeed but also defy the odds, which seemed stacked against them. My students could see how much I cared. I soon developed a reputation as the young teacher who "understood" the plight of the generation X student. I first began offering a once a week math tutorial. This soon was joined by a science lunchtime tutorial session as well. Both of these forums transformed into an open room to chill out and chat with my students.

Being an overtly observant Jewish teacher, with my beard and *yarmulke*, I instantly developed a rapport with many of the Jewish students. Similar to my parents a few years earlier, their parents' choice was not to send them to the local Jewish junior high school. Most lunch times, the students and I enjoyed chatting about Jewish knowledge and holidays. Early on in my first year, we developed almost a weekly informal lunch discussion club, discussing relevant philosophical issues.

As we approached Jewish festivals, my room was a sanctuary to my Jewish students to openly discuss memories of what it was like celebrating Jewish holidays when they were students in their Jewish parochial schools. We would openly discuss reasons why their parents had decided to choose public education over private school education and how they felt like the minority in their new environment. We invited all students from all backgrounds to hang out and even join in the discussions about the festivals and how different cultures celebrated their holidays at different times. During *Chanukah,* I brought traditional food, potato *latkes* (pancakes), and played *dreidel*, the spinning top, with chocolate money as the traditional prize. I believed finding a way to positively integrate the students in their non-Jewish environment and giving them the courage and strength to maintain their individuality was a much more positive message than providing support and strength for them to coexist in a vacuum. Being proud of their culture, religion and individuality would strengthen their self-esteem and at the same time build respect among their peers. This integration strategy proved very successful and thus the Jewish students gained significant respect from their peers.

As the school year progressed, many of the parents openly supported my candidacy as a role model for their children within the program. Many of my students came from high profile families in the Calgary business, medical and law communities. Their endorsement was an important but intangible component of my candidacy and pathway to early tenure.

All of my informal tutoring and gatherings with students was undertaken with the approval of Gary Jeffrey, who, as I discovered more and more as the year went on, was especially nurturing for a school principal. I think he felt that it was a positive message for the students of all backgrounds to feel cared for and made to feel comfortable in the multicultural atmosphere of the school. I will never forget when December came along and the early sunset dictated an early departure for me on a Friday, in order to get home before sunset when the *Shabbos* would begin.

I nervously went to Mr. Jeffrey to explain why I needed to leave early and that I was concerned that I would not have enough leave days to cover my future absences. Because of the Jewish holy days such as *Yom Kippur*, the Day of Atonement, my observance level prohibited me from working on specific hallowed days. If I hadn't had all these religious holidays included in my leave time, the early winter Fridays necessitating an early mark would certainly not have been an issue. I was shocked when Mr. Jeffrey told me not to worry. He would personally see that my classes would be covered on those early Fridays without me having to officially apply for leave. He revealed how valuable I was to his staff and how he had already seen dedication beyond the call of duty in such a short period of time. I was extremely touched by this positive feedback. I left his office after what I worried would be a difficult conversation, like I was walking on cloud nine. Not only would his gesture be something that I would never forget, but also the feedback itself, and his sincerity meant more than any financial remuneration.

Of course, my dedication at times went well beyond the call of duty, but not because I wanted to secure a long-term employment. My commitment was steadfast because of the strong work ethic, which had philosophically been ingrained in my soul from my father, mother and even my grandparents which I was privileged to witness with my very own eyes. If I look back at those years, because of this devotion to my craft, too often my family took a back seat and second priority. This was certainly not on purpose and with forethought. Sadly, however, it was just the outcome. I always felt the privilege of each and every day being in a profession that allowed me to connect to children. This responsibility is something not to be taken for granted. Children truly sense this devotion. When they feel in earnest that one is prepared to give them all that one has within, they will reciprocate equally. I have seen over the years teachers who have half-heartedly prepared lessons, and only semi-commit to their students. It then boggles their minds and these teachers question why their students are reluctant to do their homework, lack inspiration and motivation to participate or lose focus and desire to study.

It is not that these students don't want to succeed; it is rather they have not experienced the investment in the teacher-student relationship. Thus, they have not developed a desire to form a partnership with the teacher. I've always kept this at the forefront of my mind. As a student, I could always sense which teacher really cared about me and my fellow students and who was truly devoted to ensuring we had all the necessary tools to meet our potential. For these teachers, we would go to the ends of the earth to perform, just as we would feel a deep sense of guilt if we did not do our very best. We could not live with ourselves if we let that type of teacher down.

My first year of teaching was quite an exciting time for my young family and me. I look back fondly on those years, despite the immense pressure and high expectations I set upon myself. My workday would begin quite early. Even though I only lived twenty minutes or so drive from the school, and the official start of the school day was 8:30 am, it was always important for me to arrive no later than 7:45 am. This early arrival permitted me to ensure my lessons were fully prepared. More importantly, this precious thirty minutes allowed me an opportunity to connect to many of the students who would arrive early in the morning due to the extensive travelling distances. Many would travel, as I had, to benefit from the specialized late and continuing immersion programs in the school. Most of the administrative staff would also arrive early in the morning. Particularly as I was literally the new 'kid' on the block', I was eager to make a good impression. I was sure that my early arrival was seen as a positive in their eyes, especially as I was there to be making connections with my students. As the school year progressed, on many occasions, some additional tutoring would take place in those precious before-school minutes. I enjoyed the students very much and very early on developed a strong bond with many of my students as well as other students whom I did not teach.

The school day ended at 3:30 pm. Nevertheless, it was a rarity if I left the school before 7 pm. There were many duties and challenges that required me to extend my day. This was my day-to-day routine. At the time, we had our infant daughter at home, and Chaya was working on finishing her PhD. It was during those very first years of work that I developed my personal and professional philosophy never to bring my work home. No matter the challenges that every position contains, there is always a certain amount of stress that is inevitable. However, my philosophy of not bringing any of the workload into our home, allowed me to focus on the family as much as possible when I walked across that threshold. To this day, whilst this is my goal and aim, it is a constant and ongoing challenge. Not so much in terms of physical work (occasionally report cards come home for me to finish), but the emotional and mental burden of unsolved or ongoing issues.

To be truthful and honest, it would be impossible for me, given the many challenges that I faced as both as a young teacher, and young principal, to state that I was consistently focused 100% of the time in body and soul on our family while I was physically in the house. Early on in my career, one of my greatest challenges was how to handle the pressure of my position. Of course, it was largely due to my personality and values that I felt that pressure.

Often my body would indicate tell-tale signs that the stress was building to the boiling point. Even though I would tell myself things were under control and that I could handle it, my body would tell me otherwise. I began to develop a skin condition that would surface with little warning. This was an obvious indicator that the stress was becoming unbearable. However, when I reached this point, I certainly recognized the need for a pressure and stress release mechanism in my life.

This is when I found my outlet in long-distance running. At that time, I began with a run around the block. Now, over fifteen years later, I have built up to running or biking anywhere from 7 to 11 km six days a week. Not only do I enjoy the luxury of being able to eat most foods which satisfy my sweet tooth and not gain too much weight, but there is something quite exhilarating after a long day's work chock full of many pressures, to go for a long run, pounding the pavement, releasing all of the day's pressures before arriving home to my haven, to the family eagerly waiting to hear how my day went.

It is another challenge altogether to leave your work at school once you become a principal. The challenges of the workday transform to responsibility for more long-term projects. As a teacher, there are more direct day-to-day tasks that can be counted as short-term accomplishments. Usual tasks include marking, lesson plan development to be prepared for the next class. Sometimes there is test development, making sure that the lesson or unit assessments are ready for the next class. It was a conscious rule of mine that I would never bring home lesson-planning material. Consistent with my policy that home should be a haven where work should never interfere with the personal relationships and bonding that needed to take place in order to sustain a very high-pressured career. At times it was necessary to do some light marking and this was usually accomplished in bed before going to sleep. Nevertheless, ongoing term assessments and next day lesson planning were always completed in my classroom at school before I would go home.

I find that without appropriate reflection time, within the educational environment upon the day that has been, there is a residual effect from the previous day. It has always been my practice to take advantage of the quiet that the educational environment lends in providing closure and reflection at the end of a busy day. I find it allows the teacher to refocus and readjust, if need be, one's perspective for the next day.

It was for these reasons that, both as a teacher and certainly as an administrator, I have always maintained as my priority, first and foremost, to be fully committed to my students. It was this attitude that made the decision that more difficult as to whether or not I would attend Winter Camp that fateful first year.

The Extra Curricular Effect...

The immeasurable experience teachers gather from extracurricular opportunities is totally underestimated and undervalued. Too often, teachers see these responsibilities as an inconvenience, considering them a distraction, taking them away from what they perceive as their core responsibility, teaching in the classroom. Coaching sport teams and involvement in extracurricular activities take up a significant amount of time: however, the intangible rewards of these opportunities in terms of solidifying meaningful relationships with one's students are immeasurable.

True to the discussions in my initial interview, I had chosen, in theory, three extracurricular activities in addition to my regular teaching duties. One of the choices was coaching a boy's' basketball team. To let you in on a secret, it was actually my first time ever having coached this sport. To our great pleasure, mine as well as the boys, under my first-year coaching, we had a very successful first season. We even managed to sneak into the play-offs in our division. We lost in the first round, but at least we made it in. Our success actually energized the entire school. We began the season as a bunch of no-name students with a really rocky start. We began by losing our first three games, but we went on to win the last four games and just make it into the play-offs. At some point in the season, the boys somehow managed to search the archives and locate my basketball team photo in the 1985 Elboya Yearbook. They used it both as a motivation and for some gentle tomfoolery. In 1985, I had proven myself, despite my tiny size and lack of experience, on the Junior High School basketball team.

Our team making the play-offs created a new hype and excitement surrounding sport in the school. All of a sudden, there was a new wave of inspiration in the students. Of late Elboya was not known to be one of the most athletic schools in the district, nor was it known particularly as a "jock school." Changing this reputation in the neighbourhood elicited a heightened sense of camaraderie among the students, staff and parent

125

body. Once we began to win, for our last couple of games of the season and that one and only play-off game, we had standing room only in our tiny gymnasium, if you could call it that. This largest space in the school was most certainly built for stage- and theatre-style audiences, definitely not for sporting events. Everyone came out of the woodwork to see us compete. Our opponents were much taller students who, despite very much looking the part of basketball athletes, found themselves equally matched against our Elboya hearts and determination.

Becoming the coach of a sport team was not necessarily a natural progression of my having always been a sport fanatic or successful as an amateur athlete, nor even because initially I had wanted to become a physical education teacher. I had chosen to become a coach only because it was made quite clear in my Elboya interview: if I wanted to teach at Elboya I had to choose three activities and help fill in the gaping staff vacancies in the sport department.

In every one of the institutions I have had the privilege to lead, the development of sport or athletic programs has since become a fundamental strategy and rebuilding element. I learned the power of these critical school constituents early on as a first-year coach.

As you know, until Grade 9, as a student I had experienced very little academic success in junior high school. It was only when I began to get involved in the many athletic opportunities at school did I begin to flourish and gain positive self-worth. Having an outlet other than academics allowed me to excel above my peers and develop my self-esteem. Sport was an opportunity to develop individuality and acceptance among a select, visually recognizable group of students. In a large school, where anonymity is a natural causal link to loneliness, the challenge of not blending into the teenage scene and being accepted by any social group is daunting for any teenager.

For me, coming to Canada as an immigrant, not fitting into a clique-filled primary school, now transferring into a large junior high school, I was tired of being alone and having to navigate the social obstacles on my own. I was desperate to belong to a group of friends who shared the same interests. The problem was that I came from such a different background and had not developed the skills to fit into a completely foreign social environment. Coming from a primary school of a dozen graduates in Grade 6 to over 150 students in Grade 7 alone, finding a way to fit in socially was a huge challenge. As I look today at my team photos from junior high school and even the football team photos in senior high school, I was the tiny little kid who, on paper, didn't seem to fit a sporting

126

profile. But put me on the field – my desire and heart, perhaps a deep desire to beat the naysayers who didn't think I deserved to make it, who always pushed me down; oh, and my speed, to keep away from the bigger boys – I shone above the rest of the crowd.

Playing contact sports helped me define my image as an explosive, dynamic underdog, with a burning desire to succeed. Coaches picked up on this very quickly and this competitive edge, which I have transferred to every area of my life, provided me with many opportunities which I am very privileged to have experienced in my schooling, both high school and university, but I can truly say in almost every other area of my life. My goal was to pay these invaluable experiences forward and try to emulate the same circumstances and opportunities for growth for my students as I had experienced in my schooling.

One such opportunity was staring me in the face in my first basketball coaching assignment at Elboya. I did not need too much of a heads-up that John, one of the students in my Grade 9 continuing immersion mathematics class was a handful. From Day One, he was pushing the boundaries. At first, I thought it was just me and a boisterous, energetic student, giving a first-year teacher a run for his money. It was a rite of passage among students to see who could crack the new teacher on the block. After all, this was something that I would do and had done on many occasions when I was a student. My university program had been strategically designed with plenty of classroom practica to put teachers front and centre with a class, simply to gain experience with mob control. If one truly contemplates the big picture, adolescents spend much of their energy on self-amusement. By design they need to be stimulated, to be convinced that there is a reason to stay focused in class. Being more animated and uninhibited, boys were usually the risk takers willing to put themselves out on the line. With this in mind, I would strategically cultivate an environment where all students were encouraged to be academically adventurous. I would tell the students that it takes courage to be the first volunteer, to sit in the front of the class and to lead the way. I worked hard to develop a culture of open discussion as to why the answers were so, and to share multiple methods founded upon the philosophy that there is no one right way.

For many students, this was a novel approach and most students appreciated and took positive advantage of the academic freedom to be adventurous and creative in their thinking. Most had never been granted the opportunity to be an academic risk taker. I also worked very hard so the students could see me as a role model who was current in the understanding of their stage of life. At lunch time, I would spend time in the gym playing 21 or a one-on-one basketball with students. At times, I would just walk the hallways or lunchroom engaging some of my students and their friends. I wanted students to see me not as just the strict teacher, but someone who truly was interested in how they were getting on outside of my classroom. Initially it was awkward for my students, as they had never seen such behaviour from a teacher. Slowly but surely, they began to accept me for my earnest desire to care about them beyond my own four walls – my mathematics or science classroom.

For John, much of the above didn't seem to have too profound an effect. For the most part, he faded into the background in my class. In staff meetings, specifically when the topic was students who had academically popped up on the radar and were cause for concern, John was usually the main topic of conversation. He seemed to work on developing an intimidating character. He was twice my size and many of the female teachers had expressed concern at his anger and his inability to control his frequent outbursts of frustration. He wasn't doing well academically and there were signs he had begun slipping into a state of despair.

I had not seen any of these signs but certainly maintained a heightened level of vigilance, watching for any signs of aggression. Early on in my career, I formed an opinion that too much information was not healthy for a teacher when it came to teachers disclosing student behaviour issues. Quite aware of the Pygmalion effect and the stereotyping of students, I tended to fade into the background during these conversations, rarely offering anecdotal examples of student behaviour. The staff room was a potentially toxic environment where teachers, needing to unload from the daily pressures of teaching stresses, at times would not be as discreet or discerning in their "stress relief" divulgences. The camaraderie of the staff room gave teachers the opportunity to vent after a challenging day. The problem is that too often, the discussion of student reputations become the focus of this teacher inspired regurgitation. Always wanting to see students in a better light, to give them the benefit of the doubt, I have never been a proponent of the staff room social scene. I understand the need for it, but truly believe it is a dangerous minefield for the unsuspecting, naïve teacher.

So when teachers were unloading their daily grief about John, I at first just listened and superficially took it in. As the year wore on, I began vocally speaking up in his defence, assuming the role of his advocate defendant, so to speak. I had hard-core evidence and found myself going the extra mile to compensate, to try and reach out to John.

I had the perfect opportunity. Lo and behold, front and centre, none other than John himself stood in front of me as I walked into the gymnasium for the first afterschool try-out of the senior boys basketball team. He took me by surprise. I had never seen him in the gym during recess or lunch time playing hoops with the rest of the school jocks. I had come to know the sports enthusiasts very well as I was often frequenting the gym during lunch hour. I made a point to connect to these boys as my identity as a sporting teacher brought me "street credit" with the students. If they could identify with me, they would more than likely connect with me. I could more easily reach them. My extracurricular involvement would translate into positive relationships in the classroom.

When I saw John that day in the gym, I knew I had a shot to build a positive relationship with him. I could not show favouritism nor make it look like I was trying too hard. The effort and initiative would have to come from John. If he for one moment thought that I would "gift" him onto the team, and that his accomplishment was not due to his personal effort, the opportunity would be wasted.

I could see that he badly wanted to be on the team. There was special peer status from being part of the senior sports teams, and along with this status came intangible privileges. The school population looked up to these visible role models. It wasn't just because of my newly-instilled game day ritual that required team members to dress up. At first, they all felt a little nerdy wearing dress shirts and ties under their basketball singlets. As they walked through the hallways, among the rest of the student body, heads automatically turned. They were looked upon with respect and admiration. They were a special group and their peers had no choice but to stand up and take notice.

I strictly enforced that all students would have to maintain a C+ average in all of the classes to be part of the basketball team that year. A minimum of a 65% average became a threshold that John began to achieve in all of his classes. Some were sceptical that he could keep it up. Other teachers began to see him in a new light. John earned a position on the team and he was proud of himself. He walked differently in the hallways and you could see the positive self-respect he had in himself. A new reputation doesn't come easy. The basketball season was only two and a half months long. As the conclusion to the season was in sight, I began having conversations with John about how to maintain his new identity and self-confidence. I could see that he was having difficulty looking past his persona and finding a new goal and purpose. He had become quite fixated on his new image but could not see past the here and now.

Despite the numerous conversations and attempted forward planning, the conclusion to our basketball season came, and so did John's downward spiral. John had maintained an above 70% average in mathematics and was struggling to keep it together. His attitude began to wane. Thursday afternoon mathematics class was the period right after lunch time. As the students piled into class, there was an unusual amount of chatter and commotion amongst them that day. I was not exactly aware of what the buzz was all about. Once all the students were settled, I noticed John saunter in and plop himself down in another student's assigned seat. Everyone knew I was quite particular about the seating plan and the routine beginning the class with the quiz about the previous day's lesson. The daily routine required calmness and order, but today was quite out of the ordinary.

I quietly approached John. I could see that he was quite agitated. His bloodshot eyes were very red and dilated and he had a very potent aroma about him. Slumped in his chair, he was speaking in very low tone with a quite belligerent manner. The source of all the buzz and chatter was now very apparent. John had clearly taken some sort of narcotic at lunch time and now was very clearly affected. I asked John if he was okay and if he wanted to go get a drink of water. My goal was to calmly get him out of the classroom and as quickly as possible. I hoped to contain him in the hallway for the vice principal to deal with him in isolation from the other students. Of course John, being as bright but as troubled as he was, was clued in right away to my intentions. He dug his heels in and was adamant about not leaving the classroom. He stood up and quite belligerently swore there was no way he would leave my classroom and go see the vice principal. He became so angry and threatening that I needed to take swift action. My efforts to calm John were in vain and I calmly walked toward the phone in the corner of the classroom and called the vice principal's office. I tried not to speak too loudly so no one else could hear my conversation. It wasn't too difficult to be discreet as John was now in a shouting fit with some of the other students who were trying to cajole him to calm down, not to get himself into more trouble. I spoke to the main secretary and told her that John had taken something illegal and was very agitated. I needed her to get someone into my class now to remove him.

I hung up the phone and did my best to try and calm John. I tried reasoning with him. I also tried to change the focus of our discussion as it became very clear that he had worked himself up into quite a frenzy. It took a bit of time, but, before I knew it, there was a knock at my classroom door. Before someone could open the door, two policemen walked in. The vice principal remained in the hallway outside my classroom as the policemen approached me and asked me which student was the cause of concern. I motioned toward John and indicated as discreetly as possible that it was quite obvious that he was under the influence of some narcotic. You could have heard a pin drop in the classroom as the policemen approached John. I was in a bit of shock myself, not knowing exactly how I should react both to a student so completely under the influence of a narcotic in my classroom and to the arrival of two law-enforcement officers about to remove a student under my care.

As the policeman approached, John stood up, a little shaky, and asked if there was a problem. The policemen replied, "We would just like to talk to you outside. Would you mind coming with us?"

Knowing John the little bit I did, I could tell by the blushing look on his face that he knew he was in some serious trouble. He smiled, trying to break the tension and save some face in front of his peers. I breathed a sigh of relief when he simply responded, "Sure."

The policeman escorted John out of the classroom, closing the door behind them. I quickly tried to direct the students' attention back to the lesson I had prepared, attempting to act as if that most calamitous experience had never taken place.

This was the last time I would ever see John. Often I think about him and the potential he had. In the end, each student has to make decisions for himself and accept the consequences of his actions. However, the best lesson I could have learned from this tragic episode is that teachers have extraordinary opportunities for influence outside the classroom to motivate students. Those powerful 'educational' opportunities sometimes make the world of difference for a child. Because in the end, are we not here to guide children in learning how to navigate their way through the challenges of the world? And these critical opportunities need to be capitalized upon from the earliest points in a child's educational career. In John's case, I learned that as much as a teacher wants his student to achieve, an educator's success is dependent on the willing partner who must choose to actively participate in the experience.

The Curriculum Effect

The educational environment was very unstable. It was well documented in the newspaper that the Board of Education was not only in a hiring freeze but was looking to cut temporary contracts as a means of reducing its overextended budget. Thus when I was called into Mr Jeffrey's office in late May, just one month before the end of my first year, I was expecting the worst possible news. The vice principal was also in the room. Before I had a chance to process anything, with a broad smile on his face, Mr Jeffrey placed a piece of paper in front of me and said, "For now, this is the best I can do…It's not a permanent contract but at least it's an extension of your terms."

I was one of the lucky ones. Some of the other provisional first-year teachers at Elboya were not. I had been offered a year's extension to my temporary status.

That first year of teaching could not have gone more according to plan. I instinctively felt that my entry point into the public school system would be a stepping stone to a long career despite the education crisis in the province and country. Even though the school system was not offering permanent contracts, if I happened to be of good fortune to be hired under a temporary contract, I knew I would have one foot in the door. Very simply, I would just need to come up with the next part of the plan before the conclusion of this contract extension. And this is precisely what I did.

When accepting the teaching position and the split load of both mathematics and science, I was not aware of the fortuitous situation I had made for myself. It turns out that I had filled a gaping hole in the Elboya staffing grid.

If there weren't many male mathematics teachers who were qualified to teach in French, there were even fewer in the science stream. Despite having been given a shot to demonstrate my worthiness to remain in my position, there would be no guarantees. My principal would be required to submit detailed reports about my effectiveness as a first-year teacher, which included the submission of three mandatory, documented lesson observations.

At Elboya that year, there were three other first-year probationary teachers who found themselves in the same position as myself. The only difference was that they were not all French bilingual teachers. One was an English/social studies teacher, one a French language teacher, and the other an English language arts teacher. One candidate was filling a maternity leave position and thus was most certainly not going to receive even a chance of a permanent contract. With all of us being in the same situation, in limbo without a definite position come September 1994, when the stress began to mount in February 1994, after a year of serving our temporary contract, we naturally formed a support group to share the emotional burden. At times, we would congregate after school in the staff room, just talking about our options and how we were feeling. There was a sense of comfort knowing that you weren't going through the torture alone. Generally, I was not the type of teacher who would hang out in the staff room joining the gossip team. There were a few teachers who were known as the "gossip gang," who despite the intense workload always had time to sit around at the end of the day chatting about everything under the sun.

I learned from my mentor that one had to be careful to protect one's reputation and not sink to the lowest common denominator. I eventually adopted the model of many other teachers who would float in and out of the staff room, chatting here and there to make sure they were still seen as part of the team, even though they were careful not to condone and be seen as approving the hard-core gossip. This was the model I have maintained throughout my professional career.

In the late spring, early summer I had time to spare on, of all days, Friday afternoons. Once the clock changed, my rush about Friday sunset times and arrival of the *Shabbos* simply wasn't a pressure anymore. Every now and then, occasionally on some of those Friday afternoons, I would sit for a half-hour or so, chatting and joking around in the staff room. I developed a genuine relationship with my new colleagues based upon mutual passions and interests. There were some who were genuinely interested in my religious observance and love of sport. Most were surprised that an Orthodox Jewish person would be integrated into the mainstream workforce and still have a passion for ice hockey. This seeming dichotomy made for great discussion. My willingness to open up and share some personal feelings ingratiated me with my colleagues immensely and worked very much toward a mutual feeling of camaraderie.

Despite being young and the new kid on the block, opportunities to share my personal experiences allowed me to develop a sense of confidence about what I was accomplishing in my classroom. I began to formulate some very strong ideas on my educational philosophy. I was particularly interested in how to appropriately differentiate mathematics and science, specifically when teaching boys and girls together in the same classroom. In my late immersion classes, most students were highly motivated and, for the most part, confident individuals. The students who happened not to fit these criteria after the first two or three months began to slip through the cracks in the lesson.

Despite teaching thirty students in a class, it was not too difficult to recognize the students who were all too ready to sit back and not join the flow of the lesson. In a combined, multigender class of boys and girls, it was quite common for the boys to monopolize the conversation given their dominant and vocal communication style. The shy, quiet girls happened to sit back, allowing these boys to dominate the lesson. I quickly adapted my methods and devised a scheme of how to surge the involvement levels of the girls in our day-to-day lessons. In my mathematics classes, I avoided gender-specific frames of reference. I also devised specific project-based learning activities as a way for developing independent learning. This strategy was particularly well received by some of the shy boys as well. I took more control, directing the flow of discussion to find ways to spark the usually quiet girls and boys into the main flow of the lesson. All of a sudden, I had quite a robust classroom with equal participation from all my students. I was able to easily discern who had difficulty with the subject matter and who truly was excelling. A few girls managed to stand out as truly exceptional students. With some extension activities and some personal invitations to attend my lunchtime tutorial sessions, I had developed a culture of confidence and intrinsic competition among my students. They bought into the idea of competing against themselves individually rather than with their classmates. They began striving to reach a higher level to see how they could achieve, pushing themselves to succeed. It was as if they had discovered a switch inside them that suddenly turned on, perhaps for the very first time.

Throughout those early terms of teaching, teachers like Alita Pelle, my mentor, had graciously shared all her teaching resources with me. I walked into my first year with enough resources to negotiate the challenges of planning four out of six new classes with the skill and experience of teachers having taught in these areas for over ten years. Despite having to frame the resources into my own teaching paradigm, not having to begin from scratch at least in my mathematics classes made my first year so much easier to cope with. I made sure never to take this for granted. I continuously expressed my gratitude to Alita' for her guidance and generosity. I always felt indebted to her and realise that there was not much I could do other than express this appreciation. I did take on a resolution that one day, when I had the chance, I would pay this model of generosity forward and assist new first-year teachers in the same way as I had been mentored.

Unless you have actually been a full-time teacher full stop, you may not realise what is practically involved in doing this successfully. In that first year, I was assigned six challenging classes. Words cannot do justice describing the necessary preparation and workload. Two Grade 8 math classes in French, one Grade 8 math class in English, one Grade 9 math class in French and two Grade 7 science classes in French – a mouthful to say the least. The needs of the students in the separate streams necessitated significant variation in the type of preparation. I had two eighth grade math classes; one was a late immersion class and the other a continuing bilingual class. They were almost completely different worlds lesson-planning wise, despite the identical curriculum.

Whilst I thought I understood in theory what I was getting myself into, practically the experience crystallized my twofold mission. One was getting across the content of the subject matter. The second and equally important was immersing the educational outcomes in an entirely French environment. There was no question that being comfortable with these dual content demands was critical. However, I learned my most valuable lesson in that very first year as well. I have forever after been grateful for this good fortune: I really discovered what actually matters more than anything when you are standing at the front of a classroom. Students do not care how much you know as long as they know how much you really care.

Out of the blue one day, I was handed a message to call one of the parents of a female student in my Grade 8 late immersion mathematics class. She was one of the quiet girls, who had radically turned things around from being a shy girl to one of the vocal participants, wanting more and more enrichment activities. Her mother called me to introduce herself, and to thank me for being some sort of a catalyst, inspiring her daughter. It seems that the positive influence of my math class had effects reaching far beyond the school. Her daughter had taken up karate as a pursuit, and had begun to advocate for herself in ways her parents only had dreams of.

Once they saw this transformation occurring, the parents asked her about it. They helped her retrace her path in their attempt to ascertain from where the spark had come. The girl herself identified a deep sense of empowerment. She described a sense of inner strength and new-found confidence, allowing her to advocate for herself and step out from the shadows. No longer did she have to sit idly by, and allow those who looked like they had more confidence than she monopolize her "space" of opportunity. This was how her mother described her daughter's account of her awakening. She wanted to thank me personally. I was quite taken aback, not only to receive such positive feedback, but also to see how the effect of that experience in math class was impacting the life of a student far beyond the classroom.

Toward the end of our conversation, the mother told me she happened to be a Trustee for the Calgary Board of Education and that in her position, she would have some political influence over my contract. She promised to write a letter of endorsement to the superintendent and to the human resources department of the Board of Education. I was quite overwhelmed and I told her how thankful I was for her offer of support. To this day, I'm sure her letter of reference had some impact on the outcome of my contract status.

A Life-Changing Phone Call

I had been teaching for almost two years at my alma mater. My second year was going very well. I had made significant progress as a second-year teacher in the public school system. Despite the very public contract negotiations between the school board and the teacher union, I managed to remain focused on my classroom and studies.

The state of teacher contracts had not changed from the year before. Once again, first-year teachers had been told that they should not expect their contracts to be renewed as the impending cuts would certainly create staffing redundancies. The school board publicized its aggressive new strategy to radically reduce expenses by cutting all probationary contracts. The second phase would be to cut second-year contract employees. Intuitively I knew this would be their cost-cutting approach and had worked very hard in making sure my impact in the school was felt at all levels.

In my first year, I coached basketball and track and played a subordinate role in the development of the winter camp.

This year, I had decided that I would raise my hand and offer to coordinate the entire winter camp with the assistance of one other teacher.

Even though I was already staying late at school preparing my lessons, from January onward the extra time was focused on the upcoming school camp.

Esti was now curly blonde-haired, one and a half, learning her first words, growing in leaps and bounds. Despite my meagre salary and Chaya slowly progressing on her PhD, we were managing. We had spent the summer driving around rural Alberta, finding subjects for Chaya to test and include for her dissertation data. While Chaya spent the two to three hours testing in each city/town, Esti and I would spend our time at a park, or in a local mall, just hanging out watching the time go by.

Amazingly, we travelled from Calgary to as far south as Lethbridge and up north to Fort McMurray, racking up more than 1000km that summer. We had a good time driving the long roads of rural Alberta in our little red Chevy Sprint. The Sprint, our very first car and our first major purchase together, was bought within our budget, so we had to cut costs wherever we could. We never regretted opting for the more economical manual transmission – especially when Chaya taught me how to drive manual transmission on her father's red MG convertible sports car! That summer we regretted declining the air conditioning! It wasn't easy, all that hot summer driving; we surely felt the ramifications of those tight purse strings. It was so hot we purchased a bag of ice and placed it in a basket by the car fan to try and cool the warm air circulating in the car. This became a frequent money-saving makeshift air-con strategy. I can't say that it made a huge difference to the actual temperature, but psychologically we felt a little relief. We have always been a one car family, ever since then, but every car ever since, we have found a way to include the air conditioning!

The news that we were expecting our second baby was going to have a profound effect on our lives. The uncertainty of Chaya's position at the university only added to the stress and lack of security in my position with the school board. We knew that Chaya was to have collected her data by the springtime and a first draft of her analysis was due by the summer. The timing of a new baby was certainly not perfect, but we were very excited to have a sibling for Esti.

With cell phones not yet common in the early 1990s, one truly wonders how we managed to communicate in times of emergency. Today it's as simple as a one touch call or text to get an urgent message to a spouse or a loved one. The instantaneous gratification is something we now take for granted and wonder how we ever lived without it. I look back to how those events unfolded that dramatically change the course of our lives and wondered if things would have played out differently in today's technologically connected environment.

I woke up that Wednesday morning and got ready for school like any other day. Since Chaya was spending more time at home due to the nausea of being pregnant with our second child, it was easier for me to get to school with the car. On other days, she would drive me in to school after the babysitter arrived. Esti almost a two years old now, had become quite attached to our live-out nanny, certainly making it easier for Chaya to separate. She would head off to the university and run her mandatory tutorials for her graduate students in the Faculty of Psychology. At this point in her program of study, the major pressure from her PhD advisor was to prepare the write-up of her data analysis for her dissertation. We had worked tirelessly over the summer to check and recheck the data she had collected, so that Chaya could overcome this last hurdle to complete her PhD requirements.

The pressure was on. Each step of the way her advisor made it clear that Chaya was behind the intended completion date. Her advisor would not continue to keep Chaya on as a graduate student. In the very public "publish or perish" atmosphere of the doctoral program in the university, Chaya was feeling the strain. Torn between the constant demands, deadlines and needs of a budding family, the quality family time in our home was beginning to suffer. I felt a great deal of stress needing to demonstrate a high level of proficiency and dedication to my position as a second-year public school teacher.

For a new growing family, this commitment and dedication certainly came at a price. Chaya knew my personality: when I was committed, there was no such thing as giving less than 110%. Translated into staying behind until all my work was completed meant a twelve to thirteen-hour day at school was the norm. Chaya would arrive around 8 pm and wait in the corner of the parking lot for me with our baby Esti. Chaya, for the most part, didn't mind the one-on-one time, having spent the day herself away from our precious one, working at the university. Winter months were more difficult, sitting in the cold and darkness. I would sometimes leave the school to find Chaya nursing the baby back to sleep, or even finding them snoozing together in the back seat eagerly waiting to get back home to a warm bed. As she got older, Esti would be sitting on Chaya's lap at the wheel pretending to drive.

It was always a great feeling to have such a warm welcome. I remember barely being berated for coming down late for putting in extra time and hours in my job. This was the price to pay in such a competitive career market. I was on a steep climb to learn fast how to be at the top of my game: connecting to my students and at the same time preparing four difficult subject areas for over 210 students.

It was a phone call that both shocked and stunned me, one I could never have imagined ever receiving. It was rare to hear my name over the PA system at Elboya and as soon as I heard the announcement "Mr. Glogauer, phone call line 1, Mr. Glogauer, line 1" my heart skipped a beat. I immediately ran to a phone in the nearest office. It was early in the day and I was in between periods as it was morning recess time. Not having enough time to think what the problem could be, I picked up the phone to hear someone's calm, at the same time controlled, frantic emotionality.

"Noti, it's me, there is something wrong, I think we've lost the baby. I need you to come home right away!"

Trying to remain calm, I asked her, "Did you call the ambulance? Call 911!"

The next response was something I did not understand until later. "There's no point, it's all over, just come home now, I need you!"

That's exactly what I did. I quickly ran to the principal and informed him of the situation. He was very sympathetic and instructed me, "Just go. Drive carefully. Your wife needs you!"

Time seemed to slow down and it felt like an eternity making my way through the very light traffic to get home. Every light seemed to turn red that morning. It seemed the world was against me, pushing every time obstacle in front of me during that stressful drive home. I eventually arrived to find our little baby Esti sitting outside the closed bathroom door. Chaya had barricaded herself inside. Esti was in tears not understanding what was going on, why her mommy was not able to let her in. Even in her state, Chaya had made arrangements for us to drop Esti at my parent's house and for us to drive straight to the doctor's office. Our OBGYN just happened to be linked with the Holy Cross Hospital. Every care and attention Chaya would need would be taken care of upon our arrival. Chaya had called ahead before calling me and had notified our doctor that she was in trouble. Early into her second trimester, it was quite a shock to me that such a thing could even happen. I naïvely thought we were out of the danger zone, the precarious early stages of pregnancy when miscarriages were more common. Even remembering my limited biology foundation and the stages of fetal development, it was a shock that we were in this predicament.

When I quickly dropped Esti off to the poignant care of my parents, our brief hello and my rush back out the door was still enough time to see the emotion on my mother's face and her understanding look of what we were going through. Not enough time for a conversation or reassurance, I could sense her sadness and empathy. Making our way quickly to the hospital, I was still questioning Chaya, trying to hold out hope that maybe everything was still going to be okay. "Maybe it's just some spotting, maybe everything is still okay…"

Chaya was in tears. "No, it's not, I think it's not, I felt it, it's over!" As we made our way to the doctor we began to reflect on our predicament and the stress Chaya was in. "There is a reason for everything, the lesson, who knows but there must be one…"

Chaya had come to a crossroads at the University. She had begun the final write-up of her analysis, had completed all of her coursework and was now in the last stages of her doctorate. Upon completion of her PhD, she had to secure a one-year clinical internship. The problem was that in Calgary, there were only two possible program/positions that met the university's criteria. Chaya had already received feedback from her contacts that it was quite doubtful she would be chosen for either of the two positions. Because I was in my second year teaching in the public system and things were going quite well, she had decided to creatively develop her own internship. The university had frowned upon such creative means of fulfilling the necessary program requirements because of some unofficial ruling that all programs needed to have secured funding to financially support the candidate. This was the "humane" side of the program despite the limited opportunities, which in themselves became obstacles for the students to complete the necessary requirements in order to graduate.

Chaya was ready to buck the system and develop her own program, working in a clinic *pro bono* for the entire year, receiving credit, despite the lack of endorsement or financial support from the university. It was a long shot and certainly an uphill battle. There were numerous stages to gaining approval and the steps seemed unlimited. We only embarked on that complicated path because of our deep desire to stay and develop solid roots in Calgary.

This was a huge decision to not get paid for a year, but we calculated a way to cut our expenses and break even. We calculated that I could also work extra during the school summer vacation. I was going to apply to my old job in the city where I worked as a co-op student during my business studies phase. From my mother, I would get enquiring messages from my former supervisor, who every now and then would run into each other in the elevator at work. Having left on great terms, I knew if ever I was in need, I had been cautious never to burn the bridge and thus could always go back and earn some additional money. We knew this would be difficult, but at the time we were not prepared to leave Calgary, to leave our family who had been so supportive of Chaya and me. After all, my parents lived here, we were becoming part of the community and I was gaining significant traction in the public school system at Elboya Junior High School, building the foundations of my career.

Now at that moment, we were together in the car, on the way to the doctor's office to confirm what we now both felt was a *fait accompli*, that we had lost the baby. We looked at each other and said what was on both

141

of our minds: "This changes everything. If we have lost the baby, we need to leave Calgary and get an internship somewhere that appreciates you and who we are. It's not enough for us to want to be here in Calgary. Calgary also needs to want us. Maybe there will come a time when this is the case; sadly, right now, it just doesn't seem so." And that's when she said it… "I wasn't sure if it was even worth mentioning. I got a call from Houston, but I just left it alone. But now I know it's something I will need to look into." Not wanting to divert my focus on the issue at hand I simply responded, "Let's see what happens, but there is hope."

And at what seemed like the darkest hour for our young family, a time when we were both at our lowest, we looked at each other and just knew there was some deeper plan, a purpose that had its own storyline. This was all part of the cosmic plan and we would submit to the hidden plot. We had done everything we could to keep the dream of living in Calgary alive. We would need to change course and break many hearts, but that would come later. Right now, we were headed to the doctor and with my unsure understanding; I still held a glimmer of hope.

Arriving at the doctor's office at the Holy Cross Hospital, Chaya was quickly brought into the examination room. I stayed outside as I really did not want to get in the way of the doctors examining Chaya and making the determination that would potentially change the course of our lives. It sounds a little dramatic, but the fork in the road was in front of us and the determining factor was whether Chaya was still pregnant with our second child. I sat in the waiting room for a short time, which truly felt like hours. When the doctor came out, I knew by looking at her face that the outcome was just as Chaya had foretold.

A flood of emotions came over me internally but I somehow found the strength to hold back. My most immediate need was to see how Chaya was feeling. I was glad to see her as I apprehensively walked in, not knowing how she was taking the news. To this very day, I'm amazed at how strong and resolute she was in that overwhelming situation. There are times when she is overcome with emotion and others when I know she needs to process and come to grips with all the accounted-for angles. At that time, I know only now having been married for over twenty-six years that she was processing, working through the next steps in her mind. There would be a time to mourn, a time to grieve, but now for her it was planning the next critical steps in our life. It was obvious that she was deeply disappointed. She was teary but not overcome with emotion. I would not be the catalyst in this moment for the inevitable rush of emotion that was bound to occur. I would listen and be at her side to process through what she needed.

After a few more steps and some scheduled procedures, we eventually would head home to regroup. I would have time to call my parents from the doctor's office and let them know we had lost the baby. Hearing the emotion in my father's voice over the phone was enough to spark my first emotional response. There I was sobbing in the middle of the lobby over the phone. I felt it was most necessary to allow myself this moment to release the built-up feelings rather than express this loss in front of Chaya who deserved a strong husband to be the anchor through this difficult trial. They offered to keep Esti overnight for a little sleepover while Chaya and I got some needed rest. Esti was accustomed to these little treats with her grandparents, so the space to connect and emotionally deal with the shock was well received. I called into school and spoke to my principal, letting him know the news. I asked him if it would be okay to take the day off so I could be with my wife. This seemed like an odd request from the standpoint that without a doubt a personal day would be warranted. But it was only then I realised from the conversation, that there was a much bigger issue that needed to be contemplated.

Today was Thursday. I would take the Friday off, but Monday was scheduled to be the first day of the Elboya Junior High late immersion winter camp. In that second year, I took the lead role in planning the entire camp with another teacher. Together we were responsible for over one hundred students, the entire year seven cohort of French late immersion students for three days and four nights at a mountain retreat. But the unexpected tragic nature of events of that week had proved quite emotional for both Chaya and myself. I felt a racking guilt at the thought of not being at home with my wife at such a difficult time, having to deal with losing a baby at the same time as having a toddler in the room also needing her mother. I was in a precarious state in my career and I was not sure how it would be seen if I were to take time off to be with my wife, even after such a traumatic event.

Losing the baby was so unexpected and we could never have seen it coming, but now I was unsure what I should do. I was prepared to take the necessary time to reconnect with Chaya and to determine what she needed. If she felt she needed me to be at home and not attend the camp, I would not have hesitated to stay with her. In truth, there was absolutely no pressure at all from the school to attend the winter camp. The teachers were supportive and before the end of the day, the administration had already come up with contingency plans to replace me for camp.

Nevertheless, I felt somehow I would be missing out on an important career opportunity. The ability to plan the camp on paper was one thing, but to actually lead the staff and students so early on in my career was a favourable opportunity to demonstrate leadership to my principal who had invested in me a great sense of confidence with this monumental task. Almost equally important was my impression on my new colleagues, who were only beginning to get to know me and see me on level footing in terms of collaboration and as an equal contributor.

The winter camp that second year was going to be my first real opportunity to demonstrate my leadership capacity. I was also going to co-lead the entire French department by developing activities, educational programming and social activities for the staff in the evenings, all from scratch. If there ever was an opportunity to demonstrate my professional self-worth, this was the chance. Chaya was intuitively aware of this. Throughout our discussions that weekend, having every right to dwell on our own personal turmoil, we managed to remain acutely aware of the big picture. The decision we were facing regarding the next step of our life plan was somehow staring us in the face. Short term, we were grieving at having lost our baby in the second trimester. Long term, it was the unmistakable sign that Calgary would not be suitable for Chaya to complete her internship and thus fulfil her PhD requirements.

Losing the baby became a catalyst for making some tough decisions about our future. The difficult part was seeing my career develop, gaining traction in the public school system and forming important professional relationships and allegiances among the staff and administration at Elboya. There was the realization that I had to depart from the city where I had spent many years, both growing up and now developing the early foundation of a promising career. Leaving at this stage would clearly be shutting tight a door of opportunity. It would be hard contemplating all that I had done to secure employment in the public system, only now to take the decision to leave. We were almost playing a game, calculating on which side of the scale to place all our chips. Deep down we knew that our best option would be to complete Chaya's PhD as a priority, even though we would be potentially sacrificing all I had worked to build for my career in this public school system.

I would wait a few months before telling anyone, which in itself would prove to be very difficult because of the close relationships I had built. But the decision would be made, to leave Calgary. This meant giving up potential job security, giving up my valued position at Elboya. But this also meant strengthening my resolve that I was becoming a most valued employee, that my principal would do whatever he could not to lose me. I realised there would come a time when his reference would be critical to my career and I would do nothing to jeopardize this.

Our decision was made. I would attend winter camp without fail. It would be with no one's knowledge at the time, my 'swan song'. When I was leaving the school a few short months later, this camp would be characterized in my letter of reference from the vice principal as one of the best ever imagined winter camps. I am immeasurably grateful for the experience that planning the camp gave me. As I had hoped, it was also an opportunity to demonstrate my work as an employee among my colleagues. It was in this context that we made the decision to leave the Calgary Board of Education and a promising promotion at Elboya Junior High and move to the United States of America.

Tenure at 24

It seemed like a repeat of the year before. Only this time, two other employees came out of Mr. Jeffrey's office before me, in tears! News had leaked in the staff room that today all temporary employees would receive their termination notice. Education cuts were felt throughout the city, not only in a reduction in teaching resources but especially in personnel. The union had already launched its public outcry in an attempt to gain support for the many temporary contracts that were not going to be renewed. Pupil-teacher ratios were doomed to increase as a result of the decrease in staff. Elboya had five temporary teachers. Already three had received their dismissals, effective at the conclusion of the school year. Being as the odds were stacked against me numbers wise, I entered the office expecting bad news. Of course, they had no idea that I had already made plans not to return the following year.

You cannot imagine my astonishment when I walked into the office. This time the party included the vice principal and my head of department, both sitting in front of me with Gary Jeffrey. I was pretty confused to see the broad smiles. It seemed they were unable to contain the enthusiasm spilling from their faces. I thought, at first, it was some joke, that they had developed this lively atmosphere as a means of breaking the gloomy communication. It was then that Mr Jeffrey exclaimed almost in disbelief, "Congratulations! I almost don't believe it myself, but I am so pleased to offer you a permanent contract. Someone upstairs has pulled off some kind of a miracle, but here it is, in plain black and white, your letter of confirmation that you have been granted permanent tenure with the Calgary Board of Education!"

A tenured position! I had miraculously achieved this milestone in less than two years as a teacher. It is something few teachers, new or veteran, could achieve in such an unstable educational economic climate. I realised that School Board trustee parent must have gone in to bat for me, but for her to have actually succeeded in facilitating my receiving a permanent contract with the Calgary Board of Education was unfathomable! What was more incredible was that I was about to give up such a gift!

But Gary wasn't finished. His next sentence was possibly even more surprising, given that I had only been teaching for two years. "Not only do we want you back, but we believe you would make an incredible leader in our school. We would like you to consider becoming the Department Head of Science." The current science department head had just resigned her position and informed the school that she was moving back to Montreal for personal reasons.

Luckily, my shock in response to these offers was completely understandable, given the atmosphere in the school and the education environment in Calgary at that time. I thanked them all profusely, telling them I was grateful and amazed at the offer and that I needed to go talk it over with my wife and get back to them. I felt I owed Mr Jeffrey so much. A few days later I requested to meet him and the vice principal to try to explain our situation. It was quite a shock to my principal that I would resign my tenured position. In truth, I was advised to apply for a temporary leave of absence, promising to return to the Calgary Board of Education. My leave of absence was indeed granted, which further demonstrated their confidence in me and guaranteed me a future in the profession I so loved.

Making that decision to look outside of Calgary for Chaya's internship brought up so many competing emotions. We had become quite close with my parents through the loving relationship with our baby Esti, their first grandchild. When our second baby had been on the way, it was inconceivable for us to ever contemplate tearing our family apart. The manner in which we left South Africa had always been a huge emotional issue for me, primarily for having left our extended family behind. I never got over having to say goodbye to my great-grandmother, for whom our precious Esti is named and with whom I had an extremely close relationship. Part of my heart always stayed behind with her. At some intuitive level, at seven years of age, I knew I would never see my great-grandmother again. Perhaps it was due to the fact that just before leaving my birthplace, I experienced the profound loss of my great-grandfather suddenly passing away.

I will never forget that day when, for some strange reason, we were sent to our cousins' house to stay for a few days. We were told that grandpa was ill and had suddenly been rushed to hospital. We were told it was necessary for him to stay there for a few days, and in the meantime, we would stay at our cousins. Both my brother Michael and I were to stay with them, to make it easier on our mother while she took care of baby sister, who at the time was only three years old.

Having secured a potential job and the necessary visas to allow our immediate family to eventually emigrate, my father had already left for Canada. His absence and all that entailed took quite a toll on my mother. Not only was she coping with three children on her own now, she was carrying the emotional burden from the fallout of our great-grandparents and grandparents coming to grips that we would be moving to Canada. My parents had already sold our house, packed up all our belongings and sent them forward to Canada. We were now living with my great-grandparents in the same house my mother had grown up in as a little girl.

One afternoon as we were playing outside my cousin's house, my mother arrived in my uncle's car. This alone was somewhat unusual. Uncle Maish was not due to come home so early from work, so immediately I became suspicious. My mother asked Michael and me to come over. She wanted to talk to us. She was very teary, and I knew deep down what she was going to say. Making her say the words, even though they were so difficult, was part of my rebellion and disbelief. As soon as she said, "Grandpa passed away," I angrily got up and screamed at her that she was a liar and ran from the garden. I tried jumping over the gate. I tried to run away from the menacing sorrow, realizing that I would never see my great-grandfather again. Because of our incredible bond, we would affectionately only refer to our great-grandparents as Granny and Grandpa.

I had grown very close to my great-grandparents, especially my great-grandpa. The memories I have today are crystal clear, as though they happened yesterday. I can recall my third birthday, walking up onto the veranda. They were waiting behind the door ready to surprise me with my first teddy bear! He was wrapped in a plastic bag with a blue ribbon and yellow plastic closure. To this very day, I cherish my dear old Bruno. My fond memories are filled with feelings of belonging and being protected by my loving grandpa, mixed with the painful nostalgic feeling of having left that family behind. All these experiences only made it that much more difficult for us to leave Calgary and trigger that same emotional loss for our daughter and her loving grandparents.

Once Chaya submitted her name to an international registry of internship placements, it wasn't long before the phone began to ring. The first person to call was Dr Larry Ballering from Spring, Texas. After one initial conversation, Chaya had a feeling that it was a good fit. Philosophically, she had found someone who shared the same professional outlook toward children in need of direction, guidance and a purpose. It would be a clinical position in one of the largest school districts in Texas. The only question now was how geographically close we would be to a Jewish community that would enable us to maintain our growing level of observance. We didn't know a lot about the infrastructure in Texas and had to look on a map to find the actual location of Spring. To our great delight, it looked geographically close to the main city centre of Houston. It was one easy phone call to the *Chabad* centre in Houston to find out that not only would it be feasible to commute from Houston to Spring, but also the community was well-established and had a school looking to hire a math and science teacher for the upcoming academic year. We could not have imagined this divine providence. The only question we now had was, should we take the plunge? And if so, how on earth would we tell our parents?

Chaya and I sat together that weekend and made a list, enumerating all the positives and negatives. In the end, the most influential point that was influencing us toward taking the plunge was the realization that we only needed to be in Texas for one year. We could come back to Calgary at the conclusion of the internship. With me taking a leave of absence, I would have a position to return to in the Calgary Board of Education. Yes, I would not be guaranteed my exact position at Elboya, but I would still be guaranteed the full-time tenured position I coveted so much. We surmised the experience of seeing another community would be good for us. Most of all, Chaya would be that much closer, in fact just one more stumbling block away, from finally completing her PhD.

We would do one more thing before finalizing a decision. We presented all our points to our mentor, our rabbi. We were looking to him for an impartial viewpoint from a caring mentor. We had always found him to be capable of evaluating our decision-making process, ensuring that we had not left any stone unturned. The tiny Calgary *Chabad* community, of which we had grown very fond, would miss us very much, and the feeling was mutual. We had played a critical role in its development. Still a very small group of families, one less active family would leave a gaping hole. All of this weighed very heavily on our shoulders and was a bold entry in the negative column of our decision-making list. Despite not having a formal title, I had somehow become the assistant to the rabbi in our community. We had grown considerably in observance under his guidance. Not only that, we had also developed a very close relationship in the six years we had gotten to know each other.

Regardless of his personal interest in not wanting us to leave, we received his blessing with the knowledge that our clear intentions were that one day soon we would return to Calgary. Chaya and I made the decision that we now felt was staring us right in the face, pointing us unequivocally in that direction – for our family to follow in the historical footsteps of my father and mother. We were to leave our family and home, albeit, temporarily. The necessity for Chaya to finish her qualifications as soon as possible without compromising the many years of hard work leading to this point was the next step in our journey. We had found an internship that would be 100% acceptable to the university. Completing her dissertation could enable a future return for our young family back to Calgary and me back into the Board of Education.

Sunday evening, we sat down with my parents and presented our plan. Chaya would go to Houston on a fact-finding tour. If she returned with confirmation in writing that she had a firm contractual commitment to complete the required internship, we would then look at my being able to secure full-time employment in the Houston community Jewish school. Teaching in a private school alleviated me having to transfer my Canadian credentials to teach in the American public school system. The combination of Chaya's internship and me teaching would provide the necessary finances to secure our young family's living expenses. We would move to Houston on a one-year leave of absence from the Calgary Board of Education.

My parents were visibly upset, more so my Dad, ever the one to wear his emotions openly. My father was quite choked up, but quickly regrouped and became his ever practical and philosophical self. The pertinent questions relating to the everyday ideas of how we would make enough money to survive soon arrived, easing the emotional trauma. The biggest hurdle was that this was already May. We were facing a mere four-month timeline before having to arrive in Houston. The whole plan hinged on my being able to work, and I was only a Canadian citizen. We had to secure a green card in order for me to work in the USA. We thought we could easily achieve this hurdle since Chaya was born in the United States. We also had collaboration from the school in Houston being as they had a niche I could seamlessly fill. So, we embarked with the naïveté of the young, confident that it would all fall into place in time!

Divinely Endorsed Aliens

We were juggling so many priorities. It was important to Chaya to confirm in the long-term how we would make ends meet. To me I kept emphasising how we should keep our options open. I actually was secretly considering, not returning to Calgary after the year. We surmised once we had negotiated all the hurdles for Esti and me becoming official legal American resident aliens, maybe we would stay in Houston or look at our options in America before conceivably returning home to Calgary. I obviously kept this thought very close to my chest. I wanted to maintain hope in my parents that our trek down to Houston was only for one year. To present anything but a one-year stint away would only cause more emotional distress, which is what we were trying to avoid at all costs.

You see, as you may have deduced, the first time I left home was when I got married…at 20 years of age. I often felt like the child who had not experienced the full gamut of what life had to offer, having never really truly left the confines of my parents' influence. I had tried to break from their embrace when I applied to Queens University in London, Ontario for my undergrad course. Despite being accepted, I could not commit due to the prohibitive cost.

Deep down, I knew going to Houston was my opportunity – my chance to see the world, outside of parents' onlooking eyes, and protective shelter. I wanted to take a risk and this was my opportunity. As I thought it through, I began to conclude that since my parents would already be upset at the notion of our leaving Calgary for even one year, if there was a chance we would be extending this opportunity, it would be better to prepare them now rather than break the news from a distance over the phone. Better to plant this seed now than to spring the idea on them later. I did not bargain on how harshly this dose of reality would hit them, much more than I could have suspected. From this moment, or so it seemed, my mother emotionally withdrew from me to a place from which our relationship has only recently rebounded.

There has always been some unwritten tension in our relationship. It is common knowledge amongst us siblings; one of my maternal side's family characteristics is being very unemotional, rarely expressing any demonstrative, outpouring of emotion. Thus, it was very consistent of my mother, when we told my parents that we had decided to move to Houston and might explore our options elsewhere after that, to become seemingly cold and definitely withdrawn, although a bit teary-eyed. Throughout our time in Houston, it would be rare to have more than a few minutes of conversation with her over the phone. This was a time long before the video-conferencing age, when Skype was not even a remote conception. Shortly after our move to Houston, my mother contracted a serious case of shingles. She always maintained it was because of the emotional distress she was under when we left Calgary.

One of the many incredible miracles that occurred at this time was the securing of our green cards by the time we had to leave for Houston. Looking back at the timeline and our decision to make the cross-continental move, perhaps the biggest obstacle was the red tape and international bureaucracy associated with such a massive geographical relocation. In order to be able to move from Calgary to Houston, Esti, then two years old, and I had to secure green cards. At the time, it was a long process and no one could give us any guarantee as to the length of that process. Our timeline seemed completely irrelevant to every bureaucrat who assisted us along the way. Only two and a half years into the purchase of our first home, we had now deemed it necessary to relocate to a new country; we were now in a position of needing to sell our home in an unstable real estate market. There were no guarantees that we could at least break even on our investment. However, due to our timeline in terms of needing to leave Canada, we were under the gun. Not wanting to have to pay rent in the United States and still have a Canadian mortgage to take care of, my father made things a lot easier for us by assuming the title of the house and renting it out himself. In effect, we sold the house to my parents lock, stock and barrel, in exchange for peace of mind and a clear break from our brief home owning stint in Calgary.

The next step was for Chaya to fly down to Houston and meet the director of her internship. If all went well, she would need to scope out the community to ensure we could indeed live appropriately. This meant a preschool for Esti, and if all went well, some indications of some independent schools I could apply to, in case the offer at the *Chabad* School did not fall into place. Since I was only two years out of university, having just recently received my Permanent Provincial

Teachers License, it would take a while to formally apply to teach in the Texas Public School District. Therefore, my best bet would be to find a job in an independent, private school. I would apply to as many as possible in the vicinity of a rental home, once Chaya found that suitable base location. We didn't really have much choice of where to live, as there were only really two possible Jewish areas in the city. It was a matter of checking them both out.

In the meantime, I would call ahead to the Chabad Torah Day School and speak to the principal ahead of Chaya's arrival. I hoped to make a good impression. I was quite fortunate to get in touch with the principal of the general studies department, Mrs Nancy Epstein. I was amazed to find out that they were still looking for a math/science and physical education teacher for their middle school (Grades 5-8). Mrs Epstein seemed very keen and asked me to send a resumé. Since it was before the email age, I immediately faxed over a copy of my resumé and references. It did not take long for my rabbi to receive a call from the Head Rabbi of Houston, who also happened to be the dean of the institution. His wife was the acting principal of the Jewish studies department, and he was calling to get a general reference, looking into our personal level of observance to determine a general fit into his community.

Before we knew it, I received a phone call indicating my acceptance as the Grades 5 to 8 mathematics and science teacher. A contract was to arrive in the mail indicating my formal duties and responsibilities. The salary offer was quite minimal, but with the information Chaya managed to acquire while on her trip and the property agent negotiating a year's lease, we now had a place to stay and figures on paper. We determined that it was feasible from a financial perspective to make this critical move, but we were still in a bind. I could not formally accept the position until I had a valid green card! The principal in Houston was understanding and willing to wait a few weeks, pending our initial green card interview and proposed medicals, which were already scheduled in Vancouver, British Columbia.

Chaya was officially listed as both Esti's and my green card sponsor and guarantor. Supposedly, it would be a clear-cut process. The only obstacle was filling in the application and passing the medicals in Vancouver. I took off a Monday from school, making it a long weekend and we drove down to Vancouver. Because of our persistent advance planning, within a day we were able to submit our completed applications, including medicals, to the American consulate. To our great surprise, it was only a month later that we received our green cards in the mail! Surely, it must have been some type of record.

With confirmation of employment and a green card, we began to make final arrangements for moving to Houston. Chaya confirmed the lease for the house we were to rent for the year. We were very fortunate it was very close to the school where I would be teaching, which was in the same complex as the synagogue we would be attending. The challenge would be Chaya's early morning commute and rush hour return. On paper, it was a forty-five minute drive each way. We would soon discover that in Texas, what seemed simple was usually the opposite. In fact, it became clear there was the USA, and then there was Texas…

In anticipation of our move, we had found out that our brand new car could not cross the border! We were absolutely devastated. Shortly after our summer of road trips, after I had been offered my second-year position with the Calgary Board of Education, we decided we could afford a new car. We got a turquoise green Hyundai Elantra, standard shift with air conditioning! We were so upset. Our car would be considered an illegal import due to the strict quota for imports entering the United States of America. It didn't matter that the car had initially been an import from America. We would have to trade in or sell our car for a domestic American automobile. Not wanting to lay out any further money, we settled drastically for an older, used Chrysler.

All of our Calgary loose ends were almost tied off. With the U-Haul do-it-yourself truck rental secured and moving date set, we seemed to have all our "ducks in a row." Despite the apprehension of leaving the comforts of home and security of having my parents to rely on, I was quite excited to truly head out into the unknown of the 'real world'. I felt like I was actually 'escaping' the protective umbrella of my parents. Despite having been married for five years, owning our own house, and having our first child who was now two years old, I felt like I'd never really left home. Every major decision we had made was only after a long discussion with my parents. It was time to grow up and take some risks. At least that is how I felt as a young, naïve twenty-five-year-old.

Looking back now, I am amazed at how much I had really accomplished by that stage in my life. I was married at twenty, our first child at twenty-three. My true naïveté was my belief that to be grown up I needed to make decisions on my own. Today, I have learned that a truly mature approach is to talk out the issues with those who care about you, to weigh the pros and cons with them when making a decision. I am lucky to have parents who are so caring and always looks out for my best interests, and those of my family. To this very day, I know I can count on my Dad to look at all the angles and present an unbiased point of view, despite being emotionally invested in the outcome of my decision. It was thus with a heavy heart but sparkling anticipation that we packed up all of our physical belongings on Friday, August 11, 1995. We rested on the long summer *Shabbos* afternoon and woke up very, very early Sunday morning.

The undertaking was truly too tremendous. With bureaucratic red tape sufficiently addressed, we decided not to actually drive the 'new' blue Chrysler all the way to Texas. Instead, we rented a car carrier and attached it to our moving truck. I'd rarely, if ever, driven a truck before that time. It was quite a sight connecting the trailer to the long truck, and loading up our car onto it. Of course, what scared us the most were the strict instructions not to even attempt backing up the truck!

In those years well before GPS and Internet mapping, we had our "trip tick" detailing our planned route of travel for our four-day, three-night adventure. Through the assistance of the Alberta Motor Association, our journey through five states from Calgary to Texas was planned to a T, ensuring we would arrive by 20 August, midweek. This left us enough time to begin to get our bearings before the weekend. We would then have two weeks to settle in before the beginning of the academic school year and Chaya's start date Monday, September 4. Our next biggest concern, besides not being able to back up with the trailer, was our anxiety over crossing the Alberta/Montana border into the United States with all our earthly belongings in the 28-footer behind us. Having had first-hand experience dealing with the American customs agents, our anxiety level hit maximum as we approached the border crossing in our rig. We were mentally running across every possession we were 'importing' including our most controversial – our 'newly' acquired automobile. We would need to have the car and paperwork carefully inspected and secure a document with which to register the vehicle once we established residence in Texas. We planned our departure early in the morning so we would potentially arrive at the inspection station by 7 am, before it was busy with crossborder tourist and commercial traffic. Our drive to the border crossing would be approximately five hours, thus entailing a 2 am Saturday night departure time.

So there we were at 2 am on time for our departure, loading the last few food items into the main cab. We maneuvered the sleeping Esti into her car seat, fit snugly between Chaya and me. With ample provisions in the cooler filled with ice packs, we did the last few checks to make sure

155

the main door to the truck was securely locked and the trailer properly secured. With the help of one of our friends, we managed to electrically tie in a tape cassette player to the radio so we would at least be able to entertain Esti during the long haul. It still amazes me how motor travel has changed so quickly since then. There were no iPads, iPods nor iPhones to entertain children, not even built-in DVD entertainment systems. We were content with the age-old car games: name the state car license, geography games such as name a country, city, or state beginning with the last letter of the previously-named location, and above all, our vivid imaginations. And did we ever need to come up with both creative and numerous entertainment schemes for that four-day voyage with a two-year-old!

The mental picture of my parents waving goodbye is still imprinted on my mind. It was an uneventful trip to the border and we arrived pretty much on schedule at approximately 7:30 am. Entering the inspection station, ready with our well-rehearsed spiel, we excitedly produced our green cards for the very first time, with our story at the ready. We were a bit frustrated when we realised we had been given misinformation about the duty officer who would process our paperwork. We would have to wait until 8 am when her shift began. Esti was wide awake by now. Despite my eagerness to continue our journey so we could make our first destination, Coral Springs Colorado by evening, the little break would give me a chance to check our bearings, eat some breakfast outside of the confines of the truck cab after completing my morning prayer rituals. Many other individuals began arriving, lining up for a vehicle inspection. As we were first in line when the officer arrived, we realised our good fortune and became quite content about having arrived early. It seemed we were not the only immigrants needing similar entry documents. A lesson in patience, we learned that the many steps in our journey could not be rushed. There was surely a Divine, Cosmic Plan. Patience would be the necessary ingredient linking one successful rung on the ladder of our journey to the next.

The time we took beforehand preparing the necessary paperwork for this huge bureaucratic step was well worth it. I still chuckle today at the red tape involved in bringing back a car to the United States, the same country from where it was initially imported. We satisfactorily jumped through the paperwork hoops! After a border agent's very cursory look inside the truck, by 9:30 am we were once again on our way. The landscape and magnificent countryside of Montana was quite a remarkable sight. Having left the southern Alberta prairies and wheat fields, the lush green countryside and Montana hills were a beautiful sight and refreshing scenery change.

With the size of our truck and the car trailer behind, our goal was to carefully stay on track on the major state highways, which, for the most part, were four lane highways. With rest stops and gas stations along the way, we would only need to venture off the path to find our strategically, preselected motels. It was a very calculated plan – both in terms of carefully plotting our schedule but also the driving route. We had every intention of not being caught in a position that could necessitate having to reverse our large travelling caravan.

As we left the tiny rural town, built solely to connect Canada and the USA, we would need to carefully navigate our way to the Montana State Highway. Despite always driving at the speed limit, many cars were becoming impatient, having to follow behind our 28-foot monstrosity. It amazed us that so many other travellers on the road would far exceed the speed limit, overtaking us no matter whether the intended line on the road denied the maneuver. Making our way through the winding ten-mile road to the main state highway, from out of nowhere came a speeding sports car. We could see the nightmare unfolding before our very own eyes as we approached a two-lane bridge. The sports car pursued us at a high rate of speed intending to pass us before we reached the bridge. Because of his position behind us, he could not see the car on the opposite side of the road approaching us from the opposite direction. The double white line seemed of no concern to him whatsoever. At his current rate of speed, it was clear he intended to pass us over the bridge. The two cars would most likely meet in a head-on collision on the bridge. If we slowed down, we would cause the sports car to ram us from behind. We were witnessing the scenario unfold in front of our very own eyes in slow motion. We were helpless to do anything but pray and hold our breath, which is exactly what we did. The sports car increased its speed behind us even more. Just as we approached the bridge, he overtook us. There we were, two moving objects, side by side abreast on the bridge, nowhere to veer off. Now the sports car, parallel beside us could see the oncoming vehicle rapidly approaching him. Too impatient to slow down, he sped up even more hoping to gain enough speed to overtake us before he collided with the oncoming car. I resisted the instinct to slam on my brakes for fear of jack knifing our truck and the car trailer we were pulling behind us. With Chaya as quietly as possible panicking beside me, the sports car, without hesitation, swerved in and cut us off right before he was about to hit the oncoming vehicle. We had just reached the end of the bridge, and I was

157

forced to swerve off the side of the road, doing my best not to go into the ditch while trying not to lose control and drive into a skid. With the momentum of the truck and weight of our piano hopefully still tethered inside, we could hear the contents of the truck shift and move around, despite our valuables being snugly tucked in together tighter than a Jenga tower. Honking and flashing my lights, desperately attempting to display our displeasure, the sports car left a trail of dust in its wake. He didn't slow down or flash lights, and of course, he didn't stop to indicate even an ounce of compassion for the dangerous situation he had caused. Slowing our speed to well below the limit, trying to catch our breath, we realised what a huge catastrophe we had just averted. We decided that from that point forward, to watch very carefully not only how we were driving and progressing on our journey but also to watch the other drivers and attempt to avoid anyone who would be driving precariously in our vicinity. Arriving at the exit for the state highway, we stopped off for gas and to take a brief rest, hoping to calm our racing hearts.

The remainder of the journey was quite uneventful from the driving perspective, at least in relation to other, fellow travellers. With each passing hour, I became much more confident in my ability to handle our convoy. We finally arrived at our motel late that afternoon. We were relieved to see the sign indicating "Trucks Allowed" and even an open "turn around" area … or so we thought. We quickly found ourselves in a closed-off cul-de-sac motel parking lot! With Chaya directing me and having to every now and then get out of the track to see how much room I had to maneuver, we managed to dodge a huge bullet. It seems it was possible to back the sucker up because I successfully reversed the truck, with the trailer! By now, many people had gathered and were staring at us, amused at the predicament in which we found ourselves. One or two truckers climbed out of their cabs and offered to help us get out of our quandary. With my pride at stake, true to form, never wanting to admit defeat, and never backing down from a challenge, I kindly declined their assistance and persevered with my trusty wife as navigator on the ground. Throughout our more than 26 years together, over time I've come to realise how fortunate I am to have a partner who patiently has accepted my quirks and idiosyncrasies. She has had the patience to allow me to mature and work through my insecurities, many that could have been significant impediments and obstacles to the development of our relationship, not to mention my professional future.

People had a lot to say when we told friends and family that we were getting engaged, and me only nineteen years old. Yes, there was a level of immaturity and an unwavering commitment to grow; I didn't want to do it alone but rather with a partner who was equal to the task. I felt like we could get through anything as long as we were united through a shared vision. Throughout our life journey together, we have come upon huge obstacles. Together, we have both realised that when we are in sync, not always in agreement, but are open to talking through the challenges, we can, as a couple, push through any limitation. Because we have made very bold decisions, by design our relationship and personal goals have been tested. Over time, we have learned the strengths each one of us has to offer. Through experience, we have persevered, tried, and tested our resolve; we have forged a very strong bond. It sounds a bit clichéd, but I believe it with my full conviction, metal only becomes stronger when placed in fire. Relationships can only grow stronger when they are tested.

We used the many waking hours bonding on the trip down to Houston. We used that opportunity to set our success criteria enabling us to remain focused through our year away. We came to a clear understanding and formalized a foundation of how we would evaluate our life position at the conclusion of the year. Driving through the badlands of New Mexico in the middle of the night, lighted only by the shooting stars was truly a sight we would never forget. With Esti fast asleep and Chaya keeping me company, the stillness of the night and serenity of being alone in the dark wilderness allowed us to reminisce on our life together and contemplate the complexity of the journey we had just begun. Deep down intuitively we knew that even Houston might not provide us with the community and leadership to continue our growth personally and professionally. After our year was up, we could find ourselves in the position of having to plan the next chapter in our adventure in another major city, outside the state of Texas.

One thing was for sure, the Divine Providence of receiving our green cards so quickly and easily was definitely a sign that we were meant to be in the USA for a significant adventure, perhaps one that would forever change the direction of our lives. We were on our way to Houston open-minded, ready to embrace the potential of settling in a new community. We were ready to seek out new pathways and were open to determining the meaning of the forks in the road in the journey lying before us.

Whether it was the incredible landscape of New Mexico, or being the only vehicle on the quiet roads of Texas, illuminated by only the stars and moonlight, our future seemed to be a blank slate, and together we courageously held the paintbrush, ready to awaken the two-dimensional canvas through adventure and imagination. No one could have known what the future would have in store for our family. Yet our daring spirit would open doors to unimaginable experiences.

My Great-grandparents' 25th wedding anniversary portrait.

Possibly my first portrait, and with who better than my beloved
Great Grandmother and my older brother Michael.

There I am with my sister Menucha and brother Michael at the
Johannesburg Zoo shortly before our emigration to Canada.

Graduation portrait from Hirsch Lyons Nursery School
in South Africa, 1975, age 5.

Our family reunited in Calgary, Canada 1977.

Helping my father set up for one of his trade shows.

I L Peretz Primary School Grade 3 school photo
First year in Canada.

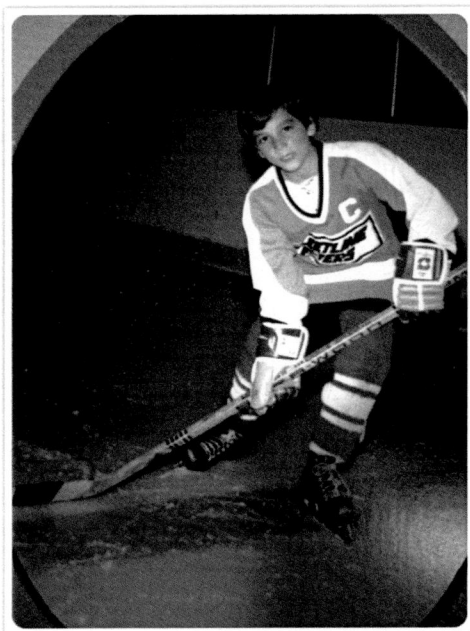

Canadian indoctrination in my second hand skates, 2 sizes too big.

Western Canada High School Grade 11 school photo.

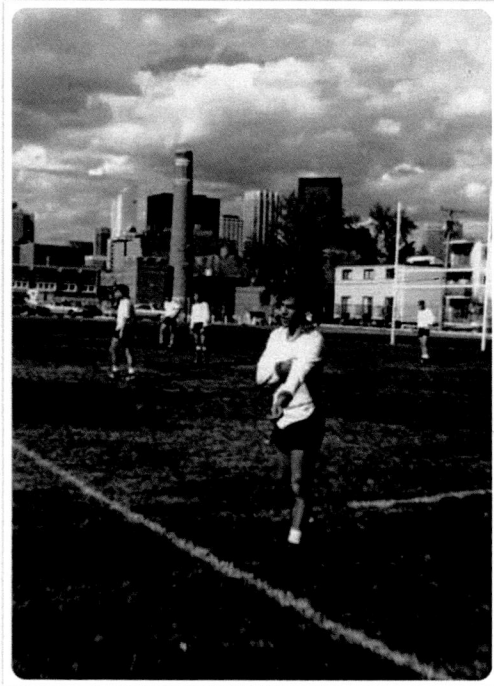

Devastating loss to Henry Wise Wood Grade 12.

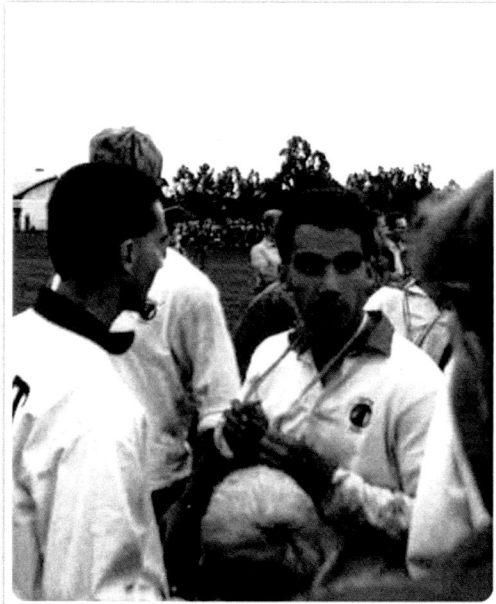

Rugby city championship - How sweet it is!
Can you tell I have a concussion?

Glogauer sparks Western Canada to high school rugby championship

By Paul Sloca
(Herald staff writer)

Arnie Glogauer had a headache.

But there was no need for aspirin, because victory was the only cure the 18-year-old Western Canada student needed and the Redmen defeated Henry Wise Wood Warriors 9-0 in the Division 1 city high school rugby final.

Glogauer, who scored Western's only try, was knocked to the pitch at Kingsland Field just minutes after his clinching 25-yard run.

What made the victory even sweeter was that Wise Wood had defeated the Redmen in last year's final and had beaten them 3-0 earlier in the season.

"There is one word for this victory — revenge," Glogauer said, still groggy from the hit. "It feels really good to beat them. We have a great team and the coaches are really the reason why we won this."

In the Division II final played earlier Friday, Ernest Manning Griffins defeated Lord Beaverbrook Lords 9-3.

The Division I game was scoreless for most of the first half, with Wise Wood carrying the majority of the play. However, when push came to shove, it was Western which was able to keep the ball out of the end zone.

"I think the key to the game was our kicking," said an elated head coach Derick Wright. "Every time we got in trouble, we were able to get the ball out."

As the first half drew to a close, Glogauer took a pass, tipped the ball into his own hands and ran in the ball for a score.

"I was trying to get as much speed as I could and just break away from the pack. Once I was clear, I knew I'd score," Glogauer said.

After a successful conversion, Western went confidently into the second half and shut down the Warriors.

Wright was sure his team could do well because it had planned on bringing the game to the opposition.

"Our goal was to win the championship, and with a lot of hard work, we finally did it. It feels good."

Reprinted with permission of The Calgary Herald.

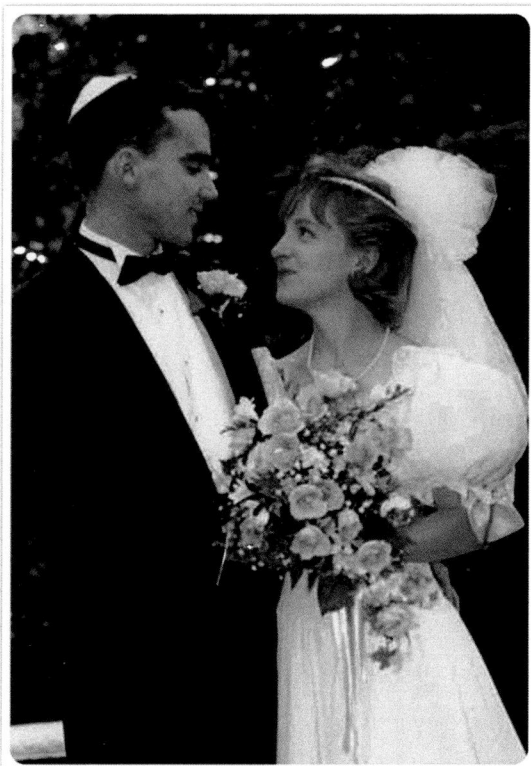

September 2, 1990 – 12 Elul 5750.

Meeting the Lubavitcher Rebbe 13th of Tevet, 5751.

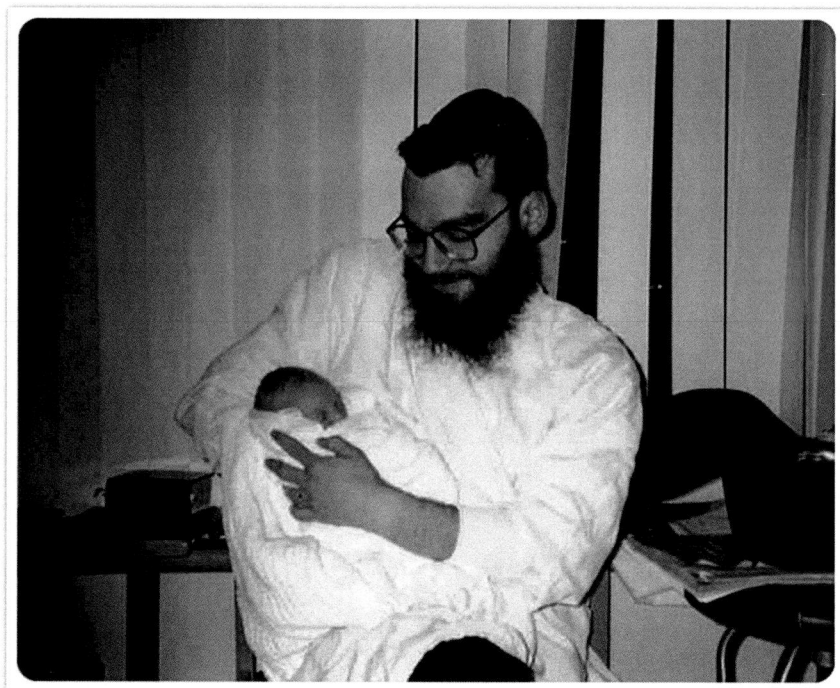
Baby Esther-Dinah June 10 1993 – 21 Sivan 5753.

I'm finally a teacher! B.A. from the University of Calgary.

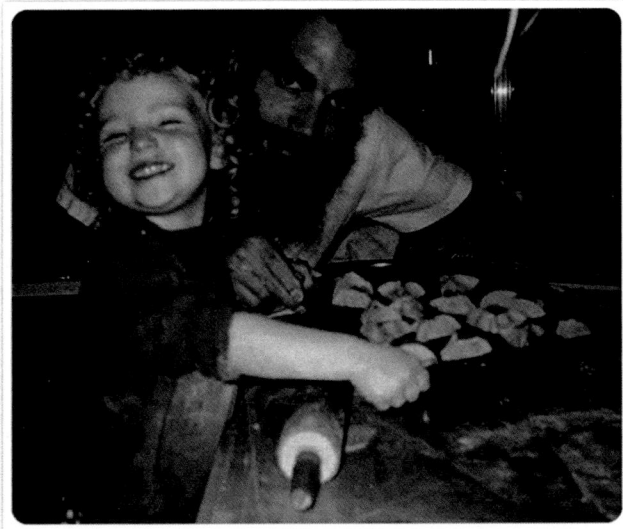

Playing Mr. Mom in Houston Texas, 1996.

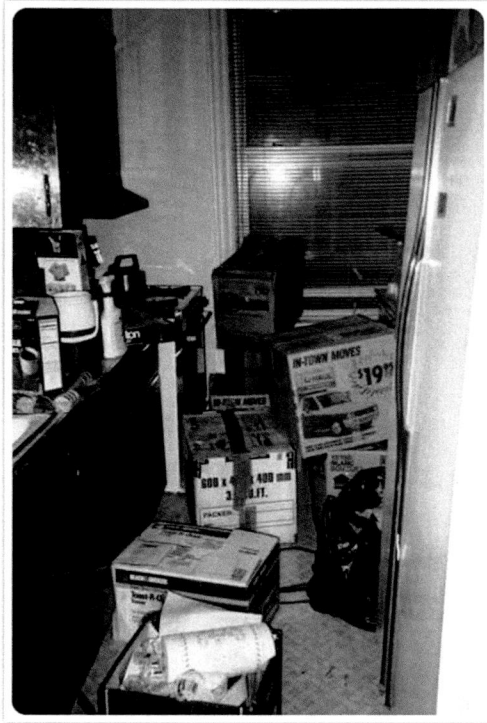

Cramming all our possessions into that tiny half apartment in
Brooklyn, NY 1996.

Jaffa, Israel, December 1998. Just passed my final Rabbinic Exam!

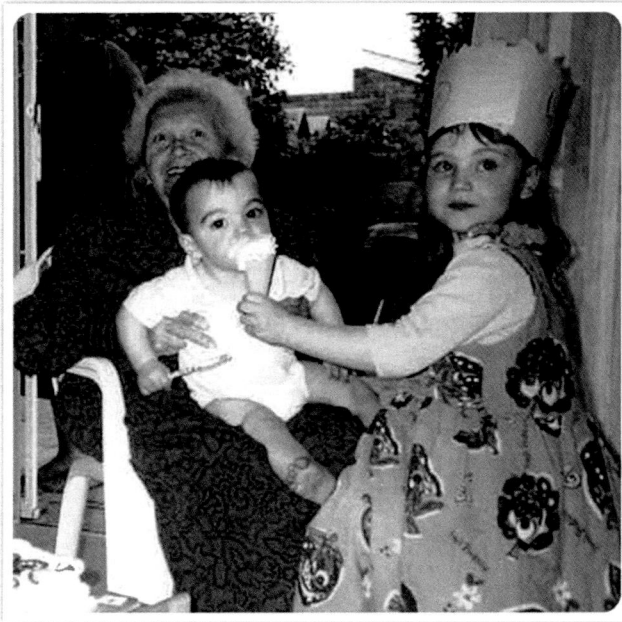

January 1999 Yossi's 1st birthday celebration in South Africa with Bobba, birthday baby Yossi and Esti.
Bobba told everyone she would never wash her dress again!

Receiving my Second Rabbinic Ordination 1999.

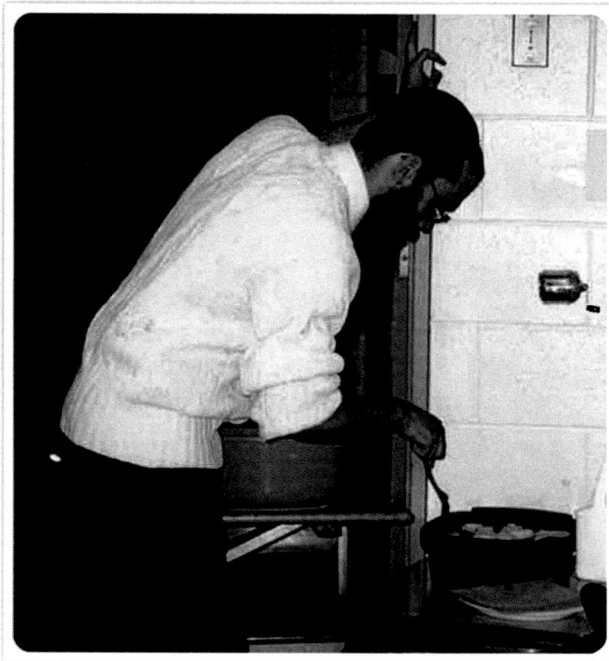

Akiva Academy Calgary, Canada.
Combining my talents teaching Year 4 Math and making potatoes
pancakes with the class for the festival of Chanukah.

Akiva Academy School choir performing at
City Hall with then Mayor Al Duerr 2000.

The morning after the school auction 2001. My surprise!

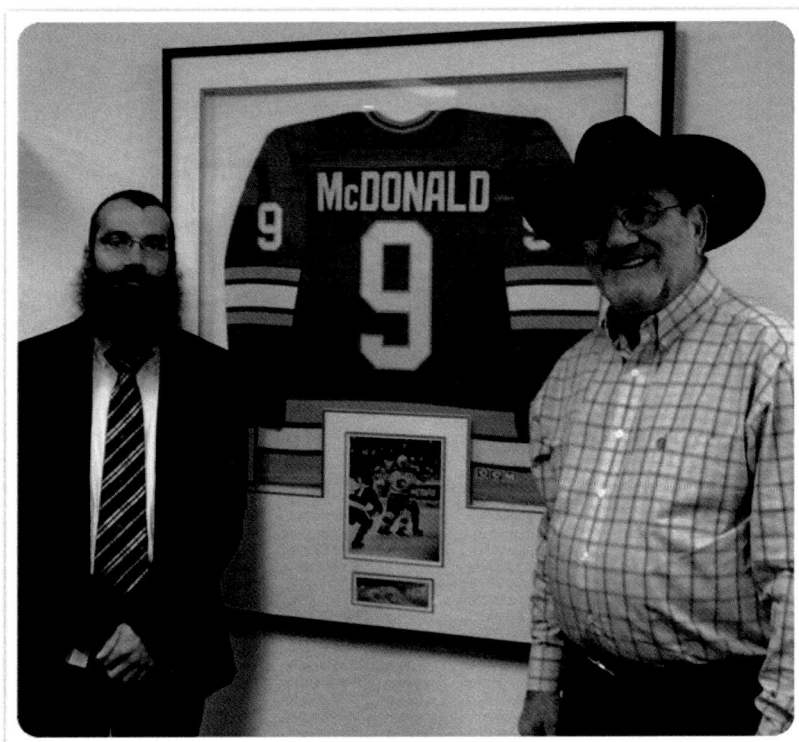

Wherever I go, Lanny's #9 goes!
2014 with my father in Sydney, Australia.

Family photo in Jerusalem.
Our youngest daughter, Rochel's Bas Mitzvah July 2015.

Houston, We Have a Problem…

Once we passed through Dallas, approaching the giant statue of Sam Houston himself in Huntsville, Texas, our hearts began to beat a little faster. Now we knew we were only a couple of hours away from our new home. Our hopes and expectations were great. Chaya had appropriately laid the foundation for our journey. I was excited to see the rental home she had secured for our stay. She tried to describe it to me, but seeing is truly believing. It wasn't long before we drove up to our house on Valley Hills Drive. As we made our way on the Beltway through Houston, Chaya pointed out the important landmarks, which would serve as critical points of reference. The most obvious for any sports fan was the Summit Stadium, located on the southwest freeway. Almost every NBA basketball fan knew that it was home to the Houston Rockets. More relevant to the Canadian hockey fan, I was excited to know that the Summit had recently become home of the Houston Aeros. Not only that, Houston would host the International Hockey League all-star game on my secular birthday January 13, 1996, a game that I would have the privilege to attend. I still have the hockey puck I managed to scramble and snatch from the bleachers when it was hit over the glass close to where I was sitting.

The drive into our neighbourhood toward the new house we would call home for the next year took us through the eternally traffic-jammed stretch of Houston Freeway called the Houston Galleria. It is an extremely upscale shopping area known for famous stores such as Neiman Marcus, Cartier, Gucci, Macy's, and Tiffany's. Its incredible architecture is truly a sight to be seen. On our list of to-dos, we included the world-famous Astrodome, Six Flags AstroWorld, and the NASA Johnson Space Centre. Having just driven over 3700 km in four days, however, the only landmark I was interested in was our house on Valley Hills Drive.

One of the arrangements we had made in advance was for a local moving company to arrive the following morning and unload our belongings from the moving van. The U-Haul return site was only one mile away from our new home, which was another aspect of our plans we deemed as divinely inspired. We excitedly parked the truck in front of our new address. All together, we eagerly walked up to the front door. Chaya had signed the lease upon her initial visit and had obtained the keys at that time.

Alas, as I opened the front door, I could not believe my eyes. The house was already occupied! At the time, it seemed to be the largest creature I had ever seen! A real live lizard ran toward me. I was so gripped by my five-year-old phobia that I was sure he had designs on me becoming his lunch. My fear of reptiles and my ability to grossly exaggerate magnified its diminutive size from one to two inches to almost half a foot. Nevertheless, both Chaya and I were none too impressed with our hospitable greeting from an unauthorized pet, or better phrased – pest. I slammed the door before the Lizard could actually meet me. I looked at Chaya with that 'look', which she had seen many times before exclaiming: "What on earth have we gotten ourselves into?"

Another benefit of our new location was a major shopping centre located just a mile up the road. Luckily, this one was filled with stores that had much more reasonable prices than the Galleria. We decided to unload our car off the trailer and take a ride up to the shopping centre to purchase some insecticide which would, we hoped, annihilate both the Lizard and whatever else was, unbeknownst to us, creeping around the house. Now you can also ask why we would drive if it was just a mile up the road and we'd been driving for days? Houston is such a car-oriented city that many of the city streets did not even have sidewalks. However, this would not have stopped us. It was, in fact, the Houston humid heat! We could not wait to climb inside the car and blast the air conditioning because it was about 95 degrees with the humidity just as high. It was as if we were standing in the vent of a clothes drier!

Chaya waited back in the truck with Esti while I quickly ran the errand. I returned with what was presumed to be the most powerful antidote to our infestation and some paper bags to dispose of the 'remains'. Together we walked to the door, negotiating at every trepidatious step who would be the one to tackle the Beast. Knowing my fears, I managed to persuade my poor wife to take on the challenge.

Slowly opening the door, to our horror, or relief, the lizard had not moved. I was holding the paper bag, ready to pass it to Chaya only after she had killed the lizard with the spray. Chaya tentatively approached the Beast. Esti, waiting outside behind me, could only hear my shriek as Chaya began the spray assault. I screamed, "More, more!" as she must have used over half a can on the one lizard. The spray was ineffective and seemed only to slightly faze the bold creature. Quickly I shoved the paper bag at Chaya and instructed her to scoop it up. Bravely, but squeamishly, she did as instructed. Gathering the scary demon, she threw the bag outside in the front yard. Incredulously we looked at each other, not really knowing what we had just done.

We caught our breath. We unloaded some sleeping bags and provisions for the evening. Tomorrow we had an early start with the movers arriving at 8 am. It was now around 5 pm and the community would be gathering at the synagogue for the afternoon and evening prayers. We decided that Chaya would drop me off and she would then go to the shopping centre to get some essential supplies for another makeshift dinner and breakfast. I waited for the main rabbi to arrive outside the *Chabad* house, which was a multipurpose building serving the needs of the community as both the synagogue and school.

It would be worth noting that at this point, I was quite naïve about the religious path we had chosen. At the time, we had no idea that, like any ideological group, ours could become rife with politics and power games. In fact, time would attest to how little I knew of the political clout and standing of the Houston head rabbi in the larger scheme of the *Chabad* movement. Looking back at this situation, I was in for an important lesson that I would definitely learn the first time!

Forever after Houston, before moving into a community, I would do much more in-depth homework as to the dynamics and religious political leanings of the main players and my potential professional associates. Had I been more aware of the philosophical mismatch between the rabbinical community and us, perhaps our one year and one week in Houston would not have been as rocky. With our hindsight being 20/20, this valuable lesson certainly influenced all our future employment decisions. It seems however, I was meant to be woefully unprepared for even the very first encounter with the Houston community that evening. That state of affairs continued throughout those 53 weeks in Texas.

More men slowly began to congregate in the parking lot until a large smiling, distinguished-looking figure appeared with the keys to the door. Once he had opened the door and many of the individuals had filed into the main sanctuary, I was greeted with a warm welcome by this rabbi whom I soon realised was indeed the main rabbi of the community. I introduced myself and before I could say anything more, excitedly the rabbi declared, "This is our new math and science teacher all the way from Canada." All of a sudden, I was overwhelmed with kind good luck wishes and enquiries about our journey and how we had settled in. When I mentioned the now, so I thought, cute anecdote about the warm welcome from the Lizard in our house and the brave action of my wife to rid our home of the Giant Beast, I was greeted with shock and horror. To my embarrassment, I was quickly put in my place for having transgressed the most significant unwritten law in Texas.

How silly of me, having removed the most important insect exterminator man could possibly have! Didn't I know that this lizard was all I had maintaining the homeostatic balance between human control of the house and a hostile takeover bid initiated by the insect world? All my fellow petitioners could do was shake their heads in sympathy in my direction. They all knew I was going to come home to the coup d'état, the hostile takeover that was soon to begin in our home.

At the conclusion of the prayers, many of the congregants eagerly introduced themselves and told me the names of their children whom I would meet in a couple of weeks when the school year officially commenced. Now it was time to get back to Chaya and share the news of my initial impressions of the community. Of course, I would have to break the news to her of the invasion that we had unwittingly aided and abetted by our part in having removed one deceptively helpful creature from our residence.

It didn't take very long to settle in. The movers arrived on time the next morning. Before we knew it, all our belongings were inside and we were beginning the task of comfortably settling our personal, familiar items creating, once again, a familiar home environment. Chaya would leave early the next morning to meet her internship adviser while Esti and I continued to unpack our belongings. In the midst of our happy unpacking, we were surprised to hear a knock at the door. When we answered, there was not a lizard. Instead our open door revealed a smiling neighbour from across the street who introduced herself as Esti's head preschool teacher. With the thoughtful welcome gift of a bottle of wine and the traditional *Challah* (loaf of bread) and salt, we were warmed by the kind gesture and offer of assistance should any challenges arise.

Esti and I continued to work together for what seemed like hours. I figured it was time for a break. It was quite a warm day outside. With the late summer temperatures of 85°F and the humidity well over 80%, I still felt it would be a good idea for Esti and me to explore our surroundings. We put on our bicycle helmets and with Esti securely strapped in behind me in her bicycle seat, we set out for the shops. This became our mode of transportation for the year. It was convenient and cost-efficient. Esti, the wind in her hair, loved it when I rode fast, not to mention the games we played. She was delighted when I would ring the bell at the scattered pedestrians walking by. I quickly learned that in Calgary there was a great need for the bell to warn all the foot traffic on the pathways. In Houston, due to those extreme temperatures, hardly anyone walked anywhere during the daytime. We soon became a well-known spectacle in the community, the dark bearded teacher and his fair blonde-ringletted child who would bike everywhere.

It also didn't take long for Chaya to realise that her geographically short commute of only 30 or 35 miles, or 55 to 60 kms, to work timewise was daunting. Chaya was travelling with the extreme traffic flow, so her morning and evening commutes were quite considerable. Not only that, she was also contending with four, five, and six-lane highways with multiple interchanges. Chaya would have to leave the house by 7 am in order to arrive by 8:30 am In the evening, Chaya would arrive home well after 6 pm. Her days were long and full. For Esti and me, we took things in our stride. We would have to make the most of our weekends in terms of quality time with Mommy.

The economic situation in Texas, with respect to supply and demand of the domestic workforce, was such that almost everyone had live-in nannies, and could well afford it too. There was ample space in the house we had rented as well. With my having to get to work by 8 am on weekdays, hiring a nanny seemed like a financial necessity, even for us, so we put the word out that we were looking to hire a Monday through Thursday live- in.

Before we knew it, our phone was ringing off the hook with possibilities. The challenge was our ability to communicate in Spanish. We quickly learned the most essential phrases such as vacuum the floors, pick up Esti from school, and drop Esti off at school. However, it was not as simple as that.

The most critical components of working in our home were all the rules of a kosher kitchen and not mixing milk with meat. The wife of one of the head rabbis came over to help us interview possible candidates and ensure they understood the basics of our kosher kitchen. With her help, we explained very clearly the strict rules on how to prepare dinner. I would do the actual cooking; the nanny would simply do the prep work while we were all at school. A main rule was for her to never actually turn on the stove or the oven. This was solely to be done by me. This rule was the easiest way to avert a mix-up with the potentially confusing kosher laws. In regards to the nanny being able to eat, all we asked her to do was to provide a specific shopping list of desired products and food types that we would purchase for her on the weekend with the acceptable kosher certification in anticipation of the week ahead. We wanted her to be comfortable in our home. We were fortunate to have a spare bedroom at the front of the house with a private bathroom attached. It was a little bit of a stretch for us financially to hire a nanny. Most people living outside of Houston, Texas would consider it a luxury.

Given Chaya's working parameters and mine, the nanny was critical. For me to prepare the many lessons I was teaching, I could accomplish most of the preparation at school after 3:30 pm until 5 pm. I could even get home in enough time to play with Esti and cook dinner at the same time in anticipation of Chaya's arrival home by 6:00 pm. This worked well for the first two weeks. Esti was quite easy-going and had settled well into school due to the incredible bond she had forged with her teacher.

We had comfortably settled into a rhythm in our life with a schedule that had Chaya leaving early in the morning when both Esti and I were still in bed. She was only to arrive home well into dinner time. We were barely getting by but we seemed to be just breaking even with the unexpected expense of the live-in nanny. We knew this would be a challenging year but we just needed to somehow make it through without going further into debt. Chaya's salary just covered the basics such as food, the nanny, and gasoline for her daily commute. My salary covered Esti's tuition and rent, so there wasn't much left over at the end of the day. The cost of the nanny was not exorbitant but due to our work schedules, it had become a necessity we had not entirely anticipated before arriving in Houston.

Perhaps it was that false sense of complacency and comfort of getting by. One evening, it all came crashing down – then and there. Chaya and I both happened to arrive home at the same time, me a little late due to a staff-training workshop, Chaya a little early due to the good fortune of light commuter traffic.

We walked into the house to the sight of the nanny frying *her* food in *our* frying pan on *our* kitchen stove. It took a split second to take in the entire scene. Our sincere, repeated inquiries to ensure that the nanny always had the food she needed to alleviate the necessity of having to cook were all, obviously in vain. She had purchased some provisions herself and was using our frying pan and utensils to cook her own food. Not only that, she had fed Esti some of the food. Chaya's Spanish by now was quite good and she managed to communicate our displeasure very well. She explained that it was unacceptable for the nanny to have cooked

180

in our house. She confirmed that the nanny had indeed understood this critical condition explained at the time of her hiring, that under no circumstances was she to bring food items into our home or to cook anything in the kitchen. Chaya asked, upon confirmation of the above, why the nanny had contravened the only rule and condition of employment we had set out in our home. We had been so accommodating, purchasing better food for her than for our family. She had no response except somewhat of a disdained look. It was as if she didn't really care.

That's when I learned something about Chaya I had never known before. To this day, I remain in awe of her composure and conviction. In her broken Spanish, Chaya explained clearly to the nanny that she was fired on the spot. Chaya opened up her purse, produced enough cash to pay her up until that day, as her payday would have been Friday. The nanny had the audacity to ask why she would not be paid for the coming Friday as well – she was insisting on being paid to the end of the week! In a very swift move, Chaya gave her the frying pan and told her she could take that in lieu of her Friday payment. Chaya told her to pack up her belongings and called her a taxi. We never saw her again.

One Sunday, not long after our arrival, we looked at our finances and realised that we would not have enough money to make it through that week. Chaya had driven home one night and, in her heroic efforts to navigate the Houston traffic, got into a fender bender. The damage to our car was negligible. In fact, it wasn't the first time that year that she had been caught in between a few cars on the beltway. Whilst there were some new dents and scrapes on our car, the precious car she hit this time was seeking compensation. Our insurance premiums would be too costly if the driver submitted a claim, so we decided to offer to settle instead. The driver accepted our offer and we felt lucky to have averted an insurance adjustment. The real problem now was the $500 we laid out was the money we would need for our weekly groceries and expenses.

Too proud to ask anyone for help, we decided to gather some belongings and head up to the local pawnshop. The most valuable items that would make an impact in securing additional funds happened to be gold jewellery. After turning in some unsentimental items, we were still short. I looked at Chaya, and she at me. Then I said what perhaps we were both thinking… We will always remember the story, and it will always mean more to sacrifice for each other than to maintain a stranglehold on physical objects. Spiritual is forever, the physical is finite.

I pawned the wedding ring that my father-in-law had made for me. He had made us both matching rings for our wedding. Mysteriously, one of our very first Friday afternoons, Chaya rushed in with barely enough time to shower and gather our things as we were invited to sleep over at the head rabbi and school director's house for *Shabbos*. Chaya put her rings on her watch and closed it to keep them safe, tossed it into the bag, grabbed the last few things and we sped over just in time. Once we had lit *Shabbos* candles and the pressure was off, Chaya pulled the circle of her closed watchband out of the bag. We watched, almost in slow motion as the rings dropped off and rolled in all directions! Somehow, the watch hadn't closed and now the search was on! Frantically we felt the bag, the carpet, reached under the furniture. We found her diamond engagement ring easily. The wedding band was gone forever... Shortly after our wedding, we had taken on the *Chassidic* custom that men don't wear jewellery, so no wedding bands. Especially as Chaya's was gone, it seemed sensible to sell mine to the pawnshop in exchange for some much needed cash. Most likely, a sight he had seen all too often. For us it made an everlasting impression, expressing our commitment to each other beyond physicality. Of course, all they would give me in return would be based on the actual weight of the gold itself. They would be melting down the ring and using it for some other type of jewellery. I don't even remember how much money we got but I do remember the pain in the pit of my stomach, knowing that I never again wanted to be in such a desperate situation to have to sell something in a pawnshop.

Fridays were a short day at school with the arrival of *Shabbos*. I was able to bring Esti home from school, as I was accustomed to. It was my job to cook the Friday night meal, purchase the *Challah*, as well as a fresh cake, and prepare the Saturday afternoon lunch. I had a system and Esti played a part in the weekly ritual. Together we would bond in such an incredible way that year despite her only being three years old; I would come to develop a deep connection with her. To this very day, we reminisce often about the special times we shared together that year.

Once we fired the nanny, Chaya spent hours calling around acquaintances in the community hoping to discover any plausible leads for a new nanny for Monday morning. The Sunday afternoon, when our desperation was reaching fever pitch, our doorbell rang. It was Esti's teacher from across the road. She had heard we were in need of some help and she was offering assistance. She said it would be no trouble to take care of Esti every day after school. It fit so well into her schedule to take Esti home after school. She was more than willing to keep her until I finished teaching and could make it home to pick her up. She also said that she would not, under any circumstances, accept money either. We were so touched by her offer and sincerely thanked her for her assistance. We told her we would only accept her gracious help if we were able to pay something. We could not accept the offer despite having no other options unless she accepted some form of payment. In the end, we came to a compromise.

Without her offer, I don't think we could have actually survived the year. We were so lucky to have someone whom we trusted and with whom Esti had developed such a close connection. After the episode with the nanny, we felt comforted that Esti was in the best hands possible. Truly, it was divine providence. Someone was watching over us.

The Epiphany

I had spoken often to the rabbi's wife. She was the acting Jewish studies principal of the school. Her role was not only to supervise the Jewish studies curriculum, but also to oversee the ethos of the educational institution. The general studies program was supervised by the secular studies principal, which included overseeing the general administration of the school. It was to her that I would report directly.

I walked into quite a relaxed educational environment where my subjects, mathematics, science as well as sport, were not taken seriously. I walked into an environment where the average student gave minimal respect to secular studies, an attitude that was not discouraged by the administration of the school. For many they invested most of their focus and energy on a challenging Jewish studies curriculum. For students in grade eight, this would be their final year living at home in Houston. I soon learned that the Houston community traditionally shipped their children interstate or overseas to pursue higher Jewish studies in high schools, usually in New York, California or Israel. The anticipated mass exodus at the end of Grade 8 affected the entire atmosphere toward education in the lower middle school grades as well. Upon graduation, the students would relocate to the larger Jewish communities with established Jewish high school programs and larger educational infrastructures. The entrance requirements were based more on their Jewish studies achievements than their secular accolades. At that time in that Houston school, secular studies were seen as an unfortunate waste of time that they had to include in the schedule in order to attract students of parents who were more professionally minded or who had themselves grown up with a secular education.

My challenge was to find ways to inspire the unmotivated. My starting point was to learn about each student, his or her personality, interests, strengths, and weaknesses. I was quite excited when my sporting reputation became known in the community news and write-ups appeared in the local newspaper, aimed at promoting the new physical education program in the school. My experience at the school further reinforced my belief that through informal education connections with students, major challenges could be easily overcome and even averted. It turned out that many of the students were extremely bright and very capable. Through sport, I knew I would be able to gain the trust and respect of the boys. Due to the religious nature of the school, the boys and girls would be taught separately for Jewish studies. They had a different curriculum arrangement however for secular studies. With the exception of physical education, they would be combined; though, the girls and boys would sit on separate sides of the classroom.

In order to develop a connection with the girls, I strategically waited a few months before reaching out. I felt that if I could first develop a relationship with the boys, the girls for the most part would take their cues from the boys. If the boys were willing to come along for the ride, the girls would be ready too.

In my science classes, I focused on the core curriculum through its practical applications using experiments. By linking the curriculum to weekly lab experiments, I hoped the students would be much more motivated toward the subject matter. The school was extremely generous in providing me with whatever materials I requested. Before the year began, I developed an extensive materials wish list and to my great surprise and delight, the list was 100% filled.

The students were not accustomed to my homework expectations; actually, they were not accustomed to much secular studies homework at all. Of course, I adopted the system from my legendary physics mentor Mr Maguire. Because I maintained my consistency, I was very quickly rewarded by fewer whines and groans about the daily quiz routine. The students began to enjoy their newly-discovered ability to self-evaluate based on their regular daily assessments. Then they deduced that they had a current, transparent calculation of their own level of achievement including when they were clearly slacking off. I began to make use of the gender card and take advantage of the incredibly competitive atmosphere that was apparent in the classroom between the boys and girls. Before long, I had the students achieving at quite a high level, focused and enjoying their lessons. What had initially been potentially a great concern, connecting to students who were not interested in my subject area, was now not a problem at all. My next step came when I found I could spend my time focusing on ways to make the subject matter more appealing by demonstrating links between scientific theory, mathematics, Jewish philosophy, and *Torah* (scripture).

At the first parent-teacher night, I was overwhelmed by the positive reinforcement from parents who recognized my efforts. Most parents expressed appreciation that their children were coming home excited about mathematics and science. I had very quickly turned around the atmosphere and motivation levels of the classes I was charged to teach. I heard many parents were calling the school's administrative body endorsing their new hire. What initially was an attitude of scepticism on the administrative side of the Jewish studies faculty now became a hot topic of discussion.

It was the first staff in-service day when I had my introduction to the full faculty. I faced the Jewish studies staff consisting foremost of six rabbis. The six of them sat back and just looked at me with a real sense of detachment. I had the feeling that they were somewhat disapproving. It became apparent I was the only male on the staff who had not received rabbinical ordination and was the only male in the room with a formal secular education. Yet, why did I still feel like I had something to prove?

The more I sat there, the more I realised they were the ones who had something to prove. I kept my feelings to myself, but as I sat there, I was amazed at the level of discussion relating to the day's topical in-service focus – classroom management. The main discussion related to the development of consistency and professionalism between the Jewish and secular studies teachers. It was apparent from the discussion led by the acting head Jewish studies teacher/director that there were many issues needing mediation with respect to the teaching staff. The commotion coming from many of the rabbis suggested there was not a lot of buy-in to the need for formality in relation to classroom structure.

The structure soon became evident. Most of the rabbis worked in the school part time to financially subsidize their communal activities and wages. That arrangement qualitatively affected the nature of many of the rabbis' commitment. Now you may or may not be aware that the word "rabbi" means teacher. However, as my experience had borne out yet again, not every rabbi can teach. Some of the rabbis were condescending and I could see the director had her hands full keeping them in line.

It became clear: the rabbis expected the students to behave simply because the subject was Jewish studies. They believed their subject held an implicit level of respect simply due to the nature of the material. The rabbis did not believe it was necessary to develop an atmosphere of mutual respect. They maintained "respect" is one way – student to teacher. I left shaking my head realizing I was truly an anomaly in that school. I kept my mouth shut. It took some effort having come from a

186

tenured department head position to realise my job was not to educate those rabbis. My job was to "keep my nose clean" and do my best by my students behind the closed doors of my classrooms. I needed to impress the secular principal. I would have very little interaction with the Jewish studies staff and the director, or so I thought.

As I looked at my class lists, I quickly discovered the names of the children of the head rabbi and director in two of my classes. It didn't take long to find out that the son was a member of my Grade 7 class and had a reputation of being defiant. He was known for taking advantage of his status and had occasionally displayed quite a temper. I decided I needed to get him onside right away. As it turned out, this was much easier than I thought. An avid sports fan himself, and quite competitive by nature, he had some suggestions on how to improve the class. Right from the get-go I eagerly demonstrated my willingness to take on his valuable insight. I found ways to empower him to the benefit of the class and everyone seemed to be on board. I only had to put him in his place once; I did so fairly and not publicly. I pulled him aside after class, thanked him for his exuberance, and explained that it was my job to ensure things ran appropriately and when I needed him, I would surely ask. I made sure within a short time span, that I did indeed fulfil my promise and seek out his 'advice'.

I was able to make good on my promise within a day or two of our initial conversation. On one of my bicycle rides to the shops, I noticed a vacant field only a block away from the school. I had been instructed to use the paved school parking lot as our field for my physical education classes. On PE days, teachers and staff were not allowed to park in the lot and had to use street parking. This allowed us a substantial area to play on, even though it was an asphalt surface as opposed to grass. The next day at school, I asked the boy to see me after class. What he initially thought would be some reprimand turned out to be my seeking him out for some advice and guidance, given his having grown up in the neighborhood and the community.

I questioned him about the history of the field, why he thought it was so well groomed, and the fact that it was not in use. It also looked like it had some sport equipment set up, but I never saw anyone making use of the premises. He turned out to be a good source for this valuable information. He told me the field belonged to a church and that the premises were often rented out in the evenings by some high school baseball teams.

I decided to be bold and called the church. I eventually got in contact with the administrator who was quite sympathetic to our plight. With true southern hospitality, we were granted full usage rights of the field once a week without any charge. I then sought permission from our Director. I excitedly thanked her son publicly in front of all the other students, for him having made it possible for us to play regularly on a real baseball field during our PE classes.

The real excitement came that first day on the field as we all made the five-minute jog with baseball gloves and bats to the field. An automatic electric baseball-pitching machine was set up on the mound, plugged in, ready for us to use! Baseball helmets and other protective gear had been left on the side for us to use too. For most of the boys, this thrill was beyond their highest expectations. We had one thing in common. Despite coming from diverse religious backgrounds, we were all baseball fans.

We made teams and devised a formal competition bracket. Our baseball game became a highlight of the week. We began our PE in-class baseball competition less than a couple of weeks before some of the rabbis made the trek over to see what all the commotion was about. It seems they were baseball fans too. Before we knew it, some of the rabbis began regularly making the trek out to the sports field. Of course, it was only natural for them to join one of the teams. Then they had the opportunity of bonding with their students over a common passion.

With an eye toward innovation, cooperation, and community support, all of a sudden we had easily found a way to create a single-minded focus toward one moment of the week. This weekly event united the boys. They could leave all their academic pressures behind and play like children together with their mentors. I found myself at times just sitting back taking it all in. How much fun and pleasure the tiny little community was having, engaged in America's favorite pastime, connecting together, students, teachers, mentors all bonding together on the sports field. This is what it was all about. Not necessarily playing sport, but developing relationships through shared interests and experiences. This was what could and most certainly would transfer into the classroom.

For me, the fringe benefits were huge. Slowly, it seemed the faculty, rabbis included, began seeking me out when they were having difficulties with their students. I had only been formally teaching for three years now, but somehow I was seen to have the key to unlocking the relationships between students and teachers. The culture in the school was shifting, and in my small way, I had become a catalyst.

Another way I had found to connect to the staff was through my passion for technology integration. The school had received a donation of 20 new iMacs. When I arrived, it was mainly individual students who were using the computers because they were quite eager to engage with the new media. Most of the teachers were quite technophobic and had pretty much stepped back from even going into the library with their classes where the new multimedia was set up for use.

I, however, saw the iMacs as a great opportunity for my classes. For the most part, the computers were free every period, so I asked permission to move one of the computers into my classroom. Soon I began developing my lessons on my computer and began integrating the curriculum material with technology. I thought about whether I could use an opportunity to offer my services to the staff. I approached the principal to ask if she would like me to develop some staff training activities after school. I developed some very simple easy-to-use spreadsheets demonstrating how to set up this useful software as a teacher grade book, as well as some simple word processing skills, which at the time was quite foreign to most of the teachers. To my surprise, I had the entire secular faculty as well as some of the Judaic staff signed up. I was amazed at their eagerness to learn and my connection to the faculty grew immensely.

A few of the secular teachers asked me to meet one afternoon privately. I was a little nervous about this strange request, not knowing what the reason could be. As I walked into the room, they could see I had the jitters. Right away, they calmed me down. They just wanted to pull me aside and thank me for contributing to such a positive atmosphere in the school. They could never have imagined that an Orthodox man could be so well educated and inspire such an effect in their tiny school. Most of them had been teaching in the institution for many years and did not have the most respect for the rabbis who were teaching on the faculty. Yes, one or two of them were committed teachers, but most had proved pretty transient. They were not emotionally invested in the school and were not seen as valuable contributors. In such a short time, I not only had the respect of my colleagues, in a new city, far from home, I had developed warm relationships with my fellow professionals, and more importantly with the students who valued my presence.

Overall, the students were not seen as an easy group of kids. There was a standing joke that the school secretary needed a separate desk just for the locked drawer full of prescription medication for the majority of the students. Somehow, I had won the respect and admiration of the students and my fellow staff members saw it. My combination of observance and secondary education became such a positive role model for the kids who for the most part only valued their Jewish studies. The teachers began to see a real connection in the student's' minds toward the secular studies and I felt that I had been a catalyst for this change. As a group, they felt that this might not be well received by the Jewish staff. They certainly wanted to pull me aside to both strengthen my resolve and more importantly to thank me.

I was genuinely touched and the overwhelming sentiments lit a spark. For the first time I thought to myself, "So why can't I make a greater change in the grander scheme? Why did it take so long to effect change in this school?" My answer was clear. Because it was one person making the change within his small circle of influence. The only way to make comprehensive change, to build upon the foundation I had developed in this school and effect similar change more globally was... to become a principal myself.

I had seen the admirable efforts of the administrator of the school. She is to this very day an incredible educator who I respect and once in a while still seek out for advice. My viewpoint had taken hold as a seed from the grassroots. All I had done was try to make my classroom interaction the best it could be at every opportunity I had.

I thought I now understood why so many Jewish schools had not succeeded both structurally, but more importantly in the minds of its students. Consistency. Kids intuitively revolt when they encounter contradictions. They thrive on structure and genuine, forthright sincerity. They need to understand the rules and know they will not change mid-game. Jewish schools that understand this simple principle have students who buy in and contribute to the whole. In an atmosphere of conflicting messages, students flounder and challenge the very foundation of the institution's mission statement.

This critical sense of order and uniformity must be embodied, subliminally implemented, through the figurehead of the institution. Having one role model, one leader of the school, who embodies the core values of the institution, both the secular and Jewish studies values, disseminates this consistent message throughout the entire institution. Most Jewish schools usually employ two principals, a rabbi or very religious female Jewish educator who oversees the Jewish studies curriculum and another qualified professional overseeing the secular studies curriculum. I thought back to Elboya, where Gary Jeffrey was running a school with three diverse streams. Yet the goals and mission for all were identical. We all understood this because we could and did look to his leadership. When there are two figureheads how do the students know what and whom to follow? This structure promotes an atmosphere of choice within the minds of the students. The older students get, the more blatant this choosing can become. The subliminal message is implanted very early on in the psyche of the student body, that there is a distinct separation between the two streams. Implicitly there is more value in one aspect of the program or the other. From that point forward, I developed my philosophical outlook that I hold on tightly to this very day. Any and every school, religious or secular, arts or sport school, whatever the special niche, it does not matter. A school must designate one leader, a qualified principal to oversee all the educational programs and streams. It is essential that this individual is not a figurehead in terms of his or her ability to supervise any one component under the purview of the school. In a Jewish context, this principal must be qualified to supervise both the secular and the Judaic curricula of the school.

This led me to the real crux of my epiphany. I thought back to my first staff in-service experience in Houston. I realised in my current situation, I could never truly be accepted as a leader in any Jewish school.

For me to become the leader of a Jewish school and successfully gain the confidence over the entire staff, I needed to become a rabbi. As superficial as it sounds, the lack of title meant that most, if not all, Orthodox Jewish schools would not even look at my resume and consider me as a potential candidate. Credentials were a prerequisite because of the inherent level of respect and recognition that would be associated with that formal rite of passage. I was lacking this critical credential and suddenly I felt a sincere need within myself to "walk the walk." I wanted to be, all of a sudden I needed to become a rabbi, but in the true sense of the word. I wanted to truly earn the title of Rabbi/Teacher. To accomplish this, I would need to upgrade my Judaic knowledge. There was only one place in North America where I could accomplish this task – New York! It would take months for this incubating thought to develop into a full-blown plan. Deep down, I knew this was the next leg of my intended lifelong journey.

Fond Memories of Houston

All of a sudden, it was February! We realised we had to begin making plans for the end of Chaya's internship. It was decision time. All the signs were clear. The results were in. We knew we would be leaving Houston. We looked as best we could into our future, realizing we had yet again arrived at a proverbial fork in the road. It was time to take the next step on our life journey. What we evaluated more so was the present in which we found ourselves. One thing we knew for sure, one year was all we could take living in the southern part of the United States of America. There were many great aspects to the location, being so close to Galveston where we took a remarkable trip. It became our first real holiday since we were married, but living near the Gulf had huge drawbacks.

It didn't take long for us to understand what a huge mistake we made removing the Lizard the first day of our arrival. On the first Friday afternoon, we were all in the kitchen together preparing for *Shabbos*. Esti was hanging around while I was baking a cake. Chaya was preparing the chicken. Out of the corner of my eye – I could not believe my eyes – a giant insect, larger than a length of my hand without taking into account its antennae, started to run toward Esti. We found out they call them tree roaches. It's because they are as big as trees! It was primal but it was a big mistake, both Chaya and I screamed. Of course, this only startled Esti who began to wail. I snatched up Esti and all three of us climbed up on the kitchen table, watching as this Beast circled around us, probably hoping to satisfy its hunger. We could not believe both its size and also the speed with which it moved. Then the negotiations began – who was going to kill it? My incredible fear of insects had been well documented in the first years of our marriage. Chaya knew deep down it was an argument not worth having.

In the end, Chaya climbed down and retrieved the spray, which we had bought the very first day of our arrival. Esti and I just watched, frozen on the table, as Chaya screamed and yelled while running either toward or maybe even away from the Beast. When the insect came in contact with the spray it seemed to freeze, but most certainly did not die. The immunity the insect had to the spray was truly remarkable. From that day forward, I must say I was never truly at peace in our own home. It certainly was not the cleanliness of our house that brought upon the plague of insects. We had a regular cleaner come in for next to nothing to clean. Nevertheless, every week we would have a similar episode. I never got used to it.

A remarkable aspect of that house in Houston was its physical layout. In the middle of the house was a glass atrium. One summer afternoon while I was reading on the couch in the living room, I noticed a strange feeling come upon me, a sense that I was being watched. Such an eerie feeling. I finally looked outside, and on one of the branches from one of the trees in the atrium, I noticed a giant green, camouflaged lizard sitting on one of the branches, watching my every move. I tested that assertion. I actually got up and sauntered across the room. His head moved slightly, following my every gesture. I truly felt like we were in the zoo, only that I was one of the creatures on display.

Once a month it was part of a lease to have the outside of the house fumigated for roaches, fire ants, spiders, and snakes. All this managed to do was deeply confirm my conviction that I was not born to live in Texas. I had a deeply-rooted childhood fear of snakes, so just the idea that they were possibly roaming around in our garden save for this regular extermination, was enough for me never to set foot outside unless I had to.

My fear stems from an incident when I was a little boy living in South Africa. Our friends had a house that backed on to the rocky side of a mountain. A great place for us, as kids, to run and play. One day, I must have been around six years old; I was running around with our friends when I happened upon a pretty large python. Of course, they teach you when you are very, very young and growing up around poisonous reptiles such as the South African deadly snakes that if you encounter one of these killers, do not move an inch. For me, this did not ever make any sense. As a pure survival instinct, I truly lived fright and flight! I quickly turned around and ran as far and as fast as I possibly could, not looking back to see if I was being chased. From that day forward, just mentioning the word snake evokes graphic reptilian nightmares.

So now, you understand. Back in my initial interview at Elboya Junior High, I was asked to consider teaching seventh grade science in order to make up a full-time load. That's why I was willing to risk not getting the job. It was a matter of my survival that I put it all on the line in that initial interview. I looked at the hiring committee and stipulated my one and only major condition. There would be no reptiles or insects as members of my classroom. I expressed my willingness to supervise an excursion to the zoo, but that was the limit of my comfort zone with reptiles. I was honest and it paid off. I obviously got the job, which included the load of two Grade 7 science classes.

Midyear, upholding my original offer, I was obliged to follow through with my commitment to take my two science classes on that excursion to the zoo. Joining the other junior science classes in the school, we all set out for the reptile sanctuary. I confessed my sincere apprehension to some of my co-teachers as well as my students. It is amazing how most people when they hear someone has ophidiophobia, a term only those who actually fear snakes bother to learn, their response usually is to chuckle and think it's cute. It is not cute!

Of course, the best time to visit the zoo and see the wildlife in action is during feeding time. I could not believe what I had gotten myself into as we walked into the reptile house during feeding time! Everyone gathered around the glass enclosure to bear witness to the unconstitutional execution of the defenceless white mice. They were let loose into the large glass 'coliseum' where the hungry python anxiously awaited the arrival of the daily prey.

Everyone stood silently, inhaling and exhaling in unison in anticipation. The tiny mice scampered around attempting futilely to avoid their anticipated fate. Keenly, the spectators edged in closer to get a good view of the impending consumption. My natural instinct was to retreat. Suddenly, one spectator's bag brushed against my leg. The sensation of the object grazing my leg morphed with the visual image of the mice being attacked by the reptilian monster. I was in my own interactive theatre of the terrified! It was enough to cause me to shriek out loud. In my same seven-year-old fight and flight state of panic, I swatted the bag from the lady's hand in one swift motion. The bag flew across the exhibit causing everyone to stare at the new attraction. Guess who had become the main event? With all the students fully aware of Mr. Glogauer's fear, the room erupted in a roar of laughter.

Standing on the kitchen table, paralysed by that same primal fear, I finally realised why we were laughed at when we first arrived. The lizards were the proverbial house pets charged with keeping the homeostatic balance in the domicile. They were the pest control agents engaged to eat these giant intruders.

At times, it felt like the insects were messengers from above – clear signs that we were not meant to be in Houston. We had our radar receptors open to receive the message. It was coming through loud and clear.

It wasn't only the insects and the occasional reptile that provided us with cosmic signs we were not meant to settle long-term in Houston. The oppressive heat was much more than I could handle. Riding my bike to school every day with Esti in the child's bicycle seat in 100% humidity and 100°F heat was oppressive to say the least. Everyone else went on heightened alert each time a tropical storm warning was broadcast; for me this was welcome news. The tropical depression that soon followed provided significant albeit only brief relief from the extreme heat and humidity.

Really, these were just mere physical conditions that, whilst close to unbearable, paled in comparison to the emotional conditions. Financially, we were struggling from day to day. This was not something we were used to, nor was it something we wanted to get used to. My family had been so stressed over money and making ends meet my entire childhood. When we had reached that desperate state, the symbolism of having to sell my wedding ring in order to scrape a few more dollars together, had a profound effect on our decision of whether or not we would raise our family in Houston. We were young and, hopefully, a growing family looking for something more in the community which Houston was not providing. The signs were pointed in the direction of leaving, as something greater seemed to be beckoning us away.

Chaya and I were both in sync. We knew I had unearthed a deeper calling. Suddenly I had discovered in myself a fundamental drive to change the status quo of Jewish education. We both realised very early on – the only way for me to achieve this lofty goal would be to obtain a higher level of influence through acquiring the prominence of rabbinical ordination. As a rabbi, I would have my "Jewish" credentials. I would be taken much more seriously than if I were to have just secular credentials alone.

It would be difficult to achieve this monumental accomplishment. We were both committed to the direction our journey seemed to be taking us. It would be necessary for me to begin on the ground level of the Jewish learning ladder. The most logical place for us to begin our odyssey would be an intensive year, studying full time, refreshing my skills, and picking up new ones in a *yeshiva*, before even contemplating entering a rabbinical ordination program. We had some prior knowledge of a program that seemed perfect for us. My sister and brother-in-law had recently relocated to such a community with a tailor-made rabbinical program that would suit our needs.

The program was run out of the Rabbinical College of America in Morristown, New Jersey. There were several tracks of learning within the college including the opportunity to upgrade my skills. Once successful, I could transfer into the Rabbinical Ordination program. We had direct access to the rabbinical admissions officer through the connection with my brother-in-law and of course our close rabbinical adviser back in Calgary. After an initial conversation between our rabbi and the rabbinical admissions officer, I made phone contact. The conversation was very positive and I was instructed to make a formal written request. My hopes were high on account of his enthusiasm and positive response to both my phone call and that of our Calgary rabbi.

We were so positive we began to look at possible accommodation in New Jersey. Not a week went by; before we knew it, I received an envelope in the mail from the Rabbinical College of America. I thought the letter would contain the official application. Instead, it was brief and blunt. It was an outright rejection from the College Dean before we even got started. My parents happened to be visiting my sister in New Jersey that week. On my behalf, they requested a meeting with the dean seeking an understanding of why I had been rejected before even having officially applied.

Something clearly seemed a little fishy. After that meeting, the muddy waters became much clearer. At first, the dean made an excuse that our inability to afford full tuition was the basis of our rejection. On the spot, my father committed to personally undertaking to cover the difference between our levels of income and the remaining financial gap. Then the truth really came out. There had been a conversation with my current employer in Houston. It seemed there had been less than a glowing endorsement. It came as quite a shock to us. We had not even made an application. Another lesson learned the hard way. The close-knit, insular connection, the 'old boys club' had denied us this opportunity to gain entrance through the fraternity's front door.

I had indeed disclosed to some of the teachers that I would be leaving Houston to embark on the process of obtaining my rabbinical ordination. I was quite surprised by the response I received. Instead of being greeted by support for this life-altering decision, many of the rabbis presented me with quite a negative response. Each rabbi had his own unique personal reason for trying to dissuade me from taking the pathway toward obtaining this milestone. "You don't need to be an officially titled rabbi to

196

run a school;" or "People don't become rabbis for employment;" or "We learn Torah for the sake of Torah, not to gain employment." All of these reasons made sense on their own merit, but I couldn't help feeling like roadblocks were being set unfairly.

The ones throwing reasons at me for not becoming a rabbi were the rabbis themselves. Deep down I knew no Orthodox school would hire me to run their institution if I did not have my rabbinical ordination. This experience just strengthened my resolve. Don't tell Arnie Glogauer something is impossible for him. I knew I would have to fight through many roadblocks if I was to achieve this new goal. I wanted to learn for rabbinical ordination through a *Chabad* rabbinical institution, or find another mechanism through a non-Chabad program and receive the ordination. This was the ticket that would allow me to achieve my dream, to become the principal of a Jewish school and alter the program significantly to do things right – I wanted the opportunity to develop a school that valued and set equal, consistent standards both in Jewish studies and secular studies. The only way to accomplish this would be to have one headmaster, one leader, one principal presiding over the entire institution. His role would be to mend the divide in the school, unite two schizophrenic institutions, discover the commonality in the inconsistent vision and begin the process of establishing governance by a unified value system. The paradigm shift would be to support one head, one vision, one school governance system overseeing the entire educational institution.

The road to becoming a Jewish school principal would be paved with huge bureaucratic obstacles. Once I made the conscious decision that this was my desired albeit ambitious journey, I realised before I even set out on the path, that neither having attended a traditional Orthodox Jewish school, nor having had the appropriate background from birth would be a tremendous impediment to obtaining the necessary certification for becoming an Orthodox rabbi. I know, now as you are reading you are asking, what's the big deal? Everyone is doing this. Coming back to their Jewish roots and then rising to the highest levels in the 'ranks'. There are now a myriad of choices in a mere twenty years since I was forging this path. Clearly, at that point, I was tapped into a vision that was ahead of the times.

I knew there were indeed a few other individuals with similar backgrounds to myself, who had succeeded in obtaining their rabbinical ordination from *Chabad* institutions. It would just be a matter of committing myself to upgrading my skills and persevering through the red tape. We began again attempting to determine the best institution to

197

upgrade my skills. Ultimately, that choice would be a significant decision affecting our entire family. Sacrifices would be made that would change the lives of Chaya, Esti and me.

The most significant realization was of course our commitment that, for the next two years, my presence as the mainstay of the family financial unit would considerably change. In order to commit myself 100% to upgrading my learning, I would immerse myself for all the waking hours in my studies. This would mean that Chaya would become the sole financial support of our family. It would be up to her to temporarily assume the burden of financially supporting our young family.

At the conclusion of Chaya's internship, we made the decision to leave Houston. We put out feelers in the next most logical location for pursuing my dream – New York. A major challenge was obviously securing full-time employment for Chaya. Not having many contacts or avenues to pursue, we nevertheless decided to take the plunge and move to Brooklyn without any job prospects secured. We realised we would have to tough things out for a while but we remained positive, keeping our eye on the bigger picture. We had minimal savings to tide us over the foreseeable difficult few months until Chaya would be able to secure a solid prospect, a full-time job. She had a few promising interviews lined up which could certainly provide the minimum income we would need to survive through my intended two-year study program. We had made the determination that I would upgrade my skills for a full year and then seek out a *Kollel* or rabbinical ordination program that would provide me with the background necessary to study for and receive my rabbinical ordination.

Looking back at our plan, we were so blessed that we did not see how naïve and simplistic we were being. A lot of steps would need to fall into place for this plan to become a reality, most of which were beyond our control. Once again, Chaya was the one who made the scouting mission. She travelled to Brooklyn ahead of our arrival with the aim of securing employment. Without any firm employment commitments, she nevertheless managed to secure at least a rental accommodation. At least she had landed some solid interviews ahead of our intended arrival from Texas.

Packing up our life in Houston was quite a cathartic experience. We knew from that first September that Houston was not going to be the community for us. We left after a year and a week. When the events that led to our having been rejected from the Rabbinical College of America in Morristown, New Jersey, were revealed, we believed this was indeed 'cosmic' confirmation we were making the right decision. We were pursuing a vision. We were steadfast in our commitment. The goal was clear. I was becoming a rabbi, and I was becoming a principal of a Jewish school.

The Vision is Born

I had seen with my own eyes how an inconsistent administrative model in an educational environment affected the attitudes of the students toward their learning. As much as the administrators tried fooling themselves that they were able to insulate the students from the internal struggles around developing a consistent voice, both in the establishment of educational policy and structure, inconsistencies nevertheless crept in which had an adverse effect on the program and ultimately the students' development.

This type of school cannot run with two principals in the same way that a body cannot function with two brains. As soon as the school sends a message that there is a General Studies Principal and a Jewish Studies Principal, students automatically seek understanding and direction from one of the leaders in an effort to understand who is the ultimate decision maker. This forces pressure on the institution to establish a hierarchy, choosing one dominion over the other. Therefore, one department automatically presides over another. Teachers deep down understand that one leader has more authority than the other. In times of necessity, resources would be allocated according to the subliminal judgment of value and the same hierarchy would thus determine staffing. Teachers entering the institution would need to fall into rank and-file, assuming their rightful role within the system. Their attitude would eventually mimic those of the student body, settling into their rightful niche within the pecking order of the educational structure. Students' attitudes toward homework and assessments, even behavior toward teachers would mimic the order of importance represented in the chain of command.

In most Orthodox schools in North America, Jewish studies will prevail, with the focus on secular studies being more of a subordinate program. Day schools struggle to promote topnotch results in an effort to demonstrate a face-value support for societal values of secular learning. With second-rate teaching staff and a lack of support financially toward the development of a general studies program, students and parents often see right through the fraudulent system being presented to them on a silver platter. Ironically, it seems the optimal way for both Judaic and secular studies to be shown equal value is for there to be one champion of both causes, allocating equitable resources to both programs.

The ideal is one voice, a role model who espouses the virtues of both systems, who consistently and evenly allocates resources, efforts, and energies to a transparent vision of equality. There needs to be a leadership model, unwavering in its commitment toward the pursuit of excellence. Only under these conditions – hope exists for a new generation. This model consists of one head, one vision, the one captain maintaining the direction of the ship toward the vision, altering the course whenever the currents threaten to shift direction toward one divergent path or another. This leader presents a new hope for the students of the Jewish learning community. The students in a school such as this would have the best of both worlds, two halves complementing each other, offering opportunity and well-rounded potential without compromise.

This was the model I believed could be developed if given the chance. It would need buy-in from some visionaries who shared my optimism that we could create this new model. First, I needed to obtain the credentials that would open the door to the Jewish world, allowing me to present my idea from a position of strength. I knew I needed to be perceived as an insider, not coming as a critic from the outside. If I were one of 'them' they would be more likely to listen, as opposed to me being a foreigner trying to convince them I had something worthwhile to sell. I innocently and quite naïvely thought that the key to the treasure chest was the rabbinical ordination and what it represented. Thus, I pushed forward despite the many voices around me persistently trying to shut me out.

Having been shut out of one path toward rabbinical ordination through the *Chabad* system in New Jersey, we came up with an alternative means that would hopefully result in the same outcome. As is the way, this apparent obstacle turned out to be the biggest blessing, once again. Having learned before in *yeshiva* in Brooklyn, I was keenly aware of my learning deficiencies and the necessary skills and knowledge I needed in order to progress appropriately to obtain my ordination. Chaya and I agreed that the most logical move would be to Brooklyn, enrolling in a program that would enable me to bridge my learning gaps. After a full year of this learning, we would re-evaluate our situation.

I was aware of other men who had enrolled in *Hadar Ha Torah*, a *yeshiva* founded to teach boys and men how to reconnect to their Jewish roots. I had attended the program for a significant amount of time four years prior during two of my university breaks between the spring and fall semesters, a four-month hiatus. I had developed a good relationship with both the head rabbi and the administrator of the institution. All it took was one phone call and an explanation of my goal. With the confirmation of my reference, our rabbi in Calgary, I was accepted into the full-time learning program. In a long conversation, I explained my goal of taking the year to upgrade my skills and my strong desire to transfer into the official rabbinical ordination program in the affiliated educational stream through the international headquarters of *Chabad Lubavitch* known as 770.

I was gently told not to focus on the end goal and that there would be no guarantee of an endorsement. All they could provide was the commitment on their part to assist my growth. It didn't take long to realise that the philosophy of the institution was not to develop rabbis, but to enhance a strong Jewish commitment and love of learning. This atmosphere was exactly what I needed for my learning. There was no doubt that this was a valuable year of upgrading my general skills. However, in terms of my goal, I would be totally on my own, building a path alone up a huge mountain against many obstacles. We decided to forge ahead, knowing the challenges yet certain that we would, one way or another, achieve our goal. There was just no way we could not succeed, because this was my purpose. As we looked back, we realised every decision I had made in life had led me to this path. I came to believe any obstacle placed in front of me was just one more test to pass, demonstrating, upon my successful completion, that this was indeed my chosen path, my destiny.

Chaya, having returned from her scouting mission in Brooklyn, came back with minimal, positive outcomes. The agreement of my acceptance into the *yeshiva* was based on my full year commitment to following the fixed schedule and timetable. It was quite unusual for someone in my position to join the program, given the fact that I had been married for six years, had a child, and was, therefore, not going to be living in the dormitory like the rest of the student body. Because of my status in America as a 'resident alien', the *yeshiva* could not access funding for me through grants. Thus Chaya would have to work full-time in order to provide income to cover rent, expenses and the cost of education for Esti, who was now three years old and starting 'kindergarten', at least in New York. The *yeshiva* understood our financial predicament, and we paid a minimal monthly fee. The benevolent philosophy of the institution allowed me to be part of the program, welcoming me every day with open arms.

Thus, we signed a year rental contract in the only accommodation Chaya could find. We decided, despite the lack of a job, nevertheless to take the bold leap and forge ahead, securing movers. Chaya tried to describe the rental market in Crown Heights and seemed very apologetic for having signed the lease, explaining that this was the only property she could find. Seeing no real choice, again we saw it as just one more test. We continued to focus on the possibilities and positivity the future held. I had given formal notice to the school administration in Houston. The school-parent body and students threw a lavish goodbye party for us all. In just one year, we had made a lasting impression on the school and students.

It started very early on in the year. Every *Shabbos* afternoon, students would gather in our home to hang out, play games, and sample my legendary chocolate cake and just chat. Our family had been a source of connection and understanding for the students to get together, share challenges of the day-to-day, talk about the present and hypothesize about the future. Many school and community initiatives that year were born from our *Shabbos* afternoon get-togethers.

One of the most memorable was the end of the year trip to San Antonio. One of the year seven students casually mentioned never having left the Houston city limits. To me this was just unfathomable. As a group, we knew we just had to change this for her benefit. In just one get-together, we had set in motion the plans for a full school fund-raising carnival on the Jewish holiday of *Purim*. We organized a silent auction with student-solicited donations from local stores around the neighborhood. Before we knew it, we had raised enough money to rent a van, secure entrance fees to SeaWorld for each student and more exciting than anything, approval from the school administration for our end of the year trip. To this day, I am in touch with many of the graduates of the school. One of the first memories they all share is that end of the year trip when the entire seventh and eighth grade classes all travelled together for a day at SeaWorld, San Antonio.

The success of the event was not the details of developing a once-in-a-lifetime trip for students who had never left the city limits, neither was it how they developed the skills to plan and execute a major school event. As we sat each Saturday afternoon with the students relaxing in what we hoped was our nurturing *Shabbos* afternoon environment, I learned the importance for students to have an outlet where they could openly discuss the issues they were encountering as adolescents without being judged by adults. It was important to initially communicate clear boundaries for respectfully sharing information and what topics were inappropriate for that forum. Most importantly, I realised that these students needed a non-judgmental sounding board, a person who could offer advice without ramming morality down their throats. It came out that many of them felt judged by their parents and were quite uncomfortable sharing their challenges for fear of being misunderstood. They avoided ramifications from their "old-fashioned" parents who simply could not understand what it was like to grow up in the "modern" world. Most felt isolated, citing an inability to gain advice and perspective from mentors or trusted advisers.

By opening our home to the students without any preconceived judgements, we had become these trusted sounding boards. Through active listening and within our safe, respect-oriented parameters, students felt comfortable to share their issues. Our environment was open but we were clear that there were still boundaries. One could not talk negatively of others, be they in the room or not. Everyone had to respect the ideas of their peers and allow a dissenting opinion with the right to politely object.

I looked forward to these get-togethers, and as the year progressed, our *Shabbos* afternoons became a very popular hangout. The last *Shabbos* before we departed for New York, we had a large turnout. The house was packed with students from near and far, making the trek on a very hot and humid August day to share fond memories and experiences of what had been an incredible year…and one week. From this aspect of our sojourn in Houston, I realised even more potently the impact informal education could have on developing relationships with students. It seemed that there was a growing need for opportunities like this for the developing youth of today.

All packed up, the moving company left the Sunday morning with all our possessions neatly jammed together in a large moving truck. We travelled ahead by car, arriving a day before in order to gain access to our apartment. In many ways, I was quite nervous, not because of the huge learning bridge I needed to cross, but more so from the financial risk we were taking. With only a three-month cushion, we needed Chaya to find full-time employment soon. Basically, our survival depended on it.

We pretty much drove nonstop. Leaving Houston, we drove through Louisiana, Alabama, Tennessee, North Carolina, Virginia, Delaware, and New Jersey into New York State. By now, Esti had become an excellent traveller. With her car seat snuggled between suitcases and other essential articles we would need to tide us over until our packed items arrived midweek, we were able to make it in relatively good time. With only one overnight stay in Nashville, Tennessee, breaking the journey in half enabled us to make it into Brooklyn by late Monday evening. We immediately drove to the rental that would become our home for the next year. We eagerly anticipated our new location and the opportunity it represented.

Big Apple, Huge Expectations

My mother's question, when I informed her of my decision to leave the Faculty of Management and Bachelors of Commerce program for the Faculty of Education, reverberated in my mind once again. It was haunting me during this transitional time: "How are you going to provide for your family as a teacher?" It was a mantra now embedded in my psyche. I encouraged its presence, more so to provide myself with the challenge that indeed. I could and would be the provider as the stereotypical male breadwinner. However, was I going to achieve that, and do exactly what I wanted as a career choice? Just as I had the first time round, landing myself the amazing position at Elboya, I would find a way to market myself into a niche that would secure the financial stability my family needed. A niche still permitting me to do what I enjoyed most, connecting to our youth, teaching them, providing them with solutions to the same problems and challenges I had when I was growing up. As you know, when I was growing up in school almost no one offered me any plausible options or solutions. Why should anyone else have to go through what I already had? If I could shine a light and help even one student not to have to go through the trials and tribulations I did, then my life purpose, my accomplishments would have been worthwhile in the grander picture.

The feelings of helplessness, the feelings of dependency; no one should have to feel so inadequate. If someone understood how to navigate these emotions, how different and empowered the self-reliant student could be. It was all about building self-esteem. I had a few teachers who did exactly this for me and thus I had a few role models from whom I realised I could do the same for others. I have been fortunate to witness times when teachers successfully reach students. Now I wanted to accomplish this with more than just a few students in my own classroom.

I was aiming for a bigger platform where I could connect to more students in need. From my discussions with students, I could see that many were disenfranchised with their schooling. Most felt like the teachers didn't care about them individually. Many students felt their teachers were self-centred, paycheck grabbers, unmotivated robots going through the motions – teaching the subject matter, not the students. I could change all of that if I were a principal. I could choose who was in charge of the classrooms in my school, empowering and motivating our students. I would have more impact determining who was connecting and shaping our youth. More importantly, I would have the ability to remove those who were not up to that challenge. These were the dreams that occupied my mind while driving from Texas to New York and whilst we settled ourselves into life in Brooklyn as best we could. For now, I was placing myself back in the starting block where I had to pay my dues once again. There were hoops to jump through and I realized quickly that I was walking into a system that was not very welcoming. I was an outsider and from the very beginning was not encouraged in the least. It was an elitist group and membership was a birthright.

To become a principal of a Jewish school, an Orthodox school, I needed rabbinical ordination. I was now categorized as a *Chabad Lubavitcher*, though not having been born into a *Chabad Lubavitch* family. I was not considered observant until the age of eighteen. Despite having been given the green light to study in a *yeshiva* that would technically upgrade my skills so that one day I theoretically could become a rabbi, there were many steps beyond that until this goal came to fruition. At first, I thought it was just because the information, religious background and vast knowledge was all too much for someone to gain in a short amount of time. I had given myself an ambitious target of two years to obtain this spiritual milestone. I learned no one would understand and appreciate my determination, so I started to keep the goal to myself. Having once made a critical error of sharing my goal, wanting to study for the sake of an *extrinsic* goal, most of the rabbis involved in the *yeshiva* were openly not impressed with my stated motives.

In my initial phone call to the head of the *yeshiva*, where I had requested permission to study full-time under his tutelage, he had been very clear that I would be following the standard course of study which would provide me with general learning skills of classical texts, the *Talmud*, the *Shulchan Aruch* and traditional *Chassidic* philosophy known as *Chassidus*. Since it was a *Chabad Lubavitch* institution, the study of *Chassidus* was part and parcel of the curriculum. The *yeshiva* was in the business of awakening the mindset of the Jewish masses. There is an intrinsic value in learning for the sake of learning. Whilst I understood that and respected it deeply, I had both goals in mind.

207

I felt very isolated, with the exception of the head of the *yeshiva*. I found it difficult developing any rapport with the other teachers. I therefore made every effort to ingratiate myself toward the main rabbi and ensure I was in every one of his classes, regardless of the level. I felt he was a role model from whom I could learn a great deal, not only knowledge but also from his teaching style. He was intent on pushing his students beyond their comfort zone and through the unspoken established hierarchy in his main *Talmud* class, the highest learning level in the *yeshiva*. Students were very motivated to climb the "ladder" and push themselves beyond their self-imposed boundaries.

When I arrived the first day in the *Yeshiva,* he met me with a great smile, making me feel instantly welcome. Even though I had not seen him in over three years, I felt like it was just yesterday when I left. The first time we met, we had come on a winter retreat in 1990 just after Chaya and I had gotten married. I had returned, rejoining the *yeshiva* in 1991 and 1992 for three months of my university' summer break. I had demonstrated my commitment to learning, having left Chaya those two summers to engross myself in the full-time study program, with the goal of upgrading my background and skills. At the time, I had earned a reputation of being a dedicated student. Those first important moments of reintegration this time in the learning program demonstrated quickly to all the onlookers that I had continued to learn over the years, despite not having been in a formal learning setting for quite some time.

I was told I would be given the benefit of the doubt and a good start in the top *Talmud* class. I was introduced to my study partner, Yehoshua. Yehoshua was a young, energetic student, eager to learn and navigate his way through the maze and complexities of the Jewish Orthodox world. In the *yeshiva* world, specifically the subculture of the youth who were intent on re-establishing their Jewish roots, many personal challenges arose. Perhaps the biggest was the need to establish connections in one's newly-chosen environment. No two *yeshiva* boys have the same story or reason for disconnecting themselves from their peer groups and families back home, embarking on a discovery mission of personal refinement. For some, it was to fulfil a personal need and desire to belong to a group, where back home, they may have been a loner. For others it was legitimate soul-searching, a sort of spiritual walkabout, seeking personal meaning in the larger picture of life. Sometimes, associating with a group of like-minded spiritual seekers enhanced personal meaning, and motivated individual growth and knowledge by pushing one's self-imposed limitations. Those who were open to confronting one's preconceived notions, receptive to examining one's paradigm, possessing courage to redefine one's borders and shaping one's personal mission statement: these students represented the "good fit" in the *yeshiva* system.

In fact, these aforementioned qualities have become what I look for in teachers, both veterans and new, young professionals. Teachers must have the ability to be open to paradigm shifting. If they are steadfast in their philosophies and unwavering, they lose the ability to grow along with their students. We say that teachers need to be lifelong learners. For me, that not only means being well versed in the upcoming pedagogy and conversant with new teaching methodologies. It's about being receptive to influences that may challenge one's personal paradigm or philosophy. The easiest way to observe these forces in action occurs when a teacher is confronted or challenged. Whether the source of confrontation is a student, parent, or faculty member, whether the issue has the potential to shatter the teacher's paradigm, one only needs to observe the teacher to gauge their reaction. Is the teacher's response defensive? Is the retort motivated to fortify personal boundaries and raise impenetrable barriers? Or does the professional absorb the new information, allowing it to shift or add new dimensions and layers to their flexible paradigm? The teacher's reaction tells me a lot about how they relate to their students. After all, how do we expect students to function in a classroom? Each and every day, the learning experience is designed to challenge students to grow, gaining knowledge, and skills. Through maintaining a grasp on the bigger picture, as teachers, we are assisting each student in defining and redefining his or her personal 'mission statement'. A teacher has the power to guide students in developing an understanding of the world around them, encouraging them to be open to change without feeling that their personal existence is being threatened. Teachers are there to support students through the times when new knowledge has the ability to completely overturn a student's perspective.

There was an additional segment of the student population in the *yeshiva* system. Students who superficially fit into the system distinguished this other tier. They were filled with the desire of needing to belong to something larger than themselves, seemingly because they could not fit into their own perceived or self-imposed paradigms. These were the students who toed the party line, regurgitated the spiritual taglines without ever having truly probed their personal relevance. The need to accept every custom and hold fast to the party line could tangibly be felt within the person. However, this apparent strictly zealous observance usually originated out of fear that 'membership' in the group could at any time be revoked. This, of course, was an illusion of that individual's core insecurity.

At times below the surface within the *yeshiva* system, there is significant conflict between these two groups of students--those who are truly a "good fit" versus those who are searching for somewhere to "fit in." This is specific to *yeshivas* that are geared toward students "returning back to their roots" called "*Baal Teshuva*" institutions such as the one in which I had enrolled.

We came to *Lubavitch* quite by accident when we were introduced to the university campus rabbi in Calgary on the Jewish holiday of *Purim*. This was a few months before our wedding in 1990. We immediately struck up a personal friendship with him, his wife, and their two children at the time. It was impossible not to, given his true, deep sincerity and warmth. As a wedding gift, he organized for us to spend two weeks in the December break at this very same *yeshiva* in New York. They had a winter program designed for university students called "*Yeshiva-cation.*" Chaya learned at the parallel women's program.

We found it a very positive experience and quite inspirational. We had the privilege to meet the spiritual leader of the movement – the *Lubavitcher Rebbe*, Rabbi Menachem Mendel Schneerson, and thus our spiritual journey began. Unlike many newcomers, we took baby steps in our growth, seeking understanding and personal relevance at each fork in the road. We were lucky to have each other, husband and wife, to openly develop significance and mutual direction together. Not only that, we had the 'good fortune' of being connected to incredible role models who guided our journey, step by step.

From the moment I met Yehoshua, I knew this match would enable me to significantly and successfully meet my ultimate goal. His thirst for knowledge and ability to push me in my learning quest was exactly what I needed. From the first day, we struggled with a textual passage and instead of taking the easy way out, seeking guidance from the rabbi for his interpretation; he pushed us to try to decipher the solution on our own. There were many days of frustration. Yehoshua was steadfast, and at times unwavering in his openness to any opinion contrary to his own. I kept coming up against his stubbornness, specifically in his inability to admit when he was incorrect. This drove me insane at first. When I confidentially approached the rabbi after one frustrating confrontation, he told me to look within myself to see perhaps if there was a deficiency within me that I hadn't recognized. He suggested that I needed to put energy into improving myself rather than trying to change someone else.

This philosophical lesson served me incredibly well. I have yet to perfect this personal attribute, but it has given me a lot of perspective in frustrating times. I go back to it time and again, especially when dealing with parents or teachers who are persistent and unwavering. I know when an issue is so intense, where there appears to be no compromise, I have to agree to disagree and look within myself for a personal lesson. This "win-win" philosophy, as described by Dr Stephen Covey, encompasses this principle for effective long-term relationships, particularly those founded upon mutual respect and mutual benefit.

Yehoshua's steadfast commitment enabled me to set a rigid learning schedule. Confidence that I had someone to rely on who was equally focused and unwavering was very welcome. Yehoshua quickly became part of our family and most nights would eat dinner with us. Knowing the food quality at *yeshiva*, this was, to him, a huge benefit of our relationship. I started each day at 7 am learning *Chassidic* philosophy for an hour, which then led to prayers from 8 am to 9 am. Prayers would last just over an hour. There was an hour allocated for breakfast. The remaining part of our day was focused on Talmudic study. With the exception of *Shabbos*, our study timetable of formal learning ran consistently six days a week. We attended a ninety-minute *Talmud* class. An hour review session with our study partners immediately followed the class as a means of solidifying the main content of the lesson. There were some classes scheduled midday but the main intent of the timetable was to provide ample opportunity to review the main *Talmud* lesson, and to prepare the new section to be learned in that ninety-minute lesson the following day.

Each day, one student chosen at random would teach the class the prepared lesson under the careful, close scrutiny of the Rabbi. If a false assumption, misinterpretation, inaccurate translation, or improper annotation of the Aramaic text was presented, immediately the student was corrected on the spot and coldly prompted to continue. It was impersonal, confronting, and challenging. We would all sit around the large table at the beginning of the class, eagerly waiting for the rabbi to arrive after his breakfast at home. Upon his entrance, the entire student body would immediately stand at attention as a sign of respect. With anticipation filling the air, in unison we students would all take our seats in a well-choreographed performance, silently waiting for him to nominate the lesson's student leader.

It was an unspeakable honour to be nominated to lead the lesson. It was a direct confirmation that the rabbi had confidence in that student's ability to meet his expectations in the delivery of the content. At times, it was also a sign that the student was coasting along, in need of a gentle prod to pick up the slack and learn a little harder. It was never meant to embarrass someone. Although if someone was not ready but agreed to lead the class, if he was struggling but making an effort, the rabbi would see that and help him out. However, if someone were on the egotistical side, showing off in front of the class through their ease of comprehension of the material or their dominance of the lesson, he would challenge them through the content of the lesson and engage them to the fullest. His knowledge was unsurpassable and no one ever got the better of him one-on-one in an intellectual debate. He knew the level of each student and we were drawn not only to do our best but also seek his approval at the same time. How he felt about us personally was significant to the growth of each student. We all respected him greatly and realised that to be accepted by him was a personal vote of confidence toward our character and essence of our being.

He had an unspoken seating arrangement around the table. His most capable students sat closest to him. Graduations, seat shuffling usually occurred at the end of the spring semester or at the summer relocation to the Catskill Mountains. At those times, everyone would vie for the coveted spots, but you had to deserve the honour of sitting closer to the rabbi. Of course, the closer you were to the head of the table meant you would be called on more often to lead the class. It was an unwritten expectation, a responsibility accompanying the privilege. The more success, the better one prepared the class and led the daily lesson. The more positive recognition a student received, the more respect showered upon the student by his peers. No one was ever jealous of the success students achieved through their learning. The envy only inspired more motivation.

It was Yehoshua's goal to be ready to lead the class each and every day. He would boldly raise his hand when he was sure we had prepared well the day before. As the year moved on, Yehoshua began nominating me, due to my reluctance and shyness to ever raise my hand. I was very hesitant at first. I was almost angry. My study partner throwing me under the bus!? When the rabbi heard that my name was raised as a possible leader, he immediately smiled and said, "Okay, let's go for it". The first time, despite stumbling a little, with his assistance and encouragement, I succeeded in leading the entire class. As the year progressed, I became more and more proficient in my studies thanks to my visionary and ambitious study partner.

There were many sacrifices living in Brooklyn. Our landlord lived upstairs from us on the second floor of a Brooklyn brownstone. The main floor of the house had been cut off from the rest of the house. Not only that, the living/dining area was closed off too. The landlord said they were renovating it for the family, so we had crammed into a tiny ground floor 'half a house' with the entirety of our belongings. Thus, our potential living area had been divided in half. Our apartment consisted of an eat-in kitchen, one bathroom, a main bedroom and two tiny rooms – one a bedroom for Esti, the other for our piano and storage.

Our access to our 'apartment' was through the driveway where we were allowed to park our car if the neighbors didn't get there first. The first come, first served basis was quite a source of irritation with the alternate street-side parking and street cleaning days during the regular week in Brooklyn. On our first Friday afternoon in Brooklyn, we read all the signs and parked our car on the street completely legally until the end of *Shabbos* Saturday evening. When we arrived home from Saturday morning services, we saw some white papers flapping under our front windscreen wiper. As we got closer, we recognized not one, or even two…five parking tickets flapping in the wind! It was a bit hard to have a restful *Shabbos* with the unshakeable horror of so many traffic tickets on our car at once!

After *Shabbos*, we retrieved the tickets. We couldn't decide whether to laugh or cry when we found the most insane reasons for the ticketing of our car. Tickets for lack of New York State emission inspection, lack of New York State license plate, improperly placed license plate just to name a few. I took the tickets up the street to the police station the next morning with photos of our car, indicating clearly in plain sight that indeed we did not have New York plates but that our car was fully registered in the state of Texas with proper out-of-state plates and valid Texas emission stickers. I was stonewalled and told to send my documentation into the New York State Comptroller with the same explanation.

The 'Welcome to New York Weekend' continued. We were schedule to take a drive later that same day. Now these were the old days, long before cell phones and GPS. We attempted to follow my sister in her car to meet her parents-in-law in New Jersey. Well, they made the light to get onto the Brooklyn Bridge, but it turned yellow as we were attempting not to lose them! We were caught following her onto the Brooklyn Bridge through the yellow light that had changed so quickly; before we knew it we received a $250 fine from the police cruiser who appeared to be waiting for the Glogauers to come along and make their day. In one weekend, we felt like we met every New York policeman's ticket quota for the month, perhaps the year! It took three full months to hear back from the New York State Comptroller. All of those *Shabbos* parking tickets were successfully reversed, but with only three months financial savings to keep us going, the time was approaching when we were close to exhausting all of our resources, as Chaya had yet to secure a full-time job.

Chaya had sent out a lot of feelers and had written her resume to diversify her skill set to maximize opportunities for employment. One of her opportunities was to support a therapist in his practice in Borough Park. He was willing to take Chaya on after September. One of his additional side jobs was the Secular Studies Principal at a local ultra-Orthodox boy's school where he was always in need of teachers. Chaya told him I was a teacher. Due to our desperate financial predicament, I approached him. He was willing to hire me on the spot to teach secular studies in the afternoon.

There was the agreement I had made with the head of the *yeshiva* that I would commit myself to studying for the entire day. We realised we had unwittingly underestimated our financial situation. We were motivated by our firm philosophical commitment not to go on welfare or food stamps. I had no choice but to seek out a part-time job that fit into the study schedule of *Yeshiva*.

When I first called from Texas about coming and studying full-time, the administration of the *yeshiva* was somewhat reluctant and hesitant for the reasons that had just come into play. Their valid concerns related to my ability to financially support my family and how that might affect my level of commitment, giving the additional burdens, which were not prevalent in a single student's situation.

From 2 pm to 4 pm the *yeshiva* students engaged in individual study time. This period allowed for consolidation and review of the day's material. In addition, most *yeshiva* students engaged in some type of outreach program. Our *Yeshiva* was an active recruitment centre for the well-documented "New York City Public School Release Time Program." Young *yeshiva* students volunteered their time, going into public schools teaching uninformed students about Judaism. I met with the head of the *Yeshiva* and explained our financial predicament. I promised that I would keep up with my studies. I proposed that I would not participate in the "release time period." This would allow me to take on a part-time teaching position to bring in additional income. I would be able to teach from 3 pm until 6 pm, returning in time for the night-time study period.

The head of the *Yeshiva* agreed to my proposal. I must say that I was always very impressed with his understanding of my predicament.

Ultra-Orthodox Education – Welcome to the Ghetto

Life was tough surviving on one income and the challenges to keep our head above water were immense. Nothing could have prepared us for just how expensive it was to live in New York. With approval secured from my head rabbi to use my late afternoon review time to earn money to help relieve the burden on Chaya, an amazing opportunity arose for me to teach in an ultra-Orthodox boys' *yeshiva* in the heart of Brooklyn, in Borough Park.

In this specific *yeshiva*, the boys learned Jewish studies from 7 am to 4 pm. In order to receive partial government funding, secular studies, specifically Mathematics and English, were taught from 4 pm to 6 pm. The secular principal was in dire need of a Grade 6 teacher to teach the last elementary grade in the school before the boys graduated into a full-time Jewish studies program. His *yeshiva* was affiliated with a specific *Chassidic* sect who happened to be experiencing a significant issue: their Grade 6 boys were dropping out at a high rate.

As the principal explained, many boys were becoming disenfranchised with the learning due to a growing awareness that their older peers were finishing school and unable to secure employment upon graduation. At that time as well, there were new influences creeping into the community. Once upon a time, it was quite easy to safeguard students from outside influences. This was a time before the internet and the widespread distribution of cell phones among the youth. Technology however, was becoming a connector for a community who prided itself as isolationist and insular. Young boys were now communicating with members of other sects and even though it was quite hush-hush, communicating with members of the opposite gender. This was all playing out in the homes of children who would leave home at the crack of dawn, before 7 am, only returning after 6:30 pm, sometimes 7:00 pm. They were able to evade the watchful eyes of their parents and anyone else who could notice patterns of emotional change. To complicate the community dynamics even more, it was abnormal for a family to have less than seven or eight children living at home at any one point in time, with often no more than a year in age gap from one child to the next. The poverty level was high. Most families were dependent on welfare and the food stamp system. For these children, education, especially secular education, and keeping up with their studies was not a high priority. For most of them, their prime objective was to get through the day somehow, with whatever self-initiated amusement they could devise to inject some life for themselves into what they saw as the tedious, habitual, unchanging schedule that was particularly demotivating for a large majority of students.

Motivation is a psychological feature that evokes a desire to attain a certain goal. Due to the absence of communal aspirations for personal career achievement, these boys had no intrinsic motivation.

The typical expectation was that each boy would complete his Jewish studies and continue in his family's business. The brightest students were to become rabbis and the rest to perpetuate the expectations of getting married, producing large families, and maintaining the community status quo of their sect through the proliferation of children. The problem was twofold. First, outside influences paved the way for alternate, sometimes secretive lifestyles. The second was overt rebellion. A large portion of the students began dropping out of the system, usually before any intervention could be initiated. Students would leave home in the morning and return in the evening unbeknownst to their parents that they were simply not at school. Often the school was aware and kept track of their attendance; sometimes the school was unable to track patterns of absences indicating long-term truancy. Elementary schools were stricter simply because there was a government rule mandating an attendance report to the New York State government in order to secure funding for their 'English Studies Program'. Their religious programming did not secure any government assistance, other than to fund their breakfast and lunch programs. This benefit was due more to low socio-economic standards established in their annual school census-taking.

The food program, for most schools was not enough of a justification to judiciously track attendance. However, to secure funding for the two hours of secular studies for many *yeshivas* was indeed a cause for diligence.

After Grade 6, there was no longer any funding available and thus students were not tracked at all within the system into which I was hired.

In this particular ultra-Orthodox *yeshiva*, I was asked to join as a teacher; there was a great desire to make one last effort to connect to the

217

students who had nine toes on the street as well as a well-established track record of truancy. I was hired to try to motivate these boys, not so much to establish the relevance of secular studies, but more so to keep them in school for this last year, before the option was presented to them to officially drop out and join their family' business. Mind you, there was not a manual explaining all I have just shared. I was not introduced upfront to all of the intricacies of these challenges. However, it didn't take long at all to deduce from what I could see before my eyes. The challenges these boys were having were unmistakable, often because of the strict rules set out to maintain a distance between them and the "evil outside world."

It was only a thirty-minute community bus ride to and from Borough Park. With permission granted, I successfully passed the interview at the secular principal's private office and set out to meet the Dean of the boy's' *yeshiva* at the school. In passing this final interview, I would be introduced to the boys and start the next day. I arrived by bus at the address of the school and waited outside for the secular principal to arrive.

Standing outside the supposed location of the school, I wondered whether I perhaps had scribbled the address down incorrectly. My eyes could not believe what they were seeing. In front of me was a large building, but its large windows were covered over by large plywood sheets, effectively blocking out the light. The front doors were chained shut. I decided to wait a little longer as perhaps this was just a meeting place and together we would walk to the actual school located elsewhere. To my relief, the principal showed up with a smile and pleasant handshake. He then proceeded without a skip of a beat, "Here we are, follow me!" as he navigated the broken steps climbing toward the chained front door. I don't know how he failed to see my utter dismay, disbelief, surprise, and astonishment…

He managed to crack a slight wedge in the door, without opening the chain. He squeezed through the small opening he had made. He instructed me to do the same and follow him as we made our way together through the dusty large entrance hall. I could see that extremely far back in time this must have been a majestic building with soaring high ceilings and light filled hallways. Now the corridors were dark, cavernous tunnels that had a penitentiary, institutional feel. We walked up some stairs, carefully negotiating the broken steps to the main office. He knocked on the door. A tall, slim, distinguished man with a long grey beard appeared.

I was introduced to the Dean of the *Yeshiva* as the new Grade 6 English teacher. He invited me into his office and asked me if I was able to speak Yiddish well enough to communicate with him. I told him it had been a while since I spoke Yiddish but I understood it very well. He continued speaking in English and tried to relate what he saw as my objectives in teaching the boys. He related his concerns that many of the boys would soon be dropping out, and that he wanted to keep them in school at least for the remainder of the year until they would transfer, perhaps into their feeder institution, their high school located in another section of the Borough Park neighborhood. He was clear that I was to use only the books provided and not to deviate from the provided curriculum. He was not concerned with their proficiency in English. My job was to keep them in school, occupied until 6 pm. I got the hint, loud and clear. It was not a subtle message; he didn't care too much what I did with the students so long as I did nothing further to 'corrupt' the boys. I was to be a good babysitter or even better, a good prison guard charged with keeping them at bay.

I kept thinking, "How bad could it be?" These poor, misunderstood boys just needed a caring teacher who could motivate them, uncovering the light of their inner wisdom through inspirational instruction. I was relegated to the status of a gatekeeper, but I was itching to be their guide toward knowledge, fulfilment, and enlightenment. I felt inspired to be "the one" who could motivate them to see the value of learning and the relevance of my subject matter. I just needed to get in there and meet my "clay subjects," whom I naïvely believed were all ready and waiting, eager to be moulded into the potential saviours of their community.

"Oh, and one more thing before I introduce you to the boys: they are not permitted to speak any English outside of your classroom. Understood?" Trying to keep the shock and bewilderment from my face, I nodded and was thus led out of his office down the hallway to what was to become my "cell." The dean knocked on the door of the classroom, and before receiving an acknowledgement, he opened the door. In front of us were thirty boys sitting in their desks. When the door opened, I think many of the boys had stopped mid-sentence. Now they were all silently staring at us. You could hear a pin drop as they all stood at attention in a united display of reverence for the principal. It was hard not to be impressed and overcome with awe at their show of respect for their Principal. At that moment, I was eager to be a part of their institution.

In Yiddish, the principal introduced me as Mr Glogauer, their new English and mathematics teacher. Some of the boys started to laugh, I thought out of excitement, only to stop once the principal cleared his throat in marked disapproval. He told them I would be here tomorrow and to make sure they had their materials ready. He indicated for me to follow him out the door and he apologized to the teacher/rabbi for the interruption.

I was given copies of the English and mathematics books, which I was told, would be available for distribution to each child first thing tomorrow, and was wished good luck. His last words were, "If you have any problems with the boys, please feel free to call on me any time." I thanked him for the opportunity and told him that it was my sincere ambition to never have to call on him.

I had learned early on in my educational career, the educational "kiss of death" for a new first-year teacher and a sure way to lose respect and control of a class was to call on a higher authority to establish control of one's students. I have found that students will challenge a new teacher and base future interactions on how the teacher reacts in their initial trials by fire. Under no circumstances was I going to show my students or any student that I was ever less than completely in control of my domain. My classroom was my world and I was the master of my domain, and I would never relinquish those rights to anyone. I would never transfer the autonomy to anyone else. I knew this was a sign to the students that the buck stopped with no one but me. On my way out, I again met the secular principal who smiled and told me that I would be paid every two weeks.

The next day I arrived at the school, trying to overlook the entrance and not be too judgmental of the appearance of the physical edifice. I kept telling myself not to judge a book by its cover, and that this experience was going to change me as a person, as an educator. We couldn't choose our students and this would be a test of my ability and resiliency.

I had prepared a 'pre-test' in mathematics to determine the background of the students. I would go over my class rules and expectations and jump into the day's lesson with the pre-test. It was a good way to show who is boss and set my expectations. I had confidence in the boys that they could all meet my hopes and desires. It sounded good. It had worked many times before, albeit in a very different environment. Deep down I believe kids are all the same. My hard and fast rule was building self-esteem by creating opportunities for personal, individual understanding, success, and growth.

At 4 pm sharp, I knocked on the classroom door. The door opened. Surprise! I walked into chaos. Unlike the day before, the students were out of their desks. Some were eating food; others were huddled in small groups in the corner of the room. As I looked about, I saw that their teacher was actually still in the room! He proved by his quick exit he was all too keen to relinquish the wheel to what I would soon realise was a sinking ship. As I walked into the room, the rabbi told me that they were having their recess time. He also said I was never to be late, as of 4 pm he had obligations to teach somewhere else. With that, the door slammed shut behind him and he disappeared.

Perhaps he was just an apparition. Before I could blink, there was no trace that there had ever been a teacher in that classroom. I closed the door behind me and made my way to the teacher's desk at the front of the classroom. At least there was a new box of chalk on the desk. I lifted it up and down with an intentional bang to capture their attention. Suddenly I was drawn to the back of the classroom. There was a small, sudden movement of some type of creature, too large to be a mouse, too small to be a cat. There it was. A medium-sized rat ran from one side of the classroom to the other, only to disappear into another hole in the wall.

I knew this was a critical test that I could not fail. Despite my total shock and growing uneasiness, knowing that there were rats living in the walls of my classroom, I could not show the boys that I was freaked out beyond belief. I needed to show them this was just another regular episode to which I was totally accustomed in my regular daily life. So there I stood, completely still, looking at each boy, eye to eye, purposely establishing eye contact. I wanted the boys to know I meant business. No one moved until I spoke, instructing them to please take their seats.

I began by taking attendance, which turned into a twenty-minute exercise as I found myself reading out very long names, and very long list of long names, because of the sheer size of the class. For the most part, I was able to accomplish this tedious task while maintaining order. The room was quite stuffy even though the windows had been left open. The large blackboard covered the front wall. There was one large, old air conditioner sticking out of the middle window on the left side of the classroom. There were no storage closets or shelving units because the students were required to maintain their own belongings on hooks outside the classroom. There were books in the storage drawer attached to their old-fashioned "Little House on the Prairie" desks.

I was totally dumbfounded when I looked at the floor. In certain areas of the room, I could see the classroom below me through the gaping craters in the floor. I tried not to smile as I saw the teacher below me, looking up and making eye contact with me. I was looking around for the hidden camera, expecting some TV show host to pop out and yell, "Surprise!" It continued to be almost a surreal situation that had to have been scripted. No one would believe that this was really occurring exactly as I am relating it to you, but it was really happening. Here I was, on this foreign planet about to teach these foreign life forms. I told myself that if I were to be successful, I would need empathy and would have to find a way to connect.

As I went through the attendance list, in very heavy accents the boys indicated "present" when their names were called. Having completed the required attendance task, I wrote on the board – "one fact that no one knows about you."

The boys stared in a state of utter suspense at the board, not knowing what was going to happen. For most, the blank looks on their faces indicated that most were absolutely incapable of reading what I had written, and it wasn't due to my questionable penmanship. I decided for the moment to abandon my pre-planned mathematics test and I handed out blank sheets of paper. I was prepared for the eventuality that some of the boys would not have their supplies, and gave those without, the pencils I had brought with me. I asked the boys to copy the sentence as I walked around assessing this simplest of tasks. Many struggled but most attempted the request. I then asked the students if they could either write their response or keep it in mind as I was going to ask some volunteers to share their response. After a few minutes, I asked the boys to put down their pencils.

The boys looked around to see who was going to be the first one to volunteer to speak. Not one student raised his hand. I tried to encourage at least one boy with hopes of salvaging this initial exercise and demonstrating my ability to elicit some aspect of educational creativity. With no success, I decided I would go first. I told them I was born in South Africa and lived in Calgary, Canada as well as Houston, Texas before moving to Brooklyn. This generated quite some excitement when the boys heard Africa and Texas. I then asked if there were any volunteers that wanted to share something interesting about themselves. Excitedly a few boys raised their hands. To the dismay of many of his peers, I called on the first student to share his interesting and unknown fact. I asked the boy first to share his name and then continue. In a very strong, *shtetl* Polish accent, he slowly stated his name, Yoel, and declared that he had memorized the entire *Seder Nezikin* of *Mishnayos* over the summer holidays. This was no small feat and many of the boys applauded. The applause encouraged a few more hands to go up. Excitedly some of the boys called out for me to ask them to share their fact. This enabled me to reinforce my rule of talking only when called upon. I was quite encouraged. It seemed I had not only won over the boys with a tiny victory of the successful icebreaker, but I was also on the road to establishing rapport with the group.

We spent over half an hour on the task as I felt it was critical to allow each boy who expressed interest to share his example with the group. The aim was not only to establish rapport with students, but it was also an opportunity for me to informally evaluate the oral proficiency of their English. I was quite shocked to see how most of the students were struggling to put simple sentences together. Even more so, there was a small pocket of students that could not speak a single word in English. I had my work cut out for me, but I felt up to the task. It was then my goal to assess their mathematical ability. I asked them to turn the pieces of paper over as I began to write a simple three-digit addition sum on the blackboard. I asked them to copy the sum on the paper and try to solve the question. As I wrote the number 942 and wrote the plus sign, the boys began to scream and holler the same word! I had to use every auditory power I had to decrypt what they were shrieking due to the now uncontrollable chaos that had erupted. One of the boys quickly ran to the board, pointed at the + sign, shook his head, rubbed out the addition sign and said, "*Tseilem* – no good." The boys were all yelling, "*Tseilem, tseilem, tseilem.*" Unbeknownst to me, I had committed the gravest of sins, drawing a "cross" on the board, a significant no-no. The boys all looked at me with a disgusted, perplexed gaze as if to say, "How on earth could you not have known?!?" I apologized and asked Yoel, my first volunteer to come to the board and show me how to indicate the mathematical operation of addition. With me still trying to calm the class, Yoel came to the board and like he was teaching a child to write his name for the first time. He demonstrated in the simplest of ways how to join the horizontal midpoint of the addition sign with the lowest point, thus creating a new symbol for addition $\top$. Gazing now at the disapproving looks of my students, I felt any goodwill I had gained from my initial exercise had been totally and utterly lost. I would need to struggle valiantly to regain their trust and respect.

I needed a way to establish calm and told the boys to quieten down as I was going to hand out an exercise sheet only then realizing the ensuing revolt which I would instigate with the many "crosses/tzeilems" within the addition sums. I gave them blank sheets and instead wrote 2 to 3 questions of each of the four mathematical operations. This took a bit of time, and thankfully, most of the boys complied. While the boys finished their task, I asked them to ensure their names were on the top of their papers. I collected them to gather further important information, thus enabling me to plan my future lessons.

As the time of my first day's lesson was coming to a close, I quickly decided to give them some homework. Since the boys were not allowed to speak English outside of my classroom, I thought I could indirectly demonstrate the value of my future lessons with a single homework task. I asked the boys to go home and bring back one example of how English was used in their parents' business. They had to bring back some physical proof of English text. Any boy who brought back an example over the week, beginning from tomorrow, would get a prize.

Excitedly the boys all got up. A few asked me if they would really see me tomorrow. With somewhat of a puzzled look, I said "Most definitely, yes" and dismissed them for the evening. It was as if my heart had beaten over 100 mph for the two hours of this class, and that I had ceased to breathe as well. Drained and utterly in a state of shock and awe, I slowly made my way out of the building through the crack in the locked front door. I walked to the bus stop that would take me home in enough time to spend a few quality minutes with Esti and Chaya. It seemed like no time before I had to leave home to get back for the evening review session with my study partner in order to maintain my learning commitments and to ensure that we were properly prepared for morning classes.

Over the next few days, a pocket of motivated students began to develop. However, as is the way with a gang mentality, there were many others who were determined to revolt against the newly-developed classroom structure I had implemented. Six to seven boys brought examples of how English was used in their parent's' daily lives. Their concrete objects only demonstrated my uphill battle. One boy brought a plastic packaged pair of pyjamas from his parent's factory, which had both Yiddish and English writing on the cellophane wrapping.

I was really excited to see his effort. After he was tasked with attempting to read the words boldly embossed on his chosen item, I awarded him with the opportunity to choose any item from my 'prize grab bag' of prepurchased trinkets. The other boys looked on eagerly and the hands of a few more motivated and prepared participants shot up. A few boys at the back of the classroom shouted some Yiddish put-downs. I could see they were having a negative effect on some of my volunteers who in response to their comments were now lowering their hands and rescinding their initiative. I did not yet disclose my level of comprehension. I simply tried to encourage those boys who had raised their hands to step up and ignore the negativity. Most did not have the courage to stand up against these few bullies.

Then from nowhere came Yoel. He raised his hand and claimed to have an example that he wanted to share. This despite loud jeers from the now growing gallery of dissenters. I asked him to stand and share his example. It turns out that Yoel's father was a *mohel,* charged with performing the many community circumcisions. Yoel produced a business card that had Yiddish on one side. When you flipped over the card, there was the translation in English. Yoel attempted to read the English and was justly rewarded with a dip in the grab bag, to the displeasure of many of his peers. Another brave boy raised his hand and shyly asked if he could share his example. Realizing the tremendous courage these boys were displayed among the growing put-downs of their peers, I decided to push hard and encourage the few interested boys to ignore the negativity, despite my inability to squash the growing rebellion. The next boy was unable to read his example, but this courageous student proudly removed an English instruction manual from his father's photocopier machine. It was a valid example that met all of the preassigned criteria and that merited a reward.

There were no more volunteers that day, so we pressed on with the day's lesson – some simple English vocabulary with examples of common nouns, verbs, building onto adjectives and eventually adverbs. I quickly realised that my objectives and goals would have to change. The outcome of my lessons had shifted from English proficiency to developing the value and minimal understanding of the importance of the English language in their insulated community. I had to develop practical examples, which could be applicable to and personalised in the life of each child.

Out of thirty boys, I had a core of six to eight motivated students who were genuinely interested in what was taking place in my classroom. As a daily reward, at the end of the lesson, I would read from a Yiddish storybook calling on selected students to translate sentence by sentence into English. The stories were well-written so the suspense of the plot pushed the boys, for the most part, to keep it together until the close of the day when we would continue the reading. It was one aspect of my lesson during which each and every one of the students remained respectful. The challenge was getting to that point in the day.

My mathematics lessons had become "Mathematics in Yiddish." I quickly realised if I removed the English component, with the language barrier lifted, the boys could all willingly engage. It had become evident the cultural negativity associated with the English language was a unifying stimulus to revolt against the lesson. If I could remove the stimulus, at times, the students for the most part would engage. Thus, the English instructional component became less and less and the class was now structured into teaching Mathematics and the English language in Yiddish. My fluidity and proficiency in Yiddish was improving immensely and I had begun to develop a closeness to a few of the boys who openly appreciated my effort.

I began to identify significant learning issues in some of my students. I quickly realised that the source of their rebellion was not necessarily against the English language. Actually, as is often the case when there is a behavioral issue with a boy in a classroom, the oppositionality was his coping mechanism not to be caught out being unable to perform. There were a number of serious undiagnosed learning disabilities. One of the boys, Shmiel, the gang leader at the back of the classroom, had a significant hold over the boys. Before boys would participate in the lesson, many of them would look over to Shmiel to gage his reaction. If he were approving of the lesson, they would positively engage. If he gave them the thumbs down, pandemonium and chaos could ensue. As you can guess, there were some days when it was almost impossible to maintain control of the classroom. The boys were intent on disturbing every activity. I varied tasks, planned games, changed often – all to no avail. I used every trick in the book to engage the uninspired and unmotivated: however, if Shmiel and his gang were intent on disrupting the class, I would have no chance of keeping them on the rails even the few with whom I had developed a positive rapport. There were times when I actually considered calling in the dean and taking him up on his initial offer. Each time, I reluctantly refused to follow through. I knew I had to remain steadfast in my commitment to my philosophy of maintaining authority over the class and never relinquishing this control to anyone else.

Somehow, I made it to my one-month anniversary. In early October, we had a sudden heat wave in New York. The conditions in the classroom, due to the intense temperatures, even at 4 pm, had the boys jumping out of control before I even entered the classroom. The old air conditioner was working overtime and one had to yell just to hear one's own voice.

I tried walking into the classroom as I did every other day. Today, the door was jammed. It was impossible to enter. Despite my incessant knocking, no one was responding. Where the rabbi from the previous lesson was, I had no idea. I could hear the boys laughing inside, so I pushed my shoulder into the door and it flung open wide.

There stood all the boys around the perimeter of the classroom. The desks, or what was left of them, were in the centre of the classroom piled high, in pieces. The old-fashioned desks had been held together by a large bolt and nut that connected the chair and writing platform/slate together. Somehow, each and every bolt from each and every desk had been removed. Now there was a pile of wood aimlessly strewn about in the middle of the room. The boys were quietly looking at me, eagerly anticipating my reaction. Perhaps it was the heat, maybe it was the built-up frustration from the weeks before, but I had had enough.

By now, I had broken all my rules and ideas about an inclusive classroom. There was a group of six students whom I had strategically placed in front of me and was catering my lessons for and focusing my attention solely on them. I had lost my voice from teaching over the rattle of the air conditioner. When I met the dean in previous weeks to gain some knowledge about Shmiel and his gang, I was told that yes indeed, Shmiel did have some learning issues but had to remain in my class at all costs. The alternative was even gloomier as the prognosis for Shmiel was for him to drop out and hit the streets like so many of his peers. It turns out that in his Jewish studies classes he was like a picture on the wall, never disturbing anyone out of respect for his rabbi. Despite his rebellion and lack of motivation, the administration felt that if he were removed from the English program, he would see it as a sign of consent to his dropping out completely from the *yeshiva* system. I tried to explain that his public rejection of everything educational taking place in my classroom, including his hold over the entire class, had developed a negative culture that was both intimidating and educationally impacting the other boys' potential and development.

Over a two-week period, I tried as well to engage the secular principal in the conversation, to no avail. No one wanted to listen to what was going on in my classroom. I tried talking to the rabbi who taught the boys before me and all he could do was raise his hands and say, "It's no different in my class, next year will be different." For me, this did not sit well. My teaching style and philosophy was significantly compromised. I found myself ignoring 75% of the students in the class who acted as if they were not interested in learning a thing. Their prime goal was to disturb the learning of the motivated few. The conductor of the chaos was exerting his power and influence and I was impotent to affect any control or exert any influence over the other students.

On this day, something changed. As I looked around the room and saw the desks in a pile in the middle of the room and all the boys staring at me, attempting to elicit some type of a response, all I could do was walk out… and march directly to the dean's office. I calmly knocked on his door and in Yiddish succinctly stated that he needed to come to my classroom and see for himself what was going on. He calmly stood up from his desk. With me walking in step behind him, we made our way to my classroom.

You could hear the commotion behind the closed door. As soon as the dean opened the classroom door, you could practically hear the rats scurrying away in fear through the outside hallways. Normally, you could hear the lesson in the classroom beneath my room through the holes in the floor. At this moment, even they were silent. The dean, aghast, beheld the massacre before him. Desks in a pile in the middle of the classroom and Shmiel, straight-faced. His pockets were filled to overflowing with the incriminating evidence, nuts and bolts conspicuously bulging out. The evidence in plain sight. The Dean called Shmiel by name and calmly told him, *"Kim a hayr.* Come here," pointing to the floor in front of him. As Shmiel came within arm's reach, in one swift motion, the dean struck Shmiel across the face. We were all stunned, not only with surprise, but also by Shmiel's stone cold lack of response. Then the rabbi swung back again and slapped him across the face, this time hitting the opposite side of Shmiel's face. The boys gazed silently as Shmiel fought desperately not to show any response, fighting back the tears. For a brief moment, I felt sincere compassion and even a hint of shame on my part for having caused this to happen to Shmiel. After all, I was the one who had called the executioner to inflict punishment.

Then the Dean asked in English, without allowing me to respond, "Who else is causing problems?" This was my chance to re-establish order, weed out the negativity: "Who else is causing you problems?" Helplessly, it seems I was forced to succumb to the authority in his voice. I was unable to think for myself at that moment of shock. I looked around and pointed out the three other accomplices, collaborators who had continuously hijacked my lessons. I was in such shock from what I was witnessing that I truly didn't realise at that moment I had just pinpointed the next three victims whose fates were also sealed. They too were told to step forward. They received the same judgment. The dean slapped each boy once across the face. Shmiel was told to empty his pockets in front of the entire class and sure enough, all of the nuts and bolts were there piled on the floor. All four boys were escorted out of the classroom in front of their peers. I looked each student in the eye. Somehow, I felt some sense of optimism. Now I would finally be able to teach.

As you predicted, as soon as the dean left and the door closed, it wasn't even a few seconds. It was as if he had never entered in the first place. Pandemonium ensued once more. I realised at that moment that this *yeshiva* was just not the school for me.

The boys had become utterly desensitized to physical abuse inflicted upon them throughout their years of schooling. This was evident in the four boys' reaction at the moments of the violence inflicted upon them. They demonstrated next to no emotional reaction to the dean's abuse. It wasn't just a demonstration of strength, proving that the abuse didn't damage their reputations. On another level, it was clear they were used to it. They had hardened their emotionality. If I wasn't sure this was the case, the remaining evidence was gathered in the fact that the episode had absolutely no effect on the remaining students. The rest of the boys started right up again when both the dean and the four culprits made their exit.

At the moment of witnessing that physical abuse I realised afterward I became paralysed because of the flashes of my past which resurfaced, replete with the six-year-old's emotions in full play in front of my eyes and in my entire stricken body. I was back in South Africa, a tiny petrified six-year-old receiving the strap for the first time in Grade 1. The embarrassment, humiliation, and pain were instantaneously present once again, vicariously connecting to those four students. Perhaps, it was guilt that I now felt; it was me having sought the assistance of the dean that caused this pain to be inflicted on those boys. How different was I to the prefects, toward whom I had developed disdain when they told the principal of my running in the outdoor corridor, presenting it as if I had purposely knocked their library books into the rain gutter over twenty years earlier?

Deep down I knew the scenarios were completely different, but the immediate emotional connection and compassion I had was palpable and significant. If I continued to teach in this environment, it would be evidence that I condoned the punitive philosophy of the institution. Perhaps it was also the fact that the boys themselves had become immune to this antiquated 'system of discipline'. Read: institutionalized abuse. I could not continue there. I could not condone the physical violence. I had been reduced to unwittingly seeking out this form of 'discipline' to regain my classroom decorum. In reality, as would be expected, it had zero effect. The boys spent the remainder of the class time putting the desks back together. At 6 pm that day, I tendered my resignation, effective immediately. I squeezed through that padlocked front door for the very last time.

There may not be a day since this episode happened when it has not popped, bidden or unbidden, into my mind. Over time, I have reflected on it hundreds of times. Needless to say, it had a profound effect on my educational philosophy from that fateful day forward. There are many methods teachers use to instill and maintain discipline in their classrooms. Very few institutions permit corporal punishment in any form. I truly believe, having been witness to the emotional effect, short and long term and the lack of efficacy, there is no place for corporal punishment in school or at home.

However, teachers and parents have found equally damaging alternatives to physical abuse. The child protection codes have already recognized that emotional abuse is equally, if not more damaging to the psyche of a child. Today there are still teachers who employ equally damaging negative techniques that instill a fearful atmosphere as a means for maintaining control in their classrooms. I am a product of an educational system that used both intimidation and physical abuse as means of establishing order in schools. I am also a product of a culture at home in which physical intervention was the primary method for disciplining children. As a child, my father was severely abused by his father. It took many years for my father to break this cycle.

The level of self-control of teachers is evident in how they deal with provocative situations. Students have the uncanny ability to very quickly assess a teacher's weaknesses. Many students exploit these weaknesses as a means of entertainment. The most successful teachers are those who have the ability and foresight to recognize their own personal challenges. They develop appropriate strategies to address confronting situations. I believe and have seen in practice that when children are dealt with in a respectful manner and the relationship starts with dignity, respect and fairness, there is rarely a need to "discipline."

That hot Indian summer day was the result of years of institutionalized abuse, ignorance, a staunch adherence to old ways of doing things, whether they work or not. There were a myriad of missed opportunities that could have averted any and all physical abuse in that *yeshiva*. Had the dean been open to examining the effect Shmiel was having on the class and the systemic culture of reinforcing negative behavior, the entire class could have been turned around. The group would have grown immensely through Shmiel's redirected leadership capabilities. This episode also provided me with a clear understanding that every child deserves a chance to change and grow. We should have worked with Shmiel to understand his learning challenges. We should have engaged his parents more directly. We had passed the early intervention stage, however this was clearly an example of a system that was not designed to identify learning issues and provide sustained support. Nevertheless, things could have been done to help him recognize areas of weakness and implement appropriate strategies to work through them.

Perhaps the many students dropping out of that school' community were in the same situation as Shmiel. Perhaps Shmiel's acting out was due to his frustration and inability to cope because of his learning issues that were undetected, not to mention the lack of positive self-esteem that would result from that scenario. He was deemed a behavior problem in a system that was unable and/or unwilling to mediate learning issues. I remember my many attempts to help Shmiel inside and outside the classroom. My commitment every day is to help the many Shmiels in our schools who are either slipping below the radar and certainly those who have been identified as having learning or emotional needs.

All forms of abuse, certainly physical and especially emotional, must be eradicated completely from the educational system. No form of abuse can be tolerated. I had a teacher in one of my schools who was extremely capable and in fact produced the most incredible results with students who had been falling below national learning standards. She had an inspirational teaching methodology that motivated her students to read and excel academically. However, it didn't take long to see that she was a "screamer." When her frustration level rose or some of her students challenged her strict approach and routines, her method to instill order was to yell. You could hear it if you were next door. Working with her supervisor, I made it very clear; she had to agree to mandated training despite being a twenty-year veteran. She needed to work through her confrontational style, as it would no longer be tolerated in our school. She needed specific skills in both recognizing the issue as well as developing strategies to deal with her improper methods of communication. She acknowledged her challenge and made significant effort to change. Her students were happier and became much more devoted toward her as a person, not just an educator.

The decision to leave the school left a financial void for us once again; however, Chaya was fully supportive of my decision. Let me digress for a few lines. One of the secrets to my wife's and my marriage was and is to this day communication. Chaya and I have always been very much in sync with our goals, both in terms of what we want for ourselves and for our children. At first, we might be on different wavelengths, but through our open dialogue and problem solving, we seem to end up on the same pathway with our far-reaching goals firmly in sight. This time, there was no disagreement. We didn't care about the money. We would find a way to manage.

We have faced many challenges in the various positions life has placed us in, but our relationship is always strengthened against the harsh outside extenuating influences. Chaya is someone whom I have always respected for her knowledge and insights. I was always quite amazed at the gift I was given, that someone like her would be interested in me. Her wisdom and belief in me were something I had rarely experienced. Throughout all of my personal growth from the various different professional challenges I have encountered, I could not have gotten through them, without Chaya at my side, behind the scenes.

Just about that time, things seemed to be falling into place. Esti was now attending the preschool just around the corner from our accommodation and Chaya had some interviews that seemed much more promising. Most importantly, the purpose for this move was progressing well. My learning was advancing and I was succeeding in upgrading my skills. We were slowly integrating into the Brooklyn community and had begun to develop relationships with families in our area. We were becoming hardened to the challenges of living in Brooklyn.

One Saturday afternoon, after lunch, we were relaxing on the sofa in our makeshift dining/living room located in…the kitchen. Our living space was so compacted that we had our kitchen table, sofa and bookshelf all crammed into one tiny area that was designed to contain one table and three chairs. Somehow, we made do and were content. There were the usual sounds, being surrounded by two apartment buildings and many children congregating outside playing ball on the street, which included frequent sirens – of police cars, fire engines, or ambulances – racing by. Today was different. Along with the sirens passing by our apartment came the sound of three or four loud pops. Not thinking too much more about it, Chaya and I just looked at each other, not wanting to say anything in front of our little Esti who by now was four years old. We rested for an hour or so, despite the fact that many more sirens seemed to be passing by our apartment.

As it came time for me to go back to my *yeshiva* for the late afternoon prayers and class, I walked out of our door to find many policemen cordoning off our car in the alleyway with yellow police tape, indicating the location of the bullet shells under our car! There were a few questions

232

from one of the detectives and the inescapable chatter amongst the law enforcement personnel gathering on our street. It turned out some boys had been hiding behind our car and had tried to shoot some of the kids playing on the opposite side of the street, directly in front of our apartment. An ambulance passed by on its way to another unrelated incident at the exact moment the shots rang out, and instead of gunning down the intended victims, the ambulance took a hit. Luckily, no one was injured and now the manhunt was on for the perpetrators. Yes, we had become inured to our surroundings as we pretty much took this in stride. This incident only reminded us we were and would only be temporary residents living on this street Brooklyn. We had a one-year lease. This was further motivation to look for another apartment that was not only bigger, but also in a safer environment and a safer street – if that was even possible.

Chaya finally secured a full-time job in her profession in Brooklyn, not more than a twenty-minute car ride away, so we were much more comfortable financially. A family health plan came along with her new employment. Despite struggling financially, we had always resolved that no matter what, we would never become dependent on the government and apply for social assistance or welfare such as food stamps, nor would we take the chance and not have full health coverage. Thus despite our minimal financial capacity, we always had been committed to forgoing a significant part of Chaya's take-home pay and allocating it toward a family health insurance plan. When Chaya finally secured a position in a company that covered this significant expense, an even larger burden was lifted off our shoulders. With Esti going to school, come September 1997, she would make the move from daycare to kindergarten.

It became a regular part of the Friday routine to pass by the neighborhood newsstand and pick up the latest copy of the Jewish News to peruse the classified ads section for future principalships. As I kept my eyes on the prize, I anticipated this search would become a more focused pursuit in a mere year or two. I felt it was important to keep my eye on the Jewish job market.

From the Ghetto to the Q-boro

This time it was as a part time position as a Math Regents Grade 11 and 12 teacher in an all-boy's' *yeshiva* in Queens. The main challenge I experienced as an educator in this position highlighted the issues that will arise when there is an absence of parental support. Of course, as it kept turning out, that was only one of the challenges…

There are a lot of general studies teaching vacancies in the religious *yeshivas* in Brooklyn. There is a general consensus amongst the observant families who desire a strong religious education for their children to find an institution that dedicates the majority of the day to religious studies and allocates a mere two to three hours toward general studies instruction, preferably at the end of the day. This philosophy purports that as children are most attentive in the morning, the most essential subjects are scheduled during this core learning time. In the *yeshiva* system, this translates to all Jewish studies being scheduled in the morning, and the general studies most commonly scheduled in the afternoon. The vast majority of *yeshivas* subscribing to this philosophy have no more than two fifteen-minute recesses per day and only thirty minutes break for lunch. For the most part, there are no physical education classes at all.

There are many implications of these scheduling parameters. The indirect implication is the message it sends to students that secular subjects are much less important in the grand scheme. Therefore, many students internalize this message. If they are going to muck up it will be in their general studies, especially as by that time of day, their attention starts to wane and the pent-up energy of sitting in a classroom all day is all but fit to burst.

This is certainly the case in the *yeshiva* system where students are required to attend early morning prayers at the commencement of the day at 7 am. One can only imagine the challenges this presents for the average teenage boy, who is expected to remain fully focused from three o'clock to 6 pm during their intense general studies program. After having expended much of their mental energy for Jewish studies subjects, students are required to demonstrate the expected level of concentration and enthusiasm even at the latter part of the day, when certainly their energy levels are much lower. Coupled with the impression that their secular subjects are not as important, given the scheduling priorities, most behavioral challenges amongst teenage boys tend to surface during these late afternoon general studies classes. In my experience, I have seen far too many examples of the above. It hasn't mattered, whether it is the ultra-Orthodox institutions or the moderately observant communities.

With the challenges described above in the *yeshiva* systems, qualified general studies teachers to teach in these designated afternoon times are in high demand. One only needs to open up the most popular Jewish newspaper's classified section to regularly find advertised positions. I believe the overabundance of advertised positions is due to the high turnover rate, given the behavioral challenges that are to be expected as a result of this educational philosophy.

For some reason, in early January 1997, a job posting for a high school *yeshiva* caught my eye. The school was located in Queens, a short twenty-minute drive from Crown Heights. Coincidentally they were looking for a high school mathematics teacher. Even more amazingly, the hours fitted perfectly with our afternoon learning schedule. I spoke to the rabbi of my *yeshiva* and, with his permission, gave the school a call. The principal was very eager to meet me. We set up an interview the very next day.

In the initial interview, I met with the secular principal in charge of the boys' high school. We spoke about my secular background and my ability to prepare the boys for the New York State Regents exam. The *yeshiva* was primarily a draw card for the Bukharin community situated around the school in that area of Queens. I was informed my goal was to prepare the boys to take the Regents exam, even though, out of the thirty boys in the class, most likely only four to five would truly be interested in achieving this end result. The boys were all required to take the class in order to meet their high school graduation requirements, but the Regents exam itself was for those interested in pursuing postsecondary schooling. In the Bukharin community, only a minority were interested in this end goal. Similar to my experience in Brooklyn, these boys would continue in their family's business. What was different, however, was the family expectation that each boy graduate with the minimum of a high school diploma. With this major difference, I was keen to consider the position.

I was charged with teaching both the thirty Grade 12 boys and the twenty Grade 11 boys back-to-back, an hour each from 2:45 pm – 4:45 pm Monday through Thursday. I would be paid in cash, every two weeks at a rate of $50 per hour. The money was an incredible incentive and I was more than keen. I was given a copy of the two textbooks and then was told that the rabbi, the dean of the institution wanted to meet me. Because the secular principal was so positive toward me, I had a very good feeling and was not nervous for this *déjà vu* experience. Another very distinguished-looking rabbi, this time with a long black beard, sat in front of me and introduced himself with a thick Russian accent. We exchanged some pleasantries and then he got up, shook my hand, and wished me good luck. That was it. As he walked out of his office, the secular principal asked me if I could start tomorrow. Excitedly, I said yes and off I went, silently praying that this would not be a repeat of my previous experience in Brooklyn.

These after all were high school students. Looking at the textbook, the level of mathematics was substantial. If the students had some level of skill, I felt very confident that I could work with them. It was a five-month position four days a week; I felt like the time would fly by quite quickly and thought I could survive no matter what the circumstances.

After the interview, I went straight to Esti's school, picked her up and proceeded on to Chaya's work to pick her up too. As Chaya came to the car, she could see the excited look on my face and knew instantaneously that I had good news. That night we went out to dinner to celebrate the fact that we would have a little financial breathing room in the months to come. It was a rare celebration. The food tasted especially good that night with the knowledge that we were on track. The journey's destination, as far off as it was, certainly seemed in reach.

That very next afternoon, I arrived early in Queens knowing that one of my challenges that day, before even walking into the classroom, would be finding a parking spot on the crowded side streets of Queens. It was part and parcel of one's existence living in New York's five boroughs to continuously avoid the meter maids and do whatever possible not to contribute to their 'personal delight'. They lived for the click of the expired meter, pitted against the guilty menacing citizens of New York, who were illegally taking advantage of the benevolence of the New York City Traffic Authority, having granted an open space to safeguard one's automobile for an explicit period of time. The meter maids were like circling vultures that could intuitively sense a car taking advantage of even one minute of unpaid, expired meter time. For us, living on such a tight budget, one parking ticket would translate into a severe consequence for our family – less food for the month.

Therefore, each day, arriving at the school to teach and finding a parking spot held the same feeling of anticipation as winning the New York State lottery. At times, I would have to walk a significant distance, which would necessitate having to arrive much earlier in order not to be late for class. It was a juggling act. Never did I want to upset my rabbi and cut out on my learning time. After all, my motivation at this point in time was to upgrade my learning, not to earn a living. The upcoming increased expenses that we were anticipating included the desire to travel home to Calgary in September to spend the Jewish high holy days with my parents. It had been a few years since we had been in Calgary. Since our financial situation precluded us from this luxury, we took advantage of the offer of one ticket organized by our former synagogue where I would act as assistant rabbi for the month of religious services. We would now be able to save a bit of money from the new job and travel as a family, thanks to my new teaching position.

Walking into the *yeshiva* in Queens was an experience like the many others I had had, walking into a new, unfamiliar school. There were strange looks from the many students lining the hallways, gazing upon me as if I was "fresh meat" on the game reserve. I felt like a baby gazelle walking through a pride of hungry lions. I could hear them licking their chops, whispering and laughing subtly as I made my way to my classroom. I kept calm trying so hard not to show any sign of sweat. After all, any apprehension was like a drop of blood in the water to a group of circling sharks.

I walked into my classroom just as the bell rang, signalling the commencement of my lesson. Having written my name on the front chalkboard, I stood at the front of the class waiting for silence. The young men quickly got the point and I began by introducing myself. I precisely expressed my expectations for the term. Each class would begin with the quiz, one question based on the previous day's lesson. They were expected to take notes on my lesson and complete the minimal amount of homework assigned each night. There would be one mid-term exam and one final exam. If they followed my lesson closely, took notes, and succeeded daily on the quiz, they would not only do well in my class, but I promised this would translate into a sincere appreciation for mathematics. The by-product of their effort would be a guaranteed successful Regents Exam result. I handed out a summary sheet including the method of evaluation, which indicated 20% homework, 40% quiz, 20% midterm, and a 20% final exam. I asked if there were any questions. There was complete silence. Everyone seemed a little shell-shocked. I reinforced my rule of respect, raising a hand to talk, and off we were on our journey together.

It turned out the boys' mathematical aptitude was reasonably strong. For the most part, they adapted really well to the quiz strategy. There was sincerity in their effort and for a significant number of the students, they were keen to achieve at a high level. They were open with me that most of them were not motivated to go on to university or college. They all had jobs after school, mostly in cell phone stores in their hustling and bustling neighborhood of Queens. Almost universally, their shared goal was to make money. A strong background in mathematics was evidence that this aptitude was deeply ingrained early on in their environment/culture.

I made a conscious effort to link most of my examples to either sport or money. They were all deeply competitive and at times controversy would erupt over conflicting opinions relating to answers or creative methods of calculation. For this reason, the daily quiz worked very well. The ability to compete against a fellow classmate was a large motivating factor in ensuring the students kept up with the daily material. They spontaneously developed a scoreboard culture in which students began keeping track, so they would know who were the top students in the class. The boys were appreciative of being able to calculate their ongoing evaluation. With the exception of the homework marks, they were keeping a running tally, not only of their personal mark but also those of the entire class. It didn't take long for the boys to reveal their hierarchy of achievement. The deep level of competition resulted in put-downs of the nonachievers and significant resentment from the weaker students toward the stronger students. I noticed subcultures forming and worked hard to try and remediate the weaker students while at the same time trying to eradicate the cutthroat nature of the atmosphere.

With less than five months left of their entire twelve years of school, it was a fruitless hope to break the cultural environment within the students and classroom. At times, the weaker boys would physically challenge the academically stronger boys as a means of publicly saving face. I quickly learned that the easiest way to incite a confrontation would be for one student to insult another's mother. A deep, penetrating comment about some personal attributes of a student's mother, no matter if it were true or not, compelled the insulted student to publicly defend his matriarch's honour. Before one could blink, desks would be pushed to the sides of the classroom and a physical showdown, one student facing another in a makeshift cage match, ensued. It only happened once in my Grade 11 classroom. I walked in having just taught next door for the Grade 12 boys.

238

I arrived in time to find the "ring" set up and two boys going at it. Insults flying fast, one boy lunged at the other and before I could say anything, another boy's fist had penetrated through the classroom window. The boys were much larger than I was, and I surely would not have survived playing the role of referee, trying to break up the altercation. I only had to witness this event once to realise I had to very carefully monitor the attitudes of the students and prevent tempers from boiling over. With the principal's assistance, a new rule was enacted whereby classrooms would remain locked and students were only allowed to enter with the arrival of their teacher.

The boys made it very clear they did not have a lot of time for homework. At the end of the day, their focus switched, with the sound of the bell, to getting to work and making money – as much money as possible. Their parents expected they would all graduate with a high school diploma, and from then forward they would be on their own financially.

While I kept them motivated and free from physical altercations, we found a happy medium, as long as I didn't expect more than what they were prepared to give. It was my job to subtly nudge them to give a bit more and deep down they appreciated my effort, drive, and concern. They could see the results and were growing and achieving significantly. The mid-term exam was an external Regents practice test based on the units studied thus far. It was set by the principal and would clearly indicate which students were on track to achieve a significant outcome on the final State exam.

With over three-quarters of the class achieving a score of over 75%, the administration and the boys themselves were all extremely satisfied, as were their parents. My hypothesis, that learning occurs best when the student-teacher relationship is built on mutual respect and equal give and take, once again, was strongly supported. The boys were deeply affected by the positive results and a sincere admiration developed between us.

At the conclusion of the year, three-quarters of the boys succeeded in achieving over 75% on the New York State Regents exam. I was emotionally gratified when many of the boys thanked me personally. Many of them and even their parents wrote cards and letters expressing heartfelt appreciation for all I did that year.

Whilst it was a much calmer five months, I still learned a lot about myself. I learned more in terms of how to motivate competitive boys, at the same time maintaining an atmosphere of collegiality. I had to learn about their Bukharin culture and how to demonstrate respect for their background and prior experiences. At the same time, I developed more ability to inspire a level of understanding and acceptance even when their values conflicted with societal mores. Inspiring a paradigm shift was a great challenge, and having accomplished this shift without compromising my expectations of mutual respect for each individual and personal growth both academically and personally was extremely rewarding. I came away feeling a deep sense of growth and accomplishment. I was asked to come back and teach in September; however, my journey was to take me in another direction.

A Change of Direction

With June approaching, my *yeshiva* program prepared for their summer transition out of Brooklyn to the Catskill Mountains. Each year they developed a summer learning program for university students to join the *yeshiva* over the summer semester break. I myself had joined the program a few summers back and much of my personal growth I attributed to this alternative learning experience. It was similar to the winter "*Yeshiva-cation*" program that developed my initial taste for the *yeshiva* system back in 1990 and motivated my return in the summers of 1991 & 1992. I was fortunate to spend three months from June through August immersed in an authentic study program tailor-made for students like myself who were seeking understanding and inspiration to the burning "life" questions that no one else could adequately answer.

With the *yeshiva* relocating to the mountains, I had to develop some type of learning program on my own. With Chaya's job in Brooklyn, plans were for me to continue with my learning and growth. One of the rabbis in charge of the learning program and student welfare called me into his office one-day enquiring as to what my plans were for the summer. I told him my goal was to obviously continue learning and asked if he had any suggestions as to what to do to keep me on track until they returned in late August. Then the bomb was dropped...

I was told very directly that because I had not followed the traditional route of learning in *yeshiva* from elementary school through high school and then into the standard learning track post-high school, it was a certainty there was no way I would be admitted into the rabbinical ordination program through the main *Chabad Yeshiva*. It was very rare for someone with my background to be accepted into this specialized program. To make things even more difficult, the program was for single boys, not married men with families. It was just not done. I asked him why I couldn't be one of the exceptions, but he didn't really have an answer for me. The proverbial door was slammed once again right in my face. I asked him if he would set up an appointment for me to meet the head of the rabbinical ordination program. He told me he could, but that my energy was misplaced. Rather what I should be focusing on was to find an alternative program, one that was not linked to *Chabad*.

He went on to say there were many institutions that would accept me and allow me to concentrate more on my studies rather than me expending precious time and energy fighting a system that had no leeway for exceptions. I told him that I would need to talk to my wife. We had shared this deep desire. Within myself, I desperately wanted to receive my ordination through the *Chabad* track. After all, I saw myself as a *Chabadnik,* and had been drawn into the "family" because of its nurturing outreach philosophy. I could not fathom how my "family" could reject me by design, just because I was not born into the community. Wasn't this rejection contrary to our mandated philosophy? Not accepting me because I hadn't been brought up through the system seemed not only exclusionary but also extremely elitist and therefore very contradictory to most of the values we had understood to be core to this way of life! Nevertheless, I pushed for a meeting with the head of the *Chabad* rabbinical ordination program. I was told that the only one who could arrange this meeting was the head rabbi of our *yeshiva*. I had to go to the top.

Just as I had been forewarned, I did indeed run into that brick wall. The head rabbi of my program also asserted that it would not be possible for me to obtain my *smicha* from their rabbinical ordination program. He did however shine a thin crack of hopeful light when I asked him if he had any suggestions of an alternate institution that would indeed meet my needs. The rabbi said he was aware of one institution. One "graduate" of his *yeshiva* had successfully received his ordination through such an alternate method. If I was interested, I could call him and meet him. He kindly gave me the man's cell phone number. He concluded very nurturingly that I would always be welcome to study at his *yeshiva* and his parting words were to remember that the goal was to study for the sake of learning, not for the sake of an extrinsic outcome.

I was quite shaken up and upset. I left his office in very low spirits. It was midday and I immediately left the *yeshiva* and went home to call Chaya. She was in the middle of her workday but luckily had a few minutes to calm me down. Always philosophical and able to see the big picture, with her ever poignant words of comfort she once again was able to touch deeply to the core, saying "You know, we have been tested at each stage of our journey. This too is just one more test. Whatever is meant to be is meant to be. All we can do is move ahead and God will take care of the rest. Set up a meeting with the rabbi in charge of the *Chabad* rabbinical ordination program and give the contact the rabbi gave you a phone call. Request a meeting with the rabbi in charge of the alternate rabbinical ordination program. Let's pursue both options, the right path will illuminate, we just need to play our part."

I was calmed by her words of reason. She always knew the right things to say. I could not say that I was not still deeply dejected as I thought I was on the right path and that I would have a shot with the endorsement of my rabbi to join the official *Chabad* track. All I could do now was just push forward as he had said and learn for the sake of learning.

I immediately made a phone call to the rabbi who was the head of the *Chabad* program and was told he had open office hours today and that I could just come and meet him personally. At the same time, I called the phone number of the rabbi from the alternate program. I mentioned how I got his number and set up a meeting with him in the morning. As I made my way to the *Chabad* program rabbi's office, somehow I had a feeling deep down that I was fighting a losing battle. Despite the overwhelming odds that he would be shutting the door on my hopes and dreams, it would be solely up to me and I surely would find a way to succeed, one way or another.

It was a very quick meeting. I am sure he could tell how nervous I was. It was made clear that an exception would not be granted for me to join his rabbinical ordination program. Excuses of fundraising and the high cost of tuition as well as my lack of learning were all grouped together. Despite my resolve to cover any financial costs, attention quickly focused toward my limited background. I could see that I would not break the barrier and left again dejected, twice in one day. My only hope was the potential outcome of my prescheduled meeting for the following day.

Not really knowing much about the program, this alternative, at the time, seemed like my only hope in achieving my goal of becoming a rabbi, thus opening the doors to my candidacy as a future principal of an Orthodox Jewish school. Naïve as I was, having had five years teaching experience in both public school and various Jewish institutions, I just knew that with the high demand for Jewish principals, this one piece of documentation would certainly open the doors of opportunity.

Perhaps if this were my only avenue, I now would be limiting my options to only non-*Chabad* educational institutions. Knowing that there were many more Orthodox schools than *Chabad* schools, this consoling thought quickly calmed me and provided me with direction and focus, not to mention hope. I might end up aiming for a Modern Orthodox school despite my strong *Chabad* leanings. A non-*Chabad* rabbinical ordination would be more attractive to non-*Chabad* institutions and that would demonstrate my openness and moderate outlook. As I thought about it, and given how I was feeling at this moment, this perspective seemed much more welcoming. With this thought, I approached my morning meeting with growing optimism and understanding of the pathway upon which it seemed I was now being thrust.

Rabbi Shmuel laid out the program very clearly. Just like any another *smicha*/rabbinic ordination program, I would be required to pass oral examinations on the four main aspects of *Yoreh Deah*. The four subject areas of study are salting, mixtures, milk and meat, and the laws of the *Shabbos*. As it turned out, Shmuel had also tried to receive his rabbinical ordination through the *Chabad* path, but had also run into the same stumbling block of not having grown up Orthodox, observant or *Lubavitch* from birth. Since he also had not learned in the *Chabad Yeshiva* system, he was not accepted into the *Chabad* rabbinical ordination program through the official *Chabad* world headquarters known as *770*.

Rabbi Shmuel's alternate track to receiving rabbinical ordination had resulted in his being extremely well versed in the particular areas of learning related to the specific topics in the Code of Jewish Law requiring mastery. As our conversation progressed, Shmuel made the most incredible offer. For no other reason other than to occupy his time with more spiritual pursuits, Shmuel was prepared to drive each day, Monday through Thursday from deep in Long Island, New York to learn with me in Crown Heights, Brooklyn from 9 a.m. to 12:30 p.m. These solid three hours would enable me to finish the first of the four subject areas by the end of the summer, with the goal of me being tested by the head of his alternate *yeshiva*.

Shmuel made it very clear that the timetable he proposed of completing one of the four tests by the end of the summer was subject to me meeting the director of this program. This rabbi, a well-known personality in New York, was interested in offering a legitimate ordination certificate for mature, married men who were learned but unable to enter traditional programs, having realised this desire later in life. I was assured that he was quite an imposing, intimidating personality with a huge character. He would grill me to ascertain my sincerity. Once I got to know him though, Shmuel promised I would feel comfortable with my decision.

One of the conditions of entry into the program was that I was required to travel once a month up to Monsey, New York where his *Kollel* was located. The objective of these trips was a one-on-one learning session to gauge my growth and ongoing commitment in a specific area of this rabbi's rabbinic ordination curriculum, which he had predetermined for his students. This was in addition to the traditional rabbinical studies. I would be told in advance the specific area of discussion. I would carefully prepare in order to make a good impression. In truth, I didn't really have any other options and was just glad to have a clear pathway, even if it wasn't the specific quality of ordination I had initially hoped to receive. Nevertheless, my end goal of receiving rabbinical ordination would be achieved.

Shmuel facilitated my acceptance into this *yeshiva*, which would grant me my ordination. He was the bridge if you will as he was well known to the head rabbi of the program in which I had been studying in Brooklyn. The head rabbi of my Brooklyn *yeshiva* program personally recommended that I pursue this alternate approach. Given his prior knowledge of where I had been learning, I was not concerned about the authenticity of this alternate program, however I was a little perplexed as to their motivation in accepting me so willingly as one of their students.

Despite my nerves and slight apprehension, the trip to Monsey seemed to take only a few minutes despite in reality being over an hour's drive. I enjoyed the scenery of the lush green trees along the Palisades Parkway, which seemed to escort and invite me to my intended destination. It felt like fate had paved my initial encounter as I pulled up to the main building of the *Kollel/Yeshiva*. Shmuel was waiting for me outside ready to escort me in. Greeting me with his warm smile, he asked me if I was nervous. I said a little, but was comforted by his reassurance that the formality was a mere test to ensure my commitment which he had sincerely vouched for before my arrival.

We walked inside together. A large man, quite imposing, with a neatly-trimmed grey-to-white beard greeted me with a firm handshake and a welcoming smile. Ushered into his office, I sat down to what became the long convoluted discussion of my personal journey, of how I came to be sitting in the chair in front of him. He seemed very taken with me and sympathetic to my desire to have received *Chabad* ordination. He strongly promoted his program. He was looking for ambassadors for his institution and believed I would be a good candidate.

He explained that in addition to the standard curriculum of the four traditional subject areas relating to the standard ordination study program, his philosophy centred on a belief that every rabbi was required to be proficient in practical rabbinics. In order to receive ordination through his institution, all students had to pass several tests, demonstrating an understanding of practical law in specific areas relating to everyday rabbinical life. Areas such as the laws of marriage, a valuable skill included the intricacies of reading and understanding a marriage contract and how to conduct a marriage ceremony. Other laws included those of death and burial, on how to conduct a funeral, as well as basic laws of circumcision. Although the curriculum and his expectation were not specific enough to come close to understanding the intricacies of performing a circumcision, the goal was for his graduates at least to know how to lead these 'life-cycle' ceremonies. It was clear that his mandate was not just to bestow upon a theoretically successful candidate the name "Rabbi." Along with mastering the four traditional subject areas of Jewish law, there was the responsibility to be able to live up to the tasks associated with the expectations of the title 'Rabbi'.

With a firm shake of the hand, I was welcomed and he said, "Okay, let's learn something together." He pulled out an unfamiliar text, then asked me to read and translate. A little taken aback and quite nervously, I pushed through and was able to engage in a conversation on the passage from the *Talmud* relating to the concept of faith and belief in God. He shared some of his personal thoughts. Then quite abruptly, he said, "See you next month. Looking forward to seeing you again."

That was it! I thanked him and told him he would not be disappointed in his decision. As we left I gave Shmuel a big hug, thanked him and told him I would see him tomorrow at what was now going to be our regular learning time. I could not contain my excitement and if the drive seemed too quick on my way to Monsey, the return home was even shorter.

In addition to my morning studies with Shmuel, I had enough time in the afternoon to review my lessons on my own until Esti's 3:30 pm summer camp pick-up time. Then I would fetch Chaya and review some more until later in the night. Every Tuesday evening the son of the head of the community's Rabbinical Court would hold an in-depth class on the Code of Jewish Law and the specific subject area I was studying. This was coordinated in consultation with the head of the *Kollel/Yeshiva* in Monsey with which I was now aligned. This rabbi's association with the program in Monsey added additional credibility to this up-and-coming rabbinical program. It is noteworthy to fast-forward to 2012 and beyond. In the past few years, a number of reputable *smicha* programs have sprouted up, online and otherwise within the *Lubavitch* movement. These programs cater to the growing *Baal Teshuva* and mature student population who possess the desire and ability to learn for their rabbinical ordination. Perhaps I was a bit ahead of my time...

Shmuel and I were making the most of our three and a half hours of learning together. Each day at 12:30 pm, upon the conclusion of our study sessions, I would walk to the corner store and grab a cold drink in a vain attempt to cope with the excessive New York summer heat. I would walk across the street to *770* to review my studies among the few *yeshiva* students who remained in New York over the summer to intensively study for their rabbinical ordination. The rest of their colleagues ran summer camps and other programs across the world. The atmosphere was strongly conducive to serious learning, helping to focus one's intensive studies and block out any potential distractions. Since most of the entire Crown Heights community travelled to the Catskill Mountains in upstate New York to avoid the heat, only a small segment of the community remained behind. With a small cohort of the official *770* rabbinical ordination program remaining, I became a regular fixture among the select few who were diligently motivated to learn. If I had any questions relating to a specific topic I was learning, I had one or two regular faces who I could approach, having become friendly with a few of the other students learning around me.

I became very entrenched in my routine and began to really excel in my studies. Not only had I the time to review the daily lessons with Shmuel, but also I began to prepare in advance for the upcoming day's section. We were flying through the chapters of study, and with the summer's conclusion rapidly approaching, I was ready to face the rabbi for my first test of the four mandatory subject areas from *Yoreh Deah*. Confidence and nervousness, the mix of the two emotions seemed contradictory. My success navigating through the tangled complexity of the many obstacles placed in front of me, blocking me from reaching my goal, would be dependent on my passing this most significant first test.

Once again, I arrived in Monsey. Shmuel was waiting for me on the front steps of the *Kollel* just as he had the first time. We walked in together. The head Rabbi, who looked as serious and intense as I felt nervous, greeted us. It appeared that not only was I on trial, but so was Shmuel, as my teacher, and thus the program itself. The systems we had devised, Shmuel as my personal guide, and the Tuesday night sessions led by the son of the head of the community's rabbinical court were equally on trial. A good outcome would be my demonstrating a high level of understanding and proficiency. This would result in a stamp of approval for Shmuel and his future ability to mentor other potential candidates. I now understood what everyone had to gain. I was the guinea pig and my success was everyone else's success. I didn't really mind, as long as I passed.

What followed was the intense, hour-long grilling of theoretical questioning and practical applications of the law. I was permitted, as was the acceptable, long-standing custom, to look into the original text to support my answers. The rationale was and is that a Rabbi is never expected to respond to a matter of law without proper consultation of the original text. It was a demonstration of proficiency to know exactly where to look for the answer as to how to support a response by citing the original source.

With each response, Shmuel sat back in the room and warmly smiled at me as I successfully negotiated each question. His satisfaction was an additional reward. At the conclusion of my test, I was wished, "*Mazal tov,*" for having successfully passed my first exam. I stood up, shook the rabbi's hand, and gave Shmuel a strong hug. Together, we had both passed. I walked out of the room with the biggest smile, Shmuel right behind me with an equally satisfied grin on his face. As we walked outside of the building, I felt it was a huge weight being lifted off my back. I thanked Shmuel for everything he had done for me.

It was the right time to tell him that I had another exciting piece of news to share with him. Chaya and I were, after quite a long time, expecting a baby. I hadn't told him or anyone else until we had clearly passed the milestone in Chaya's pregnancy when we had lost the baby, over three years ago. Chaya was in her second trimester and this pregnancy had already been laden with concern. Shortly after our initial assumption that Chaya was pregnant and with the doctor's confirmation, one *Shabbos* Chaya began to spot, just like the last time. It began on the *Shabbos* afternoon, and immediately after *Shabbos* we went straight to the hospital clinic. I took upon myself that afternoon to say the entire book of *Tehillim*. Privately in my mind, I made the resolution that once a month, on the *Shabbos* preceding the new month, I would wake up early to recite the entire book of Psalms before the morning prayers. Initially, the task took me more than four hours. To this day, I have not missed a month and can trace back my resolution to over eighteen years ago, and that fateful *Shabbos*. I have held to this promise, twelve months a year without fail, over two hundred complete readings. The task now takes me less than two hours and I have my holy son in mind each minute of this joyous task as I think back to my original resolution when I had his unborn soul in mind.

An Inconceivable Opportunity

Continuing on the path toward my goal, I decided that the subsequent chapter of study should be the laws of mixtures. This is the most complicated of sections out of the mandatory four. Shmuel and I once again resumed our learning schedule. With the summer coming quickly to an end, the *770 Yeshiva* students and the vacationing Crown Heights community repopulated the neighbourhood. As the high holiday period was upon us, we travelled to Calgary to spend the high holidays with my parents and for me to serve as assistant rabbi in the synagogue under our rabbi who had been our initial source of inspiration.

Much of the talk and discussion in Calgary was about the path we had chiselled for ourselves and how I had completed the first step of our journey. My parents were so proud that their son was becoming a rabbi. It gave me a great sense of accomplishment and satisfaction that my parents were finally demonstrating overtly a sense of pride in their son's intellectual pursuits. This was a completely new experience for me. For so many years, I felt like I could do nothing to please them. I had pursued a career which they were vocal in the early stages was one of which they did not endorse. We had "run away" from them and Calgary to the United States with their most beloved, cherished and eldest grandchild. This was truly the first time in a long period where they communicated their pride openly.

One afternoon, my mother expressed a sincere desire to invite a friend of hers over, who for some motive, requested an opportunity to meet me, but did not want to share over the phone the reason. All I was told was that she desperately wanted to meet me. Not really having much else to do, I agreed. This initial encounter would be the first of many meetings and conversations with someone who was soon to become my mentor and confidante. The subject of the meeting, we soon learned, was the prospect of me becoming the next principal of Akiva Academy, the Orthodox day school linked to the Orthodox Synagogue – House of Jacob.

It didn't take long to see that she was clearly the most passionate, outspoken, unwavering soul one could ever meet. She was a woman on a mission and nothing was going to stand in her way. She had already done her homework on me and knew all about my teaching career in Calgary. She had been in contact with my principal as well as some of the teachers I had connected with in my past while in the public school system. She was interested in my updates and what I had done in Houston and in New York. The conversation quickly turned to my future goals after completing my rabbinical ordination. More importantly, she was insistent on getting an answer to how long I thought it would take. It was flattering that someone was so interested in me, before I had even completed my goal of acquiring my ordination. We talked in generalities and I promised to keep her in the loop about my progress. She took my phone number and she promised to be in touch.

Sometime after the visit, I approached my *Chabad* rabbi in Calgary about her idea of me becoming the principal. He smiled and actually laughed out loud. He said, "Never would the Synagogue hire a *Chabad* rabbi to lead their school." My mother's friend was a pipe dreamer, enthusiastic and persuasive, but a starry-eyed dreamer. I decided to leave the idea alone, go back to New York, and concentrate on the task at hand, completing my rabbinical ordination through the Monsey *Kollel*.

Upon my arrival back in New York, I received some sobering news at my initial meeting with Shmuel. It turned out that he was now venturing into another area for the *Kollel*. In order to bring in some needed funds for the institution, he would be acting as supervising rabbi for some of the kosher restaurants under the auspices of the *Kollel*. It would potentially only be temporary, but for now, I would have to learn on my own. I was very concerned this would place a huge obstacle in the path toward completing my goal in a timely manner. I had hoped to complete one more test before the arrival of our new baby. Chaya was as usual full of reassurance that this glitch was just one more 'test' I would have to pass on the road to my goal. I should push on without changing any of my routines. Instead of learning each day with Shmuel, I should go to *770*, sit in my regular spot, and study alone. Indeed, that is exactly what I did. The pace was different as was the intensity of my learning. Nevertheless, there was some comfort knowing that I was still progressing along the journey.

As more students began arriving for the fall semester of study, the study hall/synagogue became more and more cramped. Students jockeyed for seating preference and comfort in the limited space. As I had been learning in the same seat for six months, the boys around me recognized my consistent presence and even safeguarded my spot if I arrived a few minutes late after morning prayers and my early-morning coffee run.

A few days after settling back into my routine, I noticed a new face, sitting a few seats down from my seat. He too was learning on his own, and I decided to introduce myself. Eli was from Monsey and had grown up in a *Chabad* home, having learned in *Chabad* schools all of his life. He was enrolled in *770* and was learning the first subject area for his rabbinical ordination – the section I had just completed. His study partner had just gotten married and thus left him somewhat stranded. We chatted for a bit about my path and how I had now begun my second area of study in mixtures.

Eli had a proposition. He was learning the section on salting but was also proficient in the laws of *Shabbos*. If I learned and reviewed the laws of salting for the first part of the morning and assisted him in passing his first test next month, he would help me to prepare the laws of *Shabbos* so that in four months I would be ready to take my second test. Although the test would not be on mixtures, the laws of the *Shabbos* were a shorter and much less complicated section.

The timing fit well into his schedule. As I learned from Eli, the official examiner for his ordination was the Chief Rabbi for the *Chabad* rabbinical court in Kiryat Melachi in Israel. He regularly travelled to New York, twice, sometimes three times a year. His main purpose for coming to Brooklyn was to test the *yeshiva* students in order to confirm their rabbinical ordination, or their progress on the individual *faheren*/tests. This was actually considered unofficial competition for *770* and their rabbis who traditionally tested the boys who learned in the *Chabad* system. The administration of *770* unofficially was not too pleased with the boys who went down this path; however, Rabbi Yaroslavski had a reputation as a legitimate *Torah* authority that was extremely well versed in Jewish law. His path was one much less paved with bureaucracy and red tape. Due to his vast *Torah* knowledge and indisputable international reputation, the administration of *770* did nothing to stop this growing trend.

Expectations and discussion about Rabbi Yaroslavski's arrival regularly created a frenzy among the *770 yeshiva* students. No one could pinpoint his exact arrival and therefore students had to be ready for their oral exam once word spread in the *yeshiva* of his imminent arrival. At the time, he had certain standards and rules. One had to be enrolled in a *yeshiva* program and verbally account for one's family affiliation within the *Chabad* movement in one's initial meeting. His time was precious and, by reputation, the test would continue until he was certain that everyone in attendance knew or did not know his stuff. The verdict was always swift – it was either thumbs up or the opposite. There was absolutely no discussion about the assessment. One had to choose the language of communication – Hebrew or Yiddish – as he spoke no English. He refused to test groups of less than six in number as any fewer was a waste of his time. A select group of boys would somehow secure his phone number to frantically call him in search of his travel itinerary. Some students would even fly out to where he was located in the USA at that time, in order to join one of his testing sessions at some of the other *Chabad* institutions who paid him to examine their rabbinical students.

I had one month to intensely review the laws of salting with Eli. At the beginning, the balance was fairly even between learning the laws of *Shabbos* and the laws of salting. However, as the date of Rabbi Yaroslavski's arrival in Brooklyn approached, our learning sessions focused more on Eli's preparations than mine did. I reconciled this compromise with my understanding of how one's first test is truly intimidating, remembering how I felt during my first exam. I relied on Eli's commitment to help me, and took comfort knowing I now had a committed study partner who was as equally motivated as I was on a very similar pathway and journey. The inconvenience and slowdown were only temporary.

Before we knew it, word had surfaced that Rabbi Yaroslavski had arrived and the tiny window of testing for Eli was in a mere half-hour! Eli had thirty minutes to find at least five other boys who also needed to be tested in the same subject area. The clock was ticking and poor Eli was frantic. The group of boys who sat at the same table as us were keen to join him but that only made a total group of three. They all knew the rules. They were all concerned that to walk in as a threesome would immediately frustrate the Rabbi. They feared the initial negative impression would be a strike against them before they even began the oral examination. With the clock ticking, they decided that they would not go in as a trio but that a group of four might just be ok. They all looked at me. Would I join along to complete the group?

How could I join them? I was not a registered student in *770*. I certainly didn't have the Hebrew skills to communicate proficiently. Yes, I was helping Eli prepare, but this was a different level of intensity for which I had not prepared. I didn't think I was ready to be tested again. The boys were desperate. I wanted to help, but I was so trepidatious about the entire idea.

Of course, there was one tiny but massive lingering seed of motivation. This was my chance. Wasn't it obvious? This was the opening into the *Lubavitch* system of which I had only dreamed. If Rabbi Yaroslavski accepted me, and I passed the *faher*/exam, my pathway into the *Chabad* system would be set. No one could deny me.

As I walked with the boys, I still hadn't made up my mind! Through their continuous prodding, I kept telling them, "maybe, maybe…" Nervous and unsure of myself, the moment of truth arrived. We walked up the steps to the private residence where he was staying. The three boys looked at me in desperation. With an affirmative nod of my head, I indicated my acceptance of the challenge and Eli rang the doorbell.

A tall, distinguished, very imposing man with a long white beard, traditional long black coat, and hat opened the door. For a brief moment, he looked us all up and down. In Hebrew, he told us to enter and sit down on the sofa in the living room. No one said a word. We just followed his every command. With our bound large volume of text on each of our laps, we sat silently as he settled into one of the chairs in front of us. Looking again deeply into our eyes, he addressed Eli in Hebrew first. Who are you? Where are you from? Where are you studying? Then came my turn. I answered in Yiddish. I told my name, and then I answered with a twist – the truth. I told him I was Eli's study partner. I had learned in a *yeshiva* other than *770*. I mentioned that I had lived in Calgary. I told him the names of both the rabbi in Calgary and my head rabbi in Brooklyn under whom I had studied. That appeared to be enough for Rabbi Yaroslavski because he moved on to the student beside me.

With the formalities behind us, he began with an easy question for Eli who did a comprehensive job answering. Then it was my turn. It was not a challenging question but I struggled more to understand his Hebrew. He saw my hesitation so he quickly switched to Yiddish and I was able to respond correctly with a brief response. He then moved to the next student. The boy beside me had some difficulty with his question and from nowhere he asked me to respond. I recalled a very similar scenario, which was presented to me during my first test in Monsey, so I was able to answer in a similar vein. For the first time the Rabbi demonstrated some human quality and cracked a half-smile of approval. He was pleasantly satisfied with my response. The back and forth, down the line continued for more than half an hour. All of a sudden the questioning stopped. He looked at us and said, "*Zeh hu!*" – "That's it."

I looked at Eli and quietly said, "Now what?" He looked at me and quickly took a pen from his jacket and a blank piece of paper, handing it to Rabbi Yaroslavski. The rabbi asked Eli for his full name. Then he asked me to spell Noteh Glogauer. I told him, having to repeat the difficult spelling of my last name a few times. He omitted the student beside me, and then he asked the final student for his full name. That was it! Three out of the four of us had passed.

We thanked the rabbi, who again showed little emotion, and we hastily exited the house for fear he would possibly change his mind. As we left, I was covered in perspiration and could not contain myself – did I understand what had just happened? I was shell-shocked and ecstatic. I looked Eli in the eye and exclaimed, "We did it! I *did* it!" He looked back at me and said, "Yes you did!" I didn't know why until we got there, but Eli said we now had to go to the pharmacy. It seemed a strange statement. Somehow, being as I was still more than a little dazed and overwhelmed from the exuberance, I would have done anything he told me. We walked to the back of the store to the photocopier. Eli made two copies of the piece of paper that now served as proof we had indeed passed the first of our four tests. Eli explained this would be our "official transcript" demonstrating proficiency in this step toward our goal. Four of these allowed us to receive our official "diploma" from Rabbi Yaroslavski. It was such an antiquated system, but it seemed I had now paid my dues and was actually invited to tag along for the ride! We parted ways after agreeing to continue learning tomorrow our second subject area, the laws of the *Shabbos*. After all, Rabbi Yaroslavski was planning on returning to Brooklyn in a mere four months' time – just enough time to properly prepare.

The moment I told Chaya was one she said she will never forget. I don't remember running home to our newer, but still too small and decrepit Crown Heights apartment on busy Empire Boulevard. I burst into the house and ran calling "Chaya, Chaya, you are not going to BELIEVE what happened!" I could not contain myself and the emotion could be felt as I tried to describe to her the events that led to my taking and passing the first test in the *Chabad* system. The exuberance and elation was palpable. I was speaking so fast I could barely tell the story coherently. I was happy to repeat it over and over, as I simply couldn't believe I had been granted such an amazing gift. After a few more "I can't believe its", we both reflected on the numerous, enormous sacrifices we had both made. As difficult as they were, we both felt that they were all very well worth it! The light at the end of the tunnel was shining brightly. Despite all the people telling me it simply could not be done, that my goal was unrealistic because I had not gone through the system, I had proved them all wrong!

I took what was left of the day to call both our rabbi in Calgary and my parents explaining what had just occurred. I got perhaps the best advice from my rabbi in Calgary, telling me not to forsake the opportunity and burn a bridge in Monsey. In fact, a double ordination, from both a *Chabad* and a non-Chabad institution would serve me well in my future. One never knows what windows will open and what keys unlock closed doors. Therefore, I continued learning the practical rabbinics at the same time as the traditional areas for ordination. Throughout my study time, Chaya continued working full-time, supporting the entire family on her meagre salary. Halfway through the four-month study period in anticipation of Rabbi Yaroslavski's return to Brooklyn, the expectation of the arrival of our second child crept up on us.

But the Show Must Go On

Amid the regular visits to the doctor in order to closely monitor both Chaya and the baby, I felt very strongly that the doctor needed to understand the challenges associated with Esti's delivery. We had asked around when she became pregnant and had thought we had made a wise choice of OB/GYN practice for the delivery of our second child. It had been over five years of waiting and anticipation. The doctor's practice assigned a midwife for the delivery, something we did not have in Calgary. The midwife would assist in the delivery and if there were any complications, the doctor would be called in to take over. Not wanting to alarm Chaya or initiate any unnecessary anxiety, I felt not enough consideration had been given to what went wrong during the last delivery. We were so close to having an emergency C-section performed due to Esti's distress, I was focused on ensuring all precautions were taken. My aim was that this time we would be ready, should the same warning signs present themselves. The doctor kept pushing me off telling me not to worry. I was marginalized as a second-time father having first-time father anxiety. I tried to tell him this was not the case and that I vividly remembered the indicating signs the last time, so we should at least prepare for the same. He attempted to reassure me that he would be on call. In addition, he would put the midwife on notice should any signs of distress present, to immediately call him to take over. With that, we put the issue behind us and focused only on the positive.

It was late in December. Despite the due date set for some time in Chanukah, the festive holiday came and went. My parents had come, hoping to be there for the arrival of our second child after such long anticipation. Instead, they had to take their return flights home to Calgary with no baby having yet arrived. Mind you, we had an amazing time with them. We had not been wined and dined like that since we could not remember when. Esti was in school all day and Chaya was already on maternity leave. With no baby arriving, we went out for lunches and dinners and thoroughly enjoyed that visit with my parents. The due date had passed by more than a week prior. It was Friday, 2 January, when Chaya finally went into labor. That Friday night, we sent Esti upstairs to stay with our new neighbors. We had become good friends with our new acquaintances as we had moved in a few months prior to a larger house in a much better location in Crown Heights. With Esti safe and sound, that night the taxi was called and we headed off to the Park Slope Methodist Hospital. Chaya's labor was intense, even though it had begun slowly Friday morning. By early Saturday morning, she still had not significantly progressed. Chaya was pretty frustrated and her emotionality was beyond words at the news that they weren't going to induce her labor. In this case, there was no identifiable need to induce, nature would take its course. When Chaya was in labor with Esti, the baby had been in distress during the process. This baby was perfectly fine: heart rate fine, no signs of distress – good news about our baby – not so good news for Chaya. With the midwife trying her many strategies to calm Chaya, despite her good intentions she was far from succeeding. Chaya became more agitated by the moment.

I felt that it was time to bring in the doctor and called the midwife aside to discuss our options. I immediately saw our predicament in the midwife's personal reaction to my suggestion. It was as if I had touched a nerve and had personally insulted her professionalism. She took my request as reflecting a suggested incompetence on her part. My request to call the doctor was taken as a knock on her professional capability and she strongly resisted making the call. She pleaded with me to convince Chaya to be more receptive to her and with her at Chaya's side, we were sure to succeed. I was now extremely upset at her attitude, seeing that this was more of an issue of her "success rate" and job proficiency than my wife's wellbeing. Therefore, I as assertively as possible told her that either she would need to immediately call the doctor, or I would go over her head and do it myself. With that, she stomped down the hallway to the nurses' station. She made a scene about the frantic father-to-be down the hall in front of the other nurses and doctors, but I didn't care. She made the call.

Half an hour later, our doctor arrived to examine Chaya. After one examination, he immediately made the call that the baby was indeed stuck and an emergency C-section would have to be performed. Before we knew it, Chaya was prepared for the surgical procedure. I was gowned so I could also be in the operating theatre. A partition was set up so I could be by Chaya's head, communicating with her throughout the operation. We stated again, that we did not want to be told the gender of the baby. As the team of doctors worked quickly and methodically, before long the doctor announced, "I can see the baby now. It's looking right at me, wondering 'what are you doing here?'" With that, in moments he asked me if I wanted to cut the cord, but I declined of course. I was only focusing on wanting to see my wife and child healthy and safe. He lifted the baby up above the screen in front of us and showed us our newborn – "*mazel tov,* it's a boy!" They brought our new baby over to the warming lamp and after all the checks, proclaimed him 100% healthy. I was allowed to hold him while they finished taking care of Chaya. I followed the baby into the nursery where he was given a bath, cleaned, and dressed up before he was taken to his mother for their initial meeting. It was a while before Chaya could hold the baby but about an hour or two after the surgery, our son was successfully nursing.

I spent some time with Chaya. After a little while, our baby was returned to the nursery in order for Chaya to get some much needed rest. The doctor came to see Chaya and me to check in. I thanked him for taking care of her and subtly mentioned that my initial expressed concerns were specifically to have avoided such a scenario. I explained to him that the assigned midwife was adamant she would have no assistance, and that the doctor should have been called much sooner as I had explicitly requested. Nevertheless, thank God, all was well and I decided not to push the matter further.

It was now early afternoon. Despite the more than two-hour walk back to our home, I went back to the synagogue to offer a prayer for Chaya's recovery and the health of our newborn son. Esti's reaction to having a new baby brother was priceless. Her joy and excitement in seeing him for the first time right after *Shabbos* was one of the most memorable and emotionally-pleasing events. Their immediate bond lasts to this day, evident in how they interact and communicate, supporting each other through the good times and their personal challenges. They have become each other's support mechanisms. The two of them developed a model of resilience and reliance that was passed on to Rochel and her relationships with her siblings when she was born five years later.

With a new baby in the household, there were many adjustments. All of them were made easier as Chaya now had a mandatory two-month paid maternity leave due to her having undergone a significant surgical procedure, as her C-section was justly classified. We had eight weeks to relax our regular routine of rushing both Esti to school and Chaya to work. Of course, along with the birth of a boy came significant Jewish rituals such as the *Bris* and many relevant associated customs. As I had done for my brother's only son's circumcision, Michael came to Brooklyn to attend this most significant event. The night before, there is a custom of staying awake all night learning Kabbalistic texts to comfort the soul of the baby boy having left the holy spiritual abode in Heaven to come down to this world of coarse physicality. The words of *Torah* represent a real comfort and salvation to his soul. Both Michael and our brother-in-law Yehoshua, stayed up with me. The night also included many visitors who stopped by to offer their sentiments of congratulation. My previous study partner Yehoshua came to Brooklyn for the actual *Bris* ceremony itself. Rabbi Shmuel was in attendance as were many people who had played a significant role in our lives. My parents understandably were unable to return.

At the circumcision we were honoured to have the *Lubavitcher* Rebbe's *chazzan*, Rabbi Teleshevsky OBM sing the customary emotional blessing that formally announces the baby's arrival at the ceremony. I had to fight back the tears as the *mohel* prepared our little baby for his circumcision, but we knew he was in the best of hands as he was placed on the lap of Rabbi Zalman Gurary, OBM the father of our very close mentor, Mrs. Esther Sternberg. A full circle closed that day. It was a mere sixteen years before when I had met Mrs. Sternberg's daughter in Calgary. I was a young boy attending an introductory *Gan Yisroel* summer camp run by *Chabad* in Calgary. Mrs Sternberg's daughter, Rivky, was my camp counsellor for the few days I attended the camp. The most amazing part of the story is I was only at Camp *Gan Yisroel* for a very few days as a guest of one of my friends. Little did we know that Chaya would become extremely close to Rivky's mother years later from a happenstance meeting while they were both walking to a class one *Shabbos* afternoon. From a simple hello, the rest was history. Both Mrs. Sternberg and her daughter, now Rivky Slonim actually remembered both the Calgary camp and the little Arnie Glogauer. The Guiding Hand in our lives was truly seen through that set of amazing events. From that time on, Chaya would forever have a confidante and mentor to help guide us through the many challenging decisions we would have to make regarding our future. Ultimately, that Guiding Hand would take us to Australia, but that's another book in entirety.

It took a few days to catch our breath and for the dust to settle on what was truly a life-altering experience. Having a new responsibility to care for and the reality of there now being another mouth the feed, I was even more determined to push forward.

I was cautiously satisfied that I had passed the first of four tests toward the final goal of my rabbinical ordination through a recognized

Chabad rabbinic authority. This significant event was tantamount to my being enrolled to receive rabbinic ordination through an official *Chabad* system. During the following months, significant doubts began to creep in. Did I really deserve the perfect fairy tale? Perhaps the one-off test, which I had successfully passed, was simply an oversight I chalked up to Rabbi Yaroslavski's frustration at the tiny size of the testing group. After all, the legend stated he only tested in no less than groups of six; but there had only been four of us. Not only that, he didn't even pass one of the members of our cohort. What would happen the next time I walked in to be tested? What would be my explanation of who I was? Were the names I dropped the last time sufficient enough to get me through the door once again? These questions raced through my mind day after day, throughout my preparations and study for the next exam.

Eli and I were studying the laws of *Shabbos* together. Seated around us, many other students were learning the same. The preparation became much easier. We were all quite familiar with the topics of study, given we had all lived them for the better parts of our lives. I had also learned many of the study areas in *yeshiva* in the original text. Thus, I had a leg up on many of the other students who were learning some of the topic areas for the first time. When there was controversy regarding the bottom line, fundamental law, often the boys would look to me for the answer.

As the four months progressed, I was quite confident. I eagerly awaited news of the rabbi's arrival. One day Eli came late to learning which was quite unusual. Never one to waste a moment, I began to review with some of the boys around me until Eli arrived. I asked him what was up. With a huge smile on his face he exclaimed, "*Mazel tov*, I'm engaged!" I knew he was on the circuit, involved in the dating network but had no idea he was so close to finding his match. There was a *l'chaim*, engagement party that night. Before long, Eli became eternally distracted to the point I could no longer count on his punctuality and commitment to learning. I was lucky to have the boys around me learning and interacting with me but I was concerned about what would transpire after this section was complete, once I had passed the exam and began the next area of study. As you can see from the rant three paragraphs ago, I am well known to race twenty steps ahead of myself. Chaya has always had the ability to calm me down and focus me on the task at hand. We decided to take it one step at a time. I would approach the bridge of finding a new learning partner after I had passed my second test.

Sure enough, not even two weeks later, word was buzzing in the *yeshiva* that Rabbi Yaroslavski was coming to New York before the holiday of Passover, in April. I immediately became a nervous wreck once again with all my doubts resurfacing. Scrambling to set our group with the boys around us, we became a cohort of eight. A week later, we were walking into a side room in the *yeshiva* where we were told the rabbi was waiting for us. The door was open this time. As we knocked on the door, there he stood. For some reason he looked as anxious as we were. Most likely he was eager to get this over with, as the holiday of Passover was rapidly approaching. It was unusual for him to come at this time of year, but we were extremely pleased, as many of us were well prepared. Passing the test at this time of year would allow us to enjoy the holiday that much more, not having to review over the break. As those of you who have experience with the Passover holiday know, at least until it starts, Passover is no vacation! We could be fresh and ready to start a new subject area when we returned after the Passover observances.

Once again, we all chose seats facing the Rabbi. Each one of us deadly silent, not speaking until spoken to. The introductions began and again, he wanted to know who we were. I had my piece of paper at the ready, prepared to prove my legitimacy, having passed one test with him before. I had my *spiel* already worked out in my head. When he came to me, I repeated the same story I had shared the last time. He looked at me, nodded as an acknowledgement indicating to me that I had a legitimate right to be there which calmed me instantaneously. Each student had his story as to why they had chosen this alternate pathway towards their rabbinical ordination. Once the formalities had been covered, he began grilling us on the laws of *Shabbos*. This time he was much more animated and there was a lot of lively back and forth discussion. My strategy was to only interject when I was definite on the bottom line. It seemed some of the boys were very keen on demonstrating their ability to argue with the rabbi. At times, it really looked like their egos would get the better of them. At those times, he would shut down the conversation with a clear bottom-line finality. I could not fathom why they would potentially jeopardize their passing for the sake of being right, nevertheless I decided to keep my wits about me and engage only when necessary. He was very wise and perhaps noticed that I spoke much less than the other boys did. At one point, he proceeded to ask me some specific questions related to a more obscure topic. Somehow, I remembered a class given by the head rabbi of my *yeshiva* on the exact same topic. Not only was I able to correctly remember the law, I was able to open up the Code of Jewish Law in my lap and pinpoint a similar case that had the same bottom line. The human side of Rabbi Yaroslavski showed once again. This time it was even more satisfying. He flashed a tiny, approving grin at me before moving on to the next question. In just over an hour, we were done; all eight of us had passed the exam. This time the rabbi seemed very satisfied and wrote all of our names happily on the piece of paper thrust in front of him by one of the eager students. We all wished him a happy *Pesach* and exited as fast as we discreetly could. Once again, we rushed to the pharmacy, this time to make eight photocopies – the evidence of our success.

It was of great comfort to know I was firmly established on the pathway toward the fulfilment of my goal. The goal no one said was reachable. At the same time, I was continuing with my study of my practical rabbinics. In May of that year I was told that upon successful demonstration of proficiency in three written exams, I would be conferred my practical rabbinics certificate through the *Kollel* in Monsey.

I am grateful that I was successful in achieving this milestone; however, as you can well imagine, it paled in comparison. For me, the personal significance of passing the oral examinations with Rabbi Yaroslavski was indescribable in the meaning it held for me. His questioning was thorough and my preparation was intense. Ironically, there would be organizations and schools who would potentially value my certification more from the non-*Chabad* institution. They would not know what had been involved in either journey. That is part of the mystery of this world. What is valued is not always the most valuable.

For me the path I had to forge and the challenges I had to manage getting into the *Chabad* track demonstrated a greater measure of Divine Providence. Certainly, on a daily basis, I appreciated the lesson of never giving up, despite everyone else telling me to. Even as I had successfully passed the first two exams, I knew that the next two subject areas were the toughest.

At this point in time, I didn't have a consistent learning partner who was as committed as I was to completing the goal in a similar time frame. It was now May. Eli had not been coming regularly to learn since his engagement. With his wedding planned for June, his mind was just not in it. Nevertheless, we continued learning in our regular spot, surrounded with the *770* students planning their summer pursuits. As the month progressed, the crowd quickly began to thin out. We had decided to take on the most challenging of the four subject areas, mixtures, which I had begun to learn before meeting Eli. Not only was it the longest of the four subject areas, it was also the most intricate. I dedicated my every fibre into my learning despite the new obligations and schedule with baby Yossi at home.

We now had a new nanny who would arrive at 9 am to look after Yossi. She met me at home, as I returned from dropping off Esti and Chaya at school and work respectively. It had been very difficult for Chaya to go back to work full time after her brief two-month maternity leave, but our goal of achieving my rabbinical ordination in two years and securing a job shortly thereafter was the beacon keeping us on track. We had received a clear answer that our blessings for financial livelihood would come from my learning. So I was motivated to study and Chaya found the personal strength to go back to work after only eight weeks with little Yosseleh. My success had fuelled the desire to continue on the path, despite the significant emotional challenges of living in near poverty away from the emotional support of family. For the most part, we were alone in our quest together and had become the sole, necessary support mechanisms to remain steadfast and committed to our end goal. Deep down we knew if we just remained unwavering, at the other side of the abyss, the bridge we were building would prove more than worthwhile for our family.

From Monday through Thursday, I would leave Yossi with the nanny at 9 am and study after morning prayers from 10 am through 3:30 pm, when I would have to pick up Esti from school. On Friday, I had to pick her up by 12:30 pm in order to prepare for the *Shabbos*. With Chaya working until 4:30 pm even on Fridays, it would be my task to do all the shopping and most evenings cook dinner.

Esti and I enjoyed a lot of our time together shopping for the *Shabbos*. We prided ourselves in our ability to both shop and cook for the *Shabbos* in less than two hours. Granted there was not a lot of variety in meals, nevertheless, our efficiency and practicality was to be admired. We had our set route from which the three of us would rarely deviate. It of course included a stop at the pizza store for an early Friday lunch. Our relationship was forged once again through this personal time together. We still fondly reminisce on the memories of the time we spent together growing up in Brooklyn. It was a rare scene in the community for a father to both run Friday errands and babysit the children, but I was proud to demonstrate a new type of family unit, which I could only have done due to the special qualities, and the self-sacrifice of my wife. Her education, having completed her PhD, was a true rarity in this community. Not only was our journey rare, but also it was equally an uncommon practice for the wife to work full time and the husband learn all day.

With Eli now rarely making it to our learning sessions, I had to push on by myself. For students learning toward their ordination, routine is everything. It is amazing how we are all creatures of habit. This certainly is a characteristic that assists in accomplishing a lofty goal such as the one toward which I was working. For the committed students, and there were many in *770*, you get to know very quickly their personalities and faces. Those two years resulted in a fair few boys around me becoming regular acquaintances. Soon they began to notice I was more or less alone, as my study partner had become an absent figure. One day a new face emerged at the end of our table. One of the boys introduced me to his friend – Josh from South Africa. Josh had just recently arrived via Israel where he had been learning for a year. Now he was also looking to learn and be tested by Rabbi Yaroslavski for his rabbinical ordination. Moreover, he too was looking for a study partner! He was open to studying any of the four required subject areas. We immediately hit it off and before you knew it, I had caught him up on whatever I had learned in mixtures. We were learning at a brisk pace. His skills were quite strong and we jelled perfectly as a partnership. Josh became a close member of our family. He frequently spent evenings with us for dinner and *Shabbos* lunches over the long summer afternoons.

With Brooklyn once again emptying out for the summer, Josh and I diligently learned together on the hot summer days in the pretty much abandoned air-conditioned *770*. The quiet days allowed us to progress effectively. Before we knew it, the summer holiday travellers were returning, and with them, the upcoming September Jewish high holy days.

Unexpectedly, we got news that Rabbi Yaroslavski was passing through Brooklyn on his way to Florida. If we could get a group together, he was willing to test us. With little notice, it proved a great challenge assembling the group. Once again, just as apprehensive as before, we approached a private residence with an appointment to be tested. However, exactly like our first *faher* situation, we risked Rabbi Yaroslavski's disapproval once again. Despite all our best efforts, we were only four students making up our cohort.

Nervously we knocked on the front door of the residence. Rabbi Yaroslavski slowly opened the front door. We could immediately see his frustration as the four of us stood on the step yearning to be invited inside. This time he asked, "Where are the others?" In his very clear Hebrew, he stated that he had little time on this visit and expected a larger group. Josh was our representative. He told Rabbi Yaroslavski that there were not a lot of boys studying mixtures and that due to the brief summer break; most students were learning the section relating to milk and meat. Josh explained to Rabbi Yaroslavski, with great respect, that he consequently should not expect another group of boys seeking to be tested on mixtures today or while he was here in NY on this trip.

The Rabbi paused. After a brief moment, he fully opened the door and told us enter and to sit. It was a dark, musty basement this time. This time, he didn't care to ask us who we were. Instead, he took the volume of mixtures from the shelf behind him and began to rapidly fire questions at each of us. Questioning was at a swift pace and he did not have the patience for long, convoluted answers. He was brief and expected the same brevity in our responses. This went on for forty-five minutes. There was not a lot of time for reflection from one question to another. Sometimes someone would answer the question in a way that you could tell just didn't sit well with the rabbi. He never told you, "no – incorrect". He would just say, "But if that's your response, such and such rabbi says differently," and he would quote that opinion. Subtly, you knew you had responded incorrectly to his question. You had to keep your own score. Deep down you never knew how many incorrect responses resulted in a failure, but you waited for your next question, hoping to answer it correctly and record a tick in the "correct" column. As each question was fired toward you and you proposed your response, it was a quick determination, "did I answer it correctly?" "How am I doing?" It was an intense back and forth.

Then he just closed the volume and put it back on the shelf. We were done. We all stood up as the rabbi got up to put his book on the shelf. We were all somewhat shell-shocked, unsure of the outcome. So I boldly stepped forward and asked him if we had passed. He said yes. So then, as every time previously someone gave him a piece of paper. This time, it was me. He then said the strangest thing. He told me that there was no need for the paper. He told me that it was unnecessary: *"Ani Ezkhor Otcha"* – "I will remember you!" With that, we left the apartment in a daze. What had just happened? He said we had passed but he didn't give us a piece of paper? Will he really remember me? He must test hundreds of students over the year, how will he remember me? What if he just said that to get rid of us? Should we go back and press him further? Will he then possibly get angry? How could I contain myself until the next test? All these questions burned in my mind as I was unsure how to get past this most strange occurrence. Luckily, I had Josh who was the coolest of personalities, and at this most trying time he successfully eased my mind.

He told me, "Just how many students do you think he tells – I will remember you? I doubt many. Hang on to these words; let's begin your last area to reach your goal. He most likely will come back to New York in February or March. That leaves us with more than six months to prepare."

It was true. I was on target to take my last exam before April, thus giving me ample time to start looking for a job somewhere before the start of the new school year in September. It was now October 1998. Indeed, we were on track. Our family was slowly becoming part of the Crown Heights community, having settled in quite comfortably into our new surroundings and a regular routine of our workweek and the traditional European lifestyle of living from *Shabbos* to *Shabbos*.

It was a comforting lifestyle knowing that our weekday activities were more the vehicle for our spiritual existence, which manifested its glory on the *Shabbos*. Deep down, through all the trappings of a physical existence, our observance reinforced our higher purpose, realising that life was more purposeful. Knowing that there had to be more to our existence than working 9 to 5 Monday through Friday. Living a true connected life spiritually translated into our family connectedness, a bond linking each member to one another, not only to a higher source. The *Shabbos* activities, as well as the Friday preparations, enabled a purpose that was palpable through each and every task. Our *Shabbos* preparations were like a well-choreographed performance. The role each family member played proved that the most significant event was dependent on each participant, no matter how large or small his or her contribution.

The Friday morning shopping and the input from the kids, as to which delicacies we should buy, initiated them into the process very early in their development. For the young child who had the honour of picking out the special cake from the bakery, the anticipation started at the moment of purchase. It continued beyond when dessert was finally brought to the table at the conclusion of the Friday night meal. There was the smile on our child's face, which in turn caused special smiles of satisfaction on our faces. We were linking the child's emotional experience from the pre-*Shabbos* activity and his or her decision to the source of joy for the rest of the family. Every child's investment in the physical preparations reinforced the personal importance and significance, not only to the *Shabbos* itself, but also their involvement instilled a sense of personal value.

The input each child made to the family unit regardless of age was treasured. Expectations were that every member contributed and thus their individuality was recognised. The shopping was just one example. One spiritual example was the beautiful school arts and crafts and *Torah* knowledge quiz pages Esti would bring home from school on a Friday afternoon. We would make the biggest deal over them at the *Shabbos* meal. Those early formative years in the growth of our family were in my hands to orchestrate as my time, although largely spoken for, was far more flexible and much closer to home than Chaya's. Chaya's role was to support the family while mine was to obtain the necessary credentials to take us further toward our long-term goal – finding a place that would welcome my secular experience as an educator and my learning and subsequent Jewish credentials as a rabbi.

The Trip of a Lifetime

It was the latter part of 1998. In the background of my passing my third *faher* and preparing for the fourth and final one, my father's mother *Bobba* Ruth's health was deteriorating. My parents had made the decision to travel back to South Africa to see her. I had maintained a very strong relationship with my *Bobba* despite the vast physical distance separating us. As you know, I have always taken my family relationships seriously. I was already the next generation historian in the family, renowned for my scarily accurate memory of events most people were too young to remember. To me they were as clear as the day they happened. The traumatic experience in 1977 when I was forced to leave my great-grandmother reaffirmed my commitment to preserve a close relationship with my *Bobba* when I was older.

We were very fortunate that *Bobba* Ruth had made the long journey to Canada a couple of times. After each trip, our bond grew stronger and stronger. Having left South Africa when we were young only fortified my resolve to maintain a connection with her, as she was the last of our grandparents in the family. We shared very similar joys in life. My love for baking comes from her. This is just as true about my love for playing card games. Whenever *Bobba* came to visit, we would end up playing Portuguese Rummy. When I was lucky enough to beat her, she would joyfully exclaim that I was cheating, as it would be impossible for anyone to defeat her. We all knew she was not serious in her allegations; it was just incredibly endearing that she was playfully competitive with her grandson. We could spend hours together, virtually erasing the generation gap that existed between other youths and their grandparents in modern society.

The news that her health was deteriorating so rapidly weighed heavily on my heart. The thought of my not seeing her again coupled with the fact that she had never seen any of her North American great-grandchildren motivated me to pick up the phone. I called my mother and father to float the idea that I was keen on making a trip to South Africa at the same time as they were, for the simple reason of seeing my *Bobba* one last time. Before long, somehow my Uncle Maish from South Africa was on the phone offering to pay for our family to fly down.

Fortuitously and conveniently, the trip to South Africa was cheapest that year if one flew through Tel Aviv via El Al, Israel's national airline, linking up with South African Airways. I had never been to Israel, and it was the most unlikely long shot. When the idea came to me that we would be in Israel even for a short three-day stopover, I floated the idea to Chaya and then to Josh, that if I worked a little harder, we could finish the last subject area of study, milk and meat, before my departure date. Perhaps, just by chance, if Rabbi Yaroslavski was in his hometown in Israel in December, I could go to him and take my last test. The idea was sound and even though many pieces of the logistics puzzle would have to fall into place, it was worth a try. We decided to see whether it was meant to be for me to finish my rabbinical studies a few months earlier than we had first anticipated.

If I was not a man on a mission before, I sure was now as it hit me that this event would significantly change our life and the direction of our journey once again.

So I asked around for Rabbi Yaroslavski's home phone number and after one or two unsuccessful tries, I finally got through to him. Unbelievably, he indeed declared that not only would he not be travelling over the holiday of *Chanukah* to test other students, but also he was actually willing to test me alone, by myself at his private residence the day after I was arriving in Israel. He told me to come to his home at 10 am on the 10th of *Teves*. There it was! I was about to finish my *Chabad Smicha* on the auspicious fast day of the 10th of *Teves*.

We had a lot to learn, but Josh was keen to take part in my tenuous journey and do whatever he could to help me achieve this improbable goal. Learning the entire section of the Code of Jewish Law regarding the laws of milk and meat was truly a massive feat in the six months we had originally allotted. To cut that time in half was implausible to say the least. I was so motivated. With Josh and I learning morning, noon and night for three months, the time flew by. Sure enough, we finished the week before the designated date of our departure.

I had to contain so much excitement. Travelling back to South Africa for the very first time since I emigrated in 1977; visiting family I hadn't seen for years; the opportunity to introduce all the significant places of my growing up to Chaya and our two children. Celebrating Yossi's first birthday with his *Bobba* in South Africa; *Bobba* meeting Esti, her first great-grandchild, and Yosseleh, one of only two Glogauer grandsons of her beloved son Maxi. Then there was the fact that my route to all this emotional pride was through…The Holy Land! In addition, I would be realising a lifelong goal of visiting the Holy Land of Israel, visiting the Western Wall, the direction of my daily prayers. All these thoughts and dreams had to be put on hold as I easily could have become distracted. Our future depended on my passing this last test. Little did I know that I would have one or two other tests of faith before I would ever meet Rabbi Yaroslavski on the 10th of *Teves*.

I was strangely calm as the date approached for our departure to Israel. Chaya did the packing and took care of all the arrangements, as I remained focused on my task at hand. I used every waking moment to review my studies. I was thankful for the eleven-hour plane ride and used every moment of the long haul to focus my mind on a thorough review without any distractions. I blocked out of my mind the one niggling concern. I had tried a few days before to confirm that which was discussed three months earlier, my testing at the great rabbi's home on the 10th of *Teves*. However, I was unsuccessful many times in reaching him. If worst came to worst, I could always meet him on our way back from South Africa via Israel. However, there was no way I was prepared to rely on this shaky contingency plan and worst-case scenario. I was ready and knew I would not really enjoy my visits anywhere if I still had my last exam weighing on me. I was determined to meet him on the 10th of *Teves*. Deep down I believed that divine intervention was going to make it happen.

We arrived in Israel on the eve of the 10th of *Teves*. Immediately after clearing customs, and acknowledging we were actually in the Holy Land, Chaya went to claim our bags off the conveyor belt and I went straight to the payphone to call Rabbi Yaroslavski to confirm our meeting time for the following morning. The phone rang once, twice, three times: my heart beat so rapidly, what if he wasn't there, four times… Then someone picked up the phone. I recognized his voice immediately and quickly introduced myself. I reminded him who I was and that I just got off the plane and was ready to see him tomorrow morning. Then he said, in Hebrew, "Really, are you sure? Did you not remember that tomorrow was a fast day?" I didn't really remember initially that the 10th of *Teves* was the most significant of the 'minor' fast days in the Jewish calendar, the day the Babylonian king Nebuchadnezzar surrounded the walls of Jerusalem and laid siege to the city. It was therefore a public fast day established to commemorate this most significant event in Jewish history.

I was so focused on finishing and keeping my goal in mind that I was oblivious to anything else, let alone eating and the need for physical sustenance.

I quickly responded that despite the fast day, I really didn't want to reschedule. "I am ready to come tomorrow no matter what, as long as the good Rabbi would please see me!" There was a pause on the other side…then a quick "Okay, I will see you at my home at 10 am," and he hung up. It was set and now I had to get over the next obstacle; what was his address? It sounds strange when I look back at the fact that no one told me where he lived other than his neighbourhood. I just assumed that I would get there and it would be clear where to go. Boy, was I mistaken.

My Uncle Uzzi and Auntie Miri, my mother's first cousin and his wife picked us up at the airport. They were a pleasant sight and were most helpful in providing us with some clarity in this, my first visit to Israel. As it is the spiritual homeland to all Jews, it was not a foreign country to us at all. It was just the customs and the details of navigating around that were foreign to us as every detail attested. We had made advance arrangements to stay with a close friend of ours. When Uzzi and Miri asked us where they would be dropping us off, we simply told them the address and town. They looked at each other and it was as if their faces had dropped a mile. Only when we reached the checkpoint before the entrance into the "settlement" did we realise the reason for their alarm and concern. We would be staying near *Modiin*, beyond the Green Line – one of the hot spots of contention in the media at the time. The soldiers told Uncle Uzzi not to stop on the road once we passed the checkpoint and to drive directly to the address where we would be staying. We didn't realise the potential danger we had put our gracious hosts in, much less ourselves. With a nervous smile, Uncle Uzzi and Aunt Miri looked at us squashed together in the backseat, "Welcome to Israel!"

Driving quickly and cautiously along the dirt road, we arrived safely at the address Fruma, our old friend from Calgary, had given us. With our suitcases safely inside and plans set to meet our cousins again before we travelled along to South Africa a few days later, we had the most delicious meatballs we had ever eaten. Even one-year-old Yossi demonstrated his carnivorous tendencies after that long journey, eating more than his fair share too.

With dinner finished, Fruma helped me plan my journey that was to begin only a few hours later. I would get up at the crack of dawn to travel a couple of hours south to *Kiryat Melachi*. It wasn't a simple journey, as I would end up taking a *Hasa'ah* to a bus stop outside Tel Aviv. Then from

271

the main highway, I would take a bus to the outskirts of the town of my intended destination. From there, I would need to take a taxi to Rabbi Yaroslavski's house. As much as we tried that night, no one could tell Fruma exactly what his address was. All we could confirm was *Nachalat Har Chabad* – that's where he lived. I figured if I got there early enough, with plenty of time to spare, I would comfortably find my way.

So there I was, on a community bus not having a clue if I was even going in the right direction. I told the bus driver I wanted to get to *Kiryat Melachi*. He told me in rapid fire Hebrew to take "this and this" bus and to take a seat, as he would tell me when to get off. About forty-five minutes later, the bus stopped and he motioned for me to get out. Like a little lost puppy, I did exactly what he said. Just before I exited the bus, he reminded me that "this and this" bus would take me: "Just remember. Go south." I stood at the side of the highway and waited for a bus to come. My test was at 10 am, and it was only 8:30 am. I still had plenty of time and was not too nervous. As the minutes ticked away, not too many buses were passing by. My nerves began to rattle. Finally, a bus came and I asked the driver if he was going to *Kiryat Melachi*. He said he would be driving by the town and I should get on and he would instruct me when to get off. Again, I boarded and just hoped that I was once again going in the right direction. I was a cosmic pawn in a game Someone Else was playing. I had no clue what was going on around me and now I was one of a few people on a bus going to who knows where.

It was now 9:15 am, and the bus stopped near a sign indicating the entrance to the town of *Kiryat Melachi*. I smiled and thanked the bus driver. I got off the bus and started walking in the direction of the town keeping a lookout for the taxi that would complete my journey. Of course, not one taxi, nor any cars at all for that matter, could be seen in this ghost town in the middle of nowhere. I realised this was a more observant town, and it was off the beaten path. With it being a fast day, not too many people would be out and about. After walking for a little while into town, I came upon a few stores and decided to go in and asked directions to the rabbi's house. To my dismay, no one knew or had even heard of Rabbi Yaroslavski. I was out of luck, now what?

I decided to go back to the main street and keep walking, hoping a taxi would drive by. Surely, the taxi driver would know the significant places in town and take me to this well-known rabbi's house. I walked a mile or so. Suddenly a white car came driving by. I realised I must have looked strange – a large cardboard portfolio and my personal text of Code of Jewish Law in one hand and a satchel containing my *Tallis* and *Tefillin* in another. I figured I would pray after my test since I had had to get up before dawn to get on the road and travel. I could not have prayed that early, as it was a pitch dark winter dawn when I had to depart. I had been travelling for more than three hours already to get to where I was, which was feeling more and more like nowhere at all!

I immediately put my hand out and flagged down the white car for him to stop so I could ask for directions. To my delight, the driver stopped the car. Again, in my broken Hebrew, I asked him to tell me how to get to *Nachalat Har Chabad* – Rabbi Yaroslavski's house. He smiled and told me to get in. He would take me directly to the rabbi's house. Indeed, it was not much further, but I would never have found it on my own. He pulled up to a housing complex and pointed to number two and said, "That's the rabbi's house." I thanked him profusely and got out.

On the corner there just happened to be a phone booth. With the few minutes I actually had to spare before 10 am, I called Chaya to let her know I had actually made it, purely by the grace of God. When I hung up the phone, I even had a few minutes to compose myself. I drew in a few deep breaths before I walked up the stairs to the rabbi's house. I walked toward number two. Indeed, this was the place; his family name was inscribed on a marble plaque on the front door. I apprehensively rang the doorbell, trying not to overthink the many cosmic events that had now brought me to this location at this time.

Sure enough, before long, I could see through the glass-framed window beside the door that the Rabbi was walking toward me. The door swung open and he greeted me with a warm hello. He told me to follow him as he led me to another room. This was obviously his personal study as the walls were covered with bookshelves from floor to ceiling. A large table was centred in the middle of the study. The Rabbi pulled out a chair for me and motioned me to take a seat. In Hebrew, he told me to make myself comfortable and asked me which subject area I had prepared. I told him, "Milk and meat". He walked over to one of the bookshelves and removed the indicated volume of the Code of Jewish Law. He placed his volume at his place at the head of the table. He drew a chair for himself and began posing the first question in Hebrew. After he finished the question, I humbly requested if he would mind repeating it in Yiddish and added, that if we could continue all the further communications in this language, I preferred it to Hebrew: and so we began. Back and forth, question after question. This was a very different encounter to my three previous examinations. There was no one to deflect any questions. No hope that someone else would answer the challenging scenarios being proposed. I could not hide in this one-on-one interrogation. Looking back, I was probably the best prepared for this exam compared to the other three. At one moment, I was questioned as to the validity of my response and why I was so certain that I was correct. In one of the margins of the original text, I had written a note representing the exact case being proposed from a scenario discussed in the *Talmud*. Thus, when he asked me the very question on this issue, I was able to directly quote the name of the Tractate of Talmud, the page number as well as the name of the rabbi making the point and his concluding statement.

At that point, Rabbi Yaroslavski actually got up from the table and walked over to my volume to see my inscribed note. This was not considered cheating. The question posed was quite random. It was my job, during my preparation and study, to ascertain how the applicable law cited in the Code of Jewish Law reflected various scenarios in other holy works. I also had to determine if this example set a precedent or not by citing a similar case study. One was not required to memorise the entire Code of Jewish Law. Rabbinical training requires knowledge of where to look for precedents. With this scenario, I had proven my capability for doing just that.

At some point, I made my last response. I had not even noticed that I'd been sitting for close to an hour. The rabbi stood up and said, *"Zeh hu"* – that's it! I asked him, a little confused, had I passed? He said yes. Now the challenge… I pulled out the large cardboard portfolio I had managed to preserve all the way from Crown Heights the day before. I presented the rabbi with the large poster from within the cardboard case. I opened it up to reveal a prewritten graduation certificate with my name and the day's date. I asked him if he would sign the rabbinical ordination certificate I had prepared before I left Crown Heights. The certificate was filled out to indicate my completion and fulfilment of the necessary requirements. He looked at the certificate, which also had his name and official title printed on the top. He asked where on earth did I get such a thing? I was confused, as it seemed as if this was the first time he had seen such a thing. I had followed the strict instructions from my friends in *770* who were in the know. In New York, all the *yeshiva* boys told me they were specifically getting such certificates made for him expressly to sign in an official capacity. They were made in the exact image of the *770* Ordination Certificate with the exception of inclusion of Rabbi Yaroslavski's credentials. I told him that there was a student in Brooklyn printing them himself. I had gone to his home where I procured a copy with the hopes I would successfully pass this final test and thereby earn his full approval and his signature!

He smiled. Apparently, he was indicating approval of my confidence in having already paid for a scribe to write the day's date (10th of *Teves*) on the certificate. Then my heart sank. He asked me, "Do you have the three *tzetlach,* indicating that I tested you and you passed the other three sections?" I took out and presented him with the first two. He then asked me where the third note was for the section on mixtures. My heart almost jumped out of my throat. I reminded him of three months ago when he tested me, that he had told me not to worry as he had stated, and I quoted in Hebrew, "I will remember you!"

He smiled, took the pen and then, he signed the certificate! I placed it carefully back in the protective portfolio and thanked him profusely. I asked the rabbi if I could please give him a donation of thanks. He replied it was totally not necessary. I entreated him, asking that if he would not take it himself, could he please distribute it to someone in his community who was in need. He agreed. I passed him the modest sum I had prepared before leaving Crown Heights. With that, I picked up my satchel, thanked him again, and left.

I departed his home rather quickly. I felt once again that familiar irrational insecurity that perhaps he would change his mind. I ran straight to the phone booth on the corner to call Chaya. As soon as she got on the phone, I broke down under the immense rush of emotions and exclaimed, "We did it! Chaya, it's over! I passed!" It was an incredible load off my shoulders, realising the dream so many people deemed impossible. In less than two years, I had received my practical rabbinical ordination from the *Kollel* in Monsey. More miraculously, here I was on a street corner in the middle of Israel holding in my hand the certificate of my rabbinical ordination through *Chabad*! To have come so far in life and for my goal to be achieved in all places, the Holy Land of Israel was something I could never have dreamed. We made arrangements where to meet in Tel Aviv and I got off the phone.

The long bus ride to Tel Aviv bus station seemed like an eternity. I longed to meet up with Chaya and the children to share the moment together. I eventually arrived and made my way amidst the soldiers in the main hall of the Central Bus Station in Tel Aviv. I couldn't stand still in great anticipation of my devoted family's arrival. It certainly didn't feel like a fast day and the 10th of *Teves* would forever be a personal day of triumph for me and my family amidst the historical calamity, which befell our Jewish nation on that same day 1928 years earlier. It only served to highlight the important concept that everything in this world is under God's divine hand. Not only that: it is all good. It is sometimes just really difficult to see the good in the very hard challenges in life. That 10th of *Teves* brought that message so much closer for each of us.

As I look back on this event and my individual transformation, it is quite astounding. This date has a legacy of great personal significance. My first encounter with the *Lubavitcher Rebbe* had also taken place on the 10th of *Teves*. That first *Yeshiva-cation* we attended way back in 1990, we were present during one of The *Rebbe's* famous public gatherings. One of his public talks happened also to be on this most auspicious date. Upon the conclusion of his discourse, the entire congregation shuffled by the grand *Rebbe*. Each person was given a token dollar to be exchanged for charity. This being my first experience I had no knowledge of the proper protocol or that there even was a specific etiquette. I simply wanted to sincerely thank the *Rebbe* for the blessings he had sent to Chaya and me before our wedding. I didn't know one was not allowed to talk to the *Rebbe* at that moment. I was so overwhelmed by the *Rebbe's* presence; I felt it was the appropriate time to thank him especially since this was my first opportunity at this, my initial encounter. Shuffling by, moving with the constant ebb and flow of the crowd, I passed by the podium from where the *Rebbe* was distributing the dollar bills. I managed to pause for a brief moment. In Yiddish, I thanked the *Rebbe* at the same time as I was pulled away by one of his attendants. In the hurried encounter, the *Rebbe* said some words in response to me and gave me another dollar. I was only to discover later that what the *Rebbe* responded was a direct recognition that my words of thanks had been acknowledged and received. To this very day, I am astounded that this transformative event also took place on the 10th of *Teves*.

We had a few days in Israel before travelling on to South Africa. The memorable experiences included seeing Jerusalem in all her glory and the notable Western Wall for the first time. These joyous experiences were linked very much to the completion of my goal. For the first time in my life, I was in the Holy Land experiencing Jewish life as I felt it ought to be lived. We were eating at kosher restaurants, speaking Hebrew with our brothers and sisters, seeing ancient and new Jewish landmarks that expressed the bond between ourselves and over 3000 years of our history. The most surreal aspect of these experiences was my immersing myself in it all as a rabbi. We felt a direct tie, a forged connection between the physical and the spiritual.

In late 1998, we were very much before the days of cell phones. We were in transit, with no landline of our own. We had no way of contacting or getting word to our family about the amazing news. I could not have imagined the emotional reaction of my parents, family and even more so my *Bobba* when we finally arrived in South Africa, a few days later. We were greeted at the airport with a large contingent of family who were all overjoyed to see us.

As we walked out of the customs arrival doors, I met my father. All I had to do was meet his questioning look. That confirmed I had indeed become a rabbi. I was moved by his emotions. I will forever remember the scene of both my father, mother and my *Bobba,* with tears in their eyes upon hearing of my accomplishment in Israel. Through my *Bobba's* face, I could see her drifting back to another time, living in a tiny town in Poland with her father as one of the town's *Shochtim* and the synagogue's *Shamas*. My *Bobba*, one of the sole survivors of her entire family managed to escape from the horrors of the Holocaust in 1938. The link of the present to her past had incredibly special meaning for her. My *Bobba's* tears at that moment were testimony to the significance of my responsibility to merit continuing the family legacy.

9-11

Our return to Brooklyn from South Africa was more than surreal. We had had an incredible gift and miracle-filled journey. We rekindled relationships. We met cousins and their new spouses. Not to mention the spiritual highs of our trip to the Holy Land – not the least of which was having accomplished attaining my rabbinic ordination. Of course, this milestone was destined to be and has been just that. Accomplishing this goal is meant to be a stepping-stone to lifelong learning and ongoing personal growth. I did indeed settle back into learning, albeit on a somewhat less pressurized schedule. Our return to Brooklyn in January 1999 with my ordination completed signalled the ensuing leg of our journey. My next mission was to take on the quest of finding my first principalship in a Jewish school.

It was time to test my theory. Would the doors open now that I had rabbinical ordination? Who would take the plunge and hire me? Were there really benefits to having both a non-*Chabad* and a *Chabad* rabbinical ordination?

Of course, there was one significant fact: I had never been a principal of a school. Of course, I would and did count on the fact that I had been offered and accepted Head of the Science Department at Elboya Junior High School, even though I had never served in that position. In essence, I lacked an administrative track record, despite my conviction and confidence that this was my destined path to be a great leader. I knew this deep down and it had been confirmed by some of the best educators I had known. It was this confidence that pushed me to set up one of the most challenging interviews I had ever had.

I spent a week or so updating my resume to reflect having just completed my rabbinical ordination. It didn't take me very long to update my resume, since I had spent the majority of the past two years studying pretty much full time. After our year in Houston, I only had two part-time teaching jobs in the late afternoon. I sent my resume via email to the three potential positions I had seen advertised. The whole exercise left me somewhat anxious about my future prospect of gaining a principalship. I just had a feeling. There must be another mechanism schools were using to publicise their administrative vacancies, which at the time was evading me. So I placed a quick call to The Board of Jewish Education of Greater New York. I managed to reach a very helpful administrator in the Educational Resource Centre. I told her of my challenge in identifying schools that were seeking principals for the upcoming academic year.

The helpful person at the Board of Jewish Education of Greater New York suggested I contact *Torah Umesorah*. After a quick call to directory assistance, I managed to reach the head office of *Torah Umesorah* and the Director of Personnel Resources.

In thirty seconds or less, I managed to sum up my experience and professional background, but more importantly that I was seeking a position as a principal. The director asked me to prepare an updated resume and come in for an initial interview the following week. It was a quick but purposeful conversation that left me hopeful. I wasn't really sure what to expect from my upcoming interview. I didn't have enough time during the phone conversation to get a sense of the director. Of course, I had already updated my resume before I rang *Torah Umesorah*, so I had a bit of time, perhaps too much, to think. Realising that my best chances for securing a position would be through either *Torah Umesorah*, or the odd advertisement either online or from the local Jewish newspaper – The Jewish Press, I decided not to stress too much. I would rely on all the steps I had taken toward the foundation of my education, experience and credentials. I truly believed that the good fortune I had until now all set the stage for something positive.

During this important transition period in the next four months, I would now focus on two goals on top of my learning. I would try to secure a job to bring in some needed additional income to our family. At the same time, I would keep my eyes open for principalships for the upcoming 1999-2000 academic school year. While waiting for my scheduled interview at *Torah Umesorah,* an incredible opportunity came up. An opportunity that would come to play a significant role in reinforcing my resolve that my decision to choose education as my pathway and career was indeed my destiny.

One Sunday, we had a family get-together with my wife's cousin and his family. It was a chance to catch up after our trip to Israel. During the general chitchat, I of course mentioned now that I had completed my studies, I was looking for a part-time job in between 'career' job hunting. Coincidentally Chaya's cousin remarked how overloaded he was at work.

Was I interested in helping out? Perhaps we could both benefit from our mutual circumstances. A very successful financial advisor at Morgan Stanley Dean Witter in Manhattan, Doug was looking for a part-time assistant who could organize his client base. The goal of the job was to expand his network for the financial products and levels of the investments.

I would need some flexibility if I had to attend interviews, which was fine with Doug. It wasn't rocket science. It was a job for someone with good organisational skills and a positive disposition over the phone.

First, all of the clients had to be organised based on their current financial product and level of commitment. Then I would cold-call each client on Doug's behalf with the goal of assessing their interest in receiving further information by mail, and a follow-up phone call from Doug. It would be my job to make both the cold call and to collate the physical material to be mailed out. The interim job worked well for me as the hours were flexible and the pay was well worth the effort.

It might surprise you to know that I enjoyed the subway journey into the city from Brooklyn. It gave me some time to collect my thoughts and reinforce my energy. Maybe the most exciting part was the ride into Chambers Street Subway Station and then the walk through the mall at the World Trade Center. Douglas's office suite was on the 71st floor, Tower Two, The World Trade Center in Lower Manhattan. There was the most amassing fringe benefit of this little sojourn back in the business world. At low points, when flashes of doubt would enter my mind about my possible failure in my intended education pathway, I would think about the subway ride and fantasize that, perhaps this wouldn't be such a bad career. Doug and I often chatted about how easy it would be for me to take my security-licensing exam. Perhaps with some of his contacts he could get me through the door. To this day, I am thankful that I did not pursue this sabotaging stride away from my dream.

You never know exactly what path to take when you reach the fork in the road. Deep down you have a 'feeling' that cannot be described which somehow kind of pushes you in one direction. This little nudge kept me focused on my goal – the February meeting with *Torah Um'esorah*. Instinctively I knew I was making the right decision not being tempted by the World Trade Center digression.

Two and half years later. September 11, 2001. 6:50 am Calgary, Mountain Standard Time, I got a frantic call at home. We were all in the kitchen preparing for that day at school. It was one of the school's board members. Had I seen the news? Had I heard what happened in NY at the

Twin Towers? I quickly turned on the radio to hear the incredible words; a plane had hit the North Tower 2 at approximately 8:45 am EST.

Among the speculations of both pilot error and possible terrorist activity, we remained quite shocked and kept our radio on low, for fear of upsetting Esti and Yossi. We continued as best we could with our early morning routine, carpool, and heading off to school. Listening intently to the frequent updates, we heard the live report when a second plane hit the South Tower, at approximately 9:00 am EST. It was then we knew. There was no possible doubt any more. This was no accident.

I remember looking at Chaya and finding it hard to even say the words "What about Doug?" Our immediate worry focused on our dear cousin, and then to the people I had gotten to know in our Brooklyn community who also worked in the Twin Towers! As soon as we arrived at school, we implemented our regular morning arrival routine. And then I made a decision. A decision I stand by to this very day. I felt it was essential at the time to purposely manage the information flow of these most significant events and frame how it would impact the development of my students. From that fateful day onward, I feel it is critical in significant times, how much information and specifically what information is passed on through the guise of "education" when it comes to disclosing evidentiary facts to our youth. Everything changed on 9-11.

Realising the enormity of the events unfolding before our eyes, I assembled the high school students and told them of the events that had transpired, as I knew them. We all gathered in the staff room and I turned on CNN to watch the reports of the day that would forever shape history. It was our duty to provide an appropriate educational setting to frame the events in a learning environment. I mentioned that any students who were finding themselves too emotionally fragile could go back to the classroom and I instructed the teachers to watch carefully over the students. Knowing the students were well supervised by our teaching staff, I took a moment to actually acknowledge the deep worry and shock that had been triggered by the scenes on the CNN coverage. I took that moment and I rushed to the phone desperately trying to reach Douglas on his cell phone.

As I called, there was an ominous 'engaged' beeping sound on the other end. No one answered.

Trying to be optimistic, I figured that the circuits must be jammed due to the heavy waves of cell phone traffic in the area.

I tried to remain calm and kept trying to reach Doug. Not more that 1-2 minutes later … the cell phone was ringing…voicemail. I had no choice but to leave a message: "Doug, it's Noteh, just thinking of you. Please, give us a call when you can, thinking and praying for you! All our love."

Together, we all watched the live coverage of the events as the two Twin Towers were engulfed in flames. It hit me so hard! I could have been in that Tower! Trapped! In a state of panic! By now it was approximately 7:45 am Mountain Standard Time and reports had already come in of a plane crash at the Pentagon. This news only heightened the awareness that a top-secret terrorist plot was in motion. Watching the video was incredibly surreal.

Nothing could have prepared me for the live images at 8:00 am MST when the South Tower began to collapse. Almost paralysed, I could not even speak as my heart dropped in despair, knowing that people I knew were most certainly trapped in the building. Not more than thirty minutes later, the North Tower collapsed. The feelings of helplessness and shock were overwhelming. I could not speak as the images almost floated over the screen in slow motion. As the clouds of dust began to fill the streets, forcing those few stragglers to run for cover, I could almost taste the chalky feeling in my throat, suffocating me as I vicariously felt I too was running from the shock waves and strangling dust cloud. I too wanted to run, but I couldn't as I was paralysed with grief and disbelief.

Thinking of Douglas, I managed to get up and move back to the phone once again. I realised I could call his wife Rebekah. Perhaps she had heard from Doug. Sure enough, after the first ring, Rebekah picked up the phone. I told her it was just me, had she heard from Doug?

I will never forget the wave of relief as I heard those comforting words – Douglas is OK!

It turned out their son Evan was starting kindergarten and it was his first day of school! To kick off this special milestone, his school had held a Parent Breakfast. So Doug was late for work that day. Doug left toward the end of the breakfast and headed off into the city for work, not by train, but by car. He was driving down the West Side Highway of Manhattan at approximately 8:45 am. As he was driving, he was a solitary, tortured witness to the first plane hitting the north face of Tower One of the World Trade Center. Without thinking too much, Douglas instinctively reacted. Realising he would be caught up in far too much traffic and would never make it into work, in his state of shock, he turned around the car and headed back toward home, a short twenty minutes away. It took Douglas over two hours to get home that day.

Douglas's life changed forever at that moment. He continues to realise the incredible divine providence of his son's kindergarten breakfast and not being on time to work that fateful day. Miraculously, many of Doug's colleagues were also not on time that day for a variety of reasons. Tragically, there were also many colleagues who *were* trapped and never made it out of the Twin Towers on 9-11. May God avenge their souls.

My First Principalship

Life is about making choices. One of the secrets to success is having alternatives from which to choose, never having just one pathway one is forced to follow, never having to make a decision from a place of limitation and lack of opportunities. I have always made this a guiding principle, both in my professional career as well as in the educational philosophy of the institutions in which I have been involved. This seemingly inconsequential point would become quite significant in my future.

With a keen eye on the big picture, always focused on the end in mind, it was very easy not to get distracted from my purpose of securing a position as a principal in a Jewish school. Working for Doug was a non-stressful post that allowed me to maintain my focus on my upcoming interview at *Torah U'mersorah*. I also received two phone calls from two of the three resumes I had sent out from Internet job sites. One was at a school in Florida and the other was an international school in Hong Kong. Chaya was not too keen on the idea of relocating to Hong Kong. She quite emphatically stated "It's 1999. It's not Hong Kong; it's China! Our family is not moving to China!" I think that kind of ended the discussion before it started.

I was quite excited about the phone call I received from the school in Florida. I had one very positive initial discussion with the search committee head. She was very enthusiastic about my secular experience in public school and wanted to set up a conference call with the search committee and myself. It sounded somewhat promising despite her initial reservations that this would be my first position as a principal. An appointment was set up for one week's time. Florida seemed like a long shot. They were looking for a figurehead to head up their established program. Despite being such a long shot candidate, I remained very positive, feeling confident now that there was some interest out there. I looked forward to continuing our initial discussion after my interview at *Torah U'Mesorah*. Finally, the day of the face-to-face interview arrived. I was ready for what I hoped would be the first of more productive meetings at their main office in Manhattan.

I can look back now to my sitting in the *Torah U'Mesorah* waiting room at that pivotal moment in my life. Today I realise how naïve I was and how unprepared I was for the upcoming encounter. I was not properly schooled at that time in the politics within the Modern Orthodox world to understand the depth of the subtle and not so subtle acrimony that simmered between the religious factions governing *Torah U'Mesorah* and *Chabad Lubavitch*.

I walked into the waiting room, introduced myself, and sat down in anticipation of being called into the main office where my interview would take place. There was a distinct aura of history in the room. The waiting room had old bound pamphlets on the table of publications submitted over the years by various rabbis and educators. As I idly thumbed through the publications, I happened to note the educational themes were quite outdated and historic.

It was quite a cramped waiting room. Several secretaries were occupying the tiny front area originally designed for one receptionist. You could hear a few conversations taking place at the same time. This caused me to wonder how privacy and confidentiality could be maintained.

The secretary announced my name, as usual mispronouncing my last name, and told me I could enter. As I stood up, the Director of Human Resources opened the door and put out his hand to shake mine. I shook his hand and he ushered me into his office. This initiation into the organization left me feeling a little flat and dry. I did not feel any warmth whatsoever. I kept my guard up, hoping deep down that a spark of life; some glimmer of cordiality and friendliness would enlighten this somewhat dreary first impression.

As I sat down in front of the director's large wooden desk, it was hard not to notice the many piles of papers, somewhat strategically placed in different configurations. The main window looking out onto the city was the source of light for the dark, wood-panelled office. The walls seemed to engulf me, almost suffocating me. I drew a deep breath awaiting the initial question. This was the beginning of my long awaited opportunity – the path toward my first position as a principal of a Jewish school. Perhaps I had built up this moment to be bigger than it truly was. The anticipation of the event had loomed over me for such a long time. Now that the day was finally here, would I sabotage my opportunity with the overwhelming anxiety I had created in my own mind?

Then came the first question: Can you tell me about your family background and level of observance? It was an off-putting question, one that spiked insecurity. What type of question was this? How was it relevant to me being a professional educator? Would my ability to attain a position through this organization depend on how observant my family was twenty years ago?

I gave my standard response that covered the basics: I grew up in a traditional family in South Africa, moved to Canada and became more observant over the years. I tried to be brief and not indulge the question as I felt there were far more relevant questions that needed to be asked.

Later I was to learn that *Torah U'Mesorah* was quite particular when promoting their candidates for endorsement. At some level, this is understandable. They have an obligation to uphold their credibility as an Orthodox organization, matching appropriate candidates to affiliated institutions.

The issue I sensed, upon which I could not readily put my finger, was the probing and somewhat judgmental nature of the question. It was almost as if nothing could be said to meet the expectations for level of observance of the director or his organization. I had suspected I would encounter this subtle discrimination in the Orthodox world. I felt my suspicions were being confirmed.

I was becoming less naïve about the insular, protective nature of Orthodox groups. Each time I witnessed the biased attitudes within religious sects toward other religious factions, I filed it. It was from this cumulative data that I reasoned I had to be very calculating when formulating a strategy for securing employment in the Orthodox Jewish world. It was precisely with these thoughts in mind that I had ventured out of the confines of the *Chabad* world and decided to pursue rabbinical ordination from not one but two Orthodox institutions. In line with my philosophy of developing pathways of opportunity, the *Torah U'Mesorah* interview only confirmed my intuition that I would need to push harder for more potential job openings and not rely on this seemingly dead-end encounter.

One of my strategies was to knock on every potential door of opportunity available that could get me an interview for a principalship. The more interviews, the better chance I had of being able to find my ideal position. It turns out I was somewhat off the mark thinking there were plenty of options in existence. Nevertheless, my quiet optimism, as unrealistic as it was, gave me the *chutzpah*, the nerve, to pick up the phone and call my mother's friend in Calgary. Her enthusiasm and delight at hearing from me was most encouraging. The fact that she demonstrated confidence in my ability was a well-timed boost to my self-esteem.

I disclosed my plan to her that despite my negative impressions at my initial interview, I would nevertheless attend an upcoming *Torah U'Mesorah* job fair with the hopes of discovering some possibilities and options. From that first conversation, she was utterly confident that my attendance was unnecessary. In her mind, I was a shoe-in for the vacant position in Calgary. She told me the next step would be for me to talk to her son, the current Vice President on the Board of the School.

After that uplifting conversation, I sat down with Chaya and considered my future, evaluating all the available positions in the principal market at that time. Florida was no longer one of the options due to my lack of administrative experience. The benefits of my taking on the principal position in Calgary seemingly outweighed the challenges of which there were truly many. I now had the required documentation and could tick all the administrative "red tape" boxes. In my frank conversation with the school's VP, I learned there remained only one real major obstacle. The true challenge would be the bias of the Modern Orthodox Synagogue Board under whose auspices the school was founded and existed. They were constitutionally a Modern Orthodox institution. Would their ethos support the candidacy of a *Chabad* rabbi to lead their school? In truth, there were a lot of *Chabad* affiliations within their school – from students to teachers; however, as the school vice-president explained, common practice in the school at that time was to downplay those relationships. Rather the vision was to still consider the school to be only and exclusively Modern Orthodox.

To the outsider, these distinctions may seem quite trivial. Believe me, they were and remain until this day, very idiosyncratic! The level of investment amongst the synagogue's leadership and their feelings against *Chabad* were subtly but nevertheless very well entrenched among their inner circle.

The tiny community in Calgary was just over seven thousand Jews and had a reputation for always being very fractured despite its tiny population. Before the early 1980s, there were three synagogues, a very large Conservative synagogue, a large quasi-Orthodox synagogue (with mixed seating), and the oldest synagogue in Calgary which was Orthodox and could no longer get a Sabbath *minyan*. During the early 1980s, three important changes occurred in Calgary: The Reform Temple was established, *Chabad Lubavitch* was established and the old Orthodox synagogue was renewed. This renewal required the establishment of an

Orthodox day school, which was founded by the synagogue's then rabbi and a few dedicated women, as a committee of the synagogue, and not as a distinct legal entity.

There were only a handful of Orthodox children in Calgary at the time but the school's founders, most of whom were well-regarded educators, wanted to reach out to the non-religious community. This new endeavor met with a degree of success and, as a result, it attracted children from non-observant backgrounds. However, in time the synagogue and school attracted a core of Orthodox families who tended to look more inward.

At first, relations between the Orthodox synagogue and *Chabad* were cordial. The *Chabad* rabbi's wife taught at the school and their children attended the school. However, by the time I was looking for my first principalship, that relationship had soured. The school vice-president let me know confidentially that the synagogue board might consider me to be no more than a puppet of the *Chabad* rabbi and his policies and customs.

At the time I was looking for a principalship, the vacant administrative position had been advertised throughout Canada and the United States, without success. Certainly none of the candidates had a Bachelor of Education degree and had taught for a public school board as I had. This credentialing was a necessary requirement for the school to secure government funding. The school's largely unorthodox, educationally-minded parents were not concerned about the political affiliation of the principal. Most just wanted a strong secular education product, which would challenge their children more so than at the existing Hebrew day school at that time.

The search committee was composed of the school's executive body. However, at the end of the day, the synagogue was contractually responsible for the school and had the final say in who could be hired. Further, all non-financial educational decisions having religious implications needed to be ratified by the synagogue rabbi. Constitutionally, he was the standing religious authority over the school. It was explained to me in great detail, that approval of my candidacy would depend on a successful initial conversation with the current rabbi. I was also told that he was very knowledgeable and had a very positive relationship with the *Chabad* rabbi in Calgary. They often consulted together on various issues and were hoping that, with my successful candidacy, I could unite both communities toward a critical, common goal – providing Jewish children in Calgary, very few of whom were Orthodox, with a strong secular and Jewish education.

An additional challenge was that the synagogue was experiencing very little growth. A vibrant principal with modern, educational goals had the potential to spark the community and effect greater commitment to the synagogue. At the time, the enrolment in the school was wavering around one hundred pupils and the survival of the institution depended very much on increasing this enrolment figure. My knowledge of the Calgary education system and familiarity with the Jewish community gave me a distinct advantage over any other potential candidates.

At the time, the Alberta Provincial Government had just begun mandatory literacy and numeracy testing in Grades' 3 and 6. The results and subsequent rankings of all schools, both public and private were being publicised in the city newspapers. The school had not done very well. One of the principal's key performance indicators would be to raise the level of the school's educational profile. This was framed in the context relative to the other Jewish school in town. This more culturally focused Jewish school boasted over twice the population of the Orthodox school, and had a reputation for being the only significant option for serious-minded parents seeking a strong secular education in a 'Jewish' environment.

On paper, it was a slam dunk. I was the perfect candidate, at least to the educationally-minded board members who were immune to religious politics and not threatened by my personal *Chabad* affiliation. Of course, I would need the endorsement of the Modern Orthodox rabbi. The initial phone conference was set up. I was primed by the school vice-president, my mentor-to-be and the *Chabad* rabbi as to the issues that would most likely be raised, including the most politically sensitive.

It was now late February and the Modern Orthodox rabbi called me at home in NY. We connected well. He was sincere and a straight shooter. He told me that he didn't personally have any issues with the *Chabad* rabbi nor did he have anything against *Chabad*. He acknowledged that there were a significant number of members in his congregation who were concerned that a *Chabad* principal would not honour the customs and tightly-affiliated Zionist ethos of the school and synagogue. Some of those traditions included singing the Israeli anthem each day and reciting special prayers for the Israeli government and soldiers from time to time. The Rabbi was wondering how I would support the synagogue given that I subscribed to the *Chabad* philosophy and held a different approach to the Zionist enterprise. He asked me to respond directly and honestly.

I described my background and my journey to observance that began in a traditional home in South Africa. I shared how, through various personal connections to many religiously observant role models, I had come to the stage I was at today. One of the great role models in our journey was Rabbi David Lichtman, the previous rabbi of his synagogue who had served two tenures as rabbi prior to him. During Rabbi Lichtman's time in Calgary, we were members of that synagogue. We were married by Rabbi Lichtman. I answered as sincerely as I possibly could. As principal, I would work hard to maintain the relationship between the school and synagogue and even more so, to build a connection through joint ventures which we could work together to develop. Concerning the Zionist ethos, I would always promote the school's ideals, mission, and vision and that would include the encouragement of the singing of the Israeli national anthem, prayers for the government and Israeli defense forces. We discussed some more general issues as they related to staffing. He asked me if I had any problems with him being the religious authority over the school, and did I object to the notion that all new Jewish staff member hiring necessitated his final stamp of approval. I told him that I did not have a problem with this in theory and repeated my heartfelt intentions that it would be my goal to work closely together with him for the sake of the community. He thanked me for my candour. He even went so far as to tell me he looked forward to working with me in the future.

From this initial conversation, I was quite optimistic about the potential direction the school could take with this amicable partnership. Here was a committed leader who was so willing to support the mission statement of the school. A strong school needs passionate stakeholders and from our phone discussion, I felt that the synagogue's rabbi would be a great advocate and influence upon his congregation in terms of their attitudes toward and support for their school.

The school's structure was based on this strong link to the synagogue. With the principal and rabbi working closely toward the same goal, I was optimistic that the challenges that had been presented to me in my initial conversation with some of the board members were no longer insurmountable. Shortly after my phone conversation with the synagogue rabbi, a flurry of communication came my way. All of a sudden, many contractual issues began to surface in relation to the financial offer, the proposed length of my contract as well as minute details and clauses the synagogue wished to influence within my contract such as the location of neighborhood where we intended to live. With 20-20 hindsight, we should have realised that the pressure we were receiving in relation to many of the contractual issues should have cautioned my wife and me against accepting the position. Despite the open opposition and political challenges, the lure of living in the same city as my parents became a driving force for our relocation to Calgary.

It was abundantly clear from the couriered documents that the Synagogue Executive Board was very nervous about my allegiance to the *Chabad* rabbi. Concerns regarding my day-to-day upholding of the school's and synagogue's constitutions were openly stated. The red flags should have alerted me to the idea that there were noteworthy individuals behind the scenes, not on the actual school board itself that strongly opposed my selection as the school principal.

Despite the school's assertion that it was at their sole discretion to hire a head of school, as long as it came with the approval of the synagogue rabbi, the school board of directors naïvely felt they could ram the decision through the synagogue board and fight them if push came to shove. There was initially, albeit behind the scenes, a lot of pushing and shoving.

Shortly thereafter, I made an initial visit to Calgary for my on-site interview. There was a lot of support for my candidature, but it came from the least expected influencers. Around the school board table, the constitution declared that the sole influence from the synagogue in terms of official representation could come from the synagogue rabbi in an advisory capacity as well as one additional oversight committee member who would formally represent the interests of the synagogue board of directors. This member was a go-between for both boards and would relay any constitutional matters in need of discussion or emphasis. The school budget had to be formally ratified by the synagogue board. At that time, despite the limited enrolment, the school was somewhat miraculously hovering around the break-even mark due to significant government funding for the secular program.

There was overt pressure relating to my personal relationship with the *Chabad* rabbi. I was not comfortable with the notion of having to sever all ties with my long-time friend and mentor for the sake of the principalship. It was made quite clear to me from the synagogue board representative that the main obstacle to my being hired was this connection! It was not necessarily a philosophical issue; it was, in fact, a very pragmatic issue that had little or nothing to do with my candidacy. The issue came from the perceived jeopardy the synagogue had recently been feeling since the *Chabad* rabbi formed his breakaway congregation and the resulting new community that seemed to be forming. On paper, both synagogues were a meagre fifteen-minute drive away from each other. Far too much significance was made out of this "superficial" geographical element. For true Orthodox Sabbath observers, the prohibitive walking distance of over an hour precluded poaching between congregations.

Both congregations were Orthodox in religious observance. Arguably, there was only a small, defined population from which to entice synagogue affiliation. The limited number of Orthodox families represented only a small demographic of the community's membership pool from which the synagogue could draw. In effect, this equated most importantly to a limited amount of financial support available to keep non-profit Orthodox organizations, school, and synagogues remaining viable. From the synagogue board's perspective, both congregations would be trying to tap into the same community membership for support. Therefore, the synagogue had become very territorial. Where at first, it was very subtle in its objections to its current and potential membership attending classes and services at the rival centre of worship, as time went on, they became much more overt in their expressions of displeasure. In this context, therefore, the fact that I had a prior relationship with the *Chabad* rabbi was of great concern to the synagogue board. They attempted therefore to stipulate that if I were to be hired it would be contractually conditional upon my accepting lifestyle conditions outlined specifically by the synagogue board.

The school board, after my initial face-to-face interview, had become very interested and motivated to unrelentingly engage me as their principal. I was to find out later on, that much of their enthusiasm was due to a very strong reference from my principal at Elboya Junior High School of the Calgary Public School Board, whom they managed to contact, despite his having moved to another school. The school board was focusing on the need for a strong general studies program in their school. This would be the mechanism by which we could outreach and influence non-observant families in Calgary.

My familiarity with their public school curriculum, having graduated from a prestigious program in the local public school arena and having graduated from the University of Calgary were all advantages highlighted in my favor.

The school board was very focused on the dollars and cents of the budget. They were trying to act responsibly and address head-on the pending threat of losing government funding due to the school's low test scores and inadequate administration. Of course, these facts only came to my attention soon after my acceptance of the principal position. The conjecture among the school board was that radical times called for radical solutions. For them, a principal with a strong secular background represented the only true solution to the problem. I would also find out later that there had been only one other candidate, who had far less secular educational experience than me. No one else had even applied for the position. This detail was all the more glaring in light of the fact that the school board had mounted a rigorous international advertising campaign including engaging some major Jewish educational head-hunters.

The school made the recommendation for me to become its sixth principal in just over 10 years. The synagogue rabbi approved and endorsed my candidacy. But, the ratification by the synagogue board had reached a standstill despite the approval of their synagogue rabbi. The synagogue wanted additional contractual stipulations; conditions aimed at ensuring my limited connection to the *Chabad* rabbi. The conditions included my attendance at their *Shabbos* services on Saturday morning's at least three out of four weeks a month. They wanted to stipulate that our residence be geographically closer to the Modern Orthodox synagogue than the newly-formed *Chabad* community. Not only would I have to accept the rabbi as the rabbinical authority of the school, all Jewish staff hiring would be conducted by the rabbi. They also stipulated first priority of hiring assigned to existing synagogue members interested in working at the school.

This was in addition to the fact that the new salary offered had drastically been deflated from the initially offer. I could clearly see the writing on the wall. The obstacles the synagogue had raised were too great for me to accept the position. After legal consultation with a close adviser of ours, I informed the school board that the current atmosphere, specifically the synagogue's mission to control my personal lifestyle and determine where I would live and where I could pray, was not as they had conveyed to me when I had met them, and it was certainly not the community atmosphere where I was looking to build my family and career. I formally rejected the job offer.

The response I received was quite startling. It appeared to me that the school thought we were engaged in a game of poker. They overplayed the apparent draw card that my parents lived in the city and the immense personal motivation this held for our family to accept the position. They thought they could get away with the outlandish conditions on offer. I nevertheless stood my ground. From the point of view of not being able to reunite with my parents in Calgary, we were undeniably disappointed. Despite a longing to re-establish our family and reverse the painful decision from when we had left Calgary almost eight years prior, we could not accept the synagogue's negativity and now the school's posturing negotiation tactics.

We made the firm decision to seek out other avenues as potential sources of employment. My parents unquestionably understood all too well. Their experiences of being held over a barrel when they had to accept untenable working arrangements simply to get their family out of the apartheid state of South Africa were still stinging wounds. They had worked their whole lives to get away from those interferences. They sadly, but wholeheartedly supported our looking elsewhere.

The final communication I left with the school board president was that if they were serious about me being the principal of their school, they would have to demonstrate the desire for me to lead their institution. At the same time, they would have to allow me the freedom to conduct my family life according to the personal respect they had initially demonstrated at my face-to-face interview. I made it very clear that my goal as principal would be to strengthen the community bond with the synagogue and school and that would obviously include attending services as much as possible. I would however not contractually agree to this in writing, for fear that should something unusual transpire and I was unable to attend services one week, in a hostile environment such as the current climate of negotiations with the synagogue, this absence could constitute grounds for dismissal.

If they wanted me as their principal, there would need to be an assumption of goodwill and trust that my goal would be to grow the school according to its mission statement, which included its inherent connection to the synagogue. Of course, I closed off the conversation with the logical point of how foolish it would be for me to assume the principalship, and then work against the mandate provided to me by which my success would be evaluated. With that, I diligently began to widen my search, seeking other possible employment opportunities.

As I was reaching out to some of my initial contacts, the idea of approaching *Torah U'Mesorah* and seeking a position through their employment department again became a concerted alternative. One day, from out of the blue I received a phone call from the *Torah U'Mesorah* Director in charge of Leadership Placement. He was calling to inform me of a Recruitment Day which was to be held in Manhattan. He said he had already shopped my resume around and had at least one very keen party wanting to meet me. He asked me to attend with my wife upon which I would be introduced to the hiring representatives of this mystery institution. I didn't want to seem too desperate and in my excitement, neglected to ask any further questions. I was just so positively overwhelmed that there was a potential other institution besides Calgary showing an interest in what I had to offer.

The week crawled by in anticipation of the meeting. Once Sunday came, both Chaya and I eagerly arrived early to the designated meeting place in a hotel in Manhattan. The room was set up with tables arranged alphabetically by the names of the specific institutions and their geographic locations. Walking around the room, we noticed many schools were seeking Jewish studies teachers more than principals. We were well aware of the shortage of knowledgeable, pedagogically experienced teaching staff. We had set our expectations that at this point in my life, I would be looking for more than a teaching position. Thus, I made a conscious decision, despite the possibly bleak outlook of there not being many school leadership positions, not to depreciate my goal and entertain the idea of lowering my employment standards to that of a teaching position again. Yes, we were willing to relocate to just about anywhere, realizing that it was critical to get my foot in the door as a new principal.

My first position would be a critical, foundational step to building my career and reputation as an administrator. I was seeking a position where I could apply my young, ambitious, though undeveloped and untested educational philosophy, its lofty ideals of uniting a school under one umbrella, of striving for excellence and consistency across a dual framework of general and Jewish studies. Despite my minimal experience, I was seeking the mandate of educational control of the entire educational program and the confidence from the lay leadership to lead their institution, no matter the challenges they currently were experiencing.

Walking around the room, I was keenly aware of the institutions that were seeking established personalities as a means of selling to their communities a tried and proven professional with a name in the educational fraternity. I was under no illusions that this simply was not me. My initial position would be that of a principal hired to lead a fractured institution, most likely in desperate shape but one that was willing to take a chance, a gamble on a young idealist with limitless energy and a tireless work ethic to build up the foundation of an ideal.

As far as I was concerned, if they were interested in me, even if it was a school on Mars, it deserved serious consideration. Not because I pretty much had nothing else on offer, but for the fact that they wanted me. Not much thought or analysis went into contemplating, "Why me?" I was willing to play along with the idea that I had something to offer which no one else had. My ego needed that fuel and nourishment at this early juncture in my career.

As we continued to walk around the room, we noticed not too many people had arrived. Slowly making the rounds, contemplating which school had initiated the meeting, we noticed the arrival of the director alongside some other well-dressed individuals. My heart skipped a beat. They seemed to begin walking our way. Chaya whispered to me to take a deep breath, which I did, and together we approached the group. I was introduced to the rabbi of the community and president of the school from … Las Vegas, Nevada. They expressed their excitement upon meeting me. Of course, they had already heard a lot about me from my glowing references.

As soon as I heard Las Vegas, I think my head must have spun around. I had not realised there was even a significant Orthodox community living in "spin city" or "sin city." Take your pick. I knew that *Chabad* was in every major city in the continental United States of America. When I came to think of it, why not Las Vegas? I was soon to learn that Las Vegas was the fastest-growing city in America, and that growth included the Jewish community. It soon became apparent that this rabbi was the head Chabad rabbi of Las Vegas and Nevada. The president of the school expressed a sincere desire to seek a principal who was ready, willing, and able to resurrect a school stuck on a steep spiral toward extinction. It was presented to us that the rabbi was searching for a principal who would be able to turn the community school into a Modern Orthodox school and thus a thriving institution that could, at the same time, cater for a variety of religious observances through a guiding philosophical framework.

It seemed the school was currently composed of a large contingent of Israeli, *Chabad* and non-affiliated families. The current structure focused more on the non-observant. Thus the Orthodox families felt very much alienated in the philosophical 'community structure' of the institution. The search committee was looking for a leader who could unite the three groups under one banner of tolerance, mutual respect, and harmony. The rabbi was a long-standing influential member of the community who had, at that point in time, more out of default, supported the school both communally and financially. But now he found himself at a crossroads. If the school could find a headmaster ready to accomplish the task of enhancing the observance of its students, he was willing to throw his full support around the community and publicly endorse the school. If not, he was prepared to make his own start-up educational institution. This is why he had joined the committee. In turn, the school was very keen to maintain its connection with the rabbi. There was an inherent risk that in losing his support, the resulting formation of an opposing institution could decimate the enrolment figures of the existing school and significantly erode their critical income base.

During these initial discussions, I raised some significant points regarding the types of Jewish curricula with which I was familiar. Some were being used in various North American schools and had the potential to accommodate the various levels of family observances within their proposed institution. We also touched on several strategies that could be developed to engage the many potential varying levels of literacy and capabilities of such mixed ability students.

Before I could even take another breath, both the rabbi and president suggested we hop on a plane before the week was out and come and take a look at the school and community for ourselves. Chaya and I looked at each other, quite stunned. Could we just pick up and fly to Las Vegas with a mere three days' notice?

Viva Las Vegas

Still a casual worker for Chaya's cousin Doug at the World Trade Center, I could surely make up the hours the following week. Chaya had some personal days available at work so we thought we could manage. This was, of course, as long as we could bring along Yossi, who at this time was just one and a half years old. We were quite sure that Esti could stay with my sister and brother-in-law for the few days. We strategically told Esti that we had to go away for *Shabbos*. We exaggerated a fair bit when we said we were really close by, not wanting to tell her we were travelling on a plane across the country. Feeling somewhat guilty, we knew it was the only way to truly concentrate and evaluate the opportunity with time to focus on the situation at hand instead of busying ourselves with entertaining and minding the children. Yossi was quite an easy-going little boy. With his "go with the flow" countenance, he could easily drift into the background as long as he had his box of Thomas the Tank Engine trains to keep him occupied. Before I knew it, we were packed and on our way to Las Vegas.

On the plane, we had some time to think things over and discuss what had happened, so very suddenly. Sure, they were both quite eager to show me the school in its current state and provide me with some answers to my own lingering questions. I was sure that they would pull out all the stops to present a viable career opportunity, and more than a suitable living environment for our family.

It was exciting to be wooed. As soon as we arrived at the Las Vegas airport, and for anyone who has experienced arriving in Las Vegas for the first time, it was like stepping on a time machine from the old West into the distant future. It was not just the "one-arm bandits," the slot machines in the walkways and concourses of the airport, nor the automatic train that shuttled you from your airplane to the main terminal. It was an attitude; call it moxie, in everyone around you. You could not help feel upbeat, confident; one could even say "lucky." Having Chaya with me was a great barometer, we kept telling each other not to get carried away, but to keep our eyes on the prize. We had written down the many questions we needed to evaluate throughout the visit. They related to the school, community, synagogue, head rabbi and the other members of leadership, rabbinical and otherwise throughout the city.

What were the issues in the school? If the community was indeed growing at such an alarming rate, why had the school remained so stagnant in its enrolments? What were the obstacles to its growth? What type of administrative structure had been developed in the past and present? What were the critical changes for a viable future? Did they have a financial structure in place to support the necessary changes? What was the school's mission statement and how was it being implemented? But most importantly, what did the stakeholders see as the success of the school? What initially attracted them to the institution? Had they wavered, and if so, why? What were the obstacles to increasing enrolment?

Before we got off the plane, I felt it would be tactically important to let Calgary know I was seriously considering another option. I had to be strategic and therefore told our now close friend and vice president of the school executive board who had been instrumental in getting me this far through that hiring process. I knew that the school in Calgary wanted me and I felt that it was appropriate to exert some pressure on them with the idea that there was a real possibility they could lose me to a competing institution.

What would happen next would be valuable for me, to evaluate just how much they were willing and able to fight for me against the synagogue. The school needed to realise it was a distinct possibility that they were going to lose me to another institution. My frustration had reached its boiling point. Both Chaya and I had come to the decision that we were ready to give up on the idea of moving to Calgary. Despite the recognition that the school had many ingredients and potential that primed it toward an incredible career opportunity, I needed to know that the school board was willing to put up a fight for me against the synagogue pressure. This was the perfect test for me to learn what they were made of. Just how would they respond if they realised they were perhaps going to lose me to another school?

Yes, it was true that this was a real possibility. And no. In no way, shape or form had I shown them my cards that deep down I wanted to come to Calgary. I had emotional ties, yes. I cared deeply about the families with whom I had already grown close over the years. But now it was decision time. I firmly hit the ball into their court. It was up to them to prove how committed they were to my family and me. My sincere intentions in travelling to Las Vegas were to evaluate every aspect of the position and go from there. Time would tell and my plan needed to be executed craftily without either side knowing I was evaluating one position over the other.

As we arrived at the baggage carousel, the rabbi was there waiting for us. We quickly collected our bags, and before long, we were on our way to freshen up before our first tour of the school. I was eager to get to the school. Afternoon was approaching and I was eager to see the school in action. With two days to spend on the campus before spending *Shabbos* with the community, I would have enough time to superficially evaluate the school and staff. This provided me with some insight in determining which staff I could meet privately, with the consent of the school administration, to get a better in-depth picture of what was going on behind the scenes.

It didn't take long for me to see a fractured faculty with gaping cracks in the school's mission statement. The school was desperately trying to be everything to everyone, and in the end, no one was getting what they needed or wanted. Teachers were working at a frantic pace trying to support the many varied levels of literacy in their classrooms. With the many foreign students enrolled in the school, there were many Israeli students who spoke Hebrew fluently and little English. There were just as many American students who spoke English fluently and little Hebrew. With little educational support, teachers were not coping very well.

Many staff resented the administrative focus on the physical appearance of the campus and the aesthetically glitzy educational resources that had little pedagogic value. No funds had been allocated toward much-needed learning support. Perhaps the most qualified teacher and certainly the most motivated staff member confided in me he was considering leaving the school. He had become so fed up with banging his head against the wall receiving little support. The staff was so frustrated. I was amazed at their willingness to open up to a complete stranger such as myself. It was obvious they just needed a sympathetic ear from an educator who understood their situation.

It was very clear to me that the board had put a lot of energy into keeping the structure afloat. They had gone the route of a token hiring – a well-known educationalist with a solid Las Vegas reputation. He himself admitted, in front of his board president, that he was burnt out and had little energy to address the significant educational issues at hand. This concerned me greatly. For someone who was so open to admit this to a stranger, how open had he been with his staff? Obviously, they could read his frame of mind and attitude. I could see they had become frustrated with his ineffective lobbying of the school board to inspire educational change within the institution. It was a ship with a gaping hole, which was sinking so rapidly, it was three quarters already below the water line. I saw it to be unsalvageable.

It didn't take Chaya and me a lot of time to realise that the principalship in Las Vegas under the current conditions was not an option for us. The school foundation and leadership model, not to mention the vision and mission were on very shaky ground. We didn't feel that these were promising conditions for me to come in and effect the change necessary to rebuild it from the ground up. We truly felt they were looking for another token principal, and I was not prepared to compromise my ideals as an educationalist.

That *Shabbos* night, Chaya and I had dinner with the rabbi and his wife. After the guests went home and the children to sleep, we had a very frank discussion. Put on the spot, I was point-blank asked what I thought of the school and its future. I had nothing to lose and gave my honest, albeit initial impressions of how I saw the structure and the steep descending path toward which it was heading. Brutal but frank, the rabbi made a startling declaration. He said I was very perceptive. He agreed wholeheartedly with my insightful comments. He then told me he had already come to the same determination and was just months away from having all the necessary pieces in place to start his own school. He had full support from a large contingent of the parent body behind the scenes but was in need of a headmaster to take the lead. If I was not interested in assuming the headmastership of the existing school, would I be open to discussing the idea of becoming principal of his yet to be opened *Chabad* elementary school? It was a curveball both Chaya and I had not expected.

There we were, sitting at the *Shabbos* table being offered a principalship of a new school. We were being offered the opportunity to build an institution from the ground up – to be partners and the architect of my educational ideals. There were a lot of issues to mull over including the challenge of needing to analyse the enrolment potential because without a critical mass, which the rabbi said convincingly he could almost guarantee, my salary could not be guaranteed. This was a partnership and he wanted me to buy into it. Then, if I met certain key performance indicators, he was prepared for me to build my own salary level. It had unlimited potential but until we reached a certain critical mass, there were personal risks he wanted me to assume as his partner.

On the Sunday, we toured his facility that was in mid-construction. All of the theoretical pieces were there with the exception of a finalized physical structure. Was I ready to take a leap of faith? If Calgary came through, when both boards settled their internal differences, I would have better job security simply due to the already established infrastructure.

It was a difficult decision. I openly discussed it with the rabbi. I felt I had nothing to lose being honest and open. If we were destined to develop a future relationship, the transparency of my thought processes would only become the foundation of a strong connection. Little did I realise that the *Chabad* network was a tightly-woven grapevine. This rabbi had also done his homework. Phone calls had been made to the few places I had worked and lived. Conversations about my integrity and professionalism had been had. Character references and testimonials were made about my knowledge, without my knowledge. The rabbi had done his homework and his persistence was both flattering but also pressurizing. He had a lot of information about Calgary and the politics within the city and community. I realised that he had obviously been communicating with the Calgary *Chabad* rabbi.

Despite his strong points in favour of us moving to Las Vegas and assuming the leadership position of this institution, I deep down felt the risk of the unknowns to be too great. Unknown was the support from within his community for a new school. This was coupled with the risk I would be initially taking by signing on without a guaranteed salary. These two factors alone were enough to cause me to seriously contemplate declining the offer. We left Las Vegas somewhat confused but certainly tempted. We decided to take the week and think all our options through. We arrived back in New York Monday evening. There was a phone message on our answering machine to call the president of the synagogue school board at our earliest convenience. My strategy and personal philosophy of creating options and opportunities was in play. Sure enough, my plan had worked.

I called the president back late that same Monday evening. I was told to expect a faxed copy of a revised contract offer from the school in the morning. It was unanimous. They had sorted out all the issues. I was being offered the principalship of the school with all my conditions having been met. I had exactly what I wanted. Two viable options but two very different pathways. I would end up choosing the established institution and what seemed like a more grounded option over the risky financial path. I would forever miss out on an opportunity to build from the ground up, with all the risks that entailed.

Every now and then, I think back and wonder. Not out of regret, but out of curiosity... What had become of the rabbi and his Las Vegas dream? Today it is a thriving institution. It has become almost everything the rabbi once foretold. I am certainly hard-wired to take risks. But, I am not built to take financial risks with my family's security and the needs of a stable livelihood. Despite how things turned out in Calgary, I would have made the same choice again. The advantages of my having been in Calgary those two and a half years to this day far outweigh the disappointments. Not the least of the blessings is the lifelong friendship we were privileged to grow with the Doctor family. There is Toby, who followed us as far as she could on the next phase of our adventure.

Of course, as is the theme of this book, my experiences in Calgary forced me to grow both personally and professionally in unimaginable ways. Calgary came to be the first of three schools of which I have been principal. All three schools were in pretty dire straits. Each time I was hired to set the course for success. I have had the privilege of turning around and leading each of those exceptional institutions on an effective growth trajectory. I know that I could not have become the professional I am today if I had not trod through fire and had the trials I was to experience in Calgary. It is true that when under fire and pushed to our limits, we have two options. The first is, of course, to fold. For me, this has never been an option. The second course of action is to rise to the occasion and surprise everyone, most often ourselves.

The Calgary Stampede

Calgary was my trial by fire. All that I have accomplished today I owe to the valuable lessons I learned in the most difficult times of my life as a principal in Calgary. For over two years, there was every reason to keep working and hoping. By two and a half years, I had no choice but to move on.

It is worth stating again. I believe and maintain that God is in control of this world. Everything that happened was meant to have happened. Any and all of the events that led to my two-and-a-half-year tenure as the principal of my first institution, as trying as they were, can, in retrospect, be looked back upon now to see the Divine Providence in every moment. That in itself is a lesson for the present and the future.

The events in those two and a half years in Calgary took its toll not just on us, but on my parents as well. Within four years of our departure, my parents too, moved on. My mother, again, never recovered from our sudden, but understandably necessary departure. Her bitterness over how things transpired was an ever-present force from the moment we left. She was offered an early retirement package from her longstanding job as a contracts administrator soon after we left which she accepted immediately. My father, who had become a real estate agent, managed within six weeks to sell all his personal rental properties, including their house, and buy a house free and clear in a lovely neighborhood in Toronto. Another miracle. And since then, as Fate would have it, both my sister and my brother now live in Toronto. My mother had two-thirds of her dream come true at last. Two of her three children and the clear and rising majority of her 28+ grandchildren, all live less than 40 minutes away from each other.

But none of this was evident, much less even anticipated as we joyfully arrived back home, once again, in Calgary in July 2000. My parents had sent us photos of the house we purchased. But we really, for all intents and purposes, bought it sight unseen! How could anything be worse than a decrepit Brooklyn 'tenement' rental? From the moment we walked in, we were in love. Space! Clean, bright, sunlit space! A room for each child! And we knew we could afford the mortgage payments! Why? Because this whole four-bedroom house with a family room, back & front yards, basement and double garage was costing us practically the same as to what our monthly rent had been in that tiny, old, dark hole in Brooklyn.

My arrival meant that I was now one of three Orthodox rabbis in Calgary. It was critical to develop a strong cohesive bond as a group. There was a long-standing connection with the *Chabad* rabbi simply from our past relationship. I consciously was determined to develop a good working relationship with the rabbi of the Modern Orthodox Synagogue who in earnest was a dedicated leader of the Orthodox community. I was excited when he approached me about setting up a weekly learning partnership. In that first year, we met regularly in my office, leaving all communal issues at the door and simply learned together various topics of Jewish Law. He was certainly an intelligent person who genuinely wanted to work with me. I was excited at the prospect of having a team member who not only was equally motivated towards the success of the school, but in addition, had in his best interests my personal positive standing within his community.

What initially began as a superficial, cordial relationship soon began to blossom into professional collegiate rapport on equal footing. We each had strengths to contribute. We discovered that our leadership styles, albeit different, complemented each other. Together we presented a strong message to the board and our school community. Because of our strong relationship, there was clear evidence that there was more than just a superficial link between the school and synagogue. A great orator, I enjoyed his weekly *Shabbos* sermon which always had an incredible opening story as the hook.

I Don't Have Time to Teach…But I'd Be Crazy Not To…

One of the most important components of my administrative philosophy is that no matter how much a principal has on his or her plate, teaching in the classroom should be non-negotiable. I have not always subscribed to this philosophy. This lesson was one of my most blessed rites of passage. I had this hidden fortune forced upon me in the very beginnings of my school leadership career in Calgary. Purely due to the financial limitations in the school's budget, I was assigned as the teacher for both Prophets and Jewish Law for Grade 4.

At first, I was overly concerned that putting me in the classroom would diminish my capacity to lead the school. I was afraid that my diligence in preparing my lessons and my individual attention toward the students in my class would take away from focusing on the bigger educational picture. The issues in the school were great. Could I truly be everything to everyone as a principal as well as a classroom teacher?

As I learned very quickly, nothing could be further from the truth. The lesson I learned was a great one. It has stood me in good stead in every position I have held from then on. It goes without saying that the bigger the school, the bigger the administrative headaches and of course the responsibility. Calgary taught me that being in the classroom provides me with a unique perspective. You might think you can only keep your eye on the big picture by being removed from the day-to-day details. However, that is patently incorrect. Involving myself with the small picture in the classroom has always heightened my sensitivity to what is most important in any school – the needs of the students.

Teaching in the classroom increases a principal's credibility with the rest of the teaching staff. It's more than coming out of the ivory tower. I get to claim equal rights when I too have to pull an all-night marking session. Yes, I lose sleep preparing for the 'meet the teacher' night, sitting one-on-one with the parents agonizing over children who are struggling academically or socially. As a principal, I learned that the benefits are much, much more.

From the first day in Calgary, as I entered my classroom, I learned that my passion for education would always remain untainted so long as I spent a precious portion of each day in the classroom teaching. It would come to be my haven from the day-to-day grind that burns out most administrators. I now have a personal saying: "True principals do not go into education to become administrators. The best principals are born educators and remain teachers for life so long as they are attached to the classroom." This attitude can only remain when one remains in touch with students, in the classroom.

There were many different ways I connected with my students that year. Looking back on the challenges in my first two and a half years as a principal, I'm not sure if the creative things I did to develop relationships with my students was for their benefit or mine. I know they were learning, and I could see they were enjoying our interaction. Despite the challenges that were occurring in the community or outside my classroom door, when I entered that sanctum, nothing besides the growth of each student concerned me. I had an innate ability to shut it all out and teach in the moment. Today, as I still maintain connections with a few of my many past students, they take great pleasure in reminding me of some of the things we did together.

One of the most memorable was the lesson on measurement. Measurement? What does that have to do with Jewish Law? One of our school's strongest initiatives was integration across curriculum areas. What better way to transmit an understanding of measurement than…cooking! Lucky for me, the math lessons of measurement coincided with the winter Jewish festival of Chanukah. Perfect time to demonstrate how to make my famous Chanukah potato *latkes* (pancakes) and integrate Jewish concepts with the 'secular'. I know the site of my arrival in class wearing my tied-back baker's apron and hairnet made a lasting impression.

Certainly the fun my students had seeing their Teacher/Principal/Rabbi tear up and try like anything not to cry while hand grating the onions was enough to send them into fits of laughter. I never took myself too seriously and wasn't above making a fool of myself if it led to a learning moment or their remembering some critical educational concept. I am touched when my former students get in touch with me and begin the reconnection with a story of some crazy thing I did in the classroom.

The lasting message was that in any school, beginning with the end in mind must actualise student wellbeing at its forefront. As a principal and leader of the institution, there can be no better method of living this motto than to find time in one's busy administrative schedule to teach.

Happy New Year?!

The first real sign of the true state of the school came six weeks into the school year. It was the afternoon of *Rosh Hashanah,* one of the three holiest days in the Jewish Year. It's the day that seals one's fate for the coming year. It's the day to be focused on prayer and family, not the Calgary Herald – the local newspaper.

I had just come in from synagogue with my family. Now, as I said, this is a day of intense prayer. So much so, that the morning prayers rarely end before 2 pm. So as we all sat down to eat our afternoon festive meal, it was about 3 pm. Keep in mind I hadn't eaten since the night before because it is preferred practice not to eat before certain events that occur in synagogue that morning. There was a knock on our front door. It was quite an unexpected visit. We thought perhaps the rabbi with some worshipers who didn't have a place for lunch? Nope. It was…the school president and two other school board members!

At that time of that day, it is virtually universal, worldwide for Jewish families to be at home spending time with their family and friends. For our family, it had been quite some time since we had gathered with my parents on the Jewish New Year, having lived in different cities for over three years. Nevertheless, I invited them all in and offered for them to join us at the meal. Once they saw my parents and family, ready to sit down and begin our meal, they were, I'm glad to say, appropriately embarrassed. However, they still requested just a few minutes of my time.

How could I decline when perhaps it was an urgent issue that had brought them into our neighborhood on such a hallowed day? One had to overlook the fact that to get our house, they had more than likely violated Jewish law by driving.

We retired to the private family room as I asked my parents and family to please wait a few minutes when I would return to join them. I could see the telling expression on my parents' faces. They were quite annoyed at the *chutzpah* of these people raising issues to do with mundane matters on such a spiritually significant day. Being new to my position and wanting to make a good impression, I quickly settled our "guests" and enquired about the urgent matter that must have been so critical to disturb their day to come all the way to see me.

From nowhere, the president pulled out the Calgary Herald. Yes, the same daily newspaper that ten years prior had predicted such dire straits for the education system in Calgary. It was the year I got my job in the public school system. The president asked me if I had seen today's paper. Had I seen the city rankings of the private schools? They were rhetorical questions. Not only did I not have a subscription, I would not have read the newspaper, even if I had the time, on this holy day.

They opened the newspaper to the section where our school had been ranked 41st out of a possible 45 private schools on the Grade 3 provincial achievement exams. The exams had been sat the previous year, whilst I was still in negotiations about becoming their Principal. No, I wasn't aware that our school had plummeted so low. I had had no prior indication during the entire interview process, multiple school visits, as well as meetings with members of the administration that this was even a potential issue. All I could say was that in two days' time, when I returned to school after the holiday, I would make a full enquiry and get back to the board with more information and a proactive strategy to address the issue.

There was a fire in the president's eye. Although my response was understood, I took her passionate gaze to indicate she wanted a "heads are going to roll" response. She went on, then and there, to demand affirmative action, which included dismissal of the Grade 3 teacher and a full review of the accountability of the vice principal who was in charge of the upper elementary. It did not sit well with me that I had not even been briefed about these pending results. I kept that thought to myself at this moment in time. Deep down, I became concerned with the quality of leadership in the school. How could I not have been proactively warned that there was a remote possibility we would be sinking so low? That our school would be at the bottom of the list of the private school rankings? Our Grade 6 students didn't fare much better. The president's son had just entered Grade 3 this year. She went on to say she would not sit idly by and allow her son to receive a second-rate education which was most certainly on offer, according to our results, and most definitely with the current teacher and lackadaisical supervision in place.

All I could do at this moment in time was to listen, take mental notes. I was grateful for that opportunity to realise this aggressive individual had a results-oriented focus. She didn't care who was in her way, as long as the outcome matched her personal desires, i.e. what was best for her children and herself. I quickly realised that her personal issues framed the mandate of her leadership style. In her eyes, my success would depend on my ability to achieve her desired goals. I had clearly walked into a minefield and would need to find a careful pathway out. It was so early in the game. Already, I faced an educational crisis, the resolution of which, my success as the principal would be minutely evaluated.

Superficially, it appeared that the educational program was certainly not competitive enough. For the parent body concerned about the value of their tuition dollars, a ranking of 41st out of 45 did not equate to money well spent, which I could well understand. I would have to make a significant impact, and fast, in order to buy some time to effect positive change. Most of the parents would be patient and give me a chance to reveal my professional fingerprint on the program, but there was a sense of impatience among the leadership team sitting in my family room that *Rosh Hashanah* day. They were, at that moment, the executive members responsible for the future of the school. For them, the clock was ticking.

My first step the day after the holiday was to set out a system to evaluate the supervision structure and educational monitoring framework of the leadership in the school. The two vice principals had the role of advising the teachers and supervising them for the past four to five years. This supervision was meant to be on curriculum development and mechanisms for meeting the provincial government's educational outcomes. Standards were developed by the government and implemented by the school. Meeting the criteria afforded the school financial grants on which the institution was dependent for its survival.

I presented the newspaper results at a meeting with the two vice principals who expressed great surprise at the publicized results. Yes, there had been some concern with the Grade 3 teacher; and indeed, many parents had continuously complained throughout the past year about the low instructional level imparted to their children. Citing evidence of her at times having been unprepared, they also provided documentation. There was evidence in her file that, at times, she had neglected to evaluate student workbooks. Despite more than sufficient evidence in support of her removal from her position, no one had been bold enough to make the tough call.

Yes, they had been without a Principal for a year. Nevertheless, one of the Vice Principals was promoted to the status of Acting Principal. It was her responsibility to ensure the ongoing education and supervision of the staff and program. It was quite obvious that she had dropped the ball and simply didn't have the courage to dismiss the most responsible teacher –

someone who was a close personal friend, someone that had been teaching in the school alongside her for a few years. When asked why she hadn't acted on the overwhelming evidence and documentation that there were issues the teacher had not addressed, the response was, "It is tough to get teachers who want to teach in our school. She was the best our school could get." At that very same time, this vice principal was about to go on maternity leave, so she had only one week left in the school. It seemed to me she had very much abdicated the decision to the incoming Principal – me – to make the tough call, to dismiss the third grade teacher. Not only that, I was left in a reactive, not a proactive stance.

It appeared I had no choice, but before I made the decision, I would need to talk to the teacher. I had to see for myself if anything was salvageable. It had to be my decision to let her go, reactive or not. I was not going to be the president's puppet, nor the non-confrontational vice principal's. Despite the teacher's newly revealed lack of skill and her pedagogical deficiencies, she and I had a relationship, albeit one that was just seven weeks old. Not the least of my concerns was the fact that she was teaching fifteen Grade 3 students. It would be an emotional issue for each of those fifteen students if she were to leave, so soon into the new academic year. Moreover, what if the vice principal was right? Was it hard to get people to teach in our school?

I recognised this as my first test as the principal, working with my board president. If she felt I would capitulate and act on her every desire without having demonstrated that it was truly my decision, not hers, my effectiveness as the leader of the school would surely be limited for evermore. Everyone on the staff was keenly aware of how the president felt toward that third grade teacher. It was now up to me. Transparently as possible, I set out to evaluate the situation and determine my own course of action, based upon sound educational grounds. I had to own my decision and everyone needed to know the transparency of my modus operandi.

I immediately initiated a meeting with the teacher in question to discuss my concerns over the testing results as well as the documentation in her professional file. I carefully reviewed all the significant issues and laid out a timeline of concern, which had been loosely conveyed to her over the previous year. When clearly laid out, it was quite evident that this teacher was struggling to cope with the compacted curriculum. Being a dual curriculum school, delivering both Judaic studies and the government-mandated general studies program, she was facing the classic conflict of parochial school teachers. She was hired to get stellar results on the secular syllabus in…half the time! Her lack of experience teaching that specific grade level was also on record. She had previously taught lower grades. The administration had made the decision to move her to a higher level because of a need to fill a maternity leave position. The decision had not even been made based on her capability to teach that specific grade level.

My conclusion was that she should never have been placed in the position in the first place. She was in well over her head and she knew it. Up until this point, there was a salvageable situation; but the rest of the evidence tipped the scales the other way. Rather than ask for help, the teacher began to cover her tracks and the students knew it. Shortcuts and skipping various essential skills were her coping mechanisms for covering the curriculum. Hence, the shocking result was understandable. The students could not succeed in the government assessment of their growth and knowledge of the standard curriculum. What made it even worse was her matter-of-fact attitude and continuous attempts to cover up her limited ability and her students' lack of knowledge.

In our meeting later that day, I was presented with her refusal to accept any responsibility. There was no acknowledgement that the students were unprepared for the assessments. In fact, she actually claimed just the opposite. She felt the students had done well. She remained steadfast, expressing how she would not change anything in the coming year. Her expectations were extremely low and her demeanour demonstrated she was not going to be a team player. Thus, my determination was that she should indeed be dismissed.

I quickly learned a most valuable lesson. I learned that for the most part her skills and attitude were quite antithetical to the incredible commitment of the majority of the general studies staff. Despite the awareness of the entire faculty of her negative attitude and inability to inspire students, once she was let go, staff morale dipped quite low! Behind the scenes, the sympathy was greater for this incompetent staff member than for the appropriateness of the educational decision made for the sake of the students and their school's reputation. From this situation, I learned early on that dismissing a staff member seems to create a sense of insecurity with the rest of the faculty. A teacher's natural nurturing instinct is to protect the weak, causing staff members to rally the troops and band together out of loyalty, sometimes overlooking a sense of what is right. Perhaps it's an instinctual drive for "group" survival in a perceived defenceless hierarchy. Someone else, perhaps even they, could be the next victim. Concerns for job security have a strange way of elevating the value of incompetent faculty members. Over time, I would develop an unwavering professional code of conduct including transparent professional proficiencies. Regular workshopping our staff on these policies and a mandate of accountability for upholding them consistently would go a long way to changing the insecurities of our faculty in times of transformation.

Once I made the decision to dismiss the teacher, I informed the executive of my proposed course of action. Then the deed had to be done. Theory was one thing. Practice was quite another. It is okay to talk the good game about removing the mediocre from the system. Nevertheless, dismissing a teacher is still a really difficult thing to do. You are affecting the personal lives of people. I tried not to overthink this situation, but a light bulb turned on. I realised something that to this very day makes my challenging decision-making process easier. It may sound like I adopted a hero complex. Well, so be it.

I am a protector of children. I have been placed in a position that charges me with the mission to ensure the emotional wellbeing of children. This applies to every aspect of their being when in school. I take this very personally. Therefore, as long as I have been entrusted to make decisions that directly or indirectly benefit them in both the short and long-term, it is critical that I am able to put my head on the pillow at night and sleep well. I thank Alf Boldt for crystalizing this mindset in me that very first day of my career in education. It keeps me going when I'm faced with tough decisions such as the need for dismissing unprofessional, undedicated teaching staff.

I rehearsed my monologue and despite knowing word for word how I was going to break the news, I was still a little shaky. It was decided that the president should join me and act as a witness to the discussion. This made the whole event a little more nerve-wracking, knowing that I was most probably being judged by her at the same time. We decided to meet the teacher first thing Monday morning. In retrospect, this was definitely not an ideal plan. There were far too many people in the school. As soon as she entered my office, she knew what was up. As I began my well-rehearsed speech, she cut me off. Then she lashed out at the president for stepping in and micromanaging the education of the school. She claimed that the president had targeted her. I was merely being used as a pawn to run the school that president's way. I let her have her say. Then I slowly, methodically read through each piece of documentation gathered over the previous year that pointed in the direction of the decision I, as the new Principal, had made. I wanted to demonstrate that the bottom line had been determined independently of the desires of the president, and that the evidence should have been acted upon last year. Not having had an official principal to run the school prolonged a negative situation that should have been rectified for the sake of the children the previous year.

I could have gone on, but there was no need. I had presented a solid line of evidence and documentation that screamed of her incompetence. We handed her a severance cheque that was more than fair, which protected the school from any potential litigation. Only one issue remained. How was she going to get all her personal items from her classroom in front of the children? I had that covered. While we were in the meeting, I had my secretary arrange for all her personal items to be boxed up. The box was waiting for her right outside my door. She requested the opportunity to say goodbye to the children, which we had already decided to deny. It was best for her to leave immediately. This decision, as in all my decisions, was made in the best interests of the students. It was a set of harsh decisions. In the long term, I established a very strong precedent. The mandate was that our school was only interested in hiring and keeping the best.

As I let her go, what gave me the strength of character at the ripe old age of twenty-nine? As I said, I just kept focusing on that vision of Alf Boldt, the public school superintendent and his opening address to me ten years ago, my first day in the faculty of education. 'I am the gatekeeper and protector of the young souls that you may or may not have the privilege of inspiring. If you are here because of the two months of summer holidays and the seven-hour workday, I will do everything in my power to get you out. But, if you are here to inspire a child, if you are that eager, selfless nurturer, then I will do everything in my power to get you into the most giving, rewarding profession.' Deep down, I was able to feel the sense of accomplishment having already had an opportunity to fulfil this mission. I was now more than ever one of the "protectors and guardians" of children – children who deserved nothing but the highest level of education and every possible opportunity to achieve their potential. I was now in a position to ensure that the very best teachers possible were serving on the front lines of this life or death battle.

We immediately placed an ad in the newspapers, including the very same Calgary Herald. It took only a week to hire the most incredible Grade 3 teacher. Her dedication and experience were beyond our imagination. Her philosophy of how to connect to students and her creative strategies as to how to compact the curriculum and improve our test scores were impressive. She had just recently come off maternity leave herself from the Catholic school system. She was now looking to ease her way into teaching. A part-time position in a values-based private school was just what she was looking for. It was a perfect match. Of course, that only served to plant more seeds of doubt in my mind about the vice principal who had set me up for this saga. The showdown had been set and it would only be a matter of time when we would have to go toe to toe…

Accountability

Despite the incredible traction we were gaining in the community at large, the internal fiscal challenges our school was facing were beginning to take their toll. It was a hectic time at the board level in terms of the looming deadline for determining a new course of action for sustained long-term accommodation for our school. At the same time, I got a call out of the blue from the Educational Division of the Alberta government overseeing our provincial funding. It seemed that our very same vice principal, who had taken maternity leave just after the 3rd grade teacher incident, had also neglected to file our three-year education plan with the appropriate authority. This oversight triggered a full review and the investigator wanted to set up an immediate meeting.

I was completely taken aback! I calmly as possible explained the fact that I had just taken over the principalship of the school, not more than six months ago, and would be more than happy to go over any requirements that were lacking and correct any issues that were outstanding. I maintained my composure and tried to demonstrate a strong desire to work with the investigative team that would be now unexpectedly showing up on our doorstep any day. The parting shot was that since we were in breach, they were required to notify me that, pending the review, our funding was certainly in jeopardy.

I called the school board president immediately. As you can by now guess, as I relayed the information she flew off the handle. She was livid, to say the least. Within a few minutes, she had arrived at the school to strategize our next move. By the time she arrived, I had already assembled all the documentation from one of the files in the on-leave vice principal's filing cabinet. I had discussed the issues with the acting vice principal who had assumed many of the duties of her colleague who was on maternity leave. The acting VP was not aware that the documentation had negligently not been submitted. Upon a cursory review of the files, a letter from the government addressed to the vice principal clearly indicated a request for submission. There was also a notice of breach for not having submitted the application for an extension. The acting VP indicated no knowledge of the letter. Since the "smoking gun" was found in the personal filing cabinet of the on-leave VP, the obvious conclusion was that she had also failed to pass on knowledge and disclose the information, not to mention having neglected the actual work necessary to fulfil the registration requirements well before she left on maternity leave. It was such a significant breach that the school was now seriously in jeopardy of losing its main source of government funding. Funding that we needed to survive.

The next step was to actually contact the VP at home and get her side of the story. I had met her only briefly. Within the first month of my arrival, she had given birth to her baby and gone on leave of absence. No one had thought to prepare me for the significance of this breach, not to mention the requirements for securing the funds and maintaining our private school status with the provincial government.

It didn't take long to determine the steps necessary to rectify the situation, but we had now caused a rift between our school and the government agency charged with sustaining our lifeline to the essential funding they gave us, which, in effect, enabled us to keep our doors open from year to year. Simply put, without the funding, the school could not survive. It was now going to be my task to quickly catch up on all the necessary paperwork in anticipation of the inspection team's arrival. I was determined to mend that bridge by solidifying their confidence in me personally, the new principal charged with picking up the pieces from a negligent VP.

It was not a case of throwing the VP under the bus. Her negligence had placed her there by herself. It was a very challenging phone call. Had she only admitted to having filed the letter and forgotten not only to notify her colleague during the handover but also to not having completed the necessary documents to complete the renewal process, perhaps that would have redeemed her somewhat. Not the case. At one point during the conversation, she even tried to pass the blame onto the president for not having demanded a more thorough handover from her. This was a huge error in judgment on her part and it sealed her fate. The rest of the conversation was short and to the point. We needed access to the rest of her files and documents. From then on, I would be working day and night to prepare our application for reregistration and on securing her resignation! I could not afford to await a third strike!

The decision to eliminate this vice-principal from the staff, was at this point, pardon the pun, merely academic. Her negligence in not having developed a strategic education plan, coupled with her not having communicated in her handover the pending urgency of these necessary government requirements and the now very much past due deadline made the decision obvious. It was a little uncomfortable when we met her one morning at her house and presented her with a severance package in lieu of a notice period. Her parting shot was once again to blame the acting president for interference in micromanaging the school. It didn't make much of a difference, but I felt it was only right to back up the president by mentioning that she herself had put the school in a very precarious situation that required significant effort to fix. The damage to our relationship with the educational branch of the government was significant and would require a lot of immediate attention to repair.

Having just arrived in the school, I had not prepared for such a crisis and the difficulty could easily have been averted with some simple communication. Neglecting to inform her colleague or me was a breach of her professional duty, not to mention her having buried the notice in her personal files, which was beyond all understanding. There was nothing to be gained by accusing her of sabotage. The evidence was overwhelming and it would do her no good to shift the blame onto someone else. It taught me a great lesson that sometimes, no matter how embarrassing or compromising to one's ego, it takes fortitude to admit a mistake. Had she come forward and admitted that for some reason she had made the error, I would have had more respect for her and would have gone down the road to ensure she be given the chance to rectify the situation. Instead, she chose to shift the blame, not take responsibility and thus she sealed her fate.

When a Plan Comes Together

The following few days were intense. It was a huge learning curve to get up to speed in anticipation of the government inspection. There were benefits from these events. I now had the impetus to develop the educational plan of my own design and I was determined to take maximal advantage of the opportunity. Whilst forced into a reactive stance, we decided to see this as an opportunity to developing that educational vision. There was no sense in my holding back for fear of not wanting to be seen as too dogmatic and dictatorial. There was no choice now. It was up to me to develop that educational plan…in two days! There was no luxury of time to slowly generate buy-in from the faculty. I understood very well that the success of a vision certainly was to have commitment from all organizational members. The hope that fleeted through my adrenalin-driven thoughts was that perhaps the manner in which the plan had to come into being would just become a natural buy-in. You know, how we all bond together in an emergency? That was only a short-lived thought. I only had two days to develop the plan!

I sought out the acting VP. Together we developed a plan of action. She would act as the voice of the staff and I could bounce my ideas off her. In this way, I was able get an honest understanding of both the staff's ability and willingness to be part of the future vision of our institution. Having sat in the background for many years, I ascertained in the acting VP a deep desire for advancement. Her only lingering concern was the optics of the pending removal of her colleague. She did not want to be seen as the catalyst of her friend's termination. With a commitment from me that I would shield her from any such speculation, I had a team-mate, at least on the surface, that could not only represent the best interests of the staff but someone who could act as a conduit between the administration and any staff members who might possibly be feeling insecure about the upcoming changes.

Two firings within the first few months of the school year hopefully contributed to their realisation that there would be a strong commitment to professionalism and accountability. They had to sense there could be more potential staffing changes on the horizon. There were no unions to protect the incompetent. Staffing allocations based upon historic precedent tantamount to 'tenure' no longer held value if it protected ineffectual staff members. No longer would there be employment guarantees due to seniority or membership in the Jewish community or synagogue.

Our educational vision included an employee appraisal initiative that contained a robust professional development program. The program would not only provide professional in-servicing with a focus on teacher learning, but it contained a modest incentive program for attaining self-determined goals and outcomes that were linked to our school improvement plan. The bonus scheme related to value-adding proposals developed by the staff. The cost/benefit of having staff volunteers within this bonus scheme outweighed the outlay of funds to contract outside personnel. From the creative ideas and input of staff, we were able to develop a school beautification program that included parent volunteers.

The enduring effect of having teachers commit to our vision automatically created a significant increase in teaching morale. Teachers were staying back after school to run extracurricular programs that they themselves were interested in developing, not only because they were being compensated, but because they themselves saw the benefit in terms of developing relationships with their students and effecting the vision statement of building a true community school.

One of the faculty members was a black belt in judo. Instead of hiring someone to develop an after-school sport program, which most other schools had, our school was now able to promote an experienced instructor, a proud faculty member, for a minimal, modest fee. Parents were more than happy to keep their extremely content children for an additional hour at the school under the watchful care of a trusted, known professional. Teachers felt that the benefits of developing connections with students outside of the classroom through these extracurricular initiatives enhanced their daily one-on-one, professional relationships inside their classrooms. An obvious side benefit was those few extra dollars in their pockets. For many teachers, these initiatives generated new-found respect from their students as they revealed their previously hidden talents.

Another fringe benefit was how much positive publicity we received on the variety of programming in our new extra-curricular offerings. In the case of the judo teacher, the newspaper caught on that our black belt instructor was a gold medallist from South Africa, having participated as a young adult at the International *Maccabi* Games in Israel. What made it even more unusual was that the teacher was also one of the approved, newly-hired Orthodox rabbis, full beard and all. His hiring brought the Orthodox rabbi count in Calgary to a whopping four!

The value-added component to my three-year plan included not only a significant sport program but also an overhaul of our fine arts curriculum. Until now, our school had only paid lip service to the music requirements of the government curriculum. Our well-documented plan was to increase the profile of the school choir. With some restructuring of the daily timetable, I managed to schedule practice time twice a week as a full school initiative. Not only did each class have a music lesson once a week, now they would assemble to prepare their full group performance skills. This was only one small aspect of my proposal. Having realised the potential within the students to perform a theatrical presentation in front of the community, my plan was to build this event. Within two years, we expanded to presenting our musical theatrical in front of a packed-out audience on the main stage of the University of Calgary theatre.

We started off small and the ideas took hold. The first year was quite a hit for our parent body. By the second year, we had a full-on parent group meeting on the weekends to develop the costumes and another committee of parents building elaborate sets and painting backdrops. Our little idea of developing a fine arts program had become a significant component of the revitalization strategy of our school and a main component of our three-year plan. It would be essential for us to demonstrate the actualization of our mission statement and that we were practically meeting the needs of each individual in the school. Our fine arts program certainly demonstrated how this theoretical component was put into practice wherein every student in the school had a part in our play. Some students obviously had stronger parts than others did, while the lower grades had dance routines incorporated into the story. Of course, our finale involved a full school chorus that was met with a resounding standing ovation! With widespread publicity promoting our new-found success, the full school production was documented evidence that we were well on our way to actualizing our newly-integrated mission statement and our government-submitted three-year plan.

Despite my nerves and my efforts not to focus on what was really at stake, by the time they came, I thought we were very well prepared for the on-site inspection headed by the Alberta Government Department of Education. The focus of the visit was to determine whether our school had the appropriate structures to address the accountability requirements laid out by the Department of Education.

It was miraculous what we accomplished in those forty-eight hours! We had developed documents to clarify our board structure and constitutional affiliation to the synagogue. Each member of the board submitted a resume and personal mission statement as to the rationale for their personal involvement in school governance as well as a statement of their understanding and commitment to fulfilling their fiduciary responsibly. After all, it was not just the school's education on trial, it was also our ability to remain financially sustainable. Combined with the invaluable input from the vice principal, we developed a pretty elaborate three-year plan that I hoped eloquently described our ethos and educational purpose. We established clear priorities on how we were going to meet the educational benchmarks of our student body including some bold, realistic targets. I was frank in my assertion that we had underperformed on our government assessments. Therefore, we detailed strategies on how we would address and rectify our challenges.

Our on-site meeting took the better part of the morning. The Department of Education representatives could not help but express openly how impressed they were with our ability to develop a responsive plan that could address our educational challenges... in two days! The fact that I was honest and did not hide from the issues certainly was held in our favour. I acknowledged the fact that our school had been negligent in not submitting the required documentation. In the same breath, however, I was clear that there was a new direction with a new administration that would never let this recur. They were impressed with my drive and educational background. Especially when they heard I had come from their Calgary public system as both a student and teacher, now head of this private school.

I was humbled and shocked when, at the conclusion of the morning visit, I was told that they were going to on the spot declare our school as having passed the on-site inspection! Within the week, we would receive our full accreditation status. It was a very exciting and totally unexpected outcome. I could hardly wait for them to leave the school to give our president a call to share the news. We had dodged a huge bullet and everyone knew it. I was committed to our new vision and would not allow anything to stand in our way, especially having put my name on the line as the one responsible for reaching our documented goals. In their letter they clearly stated it was due to their "confidence in the new leadership of the school, under the direction of the Principal, Rabbi Glogauer," that full accreditation would be granted to the school. We held a special board meeting, and very kindly, a basket of fruit was presented to me on behalf of all the board and staff.

At a time when schools were under close scrutiny for not meeting student needs both academically and socially, the community had begun to recognize our closely-kept little secret of making a difference in the lives of our students.

We started priding ourselves on all the attributes for which the school was formerly criticized. We turned our seeming liabilities into our biggest assets. We were proud to be a small, close-knit community which was in touch with the needs of our students. The variety of programming and connectivity between student and teacher was acknowledged not just as lip service but a sincere reality. There was now only one more essential target we needed to reach to truly make a statement in the extended community beyond our demographic.

Before parents would be ready to take the risk of changing schools, even though deep down our product and outcomes checked 95% of their personal boxes, to send their child to an Orthodox school, a religiously observant school, despite not being a "practicing Jewish family", parents would overlook the personal, confronting issues if and only if we literally 'made the grade'. Only then could and would they see the advantages significantly outweighing any of the potential negatives.

For the most part, the desired universal characteristics that every parent wants in a school seem quite obvious. Parents want a nurturing environment that builds the self-esteem and resiliency of their child. The institution should be a place where each child is stimulated and recognised for his or her individual ability. The nurturing framework should promote engaging opportunities for the student to actively contribute to the betterment of the environment.

For parents whose personal philosophy may not exactly match the ethos of the intended institution, as long as the above is met, they may consider the possibility of sending their child to the school. I have found over the years that when the academic achievement of the school is recognized to be at a high level, parents will consider overlooking the mismatch in values systems between their personal lives and the values of the school. This became evident once our program and the strategically hired teaching staff employed to raise our test scores became a reality. Intuitively, I realised the need to significantly increase our results to the point that simply nothing below the top 10% of the province was going to do. Part of my submitted government plan was to focus on the early literacy initiatives in the lower grades leading up to our Grade 3 cohort (which was the first level of government testing).

That year we had a very strong cohort of 15 students in Grade 3. When we replaced our Grade 3 teacher just after *Rosh Hashanah*, as you recall, we successfully hired an enthusiastic, child-focused experienced teacher. I truly felt the sky was the limit. Don't get me wrong, my philosophy was not based on overtesting nor was it hinged upon teaching to the test. Rather with a warm, nurturing teacher who recognizes the value of connecting to her students and inspiring them to love learning, who maintains a strong focus on differentiation, I was optimistic we would succeed and meet my overarching ambitious goal. We strategized as a staff how to maximize resources in an effort to boost schoolwide literacy. With a newly-developed reading curriculum, one could feel the shift in the student body's work ethic and commitment to their studies.

We began a homework club after school where students could stay behind and receive extra tuition with their teachers. Student extension and remedial issues were identified early with significant interventions aimed at addressing the core of the issue. One of our incredible hiring feats was a semi-retired ex-Principal whose passion and focus was numeracy. He became the mentor of our staff who perhaps were weak in this critical learning area. I have found that it is very rare to have primary school teachers who are equally solid educationalists in numeracy and literacy. It is more common for these professionals to have an overall strength in one over the other. I had great faith in the educational product we were offering with this specialist on board to serve as a mentor and hands-on resource to our teaching staff. Teachers began working together. There was more collaborative planning of units of work that were rich and well-integrated. Our students became our best advertising mechanism, returning home talking about their daily lessons and what was happening educationally in our school.

Positivity breeds more positivity. It was not only contagious from what was happening in our staff room and classrooms, but now was transferring into the many homes of our community. Most of the time, it takes a while for positivity to catch on outside of a school community. In the public sphere focused on publishing student test results, when parents wait for the school's results to be printed in the local newspapers to determine educational choice, the educational culture sadly becomes very reactionary. Parents tend to march with their feet and Calgary was no different. This was why the president showed up on my doorstep that one Jewish New Year afternoon.

Our school community was no different. They were looking for a result that would not only solidify the resolution to enrol and take a chance on the school but also inspire long-term parental commitment to our institution. A middle-of-the-pack result on the provincial tests would only serve to calm the waters. The school board and certainly my own competitive spirit were looking for more. I believed that with a top result, coupled with the other school initiatives we had put in place, we could do better than encourage the decision to attend our school, a choice made by our current parent body. I fervently believed that we could attract non-Orthodox families to our school. For this theoretical swing to take place, we would need a significant jump in our results. All my strategic staffing decisions were aligned with this goal in mind. I had been very careful not to compromise the nurturing value system of our school for my desire to attain top test results. I believed if we did things right, kept our philosophy intact, we would achieve. And did we ever!

Our students were extremely well prepared. I was the only one who was nervous. I tried to hide it as best as I could: after all, I had a lot riding on it. My strategic plan, my hiring initiatives, the philosophy now ingrained in our staff and students somehow would be evaluated by the simple score on four days of external examinations. I gave many pep talks and motivational speeches in the weeks leading up to the provincial exams. At times, I felt more like Vince Lombardi than a school principal. I believed in my team and told them so. I commended them because I knew they had done all the necessary practice to perform on the 'game days'. I paced up and down the hallways as if it was the sideline of the football field in the Super Bowl finals, in a close game in the waning seconds of the last quarter. As soon as the teacher opened her classroom door and handed me the tests, all I could do was sigh and realize all our work was done. I remember personally sealing the official envelopes shut. With a tiny prayer, I handed the package over to the courier. The four-day government-testing marathon was done.

It would take two months and many sleepless nights replaying strategy until the news of our results landed in the local newspaper. In Grade 3, we had jumped from the bottom of all private schools to the top of the list! Our tiny school had the highest percentage of achievement out of every private school in the city! We were the long shot and had achieved exactly what we set out to do. Even our Grade 6 class had demonstrated a remarkable improvement. From out of the ashes rose the phoenix and it was truly a remarkable sight. That morning, in the staff room everyone gathered around to bask in the success of our results. It was hard not to be emotional. With members of the school board joining us in our celebration, the feeling of accomplishment was overwhelming. I thanked everyone for all their efforts and commitment to our shared vision. The level of camaraderie among the faculty was at an all-time high. It was a communal success and everyone was proud to be a part of that accomplishment. With the incredible positivity among the faculty, it was mirrored by the overwhelming emotions exhibited by the parent body. Every conversation was centred on the amazing educational turnaround we had made.

Round and Round that Rim

Our school jumped up to first place out of forty private schools in Grade 3. We had redeemed ourselves. The Jewish community was all abuzz about what was happening at our tiny school. Within that first year, everyone had been anticipating the effects of the deliberate academic improvements and those significant staffing changes. With this well-publicized improvement, and instantly becoming one of the top private schools in the city, we had little time to capitalize on the opportunity. We were aiming for the parents who were on the fence in regard to their children's Jewish education. I had to figure out how to attract a wider population into the school. Every observant, Orthodox family had pretty much enrolled their child in our school. There were no more children who fit that tiny demographic from whom to draw upon. Therefore, we needed somehow to attract those who were not necessarily observant, or overtly religious, but who were on the sidelines. I was sure they could be convinced for 'other reasons' to take a chance on our school. My job was to uncover exactly what those 'other reasons' were that could entice them to peek over the fence and take a chance.

Being a small school, the one thing that we had going for ourselves was the intimate, nurturing attention each student was given. We were a school where the principal knew the names of each student. Naturally, this meant that every teacher was deeply familiar with the gifts and talents of each student in their care. This translated into an environment where every student could excel to his or her true potential. Each student was a leader and felt like he or she was special. In addition to our judo club, we also ran a hockey program after school. Sport became a major component of the curriculum and we became active members of the Independent Schools Sports Athletic Association.

Once again, it was basketball that forged a turning point. That year we made the news as our tiny team of eight players matched up against the Independent Schools city champions in our first basketball game. We were quite a sight. Our team, wearing their *yarmulkes,* walked into the gymnasium of the Glenmore Christian Academy in front of all the opposition's screaming fans. I'll never know whether it was a sight they had never seen before: Orthodox Jewish boys playing in the majority Christian sport league, or was it because our team was made up of tiny boys all under five feet five? All I know was the crowd, in unison, went completely mute as they beheld the spectacle of our team walking toward the visitor's bench.

It was hard to hold back emotion and rally the boys. The gym was full. For many of the boys, this was their first time playing an organized team sport. I recruited a close high school friend of mine to assist me in coaching the team. We were well prepared but very nervous. During the warm-up, I could see the boys were very anxious and could not really focus on the drills at hand. Perhaps they were just in awe of the sheer size of the gymnasium and the fact that such a large fan base had assembled to cheer on their home team.

I quickly gathered the boys around our bench and gave them a pep talk. I reviewed our game plan but then waxed on about a greater purpose – we were not here to impress some professional scouts, looking to make it onto a professional basketball team. We were all playing to have fun and to support each other. This was most probably the first time our opposition had played a group of Jewish boys and we were going to set an example of teamwork, supporting each other. At the same time, we were going to be exhibiting great sportsmanship. I encourage them to play just as we had practiced and they were guaranteed to have fun. At just that moment, the father of one of the boys came over. From behind me, he began to offer some strategy. Without any prior permission, or even a request to add his two cents, he began telling the boys, based on his quick scouting report, what he thought our team should do to match up against their high-powered offence. Not wanting to cause a scene by embarrassing the man or his poor son, who had turned a deep shade of purple in response to his father's advice, I acknowledged his presence and quickly changed the focus to our cheer. We readied the starting group of boys by calling out their allocated positions.

I could see this father was annoyed. I had cut him off despite his forceful conviction that he had plenty more 'wisdom' he wanted to share. I was quite taken aback at his inclination. Known to be an intense parent, always full of advice, this was not the time nor place for his involvement. My goal was for the boys to come away from the experience, having enjoyed themselves and with a sense of unity and pride in their efforts. My assistant coach too looked stunned at the unfolding scene. This parent and his lack of social awareness, having no realization at all, had stepped well over the line.

The students got into game mode. Before we knew it, we had won the tip-off and scored a basket on our very first possession. The first half was an exciting one. The boys played back and forth, trading successive baskets. It was very close at the buzzer to end the half. We were down by only four points. The boys were pumped full of energy. You could practically see their confidence growing. Deep down the potential doubts they may have had in their inability to keep up with an established team had all but dissipated, along with that confidence they were building an even more valuable asset – the trust in each other as a team. It was the icing on the cake when, after a quick bathroom break and drink of water, the boys were all brought in to a circle. My assistant coach asked the boys to share what they thought was working. One at a time, the boys complimented their peers passing and their speed at bringing up the ball. The system we had developed was working well when it was fuelled with that good communication. When we lacked the verbal dialogue during the game, we lost the ability to make the first outlet pass after crossing midway. The boys self-diagnosed the issue, and with that, they had begun to think basketball. No one bore down on anyone else. There was a strong feeling of success and trust. Up to now, the pushy father had stayed out of the huddle and remained a silent onlooker while the boys chatted amongst themselves. At the conclusion of the huddle, he began to raise some points he felt relevant to the system we had developed. I again gathered the boys together, told them to get one more quick drink and then set the second-half line-up.

As the boys lined up at the water fountain, I quickly called the father to the side. In what I thought was a very diplomatic speech, I informed the father that this moment was not a venue for parent involvement. He could stand on the sideline and cheer like the rest of the fans, but the goal of our initiative was to allow the boys to build resilience and strength in sport as a team. This was to be accomplished by developing character as a group and building themselves through the experience, not being told how to do it from experts. Learning how to develop strategies from experience with each other was, educationally, far more valuable a life skill for students than being told by adults who already knew how. This basketball court experience was like a classroom, with the exception that the learning would be hands-on and confronting. This was the best laboratory for the boys to develop trust in each other. As adults, we need to realize how important it is to trust in our children. As difficult as it may be, to want to step in to protect and save our children from potential failure, not meeting a desirable objective itself is a great lesson and learning experience for our students. I had confidence in our students and in the preparation we had given them. All I was asking was for him to have the same. With that monologue, I asked him to please go back to the other side of the gym.

The father was stunned. It was probably the first time in his life someone had put him in his place. Throughout the remainder of the game, he was the loudest of all the spectators. Running up and down the sideline, he was quite a spectacle. At times, he was shouting across the gym at my assistant coach and me to put other children in the game or to change their positions. We ignored him and focused on the children and the game at hand. It was a very tough game. With thirty seconds left on the clock, we were down by only one point. It was our turn to put the ball in. We called our last time-out to strategize. The thirty-second time-out was enough to calm the boys down and talk about who was going to take the last shot.

The boys decided to choose one of the plays we had practiced, and that the ball would go to Donnie our tallest player. The play was designed to spring Donnie free with Yossi, our smallest player to be the second alternative to receive the ball if Donnie was covered. Yossi was very nervous. This was his first team game in any sport in his whole young twelve-year-long life. Yossi urged Donnie to make sure he got open so he himself would not be relied upon to make the shot himself. We all smiled at his great encouragement and the immense nerves of poor little Yossi. Sure enough, the opposition read our plan and covered Donnie like a giant blanket. Yossi was wide open of course, as he had not been considered a threat. The inlet pass to Yossi was a clean one. The clock was counting down to zero. Yossi caught the ball. He dribbled closer in for a better shot. With almost no time on the clock, Yossi took a shot that seemed to hang in mid-air for an eternity. It struck the rim and rolled around 360°. The crowd remained in a hush. The ball seemed to sit on the ring...before falling out! Victory was granted to the home side. We all stood in stunned silence. We were not sure what to expect as a reaction from our boys! They all ran to Yossi, patted him on the back wishing him commiserations for his great attempt. He was so close and had done his best. This was the best positive outcome, and his team-mates were all very proud.

The victory would have been nice, but the team's reaction in the face of the loss was even more priceless. Every boy had a beaming smile as they all lined up to shake hands with the opposition. What happened next was even more amazing. As our boys stood in a line at centre court ready to greet the other team, the opposition gathered as a group and in unison shouted a cheer for our school. The three cheers for Akiva Academy were met with a resounding hurray from the fans who had witnessed an extremely entertaining game with a nail-biting conclusion.

Our team had lost the game but won the respect of our opposition and their fans. I was very emotional, as was my assistant coach. We gave each other a huge hug and ran onto the court to congratulate the other team and their coaches. Our players were not disappointed at all in the loss. They were truly proud of their accomplishment. They had come together and fought a battle. They relied on each other and were proud of each other. It was testimony that we had accomplished what we had set out to do. I learned a great lesson. These crucial ingredients of being an underdog and developing pride in what you are carry great value when looking to grow a school.

That night, every player would go home and share the incredible excitement and pride in being a member of the team. I made sure every student regardless of skill played an equal amount. Their uniforms had been worn with pride the day of the game. The next morning, over the PA system, a full recap was given right after the anthems, which, that day, were sung by the whole basketball team in unison.

As each game took place, more and more parents came to watch. There were articles in the local newspaper about some no-name school playing for the first time in the Independent Sports Athletic Association. We were indeed generating significant noise in the wider community. We were becoming a force to be reckoned with, not only on the sports field but also in relation to incoming enrolments.

To my unfortunate surprise, the morning after the game, the school president called to set up a brief discussion about the complaint she had received from the parent who attended a basketball game. The parent described how inappropriately he had been spoken to. He was extremely upset with my conduct. I found myself having to defend my actions against a one-sided account of how I had dealt "unprofessionally" with a parent in front of students and in a public forum. I did my best to remain calm and recount all the facts about his inappropriate behaviour. It didn't take long to realize I had unwittingly made an enemy out of a very vocal parent with a very skewed perspective of right and wrong. It left a sour taste in my mouth that my professionalism was being called into question by a personality that was forceful, obnoxious, and well-known to have consistently behaved in such a negative manner over the years. What was more, the president had not given me any benefit of doubt. That was the more distressing aspect of the whole incident.

I didn't know at the time that this type of altercation with a parent sadly tends to occur frequently in private schools. There is often a sense of entitlement fee-paying parents adopt. I have since found the same heightened sense of privilege amongst certain board members. It took me many years to gain adequate perspective that it was not necessarily about me, or something that was said or done. Rather, it is always about their own issues. Believe me, this time I truly took it personally. It would take a strong sense of mentorship and growing professional self-confidence to manage these situations. Such leadership support usually comes from the Chair of the School Board who sets a tone of respect within the institution.

As I have gained experience over the years, I now know I don't need to take this type of situation to heart and usually I don't. I strive to deeply, actively listen when there is a complaint or disagreement with the ethos of the school of which I am principal. When there is no compromise of action possible on the part of the school, as at this fateful basketball game, letting the concerned parent know I hear what they are saying is about the best possible strategy. Quietly and gently reiterating the philosophy behind whatever the issue might be is critical, when I have judged that the person with whom I am discussing is ready to hear it. The optimal outcome is multifaceted. Hopefully, this discussion results in a deeper relationship of understanding with that parent. Perhaps there can be a laugh or two in the ideal situation as we agree to disagree, but first and foremost, is what is going on for me behind scenes. I can only act with this confidence if I know I am not going to be hung out to dry by my board. The peace of mind and confidence of knowing that your board stands behind you on upholding decisions that support the ethos of the school is absolutely essential. When you have that team support, you are never alone in your battles.

Making a Communal Impact

It seemed that no matter the magnitude of the honeymoon moments within the school, at every administrative level we were in crisis mode. Each strategy session with the school's lay leadership team signified a lack of cohesion. Compounding this issue was the fact that the school's lease was about to expire and the need to secure long-term accommodation was at the heart of the viability concerns for the existing parent body and potential enrolment recruits.

My focus remained steadfast on recruiting new students into the school. Despite all the negativity in the community and uncertainty regarding long-term viability, school enrolment began to grow.

Through some well-designed strategies and support for some critical initiatives, our tiny, well-kept little secret continued to filter out to the wider community. A lot of credit was given to me for having made some very essential decisions early on in my leadership. As much as I wanted to give credit to the actual person who had come up with the ideas I had the privilege of implementing, I could not.

I had learned a lot about the players in the community and the obstacles in the way of the school growing from one of the most invested community members, who just happened to have been persuasively encouraging me behind the scenes. In fact, before I had even come to Calgary, having no idea of the opportunity available, it was the same individual, my mother's friend who happened to be one of the original founders of the Orthodox synagogue and school. A superb educator and successful lawyer, it was her vision and passion that brought about the theoretical idea of having a true Orthodox school in the city way back in the early part of the 1980s.

This unsuspecting individual was the one who planted the seed of me becoming the principal. Infamous for her passion and commitment, her no-nonsense straight-shooting reputation generated either allies or enemies. I was immediately drawn to her for the simple underlying principle that "everything needed to be for the sake of the children." It was all about the preservation of the future of the Jewish community in the city and the continuity of the Jewish people in general, and she was talking from experience. Having come from a fairly large family, she knew she was a product of not having had a complete Jewish day school education. Every one of her siblings who had a day school education was continuing a very strong Jewish legacy with their children. Not quite so with her siblings who had attended public school. I was always amazed at how simply she could narrow down the issues, and her "take no prisoners" attitude when it came to right or wrong. There was not a lot of gray when it came to decision-making. If it benefited the goal of the preservation of the overall ideal, we needed to push ahead. If it was detracting from the ultimate goal, what was best for the children in the school, we needed to stop and backtrack. In many ways, it made life quite simple.

I instantly grew very fond of her and we developed an immediate, strong professional relationship. If ever I was in doubt over how to proceed on a difficult issue, she was on my speed dial and I could count on her to encourage my focus on the bigger picture. She was not a "yes ma'am" person who would tell you what you wanted to hear. At times, she undiplomatically put me in my place and I deep down appreciated her honesty. I indubitably learned more from her in those two and a half years than in any other professional relationship over my years in the educational field. Together we shaped the school, I on the front lines, and she behind the scenes. She had an eye for educational flair and with her intimate knowledge of the Calgary Jewish community knew how to develop a program that could attract new students into the school. She had special contacts in the community and with her strategy and my implementation we grew the school to its historically highest ever enrolment.

One of her ingenuities was to put the school on the community map within six months of my first year as principal, in an area that was both public and educationally valuable for the growth of the students. Every year, both Jewish schools performed at the public *Chanukah Menorah* lighting ceremony sponsored by the *Chabad* rabbi at City Hall. Dignitaries from the Jewish community alongside the Mayor attended this festive annual gathering for this well-publicized event. This was an opportunity to outshine the competition and demonstrate a sense of pride in our student and parent body. With my mentor's assistance, we hired one of the most well-known music teacher/choirmasters in the community. Within two months, the school's music program was revamped and a full school choir was primed and ready for its first

Chanukah performance at City Hall. Within the school, there was a renewed sense of pride, not to mention the joy we all got from the incredible harmonies resounding throughout the hallways.

We had staged a huge surprise for the community. Without a lot of fanfare or publicity, I managed to fundraise for a choir uniform. We had white button-down shirts and blouses made up with the school's embroidered dark blue crest on the right breast pocket. Our students looked incredible, wearing coordinated navy pants and skirts.

Finally, the big day arrived. We were performing in front of a packed audience and the Calgary Mayor! The crowd gasped as our students, professionally poised, all marched in sync up the steps at City Hall. No one expected the beautiful harmonies that came out of their well-rehearsed voices. I was emotionally unprepared for just how amazing they looked and sounded, but even more so for the overwhelming response from the community. For the first time, our school put the competition to shame. Strangers, community leaders and the mayor himself made a point of coming over to me to congratulate us for an incredible performance and marked improvement from years past. It was so gratifying. Deep down, I truly felt that we had only just begun. We decided to build on the momentum from the December performance. Not only did we find more venues to perform, but we also needed to get the word out as a school with a newly-developed 'fine arts' program.

As school pride within our student body began to soar, so too did the renewed vigour amongst our parent body. The school's Parents Association also became revitalized through a membership drive and they increased the level of volunteerism in the school. The mid-year family barbecue get-together was an incredible success. Most families in attendance discussed ways of strategizing practical initiatives with the sole purpose of increasing support through their involvement in the school. Before I knew what hit me, parents willing to offer their services to the school in any way possible were bombarding me with their generosity. One parent in particular came to be one of our most supportive, and from there, a lifelong friend. An artist, she told me personally that if there was ever anything the school needed in terms of beautification, she was willing to assist.

One of the challenges we had at the time came from the Grade 5 parents who were quite distressed that their children's class had to be relocated into the library. Due to an issue of space and the demand for classrooms with the expansion of the primary school into Grade 7, our first junior high class, we were one classroom short. With some creative thinking, we partitioned the library and developed an additional classroom. The challenge was that it did not have a window.

The parents by the way were the only ones who were upset. The happiness and excitement of their children did not seem to make it home. Their children were thrilled to have a larger room with all the library amenities and resources at their fingertips. Since it was right beside the computer lab, the Grade 5 children had easy access and first right of passage over the rest of the school. We felt we had to develop their priority 'status' and generate some feeling of privilege in these students, given they had the classroom without the window. The hope was that this positivity would transfer into their parents' attitudes toward the school. It worked with most of the parents with the exception of one or two that wanted to stand on principle. I had a brainwave. Despite all the students being quite content with their new surroundings, and since it was only a technicality not having a window in their sectioned area of the library (the other partitioned area did indeed have some windows), I asked our parent volunteer/artist if she could paint us a window.

It sounded a bit crazy and even patronizing, but a fresh coat of paint and something novel if properly presented would demonstrate some sympathy for the parents' point of view. Over one long weekend, when we arrived back at school on the Tuesday, everyone was stunned as they walked into the classroom. Our parent volunteer, Toby, had completely transformed the classroom wall into an outdoor scene from an 'open window'. It was better than any possible window. It was light, springtime, and sunny all year round, no matter how cold, snowy, or cloudy it actually was outside! We had our very own 'Chagall masterpiece' in the Grade 5 classroom beyond anything I could ever have imagined. It was a stunning display of the idiom of making lemonade out of lemons.

We invited the parent body into the classroom to take a look. They all had smiles, especially the two parents who had made a huge deal of not having a window in the classroom. It was a great example of our determination to keep everyone on side with limited resources and a lot of ingenuity. Toby became a huge contributor. She confided that, for the first time, she felt useful and that she had something she could contribute to the community, despite her limited Jewish knowledge and minimal observance level. She had been drawn to the school because of its unique nurturing nature and intimate size, and she always felt her children were recognized for their individuality. Her family did not have a lot of financial means to contribute, and she had always wanted to give something back to the school. I found a way to keep her involved and promote her talents. Her gift was now well known to the parent body, and before long, she had become a regular part of the parent's association fundraising committee. She designed the annual *Rosh Hashanah* greeting card, which parents throughout the entire community traditionally purchased to support the school and at the same time send good wishes to family and friends at that special time of year.

I had one more grand idea and pitched it to Toby who was overcome with emotion at my suggestion. With her unique skill and aptitude, visions were jumping around in my imagination as to how we could further build our fine arts program in the school. Every year at *Chanukah* time, the school held a special concert for the families of the school. Each class presented two songs. You can do the calculations: From the two preschool classes, kindergarten through Grade 7, that's 10 classes, two songs each. If each song lasted even three minutes in duration, with time to walk on stage and off, there were not so many happy parents who sat through the entire two-hour plus concert for the six minutes of fame for their child. It was a major source of contention and having sat through one in my first year as principal, I vowed that it would be my last. Never was I to do it again.

I have stuck to this vow; so much so, that at every successive school thereafter, I have abolished the torturous annual event wherever I have gone. Don't worry. We had a better idea. Of course, there was a real expectation that *Chanukah* was the time, before winter vacation, when every school required a performance. I needed to find an alternative.

With my new music teacher, my new resident artist adviser, and parent volunteer/maintenance crew on standby, I now had a ready and waiting fine arts development team. All I needed was the script, director and producer and we would be set for our very first whole school *Chanukah* production.

It was a global idea, a way to unite every component of our school. Focusing on one task brought the entire faculty together. My sister, the talented writer that she is, wrote an incredible story. My wife, knowing the students in the school and their abilities, adapted the story to provide lines for every student. With the chorus, songs led by our choir mistress were smoothly integrated into the play. Every student felt like they were not only essential but indispensable to the overall production. The whole was truly greater than the sum of its parts. Toby and her crew of fathers built elaborate sets and our Parents Association sewed incredible costumes. With some great publicity, my mentor had the ingenious idea to hold the event in the Jewish Community Centre auditorium. We went all out, with printed posters and postcards to all parents and community dignitaries and sales of professionally printed tickets. The auditorium was packed and sold out. Word was out that our school had done something special. For weeks afterward, the positivity and momentum carried into our enrolment drive for the upcoming school year.

Our tiny school, despite its challenges, was becoming a thriving, exciting hub of education. With the goal always on my mind of linking educational outcomes with opportunities for communal promotion, I met with the synagogue rabbi to strategize plans for the upcoming celebration for Israel Independence Day. Together we came up with the idea of holding a 'walk-a-thon' through the community. Our parent body together with our students made six booths representing the six major cities in Israel. Every student received a special passport, which had to be stamped at each "City" along the route. There was an educational theme associated with each city that was taught the preceding weeks in school and actualized on the day of the Walk-a-thon. For example, for the city of Teveriya, Tiberias, being on the shores of the beautiful Lake Kinneret, Sea of Galilee, the theme of course, was about water. The content included Israel's innovative water conservation science and technology, and of course, each child got an ice-cold drink of water handed to them by our parent volunteers at the Teveriya 'station'.

The Walk-a-thon began at the synagogue and concluded at the school. It was a great communal initiative, linking the two institutions. The rabbi of the synagogue gave an opening address and the entire school marched along the route, singing songs and waving Israeli and Canadian flags. The publicity in the newspaper and positive public relations engendered were spoken about for weeks.

The Jewish holiday called *Shavuos*, commemorates the giving of the first fruits in the Holy Temple in Jerusalem. Historically, Jews from all over the Holy Land of Israel would pilgrimage to Jerusalem with baskets of the choicest first fruits of their harvest that year to offer to God via the High Priest of the Holy Temple. One of the legacies the Jewish people still cherish is the lineage of the family of priests. Members of this family include the Cohens; yes, the Cohens, and a fair number of other surnames, but the legacy has carried on from father to son for over 3000 years!

At each staff meeting, we would openly brainstorm ideas on how to celebrate upcoming holidays. With the idea forever implanted on everyone's mind on how to forge our school's stronger relationship with the synagogue, one of our kindergarten teachers pitched an amazing idea. There was one very well-known and beloved descendent of the priestly families in the synagogue whose children happened to be alumni of the school. It was proposed that along with teaching about *Shavuos*, to have the children design and make fruit baskets. The young kindergarteners would make a "pilgrimage" to the synagogue to present the basket of fruit to the 'High Priest'. It was a great idea. The synagogue resident 'High Priest' played the part to the fullest. He hired a High Priest costume and bestowed upon each child the threefold priestly blessing in front of the many parents and grandparents in delighted attendance. A member of the press came and took photos, which were prominently featured in the local newspaper's Religion section. Indeed, our tiny school had begun to make a huge impact within the wider Jewish community.

Lanny...

One of the few fortes of the school that transcended all the issues was their most incredible Annual Parent's Association Fundraiser. It was an Annual Chinese Auction, always tied to a theme and the whole community came out for this truly five-star evening event. A beautiful venue, a kosher meal with catering in a town with no kosher restaurant! To this day, I have yet to see a more cohesive volunteer group raise as much money from the proceeds of one single event. This single fundraiser had the most significant effect on the school's financial bottom line. The Parent's Association annual goods and services auction was such a success that in the last year of my being principal, the parents managed to raise a net $100,000!

The overarching theme of my first Chinese Auction evening was "growth." The silent auction items were all on display in all their glory. When I walked into the beautifully decorated and brightly lit hall, I was greeted by a huge array of sport memorabilia on auction. It was a thrill just to reminisce first-hand over the many significant sporting event items on display. As the evening went on, a huge amount of money was raised to support the growing needs of the school, due to the significant increases in new enrolments we were experiencing already. The entire community came out to contribute large sums of money in a fun atmosphere as an acknowledgement of the significance of our educational institution, an Orthodox school in a primarily non-Orthodox community, and our immeasurable impact on the stability and growth toward the continuity of the Jewish community at large.

Through the efforts of the parents, donations of products from proprietors throughout the community, there were a variety of items and opportunities, for almost everyone to walk away with something. This was only part of this feel-good event of the year. These smaller items were part of a silent auction. At the conclusion of the meal and a few speeches from significant contributors and a guest speaker, a loud auction served as the main entertainment of the evening. The Parent's Association had hired a great professional auctioneer. With some surprise novelty items, everyone remained glued to their seats, unless they were bidding. No one wanted to miss the excitement. The competitive bidders were all vying against each other or collaborating to raise their bids higher and higher to the benefit of our school.

The "oohs" and "aahs" were aplenty as the excitement grew when competitive doctors and lawyers challenged each other in a game of 'who can outbid the other'. When the auctioneer challenged individuals not to chicken out, the excitement only mounted as the previously highest bidder's wife, from nowhere, inserted a bid, thawing her husband's cold feet. The parents who could afford to only sit back and watch still took pleasure and pride in the fact that the school was benefiting. More directly, they all knew their children were "profiting" the most.

In our second year at the school, Chaya and I contributed a "Four course meal at the Rabbi's house" as a public auction item. It went for a whopping $1600 with four families pitching in. They pooled their resources together as a generous demonstration of support, not only to the school but also specifically to me as the principal. Both Chaya and I were honoured and humbled by the gesture.

Some parents bid against each other for the right to have their child assume the role as "Principal for a day." This sum of $1500 was a significant amount used as a catalyst by the auctioneer to entertain the crowd with some cute one-liners about the 'value of my position'; "is that how much one day is worth?" and "how well is the Principal compensated annually if that's his daily salary?" The crowd roared in delight. I could only grin and show my appreciation for their support and ongoing overt commitment.

For me, the greatest delight that first year was seeing Lanny's #9 Calgary Flames ice hockey jersey right in front of my eyes. Lanny McDonald is my favourite hockey player of all time. There was his autographed jersey, bloodstain and all on his right sleeve, mounted in a glass frame up for auction. Chaya and I watched in amazement at how many of the parents drove up the bidding. The final purchase price reached just over $2800, all for the school. It was an exciting and an incredibly enjoyable evening. We all went home knowing that the school had done very well and that the final tally, which would be announced in the coming days, was surely going to be one of the highest ever.

The next morning I came into school early as usual, but something was unusual. Why were there so many board members' cars in the parking lot? That was certainly out of the ordinary. I thought it even stranger seeing that no one was really around when I came into the school. After the daily broadcast of the national anthems and morning announcements, I finally walked into the school office. I was greeted by a few of the school families outside my office door. It was such an unusual sight to see so many parents in the office area that I didn't even realise that the venetian blinds to my office were mysteriously closed so I couldn't see inside. I opened my office door, walked in and turned on the lights. Six or seven parents yelled surprise. There it was. Hanging on my wall was the very hockey jersey from the auction! Lanny McDonald, his official #9 jersey, in all his glory and splendour! I was in total shock and quite emotional. They had all pitched in together to thank me for all my efforts in building the school and achieving so much thus far. Yes, the jersey was an incredible gift, and certainly, its well-publicised price tag was overwhelming. However, the sentiments and gratitude behind it meant so much more.

To this very day, in all my years in education, I have never felt more appreciated than at that moment in time. I have probably done much more in many other positions. Nevertheless, the gesture and forethought, not to mention the deviously detailed advanced planning, truly demonstrated how they felt. It was such an emotional time that I had to hold back the floodgates from bursting wide open. The fact that they had done the research to find out that Lanny was my favorite player was truly indicative of a strong sentiment of care and a desire to express their gratitude.

In every institution since then, wherever I have been principal, the framed jersey and now additional personalized signed puck and autograph hang on my wall. Somehow, it is a reminder that no matter how hard things get, and at the most difficult of times, when bogged down by the day-to-day grind, the jersey is a reminder that it is not a thankless job. Behind the scenes, there are those who are gracious. It is also not about the physical expression of thanks, but the personal sentiments of gratitude. We are all overwhelmed in the day-to-day quagmires of our lives. We don't do the things we love for the reward or thanks; we do them because deep down the satisfaction comes from the relationships we build.

I was so touched and so grateful. The parents were notorious for expressing gratitude and this was just one of the many examples in my short two-and-a-half-year stint as their principal. These were the truly good times, and they were truly good. The school, after a very long time, was beginning to make an impact in the community. Earlier that first school year, we sent out an open house invitation to community families not yet registered in our school. We had our largest influx of curious parents who had a need to come and see what the buzz was all about.

Every new initiative in the school was strategically developed with the goal of empowering our individual students. From the choir and our very public performances, to our sports teams competing in the Association for Private Schools, to the interactive lessons in the classroom. Children felt a sense of pride in their accomplishments. In every public display, parents noted a sense of professionalism and organization, something that had been lacking in previous years. We were more than on the map. We were a force to be reckoned with. It was time for us to branch out and find creative ways to promote what was happening in our school.

Because I was so hands-on in the school, my time for anything else was quite limited. The window of opportunity to get out in the community and spread the word was at its optimum and I had to be strategic in my approach due to my limitations of free time. I chose my speaking engagements carefully and began with some community groups run out of the Jewish Community Centre. I made some key phone calls to some friends of Board members, and before long, I had some speaking engagements lined up. My first public talk was with the Calgary Genealogy Society. I spoke about the importance of Jewish continuity depending upon an authentic Jewish education. With examples from the Torah and Scriptures, I was able to weave a clear connection between the original sources and the importance of one's heritage being able to renew the bonds of family through tracing one's lineage. By underlining the importance of Jewish heritage, pretty much reiterating the mission statement of their Genealogy Society, I had developed a strong group of advocates on the communal stage for the promotion of our school. Word got out and the city Jewish newspaper ran a very positive article about my talk as well as our choir performances. From years of practically no positive press, we began to generate a significant increase of publicity on the communal scene.

Links in the Chain

Being as the auction was a very public event, it served my purpose of being able to approach some of the significant philanthropists about supporting the educational initiatives we could not afford to include in the budget. With a demand from enrolment, we extended our primary school into a junior high school program. With the financial capacity to staff the program, we hired two experienced high school teachers to develop and lead the program. Parents had indicated their initial support for a Junior High program and we promised to deliver. We had parental motivation to continue our program; however, the main obstacle was student buy-in. We would need some tangibles as well as educational incentives to make it attractive to our current student body and to be able to market this new product outside the existing school population. I was one step ahead. I had devised a curriculum that I felt was not only educationally engaging for the students, but an essential component to their personal development.

As you recall, my first public speaking engagement had been at the Jewish Genealogical Society. That too was a strategic move. I had been around many Holocaust survivors throughout my youth. I had always been emotionally and intellectually drawn to the importance of being sensitive to the value of one of the most critical periods in our modern-day development as a Jewish people. I believed in the messages of hope that could be discovered through a deep historical understanding. Deep personal eyewitness accounts were an integral component to the continuity of our Jewish people.

The symbolism of the yellow star, a mandatory physical sign European Jews were forced to wear regardless of their level of observance, was enforced by the most brutal, inhumane thugs. Yet this yellow star contains hidden within it, the most poignant spiritual message to all people. One can never judge a person by external physical traits or from overt actions visible to the naked eye. Each and every one of us, no matter our level of observance has a Jewish soul that links us all together. It took a barbaric regime perpetuating atrocities of unimaginable proportions to highlight our spiritual sparks for all to see. The Nazis did not care how removed we were from our heritage. Deep down we are all one family, one entity. Charged with upholding the continuity of our people, charged with the challenge of remaining steadfast on the path of our forefathers – this is the responsibility I am committed to instil in our young generation.

My goal was to develop a curriculum that would reveal their innate connectivity, no matter how removed they all felt on a daily basis. The core of the curriculum would be personal genealogical projects. We would have each student research their personal family backgrounds as far back as possible to detect and connect to a level of observance they may have never realised was their legacy. We would then trace forward to the modern era discovering each student's own family' journey within the context of the Holocaust. With rich resources and multimedia, the students would be engaged and motivated. All this, of course took money.

I found some willing philanthropists who had no previous affiliation to our school, but who were passionate about Holocaust education. With their significant funding, the year long study would culminate in our class trip to the Holocaust Museum in Washington DC. The personal growth of our students throughout the year of that curriculum and their appreciation for the experience was truly incredible. It was not so much about the trip as it was about their understanding of the events that created a context for who they were. They were not just seven junior high school students in the tiny city of Calgary. They became seven individuals who were an integral part of a Jewish nation connecting past and present descendants to the future hope of our people.

As our students joined some of the educational programs at the United States National Holocaust Museum over the week we were in Washington DC, I saw a keen understanding of the goals of our program come to life. The students expressed their feelings at the horrors depicted in some of the exhibits. All the experiences culminated in a deeper understanding of their desires and commitment to rebuilding their community. It fostered stronger commitment to a continuation of observant life that the Nazi regime tried to eradicate.

Truly unexpected was the interest our trip generated in the community. It was an awakening in the city that our school had been an active participant in this event. The timing of the program coincided with International Holocaust Remembrance Day. Our trip all of a sudden became highly publicised. Parents from the most unlikely corners of the community started to call the school requesting information about enrolling. Questions such as "Do I have to be Orthodox to send my kids to your school?" and "Is it okay if we do not observe the *Shabbos* or kosher laws"?

I was ready for the tough questions. One by one, one after another, our enrolment numbers began to spike. From just over 85 students to close to 140, our school began to grow. It was exciting for our existing students. Each time a newcomer walked through the doors, it was a celebration for the entire school. The excitement was contagious. Each new student was treated like royalty. They were immediately accepted into the 'family' and felt welcomed in their new environment. With each new student enrolling, with the addition of tuition and the allocated government grant, our funding base started to look more promising.

Moving Up the Downward Escalator

The school I had inherited was teetering on the edge of survival and extinction. Due to the limited Orthodox population from which they had previously drawn enrolments, at the time of my hiring, I came into a school of approximately only ninety students. This stagnant enrolment figure had a significant effect on the annual budget. Salaries and expenses were increasing though the income was not. The school government grant for each student from kindergarten through junior high school was vital. It allowed a barely sustainable school model to run on the smell of an oil rag. At the time, the school only ran up to Grade 6. One of the growth directions the school had put forward at the time of my hiring was the desired expansion toward a viable junior high school. My biggest challenge as the new principal was determining how a school, whose ethos seemed to preclude the integration of non-observant families, could grow its enrolments. There simply were not any additional families in the community who identified with the vision and mission of the school from whom to recruit.

I had some ideas on paper; untried initiatives that my gut told me had potential to discover potential families hiding in the wings. I was not under any illusions that the inviting ambiance generated by the genuine, kind welcoming committee was enough to influence families to take the plunge. I witnessed new members enter the inner Orthodox circle and veteran members feel threatened by the "newbies" who were motivated to seek more knowledge. I saw the "uninitiated" push the experienced members' comfort boundaries that threatened the established status quo. Seeming too observant or too eager to learn was not popular. The keen individuals looking to advance their observance above the status quo found themselves isolated, talked about behind their backs, quietly branded fanatics or zealots. I myself had felt this way growing up in that community, but I had hoped it had changed. It took me a bit of time to realise just how stagnant the minds of some of the perceived leaders in the Calgary Orthodox community were toward reaching out to those who were different from them. It was indeed a very insular community, despite the lip service about upholding of the Judaic principles of outreach. In that community, people felt judged and insignificant in the eyes of those who were visibly more observant. The keeping up with the "Cohens," was an underlying theme among the observant and affiliated members of the synagogue. It was obvious to see how many new followers of the *Chabad* rabbi had consciously made the decision to leave the mainstream synagogue community because they had the same common negative experience.

Deep down I knew that many of the young *Chabad* rabbi's followers had the potential to join the school community. All I had to do was ensure they felt embraced by the school community and supported as their children's growth and textual learning surpassed their own. Most of these families had only begun their personal spiritual journey while their children continued to attend public schools. Parents identified with the idea that growing in Judaism is like being on a journey. To climb higher and grow, one needs to keep moving. Jewish life, observance, and one's spiritual journey can be compared to trying to climb up a moving, descending escalator. One consistently makes an effort to ascent the escalator. Just like life, the downward movement signifies the external and sometimes internal pressures forcing one to surrender to the challenge and take a step back. The simplest rule is never to stand still on the escalator. As long as you are making an effort, even small steps, you will never stagnate. Sincere onlookers take inspiration from your growth. Be prepared that the bystanders threatened by your spiritual advancement will try to derail your journey to protect their own feelings of inadequacy.

My goal was to discover and identify those individuals who were either just beginning their journey or those who didn't yet know how to find the path. In the small community in Calgary, there were many such, unaffiliated candidates. I believed in the potential growth of the school through reaching out and connecting to many of these potential families.

As I was tackling the enrolment challenge in my second year, and a challenge it most certainly was, I soon found out that our school had two other huge critical issues to tackle. For many years, the school had been renting a facility from the Public School Board. The lease was set to expire in a mere three years' time! There had been a strategy proposed by our school's executive board to purchase the existing building. Capital funds were limited and an alternative strategy was also in the works for the school to relocate to the synagogue site. At the time of purchase, the site had initially been coveted for the long-term vision of building a school there for the community.

There were many pros of relocating the school closer to the heart and hub of the Jewish community and linking it physically to the Modern Orthodox synagogue. The land adjacent to the synagogue was most certainly large enough to accommodate the school. The challenge however was the need to reparcel the physical land and sell off a sector to private developers as a mechanism for raising the necessary funds for construction. This did not sit well with many of the synagogue members. They were concerned that the diminishing of the synagogue land size reduced the total value of the synagogue. This fear existed even though the synagogue had never even raised enough money to properly complete its own planned construction. The dream blueprints were in the foyer for all to see. Nevertheless, the concern was that any potential sale of the land would now jeopardize future efforts to complete the intended structure. In addition, any money borrowed against the mortgage of the building would now divert interests from the actual synagogue toward an unwanted, and what many members vocalized as an unnecessary, physical edifice.

The school's point of view was simple. Without a growing community, without committed young families who could afford to pay for parochial, private education linked into the synagogue, there would be no real future anyway. Therefore, there would never be a need for a larger synagogue or Orthodox community. After all, Jewish education is the basis for Jewish life. Jewish law states that the priority for building a community first lies in the construction of a school before that of a synagogue. Only if you build a school, will they come – to synagogue, that is.

At the time, the synagogue was not increasing its membership. The school's theory was if somehow the community could generate a greater commitment to ideals espoused by the school, the educational institution could consequently attract more young families. By nature of the symbiotic relationship between school and synagogue, with it all being in one location, on the same campus, the effect would not only subtly embody a link and connection between the school and synagogue, the mutually-supported ethos and ideals themselves would create a natural bond.

When the strongest leadership was required from the rabbi of the synagogue, he fell silent. I tried reaching out to him to gain support for what I believed and our school board felt would eventuate into a positive for all Orthodox parties in the community. The longevity of the school was at stake. I could not understand why he couldn't see this. More disturbing was the fact that a line in the sand was being drawn. Talk of the school seceding from the synagogue had begun among the school parent body. The opportunity to unite the school and synagogue under the banner of cohesion and mutual survival was fading quickly. Sadly, it would come down to a simple vote – the synagogue members would either support partitioning their land and build a school, or stay the course and force the school board to come up with an alternate strategy.

The synagogue membership came out in full force the evening the vote was held. Most of the members who voted had no overt affiliation to the school. Many of the members had not been seen in the synagogue for years. Yet they came out and voted to deny the resectioning of the property to build the school. As you can well imagine, the issue was a defining one for the school parent body. Most parents became immediately disenchanted with the school and its inability to carry out its mandate with the structure of parental rights and representation. As a result of that fateful vote, many of the significant leadership positions on the school board would become vacant. The running of the school by default would be taken over by the synagogue, many of whom had no children in the school and no stakeholdership in the educational vision that had been established in the then two years of my tenure. The running of the school would become a simple financial bottom line consideration, whereby all major decisions were based on the balance sheet and not educational strategy or vision. I would not give up so easily, and luckily, I was not alone. It was time to rally the troops and fight for our school.

It All Came Tumbling Down...

Despite all the amazing initiatives to positively promote the school in the wider community, there was one distinct group that was not pleased with the new influx of families into our school. Surprisingly, or perhaps not, a significant faction among the Modern Orthodox synagogue community was not impressed. In fact, it became obvious that they saw the spike in enrolment as a direct threat to the existence of the school and by extension the synagogue. Their rabbi, however, did not share this opinion. He saw the new enrolments as opportunities for outreach work. He had pitched this perspective to his board, sadly to no avail.

The changing demographics of the school were due to a large influx of non-observant, non-Orthodox families. The balance of families in the school, it was feared by some, was tipping allegiance away from the Modern Orthodox synagogue. The synagogue was very slow to react and develop a strategic response. They did not choose the path of cultivating personal relationships with the new school families. Instead, the synagogue board's response was to demand allegiance out of right and expectation as opposed to developing a relationship-based foundation for their affiliation. Surprisingly, by this stage, there was little discernible response from the synagogue rabbi on the public stage.

Many felt the atmosphere of the Modern Orthodox synagogue at that time was not a welcoming atmosphere to outsiders; the new school families often did not feel welcome attending services or programs in the Modern Orthodox synagogue. Coupled with this set of circumstances, however, was the outreach philosophy of the new *Chabad* synagogue. They were actively generating overt publicity, offering programs and adult education to the non-observant. Many of the families in the school were seeking knowledge to "keep up" or understand what their children were learning at school and coming home so excited, motivated and enthused about. It seemed the new families in the school began to flock to *Chabad*.

The board of the synagogue perceived this as a direct threat to the functioning of not only the school but the synagogue as well. The crowning event occurred on the Jewish New Year, September time, at the peak of our enrolment, 138 students to start the new academic year. As is usually the case in the northern hemisphere, just after the new school year begins, *Rosh Hashanah*, the Jewish New Year is heralded in. No matter one's level of observance, most families attend services. As you recall, from our very first year in Crown Heights, we had been coming back to Calgary for the High Holy Days. I would serve in the *Chabad* community as the assistant rabbi on the high holidays. This year, however, my regular longstanding arrangement meant that it took time away from my regular, voluntary attendance at the school-affiliated synagogue. In hindsight, this was the beginning of the end.

That year, attendance at *Chabad* had reached a new record high as well. The rabbi had made accommodation for newcomers. He had developed modifications to the traditional services by incorporating both English and Russian instead of a Hebrew-only program. Advertising a free service with no membership fee and a welcoming open door policy, attendance was at an all-time high. So much so, most of the school parents who were as yet unaffiliated synagogue members, showed up unannounced and attended *Rosh Hashanah* services that year for the first time ever…at *Chabad*.

There is a known Orthodox prohibition against use of telephones and mobile communication on *Shabbos* and on festival holy days. Perhaps it was extended families getting together to share the festival meal. Somehow, word still seemed to spread through the well-connected Jewish grapevine. After the first day holiday services, word about the huge spike in attendance at the new *Chabad* synagogue spread like wildfire throughout the community. Many Modern Orthodox regulars actually made the hour-long trek to pop into the service on the second day of the holy day to see what the word on the street was all about. They wanted to see for themselves what was so special to have drawn so many worshipers to *Chabad* on the first day of the holiday. Consequently, the High Holy Day attendance became quite low at the Modern Orthodox synagogue. Their board of management began to circle the wagons in search of an underlying threat to their insular community. We were quite unaware at the time that pressure had been heavily placed on the shoulders of the synagogue rabbi to reverse the trend of declining attendance at his synagogue. He was also charged with somehow finding a solution to negate the drainage of borderline attendees, the fence-sitters who had now developed the impulse to see what was happening at *Chabad*. We found out only later that the renewal of the Orthodox rabbi's contract, which was taking place around this time of year, had been made contingent upon his ability to reverse the membership trend away from *Chabad* and into his community's Synagogue.

What compounded the issue even further were the *Kol Nidrei* services ten days later. That year, the *Chabad* house had standing room only. With the services specifically catered to all levels of the community, the talk of the town was the incredible number of newcomers, surfacing from nowhere, to attend the Orthodox service at *Chabad*.

The Modern Orthodox Synagogue Board had been harbouring significant concern over the damaging exodus of membership from their synagogue. They were further concerned with the influx of unaffiliated school families, not seeking membership in their own institution but seeking inspiration elsewhere and of all places, *Chabad*. Charged with the mission to reverse the trend, the synagogue covertly embarked on a campaign to destabilise the community's positive disposition toward *Chabad*, and they had international assistance.

At around the same time in America, a book had just been published promoting outrageous inaccuracies and a libellous philosophical invective against the *Chabad* movement. A well-known opponent of the popular *Chassidic* sect had authored the book. This was just the vitriol members of the synagogue were looking for to discredit the initiatives I had developed to grow the school, despite the fact that all the initiatives were developed in the spirit of the school's mission statement with one of THEIR members as my behind-the-scenes mentor. Most of the initiatives had collaborative input among our staff and their very own synagogue rabbi.

Seemingly out of nowhere, public accusations were made against me by the vice president of the synagogue that I had developed a hidden agenda to undermine the ethos of the school, to repeal the existing constitution connecting the school with the synagogue and establish a new charter under the auspices of *Chabad* and its charismatic rabbi.

Throughout the following week, the school board of management was notified that letters had been written on behalf of synagogue members, none having children in the school, levelling personal attacks on me and my children, raising breaches of code of conduct of both a personal and professional nature.

I was not shown the content of the letters, nor were my board of directors. I was told there were significant breaches of conduct. I was thus summoned to an executive meeting between my school board and that of the synagogue. Levels of frustration on my part were quite high, as my board seemed quite impotent to establish solid ground to fight the one-sided secret libel. Being mandated to attend a meeting, and face a list of accusations without having any prior knowledge of the specific details, my confidence in my board to execute its mandated duties running the school reached an all-time low.

Other than my newly-elected president, not so coincidentally the son of my mentor, who was frantically trying to shore up confidence and strength in his fellow officers, the intimidation of the synagogue board appeared too much for them to overcome. School board members began dropping like flies, resigning their positions faster than they could write their names in the face of this sudden fierce opposition. With key executive members resigning, I was confronted with tackling the accusations head on with only my newly-elected President beside me. Together one evening, he and I attended the meeting at the Synagogue to face the as yet secret allegations.

What was most surprising about the entire debacle was the conduct of the rabbi of the Orthodox synagogue. He sat silently as the list of charges against me were enumerated. The main claim against me was overt destabilisation of their synagogue. I was accused of blatantly encouraging the school parent body to attend *Chabad* and not the synagogue. Their trumped-up charges were based on allegations that I had violated a supposed agreement between myself and the synagogue rabbi, which stated that I would personally attend the Modern Orthodox Synagogue services three out of four weeks of the month. I told everyone that there had never been such an agreement. At the time of contract negotiations, I carefully and explicitly refused to include any clause mandating official attendance at any synagogue. Whilst there had been a clause in the original version of the contract, it had been struck from the final contract. I looked the rabbi in the eye and asked him if he actually recalled that agreement having been made?

The synagogue rabbi and I had discussed the issue and had come to a verbal agreement that I would do my utmost to attend 2 out of 4 *Shabbos* services a month. In fact, excluding the High Holy Days, some months I had attended every single week. During the wintertime that year, in a blinding blizzard with -25°C temperatures, I had made it to the synagogue Saturday morning to find almost no one else there! Despite it being an hour's walk, I had done more than my due diligence to demonstrate my commitment to the synagogue.

I felt our joint initiatives and my support of the synagogue were well-documented and even publicised in the newspaper. I even offered my services as a rabbi to speak this *Shabbos* when the synagogue rabbi was away. Despite objections from the synagogue board to allow me to speak publicly from the pulpit, the offer nonetheless had been made to the rabbi.

The synagogue board interjected and stated that this was simply not true. Conversations they had with their rabbi contradicted my testimony and his assertions, for them, enough to refute my evidence-based, albeit defensive, position. I looked at the rabbi who remained stone cold silent and without comment. I was baffled and confused as to how the tables had turned against me. His conduct was completely out of character to anything I had seen over the past two years. It was clear that they had already made up their minds and there was nothing to be said or done to alter their predetermined verdict.

The final declaration against me came in the form of an accusation directed toward my professionalism. They alleged me working to subvert the stability of the synagogue community. They cited an agreed policy I made with the synagogue rabbi, establishing at the time of my hiring that all new members of the Jewish studies staff had to be ratified by the rabbi himself. In the two years of my employment as principal of the school, I had replaced some key members of staff, key synagogue members, with new staff who had not been vetted and ratified by the rabbi himself. The allegation was that this action constituted a direct breach of my contractual obligations. It was true that I had replaced some long-standing employees, who were indeed Orthodox synagogue members; however, I had most certainly informed and made available the applications to the rabbi for his final approval. These baseless, trumped-up allegations were most certainly put forth on behalf of the disgruntled synagogue members. In fact, the school board had overseen and ratified my decision-making process to dismiss them. The school had historically been a glorified employment agency for the synagogue community, upholding the unspoken rule that if someone could not maintain a career, a fall-back position was to teach in the school.

I had demonstrated in my government-approved three-year plan a formalized appraisal system that detailed a strict protocol that included mandated consultation with the synagogue rabbi, which had indeed occurred. The school had legally dismissed the "teachers" who should never have been allowed in the school in the first place. Those of them who had been wives of synagogue board members had taken umbrage at their dismissal. This meeting, it was now clear, was a fabricated tirade to hurl at me with the hopes that by throwing any possible allegation my way, including the kitchen sink, something would stick.

It was completely irrelevant that I had been able to refute each and every ludicrous and untrue charge. What was evident from the allegations was the blatantly clear ulterior motive behind the verbal onslaught. The synagogue had very clearly plotted their strategy for my demise. At the conclusion of the meeting, they presented a letter to our school president. One week from that fateful day, the synagogue would be holding a vote amongst *their* membership to 'resolve' the issue of long-term accommodation for the school. Suddenly it all became very clear.

The two options on the table, the two mechanisms enabling a solution to the issue of the school's long-term accommodation were quite well spelled out. In the end, the issue was going to be resolved via the outcome of this vote from the Synagogue membership. The results would clearly identify the synagogue's commitment, or lack thereof, toward the sustainability of the school and indirectly the long-term viability of their community.

Simply put, the two options were as follows: Re-partition the synagogue land. Sell a large section of it to developers to raise enough funds to buy the existing school property from the government or use the funds to build a new school on the actual synagogue property by selling off a lesser portion of the re-partitioned land. Either way, the call was for the partitioning and sale of synagogue land or simply vote to do nothing.

The school community put a strong argument forward for building a school beside the synagogue and by extension, building the community long term. Positive acceptance of the proposal demonstrated a strong message of unity to the wider community that the school and synagogue would be together joined institutions with a strong viable future. A negative outcome would mean an uncertain future for the school and a perceived lack of support from its sponsoring body.

The synagogue, in raising their allegations against me, had attempted to demonstrate my wilful lack of adherence to the constitution on behalf of the school. Their desires were now clear – to take control over the school and determine the fate without any pressure of reducing the asset size of their precious synagogue land.

Less than a week later at the vote, despite desperate pleas from school parents and the school's board of directors, the synagogue unanimously voted against any support for the repartitioning of synagogue land. The consequences sealed the uncertain fate of the school. The school now needed to approach the government to seek approval for an extension on their lease. With the uncertainty of the government's response and clear indications of the government's sincere desire to sell the school property to the highest-bidding residential builder, a favourable outlook for the school seemed very bleak. The window of stability for the school had been slammed shut by its sponsoring founder.

However, the synagogue somewhat miscalculated the effects of their vote. With the news of the vote against the school, the school's board of directors called an immediate school meeting the next night to discuss the future of the school. Every, and I'm not exaggerating, every parent arrived, including the synagogue board members and many individuals among the synagogue membership. Discussions took place prior to the meeting, on how to possibly exclude the non-school membership. In the end, every stakeholder of both institutions arrived ready to hear the pending strategy discussion. It was an emotional meeting. The president of the school stood up, with the weight of all that had transpired in the past week clear in the expression on his face. He presented the cold hard facts of the gloomy future. Many parents and school board members stood up and praised my efforts for having built such a strong institution. They were committed to me and the vision I had developed over the two years as their principal. I felt very supported by my parent body, but I had been severely affected by the abuse from the synagogue board a mere twenty-four hours earlier. I saw the writing on the wall. The institution I had helped raise from the muddy ground with blood, sweat and tears was about to come tumbling down. Citing his inability to have paved the path of stability and long-term accommodation, my school president handed over his resignation at the public gathering. One by one, members of the school executive resigned publicly, de facto handing over the control of the school to the synagogue executive.

It seemed like a victory to the synagogue board members. It was a death knell for the success of the school. In the end, the inability to maintain status quo in terms of accommodation was a fatal blow to enrolments in the school. As parents filed out of the school gymnasium, talk focused on which families would be leaving the school. As many members of the school board were not synagogue members, and their religious allegiance was to other synagogues, they no longer had any motivation or ambition to remain a part of an infrastructure set taken over by a rogue board. For many of them, with no long-term future, the pathway was clear. Sadly, it was time to move on.

That night, I had to struggle to gather my thoughts. I sat with Chaya pondering and wondering what our next step would be. As we got home, our phone was ringing. Despite my emotional exhaustion, on reflex, I picked it up, almost in a daze. It was the vice president of the synagogue requesting a meeting with me the next morning, and that was only the beginning. The phone rang that entire night. School board members called to apologize and express sincere thanks for my efforts. The writing was on the wall. The school would never be the same, unable to rebound from that fateful night's catastrophic turning point.

Just when I thought things could not get any worse, I sat at the table the next morning with the vice president of the synagogue in my office. Now, all of a sudden I was answerable to the very same individuals who had led me to the slaughter a mere twenty-four hours earlier. It didn't take very long for them to present their strategy for moving forward. I sat tongue-tied as they quickly undid the many educational initiatives I had strategically put together to both attract and support the influx of new students. As each initiative was cut, it was as if a knife was being thrust into my heart. I held back from expressing the deep pain they were inflicting on my soul. They came to the final thrust, a deep penetrating wound that sealed my fate.

The underlying motivation was a guarantee that the synagogue would never have to contribute financially in any way, shape or form to sustaining the school. The policy put forward and unanimously voted upon by their synagogue board was that any class with less than 20 students would be amalgamated immediately. This effectively decimated the educational program and current teaching staff. The Grade 6 would become Grade 5/6 and the Grade 6 teacher made redundant. The Grade 3 teacher would also lose her job, as the Grade 3 would be amalgamated with the Grade 4. Grade 2 would be grouped with Grade 1. However, because the Grade 1 teacher was a member of the synagogue, she would maintain her job. The Grade 2 teacher would be made redundant in her stead. The entire high school would be immediately shut down.

There was nothing I could do. In addition, I would now be required to teach half time so one Jewish studies teacher, one of the non-Synagogue members would also be let go. Decisions on who would stay and who would go were whisked out of my hands.

I know you were waiting for the death thrust. These pending changes would remain confidential for the time being! They would only come into effect immediately after the winter holidays, not before. This meant that parents would not have the ability to seek new placements for their children over the winter break. They would be locked into a false commitment to the 'school' until the end of the school year!

This deception would buy the school the time they wanted for their financial bottom line. They would be saving on the salaries of the reduced staffing structure. What upset me the most was the lack of notice they were giving the staff! If they were notified before the break, the two-week holiday would provide these top-notch teachers a jump-start in finding new employment! The lack of fairness and care for the teachers was just too much for me to bear. They were all non-Jewish teachers with the exception of one. The bad taste it would most certainly leave in their mouths about the Jewish community was something I could not sit idly by and watch.

The vice president told me legally I had no rights other than to support the decisions the synagogue board was making. It would be grounds for dismissal if I leaked anything to the staff. Despite my supposed position and experience leading the school, I had no input in the decisions whatsoever. I was completely neutralized.

I could not sit back and allow this to take place. I would not allow myself to be seen as party to this loathsome, catastrophic plan.

Of course, my mentor was mourning every step of this imminent demise with me. She put me in touch with another well-known education lawyer. When I finished telling this 'reality is stranger than fiction' tale, he was equally disgusted with the events that had taken place and the new direction that had been imposed upon me. He was so dismayed that he stepped up and offered his services pro bono! His conclusion was crystal clear upon hearing the events that had transpired. The conduct of the synagogue board was tantamount to summary dismissal. I had no legal obligation whatsoever to sit idly by and submit to their intimidations and their plans. He directed me in composing a letter to the families of the school… that was mailed on the night of our sold-out final *Chanukah* performance, at the University of Calgary theatre.

What came to be our swan song was the school's *Chanukah* production. It was the Thursday night – the night before the last day of term before winter break. We had grown so much we were indeed using a theatre at the University of Calgary. I had secretly posted the letter Wednesday knowing that by Friday afternoon, everyone in the school would receive it in the mail.

That Thursday night was one of the most glorious of nights in my educational career. Our school *Chanukah* production was held at the University of Calgary theatre with a sold-out full house of over five hundred parents, family, and community members. The sets, costumes and music were some of the most spectacular I have ever seen. The commitment of the parent body to our educational vision was in full force.

As I gave my final speech at the conclusion of the play, only five other people – Chaya, my mentor, my ex-president, and my parents knew what was going on deep, deep behind the scenes. In a few hours, every family would be receiving my farewell letter. It was easy for me to express my emotions of thanks and sincere gratitude for the support in building the school to the thriving, warm home away from home it had become.

What was the message? In the thickest of darkness, to create light, you only need to light one candle. Together we had expelled a lot of darkness for the sake of our precious children. I was privileged to have been their principal and to have grown with them. Perhaps they understood my message, but I wanted to thank them all.

Sadly, it was time to close this tumultuous chapter. More so, it was time to turn the page to a new path in my personal book of chronicles that was sure to be filled with many more adventures.

The next morning, Friday, I called an emergency meeting for all the staff and read them my letter. It was a very emotional time. I explained to everyone that, in the weeks to come, they would have a better understanding of why I had no choice but to leave. I had not given up, but every opportunity to protect them, the children and our shared vision was lost.

I wished them all the best of luck, promised to keep in touch and expressed my hopes that our paths would cross some day in the future.

This time, a few short weeks later, as we left Calgary, we were leaving for good. It was one of the most bittersweet moments of my life, but it was and always has been about the children.

May His Memory Be A Blessing...

It wasn't more than a few months later. We were living in Port Washington, New York. I was principal of a new school. One day I received a phone call from my beloved previous secretary in Calgary, Morah Denise Hill. She was calling me to touch base, but more importantly, to find out if I had heard the news. The rabbi of the Orthodox synagogue had left Calgary! He was now living in his hometown of Boston with his family! He and his family had left very shortly after us. "Why?" I asked. Denise asked me if I was sitting down and then she gave me the shock of my life. Denise told me the rabbi had been diagnosed with an inoperable brain tumor! He had a mere few more months of life.

Denise gave me his number. I immediately called him at home. I had a few brief moments to ask him *mechila*, for anything I may have said or done wrong during the tumultuous times in Calgary. I wished him well and a complete recovery.

I was stunned, speechless. Suddenly all became clear. In the most tragic and unexpected of ways, there were the answers, the revelations accounting for the drastic change in behaviour: why he had remained speechless in the face of the libellous accusations and how he had not remembered our conversations, our behind-closed-doors agreements that were made from a position of mutual understanding and good will. I could only shake my head in absolute awe at the complexity of God's world.

May his memory be a blessing...

Epilogue – Children and Builders

A school is about providing children with the skills to become independent productive members of society.

Educational trends come and go.

It was the wise King Solomon who summed up Education in one all-encompassing phrase.

חֲנֹךְ לַנַּעַר עַל פִּי דַרְכּוֹ -- *Educate the youth according to his way or her way... (Mishlei-Proverbs 22:6).*

I have been granted the gift and privilege of being a teacher. With this gift comes immense responsibility. The ability to affect the life of a child should never be taken lightly. Each child has unlimited potential. It is the task of a teacher to positively unleash each child's unique contribution to the world. The lessons we provide our students must be packaged with an underlying purpose. Each moral needs to be strategically taught for today's young minds to find meaning. Meaning that will inspire them to internalise our most significant values. In this way, they will develop the ability to become self-aware, self-confident, self-sufficient productive members of the community. Their strengths and their challenges become owned and valued. Only then will they be inspired to change the world for the better.

A teacher's reward is seeing a student graduate with a sense of pride and a twinkle in their eyes – that knowing glance signifying a realisation that their future is a blank canvas and they are the artist holding the paintbrush with their personal pallet of colours at the ready. Each shade of color is a different door of opportunity and they have been provided with the keys to exert their confident creative control. The canvas is their destiny and they are truly free to paint their personal vision.

Over the years, it has taken me many challenges to realise that I have been given the gift of preserving the dreams and wishes of the students under my care. Apparent obstacles only arise when there is something important to be accomplished. The challenges that surface only indicate how valuable the outcome is going to be. If it weren't important, it would be a simple task to achieve. The greatest reward is achieving the difficult. An even greater reward is helping someone else achieve that which he perceived he could not. The gift I have been bestowed is the merit to ensure that every child in a school of mine is surrounded by educators who share in this philosophy – we are not teachers but builders.

Every day, observant Jews declare at the conclusion of their prayers one of the most poignant statements, one that I believe is the creed of every educator. There is a reason why it is at the end of prayers as it should be the last thing on our minds as we engage with the world around us. For teachers, it is to impact our students. The *Talmud* (*Berachot* 64a) tells us that Rabbi Elazar said in the name of Rabbi Chanina: Torah scholars increase peace in the world, for it is stated: and all your *banayich* "your children" shall be learners of the *Torah* of the Lord, and great will be the peace of *banayich* (your children). Do not read *banayich* (your children), but *bonayich* (your builders).

The future depends on teachers connecting to students. Giving their all, realising that each teachable moment might be the one that ignites the eternal spark in that child. As we teach, we contribute to the development of our students into craftsmen, builders, members of society who have been provided with transferable skills to affect the world around them. I have been given the responsibility to be not only a builder. I also sought out the task, the honour, and the privilege and, even more daunting, the responsibility to be the foreman charged with assembling the work crew. I have learned that I am not in control of the duration of the work, nor even the jobsite. As in Calgary, it is my role to do the best I can every day with the tools I have been given. When the Manager decides that my time has come and another jobsite has called me to duty, I have to accept the outcome, punch out, and clock in at the new construction zone, ready to build a new foundation and equip a new set of builders to take on their challenges.

My most valuable training comes from reflecting upon all the individual lessons in my modest education career, today spanning a young twenty-six years. Lessons, when taken individually, in isolation, may not be as well learned, nor as thoroughly applied. My forty-six years on this earth have provided me with many challenges causing me at times to question my individual purpose. The events in my life have been filled with times of jubilation as well as times of sincere disheartenment. The classroom has been my sanctuary and the students I have been privileged to teach have given me life perspective and the internal drive to push forward and never give up.

Glossary

770 – *Chabad Lubavitch* International World Headquarters, simply referred to as 770 for the simple reason of its physical location located on 770 Eastern Parkway in Crown Heights, Brooklyn. The building contained both the residence and personal office of the sixth *Lubavitcher Rebbe*, Rabbi Yosef Yitzchak Schneerson from 1940 until his passing in 1950 as well as the personal office and sometimes residence of the seventh and last *Lubavitcher Rebbe*, Rabbi Menachem Mendel Schneerson from his arrival to the U.S. in 1941 until his passing in 1994.

Baal Teshuva – (lit. "Master of return"); a term describing someone who reconnects to God, Jewish life, observance and study; often referred to a secular Jew from a not fully observant background to one taking on a more fully *Torah* observant life.

Berachot – The first tractate of the *Mishnah/Talmud*.

Bobba – Pronounced "Bobbah" or "Buhbbee." The Yiddish word for grandmother.

Bris – The traditional religious circumcision ceremony performed on an eight-day-old male infant by a *Mohel.*

Chabad – an acronym for "Chochmoh, Binah, Da'at" (wisdom, understanding and knowledge);

Chabad Lubavitch – A *Chassidic* movement founded by Rabbi Schneur Zalman of Liadi in the latter part of the 18th century that emphasizes the importance of *Chabad*, the concept of studying and understanding God and His relationship with the world. *Lubavitch* is the name of the townlet in the county of Mohilev, White Russia, which served as the centre of the *Chabad Chassidism* for four generations.

Chabad Lubavitcher – An adjective describing allegiance to the *Chassidic* sect.

Chabadnik – An affinity describing allegiance to the *Chassidic* sect.

Challah – Soft, sweet bread loaf customarily eaten at *Shabbos* meals.

Chanukah – (lit. "rededication"); eight-day festival celebrating the Maccabees' recapture of the second Temple from the Syrian Greeks, and its rededication, marked by the kindling of lights on an eight-branched candelabra called a *menorah* or *chanukiah.*

Chassid – (lit. "pious"); (a) one who goes beyond the letter of the law (b) a member of the *Chassidic* community who studies and follows the ways of the movement's teachings and philosophy (c) an adherent and follower of a Chassidic *Rebbe.*

Chassidic – of or relating to the *Chassidim* or its members or their beliefs and practices.

Chassidim – the plural of a *Chassid.*

Chassidus – The inner dimension of *Torah* explored and taught by the Chassidic masters. Chassidus expounds through the mystical lens upon concepts such as God, the soul and Torah and makes them understandable, applicable, and practical to the modern person.

Chazzan – (lit. "cantor"); the individual who leads the congregation in prayer.

Cheder – (lit. "room"); a traditional elementary school teaching the basics of Judaism and Hebrew language.

Chutzpah – Yiddish term meaning brazen audacity and/or impudence.

*Faher(-en*pl.) – To orally test a student thoroughly on a specific topic of study.

Hadar HaTorah – founded in 1963 in Brooklyn, NY, accommodating Jewish students of all backgrounds and affiliated with all Jewish movements, the institution claims to be the world's first *Yeshivah* for Jewish men.

Hasa'ah – Hebrew term denoting a community sponsored taxi service.

Kiddush – (lit. "sanctification"); Just as the *Torah* explicitly states that God declared the *Shabbos* holy, observant Jewish families in turn sanctify it every week anew with the verbal declaration of the *Shabbos Kiddush.* Composed of scriptural verses, the sanctification is recited on a cup of wine and officially begins the Friday night *Shabbos* meal.

Kiryat Melachi – a city in Israel's Southern District, 55 kilometres from Tel Aviv.

Kol Nidrei – The holy day of *Yom Kippur* begins at sunset with the public recital in synagogue of the solemn prayer titled *Kol Nidrei.* Attendance in synagogue is at its highest rate by those both observant and not for this most solemn of services.

Kollel – (lit. a "gathering" or "collection" of scholars); an educational institution for full-time married scholars dedicated to the advanced study of the *Talmud* and other rabbinical works.

Kosher – Jewish dietary laws involving the strict separation of milk and meat and the complete avoidance of pork, shellfish and other prohibited living things listed in the *Torah*.

L'chaim – (lit. "to life"); a common celebratory Hebrew toast. When a Jewish couple becomes engaged, friends and family gather publicly to celebrate the upcoming union. The celebration is aptly named a *l'chaim* since the couple is toasted *l'chaim* ("to life").

Lubavitch – the name of the town in White Russia where the movement was based for more than a century. Appropriately, the word *Lubavitch* in Russian means the "city of brotherly love." The name *Lubavitch* conveys the essence of the responsibility and love engendered by the *Chabad* philosophy toward every single Jew (see www.Chabad.org).

Lubavitcher Rebbe – Rabbi Menachem Mendel Schneerson, of righteous memory (1902-1994); seventh leader of *Chabad-Lubavitch*, lived in Nikolayev and Dnieperptrosk (Ukraine), Leningrad, Berlin, Warsaw, Paris and New York; built upon and expanded his predecessors' work to revolutionize Jewish life across the globe; known simply as "the *Rebbe*" (see www.Chabad.org).

Maccabi – singular of the plural Maccabees, who were a Jewish rebel army that took control of Judea at the height of the Seleucid Empire and founded the Hasmonean dynasty, which ruled from 164 BCE to 63 BCE. The heroism and courage of these great warriors has become a symbol of the Maccabi World Union which is an international Jewish sports organisation spanning five continents and more than fifty countries, with some 400,000 members. Every four years the organisation holds an international competition in Israel.

Mazal tov – (lit. "good luck"); a common Hebrew phrase used to express congratulations for a happy and significant occasion or event.

Mechila – asking someone for forgiveness for anything they may have done wrong to him or her.

Menorah – an eight-branched candelabra kindled during the eight-day festival of *Chanukah* to signify the miracle of one tiny jar of oil that kindled the candelabra in the Holy Temple for eight straight days during the occupation of the Holy Land during the Syrian-Greek rule.

Merkos L'inyonei Chinuch – (lit. "Central Organization for Education"); Founded in 1943 by the sixth *Chabad Rebbe* Rabbi Yosef Yitzchak Schneerson, the organization is the central educational arm of the *Chabad Lubavitch* movement.

Minyan – a quorum of at least ten men required for engaging in public prayer.

Mishnah – (lit. "repetition"); The first compilation of the oral law, authored by Rabbi Yehudah HaNasi (approx. 200 CE); the germinal statements of law elucidated by the *Gemara*, together with which they constitute the *Talmud*; also, a single statement of law from this work.

Mishnayos – comprising all six orders of the *Mishnah*.

Modiin – a city in Israel located 53 kilometres from Jerusalem.

Mohel – a trained Jewish male who performs the ritual circumcision called a *Bris*.

Nachalat Har Chabad – the main *Chabad* neighbourhood in *Kiryat Melachi*, Israel.

Pesach – (lit. "Passover"); the eight-day Jewish festival is celebrated in the early spring, from the 15th through the 22nd of the Hebrew month of Nissan. It commemorates the emancipation of the Children of Israel from slavery in ancient Egypt.

Purim – is a Jewish holiday that commemorates the deliverance of the Jewish people in ancient Persia from annihilation in the wake of a plot by the wicked Haman.

Rabbi Yehuda Hanasi – (lit. "Judah the Prince"), also known as *Rebbi* and *Rabbenu Hakadosh* (Hebrew: "Our Holy Rabbi"), was a key leader of the Jewish community of Judea toward the end of the 2nd century CE, during the occupation by the Roman Empire. He is best known as the chief complier and editor of the *Mishnah*.

Rebbe – (lit. master) (a) A *Torah* teacher. (b) Since the founding of the *Chassidic* movement, the term *Rebbe* has been used primarily to refer to the leaders of *Chassidic* groups. (c) Today, "the *Rebbe*" is often a reference to Rabbi Menachem M. Schneerson, the *Lubavitcher Rebbe*, of righteous memory (see www.Chabad.org).

Rosh Hashanah – a two-day Jewish holiday marking the beginning of the Jewish New Year. The first of the High Holy Days or *Yamim Nora'im* ("Days of Awe"), the holiday is called the "Day of Judgment" and set the appropriate tone for the solemn day of *Yom Kippur,* the "Day of Atonement."

Seder Nezikin – (lit. "Order of Damages"); the fourth order of the Mishnah dealing largely with Jewish criminal and civil law and the Jewish court system.

Shabbos (es) pl. – the Sabbath, the divinely-ordained Jewish day of rest on the seventh day of the week. *Shabbos* observance entails the refrainment from weekday, work activities, and the engagement in spiritual activities to honour the day.

Shamas – (lit. "servant"); Yiddish term commonly referring to the synagogue attendant.

Shavuos – Known as the "Feast of Weeks" in English, is one of the three major Jewish festivals that occurs on the sixth day of the Hebrew month of Sivan. The holiday signifies the vital wheat harvest in the Land of Israel; and it commemorates the anniversary of the day God gave the Torah to the entire nation of Israel assembled at Mount Sinai.

Shochtim – religious Jews who are duly licensed and trained to slaughter and inspect cattle and fowl in accordance with strict Jewish dietary law.

Shpiel – (lit. "play"); Yiddish term denoting a long, involved sales pitch.

Shtetl – a Yiddish term denoting a small Jewish town located primarily in Central or Eastern Europe.

Shteibel – a tiny private house used for communal Jewish prayer.

Shulchan Aruch – standard Code of Jewish Law, compiled by Rabbi Yosef in 1563.

Smicha – rabbinical ordination, formal credentials certifying rabbinical status.

Tallis – a specially made shawl with ritual fringes at four corners, worn by men during certain prayer services.

Tefillin – also called phylacteries, are a set of small black leather boxes containing scrolls of parchment inscribed with verses from the *Torah*, which are worn by observant Jewish men during weekday morning prayers.

Talmud – the basic compendium of Jewish law and thought; its tractates mainly comprise the discussions collectively known as the *Gemara*, which elucidate the germinal statements of law (*Mishnayos*) collectively known as the *Mishnah* (see www.Chabad.org).

Tehillim – the Book of Psalms authored by King David.

Teves – the Hebrew month corresponding to December-January.

Tikun Olam – (lit. "repairing the world "); a modern Hebrew term which has come to connote social action, community service, social justice, and often, a liberal social agenda.

Torah – (lit. teaching) (a) The Five Books of Moses (The Bible); (b) the overall body of Jewish religious teachings encompassing the whole body of Jewish law, practice and tradition (see www.Chabad.org).

Torah Umesorah – The National Society for Hebrew Day Schools is an Orthodox Jewish organization in North America that fosters and promotes Torah-based Jewish religious education by supporting and developing a loosely affiliated network of approximately 675 independent private Jewish day schools.

Tseilem – (lit. "cross"); a Yiddish term.

Tzetlach – (lit. "notes"); a Yiddish term.

Tzitzis – special knotted ritual fringes, or tassels, attached to the four corners of an everyday worn undergarment.

Yarmulke – (Hebrew: kipah) Skullcap. The head covering worn by Jewish men symbolizing recognition of God above (see www.Chabad.org).

Yeshiva – a Jewish educational institution that focuses on the study of traditional religious texts, primarily the *Talmud* and *Torah* study.

Yom Kippur – the Day of Atonement, the holiest day of the Jewish calendar represents the climax of the Days of Awe. Observance on this holy day includes an approximate 25-hour period of fasting and intensive prayer with the majority of the waking hours spent in synagogue.

Yoreh Deah – one of the main sections of the Code of Jewish Law, this component of study is but one aspect of the time-honoured traditional curriculum required for mastery for a student to receive rabbinical ordination.